THE MOUNTAIN MEN
and the Fur Trade of the Far West
II

OTHER PUBLICATIONS BY LeRoy R. HAFEN –

1926 – *The Overland Mail, 1849-1869*
1927 – editor, *History of Colorado,* 3 volumes
1931 – *Broken Hand: the Life of Thomas Fitzpatrick* (with W. J. Ghent)
1932 – editor, *Villard's Past and Present of the Pike's Peak Region*
1933 – *Colorado, the Story of a Western Commonwealth*
1938 – *Fort Laramie and the Pageant of the West* (with F. M. Young)
1941 – *Western America* (with C. C. Rister) ; revised, 1950
1941-1942 – editor, *Southwest Historical Series,* volumes IX, X, XI
1943 – *Colorado: a Story of the State and its People* (with Ann W. Hafen)
1948 – *Colorado and its People,* 2 volumes
1950 – editor, *Ruxton of the Rockies*
1951 – editor, *Ruxton's Life in the Far West*
1953 – *The Colorado Story* (with Ann W. Hafen)
1924-1954 – editor, *The Colorado Magazine*
1954 – *The Old Spanish Trail* (with Ann W. Hafen)
1954-1962 – editor, *The Far West and Rockies Series,* 15 volumes (with Ann W. Hafen)
1960 – *Handcarts to Zion* (with Ann W. Hafen)
1962 – compiler and editor, *The Hafen Families of Utah*
1965 – *The Mountain Men and the Fur Trade of the Far West,* vol. I

Also contributions to numerous other publications and journals. For further detail see *LeRoy R. and Ann W. Hafen, their writings and their notable collection of Americana given to Brigham Young University Library* (1962, 109 pages)

A Mountain Man

From a painting by western artist Clarence Ellsworth, 1951.

THE MOUNTAIN MEN
and the Fur Trade
of the Far West

biographical sketches of the participants
by scholars of the subject
and with introductions by the editor

under the editorial supervision of

LeRoy R. Hafen

State Historian of Colorado, Emeritus
Professor of History, Brigham Young University

Volume II

THE ARTHUR H. CLARK COMPANY
Glendale, California
1965

Contents

Illustrations

For the map of the "Fur Country of the Far West,"
see the first volume of this series, at page 20.

Preface

In this, the second volume of the Mountain Men Series, will be found biographical sketches of thirty-seven more of the men engaged in the trans-Mississippi fur trade of the first half of the nineteenth century.

The sketches in this volume, as in the first, are arranged alphabetically under the surname of the subject person. This same format will be used in all volumes of the Series, with an index-guide in the final volume.

The reader is referred to the summary history of the fur trade, presented in the first section of volume I, for the general background history and the contribution of the fur men in advancing the frontier. Likewise, for the area concerned, the large map which appears at page 20 of volume I, will be of value in connection with the text of all volumes.

Again we express sincere thanks to the scholars of the fur trade era, for their cooperation in contributing the valuable biographies presented in this work.

JOHN D. ALBERT
From the *Denver Post,* November
20, 1901, where it was captioned
in error as Tom Tobin.
Courtesy of State Historical
Society of Colorado.

CHARLES BENT
As governor of New Mexico. From
an oil painting. Courtesy of
Museum of New Mexico, Santa Fe.

AUGUSTE CLERMONT (AUGUST CLAYMORE)
A photo by D. B. Chase of Trinidad, Colorado, about 1875. The scene compares closely
with that of Claymore's death. Courtesy of Pioneer Museum of Colorado Springs.
The original was given to F. W. Cragin by Eliza Walker, daughter of Dick Wootton.

WILLIAM CRAIG
Courtesy, Oregon Historical Society.

JAMES KIPP
Courtesy of Historical Society
of Montana.

Lancaster P. Lupton
Courtesy of State Historical Society
of Colorado.

Kenneth McKenzie
Courtesy of Historical Society
of Montana.

STEPHEN MEEK
Courtesy, Oregon Historical Society.

DAVID D. MITCHELL
Courtesy of Missouri Historical
Society, St. Louis.

ALBERT PIKE
At about fifty years of age.

ISAAC SPARKS
Engraved for *The Hesperian*, July 1859,
from a photograph by W. Shaw.
Courtesy of California State Library.

LOUIS VASQUEZ
From a painting by Waldo Love, 1936.
Courtesy of State Historical Society
of Colorado.

WALKARA
AND HIS BROTHER ARROPEEN
Engraved from a painting
by S. N. Carvalho, 1854.
Courtesy of Latter Day Saints
Church Historian's Office.

WILLIAM WOLFSKILL
From a photo taken by Henri Penelon
in Los Angeles, September 27, 1866.

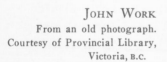
JOHN WORK
From an old photograph.
Courtesy of Provincial Library,
Victoria, B.C.

John D. Albert

by LeRoy R. Hafen
Brigham Young University

A familiar figure for many years in Walsenburg, Colorado, was "Uncle John" Albert.* For nearly thirty years preceding his death in 1899, he had lived in the Cucharas Valley. On summer evenings he often sat for hours on the bench in front of the Sporleder Hotel and while smoking his corn husk cigarettes would entertain the guests of the inn with tales of his adventures.

Even after he was seventy years old he continued to follow, in a limited way, the trapping and hunting pursuits that had brought him to the West some fifty years before. He caught beaver on the Cucharas River just below Main Street, Walsenburg, after the town was started, and every fall he brought in a supply of venison. He was a Mountain Man of the early nineteenth century trying to adjust himself to the changed conditions that had come to the West in the latter years of that century.

The ancestors of "Uncle John" came to America near the close of the seventeenth century with Francis D. Pastorius, founder of Germantown, Pennsylvania. The family later moved to Maryland, where at Hagerstown, John David Albert was born in 1806.[1] His father enlisted for military service during the War of 1812 and was killed at the Battle of New Orleans. His mother died soon thereafter. The

---

* See portrait at page 13.

[1] Data from Louis B. Sporleder, who for some twenty-five years was a fellow townsman in Walsenburg, Colorado. Mr. Sporleder wrote a biographical sketch of Mr. Albert, from which the data in this article are taken, except where otherwise indicated. The manuscript is in the library of the State Historical Society of Colorado, at Denver.

orphan then found a home with a married sister at Harrisburg, Pennsylvania.

As a young man Albert began his westward wanderings, going first to Zanesville, Ohio; next to Cincinnati; and then to Louisville, Kentucky. Here he found employment on one of the keelboats which plied the Ohio and Mississippi. In 1833 he went by keelboat from New Orleans to St. Louis, a trip which he later characterized as "the most laborious journey of his life." [2]

After spending the winter of 1833-34 in St. Louis, Albert entered the fur trade in the spring, going to the mountains with a party of sixty men. During the three succeeding years he was a trapper and trader. At times he bartered his furs at Fort Hall and at other times to the so-called American Fur Company. While in the region about the Great Salt Lake he says that his party lost track of the day of the week and of the month.

Mid-winter of 1836-37 he spent with a band of Indians near the mouth of the Cache la Poudre River (branch of the South Platte). "On the first day of December," he says, "snow began to fall and did not let up until the earth was covered to the depth of seven feet on the level, and it remained until spring. Not much antelope in that kind of snow. No sir. We lived on horse flesh. Our horses froze to death, and the meat kept all winter." [3] When spring came, Albert and his companions went south to Bent's Fort, where they obtained horses.

In the spring of 1837 a new partnership was launched by Peter A. Sarpy and Henry Fraeb, backed by Pratte, Chouteau & Company of St. Louis. Trade goods amounting to $10,909.75 were brought out to the South Platte River,

---

2 Frank Hall, *History of Colorado* (1891), III, p. 496. Apparently Mr. Hall interviewed Mr. Albert before writing the sketch of the latter's life.

3 Sporleder's biographical sketch of Albert (MS.).

where the partners erected adobe Fort Jackson.[4] Albert was employed by Sarpy and Fraeb at the fort and in the trade of the region. The company accounts show payment to him on March 1, 1838.[5] He continued service until October, 1838, when the fort was sold to Bent and St. Vrain. At that time Albert was paid $124.52, at Fort Lookout (Fort St. Vrain), "being the balance due."[6]

As trapping was becoming unprofitable, Albert decided to forsake the fur trade for farming. He settled down in Taos Valley, New Mexico, and married a "half breed Mexican, the daughter of William Pope, who came to the mountains at a very early date."[7] Life during most of the succeeding decade was not spectacular. In 1847, however, he had the most thrilling experience of his life. It came as a result of the famous "Taos uprising."

The American conquest of New Mexico under General Kearny had been effected without serious opposition in August, 1846. American control was set up with Charles Bent, long a resident merchant of New Mexico, as governor. A smouldering distrust in the minds of many natives was stirred to flame by certain Mexican leaders. A wholesale uprising against the invaders was carried into effect in January, 1847. At several places in the territory attacks were made almost simultaneously. Governor Bent and other officials were killed at Taos. An attack was made on Turley's mill, located on the Arroyo Hondo, some seven miles north of Taos. Here a number of Americans, including Albert,

---

[4] See LeRoy R. Hafen, "Fort Jackson and the Early Fur Trade on the South Platte," in *Colorado Magazine,* v (1928), 9-17, in which the original documents are cited or quoted.

[5] Chouteau-Maffitt Collection, Missouri Historical Society, St. Louis.

[6] *Ibid.,* Oct. 6, 1838. Document signed by Albert.

[7] Thomas F. Dawson Scrapbooks, I, p. 369 (State Historical Society of Colorado). This clipping, dated Oct. 31, 1885, is from a Rico, Colorado, newspaper and is copied from Walsenburg correspondence to the *Denver News.* Look elsewhere in this volume for a biography of William Pope.

were employed at the time. Extracts from Mr. Albert's
account of experiences follow.

They commenced the attack upon Arroyo Hondo by sending in to us
a flag of truce, demanding our arms and ammunition and an uncondi-
tional surrender of ourselves. I told the boys they could do as they
pleased, but I knew their treachery would lead us to certain death in
the end, and I was going to die with my gun in my hands, and not be
murdered like a common dog.

This was the turning point in the matter, and they all concluded to
fight it out as best they could. . . We of the mountains had collected in the distillery belonging to Mr. Turley, a building of considerable size, and the only one in the place that was two stories in
height. The dancing Indian was within gunshot and I killed him. Billy
Austin stood close behind me, and when another man came to drag the
body back, Austin shot him. By this time my gun was loaded and I
killed the third man. Then a hurrah commenced and the air was filled
with bullets from the guns in the hands of the men who had laid behind
the top of the hill. The bullets rattled against the house like hail. There
was not a window left in it. Although we saw we were in a trap, we
fought all day.

When the sun was setting the Mexicans made a curious charge and
set fire to the house we were in, and got under the walls of other buildings. Soon everything was ablaze; the uproar of the yelling devils on
the outside and the excitement of the men on the inner side was deaf-
ening. We tried to escape by digging through the floor down into the
granary. The house was filling with Mexicans and everything was
confusion.

Fortunately for me, in the confusion, I escaped from the house. I
don't know how many shots were fired at me, but none took effect. I
had a bullet in my clothes, one cut off the brim of my hat, and another
cut the band and I lost it from my head. In the excitement I forgot my
coat and was out in the world alone without coat, hat or friends, and
with 140 miles of mountain roads between me and safety, in the winter
time.

My comrades behind me were all killed. I was alone in a world of
snow, with not a human soul on whom I could depend, and with no
provisions and no hope of getting any unless I could kill some animal
while I was traveling. I never look back to the dark hours of that day
and to my sufferings in the days following, but the devil gets in me
bigger than a wolf. . .

I traveled the entire night and reached little Red River just as the rays of the morning light were creeping over the Sierra Madre Mountains. I thought I would freeze, it was so cold in the last hours of the night. I arrived at Costilla about midday and at Indian Creek at the setting of the sun. Here I took my first rest. . .

When the light of morning came I went to the trail and had not gone far when I saw two large deer standing near the trail. I shot and broke the back of the largest. As soon as I could I opened it and cut out a piece of liver and began to eat. I had eaten raw liver and raw meat many times before without any inconvenience, but this made me sick. I laid down upon the ground and snow with my head upon the dead animal, and for an hour or more suffered all the pains of death. When that passed away I was as anxious to resume my march as ever.

Fifty miles remained between me and the trading post at Pueblo, my nearest source of relief. My appetite for venison broil was gone for the time. I took the skin of the deer and wrapped it around my head and shoulders as a substitute for a coat, the hair next to my body. It served a very good purpose. Then, taking a small cut of venison, I started on my journey.[8]

He finally reached the Pueblo on the Arkansas, obtained relief, and told of the uprising in New Mexico. Word was sent down the river to Bent's Fort, to William Bent, brother of the murdered governor. Mountaineers made up a party and headed for New Mexico. The uprising was put down by the military forces under Colonel Price, as is well known.

We shall not attempt to follow Albert's subsequent career. His remaining years were spent in New Mexico and Colorado. In the early seventies he settled at Walsenburg and here built his home.

Mr. Albert was married three times. "A custom he followed was to divide his property among the children when a wife died and start life anew with any subsequent alliance." He had twenty-one children.

Mr. Louis B. Sporleder, who knew Albert well and as a

---

[8] As told to L. B. Sporleder and reported in his manuscript biography of Albert, cited above. See LeRoy R. Hafen (ed.), *Ruxton of the Rockies* (Norman, Okla., 1950), 219-20, for a contemporary account of Albert's ordeal.

young man accompanied Albert on one of the old man's last hunting trips, says of him:

The old patriarch smoked corn husk cigarettes incessantly, sometimes twenty at one sitting — without batting an eye. Fond of a little good liquor, he yet never drank a drop more than he could stand. Cock fights interested him greatly and he himself bred game birds for a number of years. He was quiet and unostentatious, preferring his own fireside to the glamours of gambling and the deviations from moral rectitude, differing in that respect from most of the old mountaineers. Although himself not a member of any denomination, and not a church-going man, he revered, above all other things, an old German Bible, which his mother had left him. This book he carried with him constantly, considering it, perhaps, as a talisman to protect him from harm.[9]

On April 24, 1899, John D. Albert, one of the last of the Mountain Men, passed away. He lies in the Catholic cemetery just south of Walsenburg, Colorado.

---

[9] Sporleder, *op. cit.*

Charles Bent

by HAROLD H. DUNHAM
University of Denver

Charles Bent, fur trapper and trader, Santa Fe trader, part owner of Bent's Fort on the Arkansas, and governor of New Mexico, was born November 11, 1799, at Charleston, (West) Virginia.[1] His father was Silas Bent, a native of Rutland, Massachusetts, who had been sent west as a young man in 1788 to select a home site for his parents at the Ohio Company's new village of Marietta.[2] A short time later, Silas moved to Wheeling to study law, and afterwards he went to Charleston to become a storekeeper. There he married Martha Kerr, of a Virginia family, and their first child was Charles. Silas subsequently received an appointment as deputy surveyor, then judge in a Common Pleas Court in Washington County, Ohio.

When Charles was six years old, his father was appointed deputy surveyor for Louisiana Territory, so the family embarked for St. Louis, arriving there during the middle of September, 1806, a few days before Lewis and Clark returned from their epic trip to the Pacific Ocean. Silas promptly assumed his duties as surveyor and found them somewhat arduous, first because of the extent of territory for which he was responsible, and second because of complica-

---

[1] A. H. Bent, *The Bent Family in America* (1900), 121. The most extensive coverage of the life of Charles Bent may be found in D. Lavender, *Bent's Fort* (Garden City, N.Y., 1954). See also H. H. Dunham, "Governor Charles Bent: Pioneer and Martyr," in N. Mumey (ed.), *The Westerners Brand Book, 1951* (Denver, 1952), 219-67; P. A. F. Walter, "The First Civil Governor under the Stars and Stripes," *New Mexico Historical Review,* VIII (Apr., 1933), 98-127; and I. W. Cason, "The Bent Brothers on the Frontier," M.A. thesis, MS., University of New Mexico, Albuquerque, 1939. See Charles Bent's portrait, page 13 herein.

[2] Bent, *Bent Family,* 58.

tions resulting from the existence of Spanish and French land grants in the area.[3] There is a certain relevance in these factors for the life of Charles, in that he became classified as a surveyor in New Mexico, and that he was instrumental in the promotion of some extraordinary land grants in New Mexico during the early 1840s.

After serving less than a year as Louisiana surveyor, Silas again transferred to the judicial field and filled successively positions of increasing responsibility, the most important of which was that of Justice of the Supreme Court of Missouri Territory, 1813-1821.[4] He lived an honorable life with his large family (Charles had a total of ten brothers and sisters), in a fine residence in Carondelet, then a suburb of St. Louis. He became associated professionally and as a friend with the region's leading citizens, including fur merchants such as Bernard Pratte and Auguste Chouteau. These latter persons may well have been significant in the subsequent lives of his sons, four of whom took part in the fur trade.

Charles Bent grew to manhood under comfortable family circumstances and in the environment of a city that was emerging from its more primitive and provincial characteristics. As St. Louis grew to become America's western fur capital it lost some of its French cultural orientation. Doubtless Charles was aware of these changes and opportunities, but as a matter of fact, not much is known about his youth, including his education, either along the Ohio River or in Missouri.[5] Sometime during his teens he did attend school at Jefferson College in Canonsburg, Pennsylvania. His brother John studied at the same institution, although neither boy received a diploma. Reports or indications of later times demonstrate that while Charles possessed

---

3 Lavender, *op. cit.,* 20-21.

4 Bent, *Bent Family,* 59. A picture of the Silas Bent home is contained in C. W. Hurd, *Bent's Stockade* (1960), 18.

5 Lavender, *op. cit.,* 25-6.

an erratic method of spelling, he probably picked up some beneficial training in mathematics and medicine. Assertions that he attended or graduated from West Point are not substantiated by the official records of the Academy.[6] Nevertheless, in maturity, he displayed a keen, vigorous, clear, and logical mind.

In view of his later classification as a surveyor,[7] it is possible to speculate that Charles engaged in surveying work as a young man, but whether he did or not, it is certain that he entered the fur trade. One author declares that he enlisted with Gen. William Ashley's first group of trappers and went up the Missouri in 1822, although for some undisclosed reason he returned to St. Louis within less than a year.[8] The family historian places Charles with the American Fur Co., by 1823,[9] but later research has shown that at that time he was identified with the Missouri Fur Co. Within two years it is recorded that he had become a partner in that firm, and within two more years he joined the partners in an expedition to the Colorado River of the West. Despite the lack of adequate information and in the face of some conflicting records, it seems likely that for the period of the early 1820s Charles had served the Missouri Fur Company in St. Louis and had been able to participate in its activities on the Big Muddy, so that first a brief review of the company's history for the period is in order; then Bent's known connections with it can be described more fully.

Upon the death in 1820 of its founder and mainstay, Manuel Lisa, the Missouri Fur Co. had been taken over by Joshua Pilcher.[10] He began to re-expand its area of operations in the western fur trade revival that commenced about

---

[6] *Ibid.*   [7] *Ibid.*, 164, 393.   [8] Hurd, *op. cit.*, 20.

[9] Bent, *Bent Family,* 121. See also *Dictionary of American Biography,* II, p. 205.

[10] H. M. Chittenden, *A History of the American Fur Trade* (2 vols., 1954 edition), I, p. 150; and P. C. Phillips, *The Fur Trade* (2 vols., 1961), II, p. 391.

that time. In 1821, Pilcher pushed beyond the old headquarters at Council Bluffs and built Ft. Recovery at the
mouth of the White River in Sioux country. He sent Robert
Jones and Michael Immel to the mouth of the Yellowstone
to trade with the Crows. A year later, the company erected
Ft. Vanderburgh in Mandan territory.[11] Government licenses issued to Indian traders that year, 1822, show that
both in April and September, Pilcher's company declared
the valuation of its capital goods at $50,000.[12] It is said to
have employed 300 men along 1,000 miles of the Missouri
River, from Council Bluffs to the Yellowstone.[13] Meanwhile, competition along the river steadily increased, entering a new phase when in 1822 the American Fur Company
created its Western Division and began its efforts to dominate the trade.

David Lavender asserts that by 1822 Charles Bent had
become "firmly established in the lower echelons" of the
Pilcher outfit.[14] Yet it is not known whether he served the
company at Ft. Recovery, at Ft. Vanderburgh, with Immel
and Jones, at Council Bluffs, or elsewhere. And for the next,
or fateful year of 1823, when the Blackfeet Indians de-
spoiled Jones and Immel and attacked Andrew Henry,[15]
the Aricaras repulsed William Ashley, and Colonel Henry
Leavenworth's expedition encountered mockery from the
Aricaras,[16] there is no unequivocal word of the role played
by Bent. It does seem fairly certain that after these events
had occurred, he spent the following winter at Ft. Recovery
in the Sioux country.

In the spring of 1824, Charles Bent, identified by a con-

11 P. C. Phillips, "William Henry Vanderburgh: Fur Trader," in *Mississippi Valley Historical Review,* xxx, (Dec., 1943), 381-2.

12 *Ho. Exec. doc. 7,* 18 Cong., 1 sess. (ser. 93).

13 Chittenden, *op. cit.,* I, p. 150.   14 Lavender, *op. cit.,* 31.

15 H. C. Dale (ed.), *The Ashley-Smith Explorations and the Discovery of a
Central Route to the Pacific, 1822-29* (Glendale, Calif., 1941), 65.

16 Dale Morgan, *Jedediah Smith* (Indianapolis, 1953), chaps. 2 and 3.

temporary as employed by the Missouri Fur Company, accompanied one of the Papins down the River with two fur-loaded keelboats.[17] On May 4 the men put their boats ashore at Ft. Atkinson, the Army post located at Council Bluffs. There Bent donated ten buffalo tongues to James Kennerly, the post sutler. Such a courtesy suggests previous acquaintanceship with the staff at the post. Undoubtedly Bent resumed his river voyage and landed at St. Louis to unload his furs. Perhaps he subsequently returned upstream with a shipment of fresh supplies and barter goods.

In any case, by 1825 Bent became one of the partners in the reorganized Missouri Fur Company. The losses which it suffered in 1823 seem to have crippled it greatly. Pilcher's license for October 27, 1824, showed that the total capital to be employed was listed at only $3,175, a mere fraction of the amount for the previous year.[18] Dale Morgan has found that the company became bankrupt by 1825,[19] and yet it was at that time that Pilcher was able to effect another company reorganization. In the new concern, Bent stepped up to full partnership, with Lucien Fontenelle, William Vanderburgh, Andrew Drips and Pilcher. On July 4, 1825, the partners obtained a license from Superintendent William Clark "to trade at the mouth of the Kanzas River, Bellevue Trading establishment, eight miles below Fort Atkinson, Pania Villages; at the mouth of L'eau Qui Cours [Niobrara River], Fort Lookout [Ft. Kiowa]; mouth of the Cheyenne River, Ricara and Mandan Villages; and mouth of the Yellowstone River." [20] The amount of capital involved was $7,712.82.

Where Charles Bent operated that year, as well as the next, when the company license showed little change in the

---

[17] E. B. Wesley (ed.), "Diary of James Kennerly, 1823-1826," in *Missouri Historical Society Collections,* VI, p. 69.

[18] *Ho. doc. 54,* 18 Cong., 2 sess. (ser. 115).

[19] Morgan, *Jedediah Smith,* 298.

[20] *Ho. doc. 118,* 19 Cong., 1 sess. (ser. 136).

amount of capital employed and areas of trade, is a matter
of guesswork, at present. William Waldo's later comment
on Bent's experience prior to 1829 that he "had spent some
years in the Rocky Mountains," offers only general information for locating Charles during the period.[21] However, it
was during 1826 that he was officially recommended for the
post of sub-agent to the Ioway Indians,[22] and in 1827 his
appointment was approved. This position might have at
least proved interesting, but Bent could not take it, and
within a few months of his appointment, another man was
assigned to the work.[23]

Later in the year Bent accompanied his partners on a
trading and trapping expedition to the Colorado, or Green
River, as previously mentioned. Pilcher has described how
he arranged for "more extensive operations," in 1827 than
his outfit had attempted for some time.[24] He organized a
party of forty-five men, including all his partners and probably William Bent, Charles' nineteen-year-old brother.
Stocked with ample merchandise for trade, the expedition
headed west from Council Bluffs in September, struck the
Platte River, and continued up its north branch. When they
reached the mountains, the Crow Indians stole all but a few
of their horses, so it became necessary to "make a depot
[cache] of merchandise and property . . . by burying
it in the ground." Thereafter the expedition resumed its
journey, on foot, through deep snow across South Pass.

---

21 Wm. Waldo, "Recollections of a Septuagenarian," in Missouri Historical
Society, *Glimpses of the Past,* v, (April-June, 1938), 72. Waldo also testifies that
Charles Bent and David Waldo were partners in trading and trapping at a very
early period. *Ibid.,* 62-3.

22 LeRoy R. Hafen, "When Was Bent's Fort Built?" in *Colorado Magazine,* XXXI,
(Apr. 1954), 111.

23 Letter from Wm. Clark at St. Louis, April 27, 1827, to M. L. Clark (his son).
MS. Missouri Historical Society, St. Louis. Photostat in the possession of the
author. See also Lavender, *op. cit.,* 46.

24 Chittenden, I, pp. 155-6; Morgan, *Jedediah Smith,* 298-9; and *Sen. doc. 39,* 21
Cong., 2 sess. (ser. 203), 7-8.

The rest of the winter of 1827-28 was spent in camp on the Green, or what Pilcher called the Colorado, River. When spring returned, most of the party either hunted or trapped, while one of the partners obtained horses from the Snake Indians and returned to the depot on the Platte. To his dismay he found "a considerable part of the merchandise destroyed, the water having penetrated the place where it was buried." The goods which were still usable were carried back to Bear Lake, "then a rendezvous for hunters and traders." There at the rendezvous of 1828, Pilcher, Bent, and the other partners traded for what additional furs their diminished supply of goods would permit, and ended up with a total of less than twenty packs of beaver. This was a discouragingly small return for forty-five men, in view of their labors, losses, and expenses; so the company was dissolved.

After the break-up of the partnership, Bent, Vanderburgh, Fontenelle and a majority of the party embarked during July on the return trip to Council Bluffs via South Pass and the Platte River.[25] Enroute, the expedition suffered an attack by the Crows and lost two men.[26] When the survivors finally reached the old company headquarters, they learned that the American Fur Company had achieved a virtual monopoly of the Missouri River fur trade during their absence. The former partners appear to have accepted the situation for what it was and approached the American Fur Company official, J. P. Cabanné, at a nearby post, requesting the necessary financial backing to return to the mountains.[27] Only Bent seemed to have had certain reservations about undertaking a new expedition, though on what grounds is not stated.

---

[25] Morgan, *Jedediah Smith,* 299; Lavender, *op. cit.,* 82.

[26] *Ibid.*

[27] Letter from J. P. Cabanne at "Pres du Bluffs" Oct. 14, 1828, to P. Chouteau, Jr. MS. Missouri Historical Society, St. Louis. Photostat in the possession of the author.

Cabanné debated their request for, as he wrote Pierre Chouteau, Jr., he recognized that by enlisting these experienced traders under the company banner there would be less competition in the year ahead. Yet he decided not to back them because they could contribute so little in the way of supplies and equipment. Bent's financial status seems to be indicated by the fact that he was forced to borrow money from Cabanné in order to return to St. Louis that fall, 1828.

The following winter marked a turning point in Charles Bent's career. His interest became drawn to the Santa Fe trade. Whether this resulted from a meeting with Ceran St. Vrain, his future partner, operating out of Santa Fe during the time of the 1827-28 Pilcher expedition to Green River, as Lavender surmises,[28] or from persuasion of his long-time friend, David Waldo, who had recently returned to St. Louis from a trip over the Santa Fe Trail, or from some other cause or causes, is difficult to determine. But whatever the reason, by the spring of 1829 Charles was determined to join a Santa Fe caravan with Waldo. During the latter part of May of that year he brought his goods to Round Grove, the rendezvous center for traders, forty miles west of Westport.[29] Here he found a party of seventy-eight, possessing thirty-eight wagons loaded with trade goods.

At the suggestion of David Waldo, Bent was chosen captain of the caravan, and so became responsible for conducting the outfit over the 775 miles of prairie and mountain trail to the New Mexican capital.[30] Charles' brother William became a member of the expedition, as he had done with some of those of the fur company on the Missouri River. Captain Bent's party became marked by two firsts: one was the protection afforded by four companies of U.S. infantry under the command of Major Bennett Riley; the

---

[28] Lavender, *op. cit.*, 79.　　　　　　[29] Waldo, "Recollections," 72-3.
[30] O. E Young, *First Military Escort on the Santa Fe Trail, 1829* (Glendale, Calif., 1952), 75.

second was Bent's testing of oxen on the western part of the Trail, after Major Riley had brought them as far as the Arkansas River.[31]

On June 12, 1829, Bent started the expedition with its escort out of Round Grove, and by July 9 it had reached the international boundary at the Santa Fe crossing of the Arkansas. Here the military escort was to wait while the traders took their goods into Mexican territory and returned; Bent promised to be back at the river early in October. Bent also borrowed a yoke of oxen from Major Riley, and the subsequent trip proved that they were able to get through to Santa Fe better than the mules.

After fording the Arkansas River, the caravan set out on the Cimarron branch of the Santa Fe Trail. It had progressed only nine miles beyond the crossing when a large band of Indians, perhaps 500 Kiowas, violently attacked it.[32] At one point during the assault Captain Bent is said to have charged alone at a group of fifty Indians that were pursuing a trader, and he dispersed them by his audacity. Meanwhile, he dispatched messengers requesting assistance from Major Riley. Ignoring the international boundary, the latter came to the rescue of the caravan, and then accompanied it for a few days toward the Cimarron, before returning to his vigil on the Arkansas.

The traders continued westward under Bent's leadership with some apprehension because of a report from Mexicans of large numbers of marauding Indians.[33] The Mexicans joined the traders for safety's sake, and later a protecting force of nearly one hundred men under the leadership of Ewing Young escorted the combined group into Taos. The members of the caravan then pushed on to Santa Fe, where they were well received, and judging by the value of their

[31] *Ibid.*, 86; *American State Papers, Military Affairs*, IV, p. 277.
[32] Young, *op. cit.*, 89-91.   [33] *Ibid.*, 140-1.

return cargo they enjoyed a profitable sale of their merchandise.

The return journey to the states was begun under the protection of a Mexican military force, and in company with a party of wealthy Spaniards who were being expelled from Mexico. According to William Waldo, Charles Bent again was the captain of the non-military part of the expedition, and he rendered significant aid to the New Mexican military force on whom the Indians attempted a trick.[34] The caravan's cargo consisted of furs, specie, and mules to the value of $240,000 (amounting to one hundred percent profit on the goods that had been brought out).[35] The caravan reached Major Riley on the Arkansas in October, just as he had started to return to the States because he believed it was not coming through.[36]

One confusing factor about Bent's captaincy arises from a document showing that early in October he was assigned a guide in Santa Fe to accompany him on a trading trip to Chihuahua and Sonora.[37] There is a similar conflict of evidence for his activities in 1831. Nevertheless, it is helpful to learn from his 1831 passport that he stood five-feet seven-inches tall, possessed a high forehead, common nose, mouth and chin, and gray eyes and black hair.[38] In later years the Indians were to call him gray-haired whiteman.

In the second year of his life as a Santa Fe trader, that is in 1830, Bent established a business agreement with another trader-mountain man, who was the courteous, capable, ex-

---

[34] Waldo, "Recollections," 75.

[35] *Ibid.*, 59.   [36] Young, *op. cit.*, 139.

[37] Charles Bent – Declaration of Goods and Petition for a Guide, Oct. 8, 1829. Folder 2330. R. E. Twitchell Collection, New Mexico State Archives and Records Center, Santa Fe. It is possible that this applied to a trading venture of his brother William and Robert Isaacs west of Santa Fe in 1830. See an account of the trip in an abstract from Isaac's Journal in the *Missouri Intelligencer* of Columbia, Oct. 6, 1832.

[38] L. H. Garrard, *Wah-To-Yah and the Taos Trail*, R. P. Bieber, ed. (Glendale, Calif., 1938), 179.

perienced Ceran St. Vrain. The latter had gone to Santa Fe
as early as 1824, and had established business contacts with
Bernard Pratte and Co., fur merchants of St. Louis.[39] Bent
and St. Vrain may have known each other in St. Louis, they
may have discovered their common business interests while
accompanying the 1830 spring caravan to Santa Fe, or possibly they met during the winter of 1827-28 on Green River,
as mentioned earlier. It is assumed that Bent traveled with
the 1830 caravan, one which consisted of 140 men, seventy
wagons, and $120,000 worth of trade goods.[40] But whatever
the origin of their agreement, Bent seems to have under-
taken the return trip to the States in September, after St.
Vrain lent him a wagon.

Returning to Santa Fe again, it is certain that before the
year 1830 had closed, the two traders reached an understanding whereby St. Vrain purchased half of Bent's goods
for cash and agreed to remain in New Mexico to sell them,
while Bent crossed the plains to St. Louis in order to obtain
additional merchandise for both.[41] Thus commenced a business association which endured until Bent's death in 1847.
Known first as Bent and St. Vrain, it later was called Bent,
St. Vrain and Co., and it became the largest and strongest
merchandising and fur trading firm in the Southwest.[42] Important as were the contributions of both St. Vrain and
Charles' brother William, it appears that Charles Bent
played the dominant role in the firm's operations.

As indicated above, just how or when Bent traveled back
to Missouri early in 1831 is not clear. He may have gone
directly there from Santa Fe, for he carried St. Vrain's letter
of January 6 to B. Pratte and Co., telling about the arrange-

[39] Hafen, "When Was Bent's Fort Built?", 108.
[40] *Ibid.,* 112; Lavender, *op. cit.,* 123.
[41] Letter from Ceran St. Vrain at Santa Fe, Jan. 6, 1831, to B. Pratte & Co. MS.
Missouri Historical Society, St. Louis. Photostat in the possession of the author.
[42] Waldo, "Recollections," 62, fn.

ments for trade the two men had made. On the other hand, since Bent had obtained a passport for Mexican provinces to the south of New Mexico, he may have gone southward and then either returned through New Mexico or headed for the east coast of Mexico and taken a boat to New Orleans and thence up-river to St. Louis.[43] Whichever route he followed, he was loading goods in the latter city by May, and Josiah Gregg has indicated that he preceded Bent in his summer crossing to Santa Fe.[44]

Granted that Gregg's report is accurate, Bent must have made a hurried journey back to St. Louis, for he obtained a passport there in July,[45] and early in August was preparing to head westward along the Trail again.[46] At Independence in September, the party of seventy-five men, with ten wagons, purchased some oxen, repaired their wagons and added to their stores before pressing on to Council Grove. One member of the party was Albert Pike, the later famous author, lawyer, and soldier.[47] He has related how Captain Bent's train made a much slower than expected crossing of the prairie and then was caught in a blizzard in the mountains east of Taos, so that not until the middle of November did all the travelers reach the haven of that town.

According to Hiram Chittenden, in both 1832 and 1833 Charles Bent captained the principal westbound caravans over the Santa Fe Trail.[48] He seems also to have brought in to the States the major returning train in 1832, one which carried with it $100,000 in specie and $90,000 worth of other property. The outgoing caravan of 1833 consisted of 184

[43] Lavender, *op. cit.,* 127.

[44] Josiah Gregg, *Commerce of the Prairies,* M. L. Moorhead, ed. (Norman, Okla., 1954), 51.

[45] Garrard, *op. cit.,* 179.

[46] A. E. Jones, "Albert Pike as a Tenderfoot," in *New Mexico Historical Review,* XXXI, (Apr. 1956), 141.

[47] M. G. Fulton and P. Horgan (eds.), *New Mexico's Own Chronicle* (Dallas, 1937), 103-4.

[48] Chittenden, *American Fur Trade,* II, p. 510.

men, 103 vehicles and cargo worth $100,000. One report credits Bent with the ownership of goods valued at $40,000 in this expedition.[49] It was escorted by a force of U.S. Mounted Rangers, the first military convoy since 1829. A special feature of the caravan was that its members fell into a dispute about the election of a captain at Council Grove, and decided to push on to Diamond Spring without agreement; at the Spring, however, Bent was finally selected.[50]

Obviously by 1833 Bent was recognized as one of the leading Santa Fe traders. Moreover, he and St. Vrain had established a store in Taos, at least by that year, and later they were to add another in Santa Fe. Charles' frequent crossings of the prairie seem to reflect an increase of trade, and he was to continue to average one round-trip a year until the time of his death. In this connection, a new phase and increase of the business is associated with the year 1833, for, as will be described shortly, it was marked by the construction of Bent's Fort on the Arkansas River. This meant that Bent, St. Vrain and Co. would trade with several Indian tribes at or near the Fort, send out trappers and traders to deal with Indians, later erect two additional forts (one on the South Platte and one on the Canadian River), enjoy the increased business of supplying the necessary trade goods, and haul wagon-loads of furs to Missouri markets annually. So after 1833, Charles Bent's trail travel was apt to proceed by way of Bent's Fort.

Charles was the leader in the company's efforts to plan for and to erect Bent's Fort, or Fort William, as it was also called, because William Bent supervised much of the construction and the management of the establishment.[51] There has been considerable controversy over the dates for the

---

[49] Hafen, "When Was Bent's Fort Built?", 114.

[50] O. E Young, "The U.S. Mounted Ranger Battalion, 1832-33," in *Mississippi Valley Historical Review*, XLI (Dec. 1954), 463.

[51] Lavender, *op. cit.*, 132, 136.

building and completion of the fort, though more recently the year 1833 has been accepted as the time when it was finished for the opening of Indian trade.[52] It became one of the leading three or four fur trading posts in the West, and certainly it was the most outstanding one in the Southwest. Its ground plan showed measurements of approximately 180 feet by 137 feet; its adobe walls were three feet thick and fourteen feet high, with two watchtowers eighteen feet high.[53] Attached to the main courtyard with its shops, living quarters, and other facilities, was a large enclosed courtyard for the protection of animals. The fort served as a business emporium, a haven for travelers, a rendezvous for the military, a home base for trappers, and a center for Indian trade and conferences. At its peak, the fort might place anywhere from 100 to 150 men on its payroll.

Rather curiously, Bent and St. Vrain did not obtain a license to trade with the Indians until December 13, 1834.[54] Furthermore, the license was issued by Indian Superintendent William Clark to Charles Bent, rather than to the company or partnership. It was, nevertheless, to be valid for two years, and it showed that the total amount of capital to be employed was $3,877.28, and the number of employees, twenty-nine. As to places and tribes for trading purposes, the license stipulated:

at Fort William, on the north side of the Arkansas, about 40 [80] miles east of the Rocky Mountains, about 20 miles north [90 miles northeast] of the Spanish Peaks, and about five miles below [above] one of the principal forks of the Arkansas, near the foot of the Rocky Mountains, about ten miles below the Black Hills [Black Forest?]; and at a post near the mouth of the Bear river, on the waters of the Grand River, or the Colorado of the West; with the Arapohoes, Cheyennes, Kiawas, Snakes, Sioux and Aricharees.[55]

---

[52] *Ibid.*, 386; and Hafen, "When Was Bent's Fort Built?", 119.

[53] N. Mumey, *Old Forts and Trading Posts: Bent's Old Fort and New Forts* (Denver, 1956), 23-4.

[54] *Sen. doc. 69*, 23 Cong., 2 sess. (ser. 268), 3. Lavender has given the license the date of 1833, which I believe is in error.

Licenses issued at later dates show certain changes as to location of trade and Indians with whom to trade. For instance, in 1838 the names of the Snake and Arickaree Indians no longer appear, nor does the Grand River;[56] the names of the Comanches were included.

Charles Bent's trips to or by way of Bent's Fort might find him present when military groups made periodic visits there. Some well-known military visitors were Colonel Henry Dodge, Colonel John C. Fremont, and Colonel Stephen W. Kearny. Bent was present in 1835, for instance, when Colonel Dodge stopped in after nearly completing a sixteen hundred mile sortie out of Ft. Leavenworth to conciliate plains Indians.[57] Early in August he and his officers were accorded a hospitable invitation by both Charles Bent and Ceran St. Vrain to dine at the Fort.[58] The Colonel believed and reported that Fort William was favorably located for establishing an Indian agency to deal with the upper bands of the Kiowas and Comanches, as well as the Cheyennes, Arapahoes, Gros Ventres, and Blackfeet that frequented the vicinity.[59] To one of the other officers, Captain Lemuel Ford, Bent and St. Vrain appeared to be conducting a lively fur trading business with the Indians.[60] He observed the loading of fifteen wagons, or packs, principally of buffalo robes, for transporting to Independence. He seemed to be impressed by the fact that the proprietors purchased each robe for about twenty-five cents worth of

---

[55] Because Col. Henry Dodge visited Bent's Fort during October, 1835, about ten months after the 1834 trading license was issued to Charles Bent, and because Dodge reported that the Fort was located about 130 miles from the Rocky Mountains, I have assumed that the license referred to that fort, rather than to any other Bent's Fort. See: *American State Papers, Military Affairs,* VI, p. 145.

[56] Mumey, *Old Forts,* inset, opposite p. 12.

[57] *American State Papers, Military Affairs,* VI, pp. 130ff.

[58] L. Pelzer (ed.), "Captain Ford's Journal," in *Mississippi Valley Historical Review,* XII, (Mar. 1956), 566.

[59] *American State Papers, Military Affairs,* VI, pp. 140-2.

[60] Pelzer, "Captain Ford's Journal," 566-67.

goods, and later sold it in St. Louis for five or six dollars. A further indication of alluring profits for the company is evident in the report that a gallon of brandy which cost two dollars in New York was sold for twenty-five dollars at the Fort.

Since Charles Bent frequently captained the annual fur-ladened caravans sent to Missouri from the Fort, a few of his experiences on the Trail are relevant. For instance, in the late spring of 1839 his caravan consisted of thirty men and ten wagons loaded with peltries.[61] On the Trail about the middle of June, the train had halted for the evening when a party of hunters came up from T. J. Farnham's Oregon-bound party. Bent and his associate, probably Antonie Leroux, treated the hunters kindly, served them an evening meal, and offered to share the shelter of their tent for the night. It is just possible that Captain Bent hoped these hunters would subsequently keep a sharp lookout for thirty mules and seven horses that had run away from his train a few days before, and if he did, his hospitality was rewarded, for the strays were found and driven back to the Fort. The 1839 caravan drove with it two hundred sheep for marketing in Missouri. News of Bent's cargo preceded him to St. Louis. On June 1, J. F. A. Sanford, writing from that city, informed Pierre Chouteau, Jr., that the Bent and St. Vrain train was expected to bring in about six hundred packs of robes and ten packs of beaver by the end of the month.[62]

Again in 1840 Bent captained the company shipment of furs from the Fort to St. Louis. The *Missouri Republican* for June 12, 1840, reported that the firm had enjoyed remarkable success during the previous season, for it had obtained fifteen thousand buffalo skins. Again the following

---

[61] LeRoy R. and A. Hafen (eds.), *To The Rockies and Oregon, 1839-1842* (Glendale, Calif., 1955), 36, 99.

[62] Letter from J. F. A. Sanford at St. Louis June 1, 1839, to Pierre Chouteau, Jr. MS. Missouri Historical Society, St. Louis, Mo.

year Bent supervised the firm's eastbound caravan. He reported from Bent's Fort that the company had made a fine trade during the winter, that eighteen company wagons loaded with "peletrys" had started for the States.[63]

During the journey of the 1842 caravan, Bent was able to arrange for special trading relations with the Comanches and Kiowas. As early as the spring of 1841, while he was in Taos, Bent learned from the Fort that thirty-one Comanches had come to make peace with the company.[64] Apparently this move was preliminary to what was described as "a kind of peace or truce" that Bent himself made with both the Comanches and Kiowas during the summer of 1842.[65] It occurred on the Trail when he met a combined band of those two Indian tribes and drew up the "truce." Consequently, that fall Bent established a trading post on the Canadian River, within the present Panhandle of Texas, and began a more systematic trade with what Captain Phillip St. George Cooke estimated were approximately six thousand Comanches and twelve hundred Kiowas. From them, one or the other partners of the firm obtained buffalo robes in trade each year, at least through 1846.[66]

One other of Charles Bent's eastward trips might be noted because of two distinctive features associated with it, namely, cattle and boating. The summer fur caravan from Ft. Bent in 1843, consisted of fourteen well-laden wagons drawn by ox and mule teams.[67] Additional hides were being trans-

---

[63] Letter from Charles Bent at Ft. William, Apr. 30, 1841, to M. Alvarez. *New Mexico Historical Review*, XXX (Apr. 1955), 159.

[64] Letter, same to same, Mar. 15, 1841. *Ibid.*, 155. Six years earlier, that is in 1835, Col. Henry Dodge reported that on August 8, Mr. Bent (Charles or William?) had arrived at Bent's Fort after a visit to the Comanches on the Red (Canadian) River, where he had been treated with great kindness. *American State Papers, Military Affairs*, VI, p. 145.

[65] W. E. Connelley (ed.), "A Journal of the Santa Fe Trail," in *Mississippi Valley Historical Review*, XII, (June 1925), 239.

[66] Letter from Charles Bent at Taos, N.M., Mar. 6, 1846, to M. Alvarez. *Ibid.*, XXX, (Oct. 1955), 352.

[67] Connelley (ed.), "Journal of the Santa Fe Trail," 85.

ported on hoof, for Bent was taking a drove of cattle raised
near the Fort to his farm in Missouri. This trip was held
up about ten days near Walnut Creek, largely because his
chief partner, Ceran St. Vrain, was coming up with five
more wagonloads of peltries.[68] St. Vrain's delay had been
caused by what Captain Cooke described as a not altogether
successful experiment in conveying furs by boat down the
Arkansas. The wagons had had to be called up to take over
from the boats.

Of course, not all of Bent's time was spent at the Fort or
on the Santa Fe Trail. By 1832 he had established his residence in Taos, seventy miles north of Santa Fe.[69] Probably
in 1835, Bent married Maria Ignacia Jamarilla, a beautiful
widow who was related to several prominent families in
Taos. The couple's life together appears to have been most
congenial, and to them were born three children: Alfred,
Teresina, and Estefina. Domestic felicity and local business
enterprise were accompanied by a certain political prominence amidst the factionalism of Taos.[70] Charles not only
held minor political positions, but established friendship
with such prominent men as Cornelius Vigil and Charles
Beaubien. Yet he developed a strong antipathy to the polit-
ically powerful Martinez family, headed by Padre Antonio
Martinez, the most outstanding religious leader of the
region.[71] The antipathy between Bent and the Padre was
mutual, and the latter denounced certain practices of Anglo
traders like Bent and St. Vrain, and sought to thwart Bent's
activities in connection with land grants.

[68] *Ibid.,* 86. Again in June, 1844, Charles Bent's train was held up at Walnut
Creek, but on that occasion by flood waters. However, his brother William, who
had crossed the Creek earlier after a trip from Chihuahua, reached St. Louis
ahead of the flood. "Letters and Notes From and About Bent's Fort, 1844-45," in
Colorado Magazine, xi, (Nov. 1934), 223-4.

[69] Dunham, "Governor Charles Bent," 231-2.

[70] *Cf.* Election List of Taos, N.M., March, 1842. Item 6750, New Mexico State
Records and Archives Center, Santa Fe.

[71] Dunham, "Governor Charles Bent," 237-8.

Bent's contacts naturally extended to leaders at the capital, Santa Fe. Besides American traders with stores there, particularly the U.S. Consul, Manuel Alvarez, Bent became well acquainted with New Mexican traders and political leaders.[72] He developed a special standing with Governor Manuel Armijo, who held the chief political post throughout most of the period 1837-1846. Bent's connections enabled him to secure an occasional reduction in tariffs on merchandise his friends brought into New Mexico and to promote the acquisition of title to large sections of public land in this northern Mexican province.[73] All of which is not to say that Bent avoided antagonisms and even periodic assaults, from the governor down to the lowliest citizen, that were directed toward Anglo traders. Moreover, the government could and did adopt discriminatory practices toward that group. To his credit, Charles Bent stood in the van of those who protested such treatment, and persisted in demands for justice where too frequent official shortcomings occurred in regard to his fellow countryman.[74]

Another way in which Bent sought to help Santa Fe traders and fur traders, including his own firm, was to support the movement seeking to allow drawbacks to traders.[75] Drawbacks meant that traders who imported their goods from abroad and paid the standard U.S. tariff rates, and then transported their merchandise to New Mexico and paid the Mexican tariff, should be permitted a refund on their United States duties. This movement was finally successful shortly before the Mexican War.

Another benefit for traders along the Santa Fe Trail could have come from the establishment of U.S. Army forts in appropriate locations. In 1842, Bent responded to a

---

[72] The available letters from Charles Bent to Manuel Alvarez have been published in the *New Mexico Historical Review*, XXIX (1954), no. 3 et seq.

[73] Dunham, "Governor Charles Bent," 247-9.

[74] *Ibid.*, 250-3.

[75] *Ibid.*, 254.

request from Senator L. F. Linn of Missouri for advice on such a fort, one that would offer protection to Oregon immigrants as well as Santa Fe traders, by holding in awe Indian tribes living between the two routes indicated.[76] Bent's suggestion was that the junction of Fountain Creek with the Arkansas River was the most likely spot, near the trading post called Fort Pueblo that had recently been established. A further step by the government that might have benefited Bent's firm much more than traders in general related to the Cheyenne and Arapaho Indian tribes. The issue had developed earlier, that is, after 1835, when Colonel Dodge promised those two tribes that official tokens or medals would be presented to their principal chiefs. Some kind of delay occurred so that by 1838 the medals had not been delivered, and as a consequence Bent then urged that these tokens of friendship be supplied.[77] Indian Superintendent William Clark favorably endorsed Bent's proposal, but the available records do not indicate the outcome.

The latter portion of Charles Bent's all-too-brief life is highlighted by two features arising partly from the so-called forces of Manifest Destiny and their relation to the onset of the Mexican War. The first feature is associated with the promotion of land settlement in New Mexico and grew out of the opportunities for obtaining extra large land grants during the 1840s from New Mexico's authoritarian governor, Armijo. Bent was reputedly instrumental in securing for various claimants the Beaubien and Miranda (or Maxwell) Grant – 1,714,000 acres; the Sangre de Cristo Grant – 1,000,000 acres; the Vigil and St. Vrain (or Las Animas) Grant – claimed amount, 4,000,000 acres; and the Nolan Grant – claimed amount, 500,000 acres.[78] They formed a

---

76 Letter from Charles Bent at Taos, Sept. 19, 1842, to M. Alvarez. *New Mexico Historical Review*, xxx, (Apr. 1955), 161-3.

77 Letter from Wm. Clark at St. Louis, Apr. 30, 1838, to C. A. Harris, Com. of Indian Affairs, Wash., D.C. Photostat copy in the Missouri Historical Society, St. Louis.

compact unit athwart the trails running to and from the upper Arkansas River and Taos and Santa Fe. While Bent's name does not appear in the original title papers to these grants, the records show that he soon obtained possession of a portion of three of them from the original grantees. Two of the grants, the Beaubien and Miranda and the Vigil and St. Vrain, developed stock ranches and settlement projects at Bent's instigation between 1844 and 1847. On his last trip to the States, in early June, 1846, Bent accompanied a group of settlers from Taos to the company's Poñil ranch or farm on the Beaubien and Miranda grant, some miles south of Raton Pass.[79] Perhaps Bent and his associates had become aware of the value of such foreign-made grants to claimants when the United States acquired the territory from another country, because of their knowledge of the value of French and Spanish grants along the Mississippi, especially in Missouri after 1803.

The other prominent feature in Bent's later life was political, for in September, 1846, he was appointed the first U.S. civil governor of New Mexico.[80] Two years before, he had become concerned over the election of James K. Polk as President of the United States, apparently because it threatened war with Mexico. Subsequently, Bent had established friendly relations with Colonel Stephen W. Kearny, at least by the time of the latter's 1845 visit to Fort Bent. In the late spring of 1846, with American preparations for war in progress, particularly those for raising Kearny's army that was to invade New Mexico, Bent and his partner Ceran St. Vrain hurried from Santa Fe to Ft. Leavenworth, conferred with Col. Kearny, and assured him of the possibility of an easy and perhaps peaceful conquest of the department. Ostensibly, too, arrangements were completed at

[78] Dunham, "Governor Charles Bent," 249-50.

[79] Letter from Charles Bent at Taos, June 1, 1846, to M. Alvarez. *New Mexico Historical Review,* XXXI, (Apr. 1956), 164.

[80] Dunham, "Governor Charles Bent," 257-61.

that time for assembling Kearny's Army of the West at Bent's Fort.

When that army entered Santa Fe on August 18, 1846, without having fired a shot, Bent had not yet returned from St. Louis. Nevertheless, he reached the New Mexican capital a few days later, and within a month was appointed governor.[81] Other high ranking territorial officials were selected from American or Mexican residents of the territory, and several of them were connected with the large land grants mentioned above. The new governor promptly undertook to fulfill the burdensome and exacting duties of his office, and seemed to succeed except in gauging the degree of social unrest resulting from General Kearny's conquest. During December, 1846, it is true, Governor Bent was able to forestall an incipient revolt because he was secretly advised of it in time. Believing that he had scotched any further efforts of the kind, he sought a vacation in his home at Taos.

Unfortunately the forces of discontent had persisted, and they burst out in connection with a disagreement over the treatment of local prisoners so that there resulted the Taos Revolt of January 19, 1847.[82] Governor Bent was brutally slain in his own house, and other officials and citizens also lost their lives. The revolt was suppressed by troops under Colonel Sterling Price, assisted by a body of volunteers commanded by Ceran St. Vrain. The Governor's death cut short a life of great accomplishment and great promise. Among the many tributes that have been paid him by his contemporaries, that of William M. Boggs seems particularly fitting: Bent "was a noble man and was a great business man." [83]

---

[81] *Ibid.*, 262-5.

[82] R. E. Twitchell, *Military Occupation of New Mexico, 1846-1851* (Denver, 1909), 125-32.

[83] L. R. Hafen (ed.), "The Wm. M. Boggs Manuscript about Bent's Fort," in *Colorado Magazine*, VII, (Mar. 1930), 57.

Thomas Biggs

by JANET LECOMPTE
Colorado Springs, Colorado

Born in Pennsylvania about 1812, Thomas Biggs was in the Rocky Mountains by 1834, trapping with James Bridger's fur brigade. During the winter of 1834, Bridger and his men wintered on the Snake River near Nathaniel J. Wyeth's new trading post, Fort Hall. In February, 1835, the Blackfeet stole eighteen horses from Bridger's camp. Kit Carson, Mark Head, and ten others, including Thomas Biggs, were sent to recover them. They succeeded in finding the Blackfeet and capturing five of the horses, but not without a battle.[1] On February 26, 1835, on the way back to camp, Carson and Biggs stopped off at Fort Hall. There Biggs bought sugar and coffee and paid for it with beaver; Carson paid for his purchases with "one grey horse unbroken." The clerk at the fort treated the visitors to a half pint of rum, hoping perhaps to induce them to join his company, but the trappers returned to Bridger's camp.[2]

After his brief visit to Fort Hall, Thomas Biggs disappears from the records for nearly three years. In November, 1837, however, he was working for the American Fur Company as leader of a small party of French *engagés* on its way to make camp fifteen miles up the Platte from Fort William, the American Fur Company post later known as Fort Laramie. Biggs stopped at the fort and found there six unhappy American Fur Company trappers who had arrived on foot, having lost all their horses and belongings to the

---

[1] *Kit Carson's Own Story of His Life,* ed. Blanche C. Grant (Taos, 1926), 33f.

[2] Fort Hall Journal, Oregon Historical Society, microfilm copy courtesy of Dr. Richard G. Beidelman, Colorado College, Colorado Springs.

Crows. Their misery had been aggravated by the refusal of the bourgeois of Fort William to outfit them with more than some moth-eaten buffalo robes for bedding. Biggs immediately took charge of the trappers, obtained their necessities from the stingy bourgeois, and moved them up to his own camp, where they shared his powder and lead, his thirty broken-down horses, and even his precious tobacco. One of the trappers, Osborne Russell, held Biggs in high esteem. Russell's journal calls him "Mr.," a title the journal ordinarily reserves for brigade leaders and gentlemen, and it quotes Biggs's speech to the trappers, revealing him as a man of good sense, generosity and firmness. On December 20, 1837, Biggs's party on the Platte moved to the main winter camp on Powder River – and again we lose sight of Thomas Biggs for a time.[3]

On September 25, 1839, Thomas Biggs, now working for Sublette and Vasquez, arrived at Brown's Hole in northwestern Colorado to trade with the Indians.[4] Also at Brown's Hole that fall was a Bent, St. Vrain & Co. trader and a group of traders at Fort Davy Crockett. Opposition was so high that even the common courtesy of carrying each others' letters was unobserved. When Biggs wanted to send a letter to his employer at Fort Vasquez, he had to give it to a neutral party to hand to the Bent, St. Vrain & Co. trader who would be passing the fort.[5]

---

[3] Osborne Russell, *Journal of a Trapper* (Boise, Idaho, 1921), 79-82. Fifty years later Isaac Rose remembered that Tom Biggs went to Fort Laramie in 1837, and he also recalled an incident the following spring that reflects no credit upon Biggs but a large amount upon himself. According to Rose, when Biggs's party failed to return to Bridger's camp on Wind River, Rose and others were sent to Fort Laramie to find it. There they all spent a pleasant winter and in the spring they set out for Bridger's camp. On the way they met fifty Gros Ventres who demanded their pack horses and packs. Thomas Biggs, "showing the white feather," would have given the Indians their animals, but Rose exhorted the men to resist the Indians, and then in a heroic speech, talked the Indians out of their demands. James B. Marsh, *Four Years in the Rockies, or, The Adventures of Isaac P. Rose* (New Castle, Pa., 1884), 211-14.

[4] Robert Newell, "Memorandum of Robert Newell's Travels in the teritory of Missourie," MS in the library of the University of Oregon.

Upon learning that the Sioux intended to attack in the spring, some of the trappers determined to cross the mountains and return to Fort Vasquez on the South Platte. They left on January 24, 1840, a party of twenty including four Indian women, two children, and a string of horses carrying equipment and furs. As they set out the weather was warm and pleasant, but in a few days the snow began to fall and soon measured six feet deep in the hollows. There was no game; the horses began dying off for want of food and water. Soon the party was subsisting on dead horses and a few dogs, cooked lightly in a brief sagebrush fire. When the pack horses were almost gone, the men cached their furs high above the snow on a scaffold among the trees. On February 24 they reached the valley of the North Platte, where they made camp and built a log fort for defense against the Indians, for they were still 150 miles from their destination and almost without horses. Four men left for the South Platte to obtain horses, but sign of the hostile Sioux made them return to camp. A few days later Thomas Biggs and a half-breed took one horse to carry blankets and provisions, and set out on foot for Fort Vasquez by a route which promised no Indian interference. In forty-two days they returned with Mr. Vasquez himself and horses. Immediately Biggs went to fetch the beaver left behind on the scaffold, returning in five days. The party finally reached Fort Vasquez on April 24, four months after they had set out.[6]

In the next year or two Biggs found himself out of a job, for Fort Vasquez changed hands and then was abandoned. The last rendezvous was held in 1840, the American Fur Company closed its business in the mountains in 1842, and

[5] "The Peoria Party – Shortess," Hafen & Hafen, *To the Rockies and Oregon, 1839-1842* (Glendale, Calif., 1955), 105-6.

[6] "The E. Willard Smith Journal," Hafen & Hafen, *op. cit.*, 180f.

hundreds of trappers began looking for new occupations in new localities. Thomas Biggs went to Taos, New Mexico, and asked Charles Bent to get him a passport to California. Bent wrote the U.S. consul on September 4, 1842:

> Thare is an American gentleman heare, a native of Pensylvania, about thirty yeares of age, by the name of Thomas Biggs, who wishes to procure a pasport for California, so far as I have acquaintance with him, he is a worthy man, and one I have no hesitation in vouching for his good behavior. You will pleas doe me the favor to procure him a pasport if possible, and forward it to me, let me know the cost and I will refund you the money.[7]

If Biggs did get to California, he had returned by April 24, 1844, when either he or his deputy cashed a draft on Bent, St. Vrain & Co. at the St. Louis store of P. Chouteau Jr. & Co., in the amount of $1240.[8] There is no hint as to what goods or services Thomas Biggs provided for this large sum. It is possible that he obtained horses in California and sold them to the Bents, but proof is lacking.

Thomas Biggs was in Santa Fe at the time of the 1847 insurrection and served in Colonel St. Vrain's company of "mountain volunteers" which routed the insurgents at the Taos Pueblo in February, 1847.[9] After the company was mustered out at Taos on February 20, 1847, Biggs returned to Santa Fe and engaged in placer mining at Old Placer, twenty-seven miles south of Santa Fe.[10] He was still in Santa Fe in 1849.[11] In September, 1851, Biggs was living at Socorro, New Mexico, where he wrote Governor Calhoun regarding the loss of ten mules stolen by Apaches.[12] By 1852

---

7 Bent to Manuel Alvarez, September 4, 1842, Benjamin Read Collection, Museum of New Mexico, Santa Fe, N.M.

8 Cash Book HH, Chouteau Papers, Missouri Historical Society, St. Louis.

9 L. Bradford Prince, *Historical Sketches of New Mexico from the Earliest Records to the American Occupation* (Kansas City, 1883), appendix.

10 *Santa Fe Republican*, May 3, 1848, p. 2, c. 2; June 27, 1848, p. 2, c. 1.

11 Hafen & Hafen, *Fremont's Fourth Expedition* (Glendale, Calif., 1960), 247-8.

12 Ritch papers, Henry E. Huntington Library, San Marino, Calif.

he had bought a ranch on the Rio Grande opposite the ruins of Valverde, in partnership with one Smith,[13] which was sold to Henry Beckwith in 1857.[14] Biggs, in the meantime, had moved to Salt Lake City where on October 22, 1855, he bought a lot from Hezekiah Duffin for forty dollars.[15] There we must leave him, for his trail becomes too faint to follow.

[13] "Private Land Claims in New Mexico," *House Exec. doc. 14,* 36 Cong., 1 sess. (ser. 1047), 229.

[14] Socorro (N.M.) County Records, Book D, 390.

[15] Salt Lake County (Utah) Records, Book A, 60.

Francis Ziba Branch

by JOHN E. BAUR
Los Angeles, California

Branch was born in Scipio, Cayuga County, New York, on July 24, 1802.[1] His grandfathers both served in the Revolutionary War. Branch's father died when he was too young to remember him, and since his mother was poor, the children were scattered among relatives. At eighteen, young Ziba left his home and became a sailor at Buffalo, working for about five years on Lake Erie boats. His activities during this period are untraceable.[2] Later, he went to St. Louis. In 1830, he joined a trading company commanded by one Captain Savory [St. Vrain] en route to Santa Fe, where the party, according to Branch, consisting of 150 men and 82 wagons, arrived safely in July.[3] That fall, Branch joined William Wolfskill's party which planned to trap in the Tulare Valley, California, after entering by way of southern California.[4] They hoped to get beaver in the San Joaquin before returning by way of the Great Salt Lake.[5]

According to an interview Branch gave a generation later, they journeyed from New Mexico towards the Great Salt Lake, crossed the headwaters of the Colorado, and struck a stream they called the "Pooneca," supposedly the Sevier

---

[1] *San Luis Obispo Tribune,* May 16, 1874. In Mrs. F. H. Day, "Sketches of the Early Settlers of California: Ziba Branch," *The Hesperian,* October 1859 (San Francisco) III, p. 337, it is stated that he was born in 1803.

[2] John Adam Hussey, "The Wolfskill Party in California," M.A. thesis, University of California, Berkeley, May, 1835, p. 170.

[3] Day, *op. cit.,* 338.

[4] "The Story of an Old Pioneer," Wilmington (Calif.) *Journal,* October 20, 1866, p. 1.

[5] Hussey, *op. cit.,* 53.

River. In November the country was covered with snow. They struck off south of the Colorado and spent nine days crossing the region, breaking a path through two or three feet of snow. Branch and his companions found few beaver and no game and soon had entirely exhausted their supplies. They had left Santa Fe with four oxen, but killed the last one near Little Salt Lake and thereafter lived on mules and horseflesh. A welcome surprise was the kindly treatment of the Mohaves, then notoriously hostile, who gave them bread, pounded corn baked in ashes, some dried pumpkins, and small white beans.[6] After two days with the Mohaves, during which the party traded red cloth and knives for food, they set out west again, arriving in the San Bernardino area by February of 1831. The Wolfskill party had opened a new route between New Mexico and southern California previously only traversed partly by others. This, the Old Spanish Trail, had been proved feasible for travel from Taos to Los Angeles.[7]

Soon thereafter, the tired wayfarers proceeded to Los Angeles where the party disbanded. Very few of the men planned to remain permanently in California. We do not know if Branch felt the same. In any case, his brief days as a Mountain Man were over. He was destitute and, like the rest, had to earn money in order to return to New Mexico or survive in California. There were no trapping prospects until late fall, so Wolfskill made no attempt to hold his men. Branch's interviewer, Mrs. F. H. Day, in 1859, stated his typical predicament: "Mr. Branch, like so many more of those early Pioneers, reached California with nothing but his gun by which to make his living. This, however proved in his skillful hand, to be all the capital he needed, and

---

[6] Day, *op. cit.*, 338.

[7] See L. R. and A. W. Hafen, *Old Spanish Trail, Santa Fe to Los Angeles* (Glendale, Calif., 1954), 139-54.

with it he shot otter, the skins of which were very valuable, and always brought the ready cash." [8]

After three years of sea otter hunting at a time when these animals were becoming scarce, Branch turned to general merchandising in Santa Barbara. He seems to have been associated with Lewis T. Burton, another of the Wolfskill party of 1830-31.[9] Later, Branch sold out his interests to Alpheus B. Thompson, a native of Maine.[10] In 1835, he married Manuela Carlon, daughter of Seferino Carlon, a soldier of Santa Barbara. She and Branch had eleven children. By 1836, Branch was listed as a Catholic. The next year, he and Burton were running a boarding house in Santa Barbara. [11]

On April 6, 1837, Governor Juan Bautista Alvarado granted Branch the Rancho Santa Manuela on the Arroyo Grande in the San Luis Obispo area. In this wilderness he built an adobe house. The Arroyo Grande was then a favorite route of valley Indians attacking coastal ranches! [12] At first, Branch pursued the Indians alone and single-handedly faced the grizzly bear problem as well. Because of Indians and bears in the Arroyo Grande region, Branch kept his horses in a large corral, with one belled in order to warn him of a disturbance. Once he and other ranchers had to organize and ride against horse thieves. On another occasion he dug a pit with a companion, covered it with brush, climbed in, and waited to catch a bear which had killed one of his cows. The bear proved to be a female with a cub. Branch shot the cub and so infuriated the mother that neither man in the pit dared reload and fire, so they had to stay there until morning, when the she-bear left.[13]

[8] Day, *op. cit.*, 338-9.

[9] Hussey, *op. cit.*, 170.   [10] Day, *op. cit.*, 338.

[11] Hussey, *op. cit.*, 170.   [12] *Ibid.*

[13] Annie L. Morrison and John H. Haydon, *History of San Luis Obispo County and Environs* (Los Angeles, 1917), 54-55.

Meanwhile, Branch was running 700 to 800 head of cattle on his new ranch. Later, his land holdings became more extensive and included the Pismo, Corral de Piedra, and Bolsa de Chemisal ranchos. He took no part in the Mexican War, though Frémont's men appropriated sixty-five of his best horses. At one time he was the wealthiest man in San Luis Obispo County, owning over 37,000 acres and great herds, but before he died much of his stock had disappeared, chiefly due to the droughts of 1862-64. Their numbers fell from a peak of 20,000 head to only 800.[14] He said that early in 1863 a cattle buyer had offered him $28 a head for his animals, but he had refused and thus, due to the drought, lost $96,000.[15] In December, 1867, Branch paid $371.22 as his state and county tax on property valued at $9,280.26.[16]

During the land title litigation following American occupation of California, Branch had retained the firm of Hinchman & Hoover to defend successfully in the U.S. District Court his titles to ranches at Santa Manuela, Arroyo Grande, and Huerhuero.[17] Branch had purchased from Isaac J. Sparks in 1858 the Huasna Ranch for $20.000.[18]

As a result of a dispute over Branch cattle using neighboring lands, inspectors on April 2, 1846, had reported his estate as "covered with fine pastures, and that there being 2,500 Branch cattle according to the prevailing count by the previous year's branding, there was enough land to pasture these cattle and two or three thousand more."[19]

---

[14] Hussey, *op. cit.,* 181.   [15] Morrison and Haydon, *op. cit.,* 55.
[16] Tax receipt, San Luis Obispo County, December 12, 1867, of Francis Ziba Branch in Branch Papers, Bancroft Library, University of California, Berkeley.
[17] Receipt in Branch Papers, Bancroft Library, dated March 18, 1856.
[18] All the notes given by Branch to Sparks in 1859-1861 are in the Branch Papers, Bancroft Library.
[19] Papers in dispute between José María Villavicencio and Francis Ziba Branch; T. W. Norris Collection, Bancroft Library. Testimony before Victor Linares, March 18, 1846, n.p.

Francis Ziba Branch kept journals rather sporadically during his ranching years. He was a fair speller. He paid for his drygoods and hardware purchases with hides, tallow, onions, and potatoes in the 1840s.[20] Later notations tell of rodeos, calf branding, sheepshearing, building a grist mill for his and his neighbors' grain, contain the lists of Indian men and boys working for him, and record his receiving a share in a quicksilver mine near San Simeon and his inspection of it in 1860.[21] Later entries grew briefer, speaking of his interest in pioneer beekeeping and his attending the school trustees meeting when a new teacher was hired. Branch was civic-minded, active in local politics from the time San Luis Obispo County was organized in 1850. He was the first county assessor, and in 1851 became *juez de campo,* a worthy position for the area's leading cattleman. He was also a member of the county board of supervisors in 1852.[22]

One room of Branch's old adobe ranch house was used as a schoolroom where fifteen children, mostly relatives, were educated.

A San Francisco visitor in the spring of 1865 found the ranch as idyllic as the Mexican inspectors of 1846 had. He was impressed by the gentle manners of the "old, very old pioneer," and described the oak, cottonwood, sycamore, and willow as well as the abundance of water from Arroyo Grande. In these latter years, Branch was interested in petroleum. Tar springs about half a mile from his residence were now attracting attention, though for twenty years Branch himself had used the liquid for wagon grease. He

---

[20] Branch journals, 1842-47 *passim,* Branch Collection, Bancroft Library.

[21] Branch journals, 1858-68 *passim,* Branch Collection, Bancroft Library.

[22] Morrison and Haydon, *op. cit.,* 131.

had recently made a lease to eastern capitalists of the mineral oils of his ranch.[23]

Francis Ziba Branch died of bronchitis at his home on May 8, 1874, and was buried near the Santa Manuela house.[24]

---

[23] "Notes of a Tour through the Southern Coast Counties of California. No. 1; The Estate of Mr. Branch," San Francisco *Alta California*, May 3, 1865, p. 1.

[24] *San Luis Obispo Tribune,* May 16, 1874. See also, Yda Addis Storke, *A Memorial and Biographical History of the Counties of Santa Barbara, San Luis Obispo, and Ventura, California* (Chicago, 1891), 422.

See page 14 of this volume for Branch's portrait.

Calvin T. Briggs

by JANET LECOMPTE
Colorado Springs, Colorado

Calvin T. Briggs was born in 1808 at Brattleboro, Vermont.[1] By 1834 he had come as far west as St. Louis, where Nathaniel J. Wyeth hired him on April 14 to accompany a trading expedition to the Rocky Mountains. Briggs was to be paid $250 for 18 months, or $15.88 per month, a salary that indicates his inexperience as a Mountain Man.[2] At the rendezvous on Ham's Fork of the Green River, the partners of the Rocky Mountain Fur Company refused to accept goods Wyeth had contracted to bring out for them. Stuck with a large stock of trade goods, Wyeth went on to Snake River and built Fort Hall near the mouth of the Portneuf, where he intended to sell the goods to trappers and Indians. On August 5, Wyeth left the fort in charge of a small number of men and set out for the mouth of the Columbia to establish a salmon fishery. With him was Calvin Briggs, who, on August 27, 1834, was named in Wyeth's journal as one of two men who stayed at the rear on the march to collect the worn-out horses.[3] In November Wyeth sent his men, including Briggs, back to Fort Hall under Captain Thing,[4] arriving on Christmas Eve.[5]

From Christmas through New Year's there was bibulous celebration at Fort Hall, but Calvin Briggs did not join in –

[1] H. H. Bancroft, *Works*, XIX (San Francisco, 1885), 730; *Memorial and Biographical History of the Counties of Fresno, Tulare, and Kern, California* . . . (Chicago; n.d.), 820.

[2] Fort Hall journals, Oregon Historical Society library. Microfilm copy loaned to author by Dr. Richard G. Beidelman, Colorado Springs.

[3] "The Correspondence and Journals of Captain Nathaniel J. Wyeth, 1831-6." *Sources of the History of Oregon*, I (Eugene, Ore., 1899), 230.

[4] *Ibid.*, 148-9, 235 *passim*.

[5] Osborne Russell, *Journal of a Trapper* (Boise, Ida., 1921), 15.

or at least the ledgers of the post record no purchases of whiskey and rum by Briggs. In January he bought tea, sugar, soap and rice; in February he bought needles and thread; and on February 14 he bought two papers of vermillion, an Indian cosmetic, signifying perhaps the beginning of his relationship with the Shoshone (Snake) woman who was to be his lifetime companion. Between April 1 and May 20 Briggs was out on a beaver hunt, and on June 15 he joined Joseph Gale on the big fall hunt which lasted until October 16, 1835.[6]

In October, 1835, Briggs's contract with Wyeth expired, and was not renewed. For four months Briggs remained at Fort Hall, buying on credit such items as playing cards, liquor, tobacco, beads and dressed deerskins (for his wife?), and fish hooks. On February 15, 1836, he bought $595.32 worth of trade goods in partnership with Moses T. Collins, Charles Schriver, and Alexander Wade, and set out for the country north and west of Fort Hall to trap and trade with Indians. On the first of June they brought into camp at Walla Walla 35 beaver ($175), 31 otter ($114) and 14 muskrats and mink ($3.50). They were also credited with two horses delivered at the Grande Ronde on April 3 ($140) and the goods they had not traded. For four months' work each partner earned only $20.22, but with the traditional abandon of the free trapper, Briggs proceeded to increase his debt to the company by buying a number of things from the Fort Hall store, including a "superior rifle" ($60) and a three-point blanket ($13). He also bought more trade goods in partnership with Collins and was out trapping and trading until October 7. This time Briggs's share of the profits was $78.62.[7]

In his year as a free trapper Briggs earned far less than he had spent at the Fort Hall store and was obliged, on October 14, 1836, to enter the service of the company again,

---

[6] Fort Hall journals, *loc. cit.*   [7] *Ibid.*

without a contract but at a salary of $25 per month, or twice as much as he was originally paid. On this salary he remained at Fort Hall through the winter of 1836-37, trapping in nearby streams or trading at nearby Indian villages, until on April 4 he decided to trap for himself again – and this time he was successful. On May 26 he turned in 13 beaver, 1½ otters and 1 muskrat, for which he received $71.25; on June 10 he brought in 4½ beaver; on June 28 he brought in 6 beaver. On August 2, 1837, he turned in 5 beaver and bought one spur ($0.37½) to balance and close his account with Wyeth's company, whose assets including Fort Hall were taken over by the Hudson's Bay Company shortly after.[8]

Calvin Briggs's three years of trapping for Wyeth would have netted him little besides a "superior rifle" and a wealth of experience, except that sometime during this period he had gathered to himself two of life's inestimable treasures – a good friend and a faithful wife. The friend was John J. Burroughs, a trapper from Kentucky whom Briggs met first at Fort Hall in January, 1835. They were together on the fall hunt in 1835, when each was charged one beaver skin for damaging a rifle in Bridger's camp.[9] Their friendship was cemented when they married Shoshone sisters, and their marriages were remarkable in that both men returned to civilization in later years taking their Indian wives and half-breed children with them. Briggs's first child, Thomas L., was born in the present state of Colorado on March 1, 1839, and later became a wealthy and respected businessman of Bakersfield, California. Briggs and his wife also had three other children.[10]

Calvin Briggs's movements are vague for the next few years. Bancroft indicates he may have been in California in 1837.[11] Dick Wootton says that Briggs was a member of a

[8] Ibid.   [9] Ibid.   [11] Bancroft, op. cit., 730.
[10] Memorial History of Counties of Fresno, Tulare, and Kern, 820.

trapping party of seventeen men who left Bent's Fort in June, 1837, trapped the Rio Grande del Norte, the Arkansas and "pretty much all the streams of Colorado and Wyoming," wintered in Wyoming, and returned to Bent's Fort in March, 1838. Wootton's date is in error, for we know Briggs was at Fort Hall until August, 1837, but he gives an interesting account of Briggs, Burroughs and their wives:

> We had two men in the party, one by the name of Briggs and another named Burris who were in partnership. These men were brothers-in-law, they having married two Indian women belonging to the "snake" tribe, who were sisters.
>
> These two squaws shared the hardships of the trip, traveling along with the party. They did the cooking for their husbands, mended their moccasins and clothes, and took care of themselves quite as well as any of the men. Both Briggs and Burris, with their squaw wives, afterwards went to California, and settled in the neighborhood of Sacramento, where they became very wealthy.[12]

George Simpson describes a reunion of Briggs and Burroughs and their wives after a separation of a few months. In the fall of 1839 Briggs joined one of the several fur companies operating in U.S. territory, and Burroughs took their Shoshone wives to Fort Hall. While Burroughs spent the winter trapping for the Hudson's Bay Company, the Indian sisters visited their Shoshone relatives. In June, 1840, Briggs, George Simpson, Bill Williams, Lew Anderson, and Charles Kinney camped on the Portneuf near Fort Hall and were joined by Burroughs and the two squaws:

> With Briggs, the meeting with his partner was a red letter day, at least he said it was, or something like it, for he was also reunited with his Sarah Ann, who, like Burroughs' Susan, had been having a "high old time" with her people, the Shoshones.[13]

By 1843 Briggs and Burroughs had begun to live on the

---

[12] H. L. Conard, *"Uncle Dick" Wootton* (Chicago, 1890), 55.

[13] Senex [pseud. of George Simpson], "Pah-U-Tah," *Trinidad Daily News,* undated clipping, probably October or November, 1882, Dawson Scrapbook I, p. 409, Colorado State Historical Society library, Denver.

Arkansas River in Colorado, at or near Fort Pueblo, one of the little settlements founded by trappers who had been forced out of work by the decline of the fur trade.[14] One of their friends here was John Brown, who later wrote a book about his experiences as a trapper and as a spiritualist. In the book Brown says he lived in an Indian lodge with Burroughs and Briggs in 1843-44 on the Arkansas near Pueblo. One night Brown's "spirit guide" told him in a dream that when Calvin Briggs went out to hunt deer the next day, Brown must stay with him or else something terrible would happen to Briggs. In the morning Brown and Briggs started off to go deer hunting together, but at the junction of the St. Charles with the Arkansas they separated, having forgotten the prophecy. Soon Brown had clear warning from his "spirit guide" to return to Briggs, whom he found lying prostrate on the river ice, his hand and arm caught fast in a beaver trap he had set several days earlier and was checking as he passed by. The hole in the ice was too small to withdraw the trap, and here Briggs would have died, frozen to the ice, had Brown not reached him in time.[15]

Between 1846 and 1848, and probably for several years before, Briggs and Burroughs lived in jacal cabins on Hardscrabble Creek, several miles above the Hardscrabble settlement and below the log headquarters of Mathew Kinkead's cattle ranch.[16] They undoubtedly worked for Kinkead part of the time, but the diary of Alexander Barclay, who lived at the Hardscrabble village, showed that they did other things in other places: From November 20 to November 24, 1844, Briggs was at the Hardscrabble village; on March 19, 1845, Briggs and Cosper killed their hog which weighed

[14] Mrs. George Simpson to F. W. Cragin, interview, October 31, 1904, El Paso, Tex., Cragin Collection, Pioneer's Museum, Colorado Springs.

[15] John Brown, *Mediumistic Experiences of John Brown, the Medium of the Rockies* (San Francisco, 1897), 190-2.

[16] Mrs. Felipe Ledoux, interview with F. W. Cragin, Las Vegas, N.M., June 17, 1908, Cragin Collection.

380 pounds with the head; on March 24, 1845, Briggs and Cosper went to trade with the Utes camped on the Arkansas; on April 3, 1845, Barclay settled his account with "Burris" and Briggs; on July 2, 1845, Briggs and Saboren arrived from a trapping trip with 17 beaver; on August 24, 1846, Briggs arrived in Hardscrabble from Pueblo and on November 1 he returned to Pueblo; on November 30, 1847, Rube Herring and Briggs arrived at Barclay's houses two miles above Pueblo, and on December 2 Briggs went on to Hardscrabble.[17] In 1848 Barclay moved to New Mexico and his diary does not mention Briggs again, but Lancaster Lupton's account book for his Hardscrabble store shows that Lupton paid "Biggs & Burrows" five dollars on December 10, 1847.[18]

Hardscrabble and Pueblo were abandoned in 1849 and a number of the inhabitants, including Calvin Briggs, John Brown, and probably John J. Burroughs, set out for California, arrived at Salt Lake City July 4, 1849, and Sutter's Fort September 1, 1849.[19] Briggs and Burroughs first settled near Sacramento, where Briggs sold milk. Four years later Burroughs returned with his large family to Kentucky [20] and Briggs moved to Tulare County and began raising stock on Dry Creek. In 1859 the family moved to Kern County and raised cattle on the open range here and in San Luis Obispo County.[21]

Calvin T. Briggs died at Sacramento in 1868, aged 60.[22] In eulogy his friend John Brown wrote of him, "Mr. Briggs was a good man, and is in just such a heaven as he made in earth-life." [23]

---

17 Diary of Alexander Barclay, microfilm copy in Colorado State Hist. Soc.

18 Lupton papers, Colorado State Historical Society library.

19 L. A. Ingersoll, *Ingersoll's Century Annals of San Bernardino County, 1769 to 1904,* (Los Angeles, 1904), 650; John Brown, *op. cit.,* 192.

20 John Brown, *op. cit.,* 192.

21 *Memorial History of Counties of Fresno, Tulare, and Kern,* 820.

22 John Brown, *op. cit.,* 192; Bancroft, *op. cit.,* XIX, p. 730.

23 John Brown, *op. cit.,* 192.

Lewis T. Burton

by JOHN E. BAUR
Los Angeles, California

Lewis T. Burton was born in Henry County, Tennessee, in 1809.[1] In 1831, he came to California with the famous William Wolfskill expedition. When the Wolfskill party disbanded, Burton settled in Santa Barbara and engaged in sea otter hunting, trading, and, eventually, in farming. In 1836, he described himself as a bachelor in business with Francis Ziba Branch, another former member of the Wolfskill group.

In 1839, Burton married María Antonia, daughter of Carlos Carrillo, and was naturalized as a citizen of Mexico in 1842. In 1845, Thomas O. Larkin praised Burton highly. After the Mexican War, Burton was a claimant for the Jesús María and Chemizal ranches.[2] After the death of his first wife he married a daughter of José Antonio Carrillo. He himself died in Santa Barbara in May, 1879.[3]

---

[1] *Santa Barbara Press,* May 24, 1879.

[2] In 1843, Burton had purchased from Francisco Quijada half of the Rancho Bolsa de Chemizal and the rest of it between 1846 and 1852. This tract contained 14,335 acres. The United States Land Commission granted Burton clear title to it in 1855. In 1851, Burton had purchased 2/3 of Rancho Jesús María in Santa Barbara County, containing 42,184 acres. See John Adam Hussey, "The Wolfskill Party in California," M.A. thesis, University of California, Berkeley, May, 1935, pp. 187-8.

See also J. P. Harrington, *Exploration of the Burton Mound at Santa Barbara, California* (Washington, D.C., 1928), 31-3 and 58-60.

The Burton papers at the Bancroft Library, University of California, Berkeley, refer to claimants of the Jesús María and Chemizal ranches.

[3] Hubert Howe Bancroft, "Pioneer Register and Index," in *History of California* (San Francisco, 1886), II, p. 738. See also, Abel Stearns Papers, Henry E. Huntington Library, 15 items, Burton to Stearns, covering business correspondence, 1836-56. At the California State Library, Sacramento, in the William Heath Davis papers are three letters from Burton to Davis, written from Santa Barbara, 1849, 1850, 1851, regarding routine business transactions.

At the time that Burton was seeking sea otter in California during the 1830s, it was impossible for a newcomer to get a hunting license, but Captain William Godwin Dana, captain of the port of Santa Barbara, had such a license, so Burton, Isaac Sparks, and other hunters, used it, paying Dana a share of their skins. Burton, Sparks, and another sea otter hunter, Job F. Dye, went aboard the newly-built Mexican schooner, *Peor es Nada,* at Monterey and sailed for Lower California during the summer of 1835, returning that fall after a very poor hunt which brought only twenty-five skins, when they should have secured two hundred.[4] In 1841, Captain John Wilson got financial aid from the prospering Burton to outfit a sea otter voyage. Men, canoes, and supplies were put aboard a brigantine belonging to Wilson and his partner for an extended trip along both the upper and lower coasts of California. The returns seem to have been good, but Burton and Wilson were reported to have been so stingy that they did not sufficiently feed the hunters, several of whom refused to work and left the ship![5]

In March, 1849, Nidever and Burton went to the gold mines between the Tuolumne and the Stanislaus rivers, but apparently Burton did not stay long.[6]

A prominent citizen of Santa Barbara, Burton became assessor for the county in 1850.[7]

---

[4] *The Life and Adventures of George Nidever,* ed. by William Henry Ellison (Berkeley and Los Angeles, 1937), 36-7.

[5] *Ibid.,* 58.

[6] *Ibid.,* 75.

[7] Consult Jesse D. Mason, *History of Santa Barbara County, California* (Oakland, 1883), 48; and Yda Addis Storke, *History of Santa Barbara County* (Chicago, 1871), 36-7.

John Pierre Cabanné, Sr.

by RAY H. MATTISON
National Park Service

Described as a "merchant" and also as "prominent in the fur trade for exceeding forty years," John (Jean) Pierre Cabanné was the son of Jean Cabanné and Jeanne Dutilh. He was born in the city of Pau, Bearne, France, October 18, 1773. After receiving a good education in France, he migrated to New Orleans where he remained for a time and then came to St. Louis in 1798. He soon became identified with the prominent French families of that town by marrying Julia, the eldest daughter of Charles Gratiot, Sr., a fur trader and merchant, on April 8, 1799. Sylvester Labbadie and Pierre Chouteau, Jr., both very active in the fur trade of St. Louis, were Cabanné's brothers-in-law.[1]

Apparently, Cabanné entered the fur trade soon after his arrival in St. Louis. On April 26, 1800, Gregory Sarpy and Cabanné, stating they had been exploiting the post of the Kansas Indians for two years, petitioned for the exclusive trade of that tribe, in consideration for which they would make a treaty of peace with those Indians.[2] In July, 1801, the Spanish government gave the partners exclusive trading privileges for two years.[3] Cabanné soon developed a thriving mercantile establishment and played an important part in breaking up the Clamorgan monopoly in the Spanish fur trade.[4]

Cabanné early established a close relationship with the

---

[1] Frederick L. Billon, comp., *Annals of St. Louis in its Early Days* (St. Louis, 1886), 473-5.

[2] A. P. Nasatir, *Before Lewis and Clark* (St. Louis, 1952), II, pp. 614-16.

[3] *Ibid.,* 592.

[4] Richard E. Oglesby, *Manuel Lisa and the Opening of the Missouri Fur Trade* (Norman, Okla., 1963), 168.

John Jacob Astor fur trade interests in the East. In 1812, in
violation of the Embargo and Nonintercourse Acts, Cabanné and one Chenie, another St. Louis trader, who may
have been acting for the Chouteau interests, attempted to
smuggle furs into Canada. They were arrested and six hundred packs of furs, some of which belonged to Astor, were
seized and confiscated.[5] On September 6, 1816, Cabanné was
granted a license to trade with the Iowa, Sac, Fox, and
Sioux in Missouri Territory.[6] On August 18, 1817, Cabanné
& Company were granted a license to trade with the Indians
on the Upper Missouri.[7]

Cabanné's family home in St. Louis was described as "a
seat of pleasant hospitality; but like many of the fur traders
he spent part of each year in the Indian country . . ."[8]
He was one of the stockholders of the Territorial Bank of
Missouri and a Trustee for the town of St. Louis.[9] Cabanné
belonged to a political group dubbed "little junto" which
was dominated in the economic field by Auguste Chouteau,
his innumerable relatives, and by Bernard Pratte, Charles
Gratiot and Jules De Mun; and in politics by Governor
William Clark, Edward Hempstead, and his brother, John
Scott of Ste. Genevieve, and some others.[10] Cabanné had a
country homestead; in 1833, he built a city residence located
at No. 20 Vine Street, St. Louis.[11]

In an attempt to achieve a monopoly in the fur trade on
the Missouri River following the War of 1812, the reorganized Missouri Fur Company, which had been formed

5 Paul C. Phillips, *The Fur Trade* (Norman, Okla., 1961), II, p. 251.

6 Clarence E. Carter (ed.), *The Territorial Papers of the United States*, XV, The
Territory of Missouri, 1815-1821 (Washington, 1951), 191.

7 *Ibid.,* 378.

8 Reuben G. Thwaites, ed., *Travels in the Interior of North America by Maximilian, Prince of Wied* (Cleveland, 1905), I, pp. 271-2.

9 *Bulletin of the Missouri Historical Society,* IV (1948), 211; VII (1949), 74.

10 *Ibid.,* V (1948), 5.

11 Elliott Coues (ed.), *Forty Years a Fur Trader* (Minneapolis, 1962), I, p. 161.

by Manuel Lisa and Theodore Hunt in June, 1814, decided in 1817 to broaden the base of its operations. Lisa took into this new partnership under the name of Cabanné & Company, Bernard Pratte, Bartholomew Berthold, Pierre Chouteau, Jr., and Hunt, several of whom later were partners in the Western Department of the American Fur Company. This new company was worth $60,000, of which Cabanné furnished $15,925.[12] In a short time, Cabanné and some of the others decided to divest Lisa of his control of the new company, so the partnership dissolved by mutual consent June 1, 1819.[13] By 1821, another organization, Berthold, Chouteau & Pratte, known also as "the French Company," of which Cabanné was a partner, was operating on the Missouri. After changing its name in May, 1823, to B. Pratte and Company, of which Cabanné, Pierre Chouteau, Jr., and Berthold were members, the partnership in December, 1826, merged with Astor's American Fur Company, which had set up its organization in St. Louis in 1822, and became its Western Department. In July of the following year, the Western Department and the Columbia Fur Company, an opposition company, also merged. By a new trade agreement, the Western Department agreed to confine its operations to the Missouri Valley south of the Big Sioux River.[14]

Meanwhile, in 1819, Cabanné was sent to take charge of the French Company post at Council Bluff,[15] in competition with the Missouri Fur Company. In 1823, after Berthold, Chouteau, and Pratte and Company had founded a post near Fort Atkinson, Cabanné was the resident partner.[16]

---

[12] Oglesby, *op. cit.*, 167-170; Dale L. Morgan (ed.), *The West of William Ashley, 1822-1838*, xlix-l.

[13] Oglesby, *op. cit.*, 171-2.

[14] Hiram M. Chittenden, *The American Fur Trade of the Far West* (New York, 1936), I, pp. 327-8.

[15] David Lavender, *Bent's Fort* (Garden City, N.Y., 1954), 41.

[16] Morgan, *op. cit.*, 243.

Cabanné remained intermittently at Council Bluff for over a decade.[17] While at that post, Cabanné and his company engaged to a limited degree in the emerging Santa Fe trade.[18] The expedition sent out by Cabanné in 1825 had a member, James Ohio Pattie, who later published a famous account of his adventures.[19]

When Maximilian, Prince of Wied, and the artist, Charles Bodmer, made their journey up the Missouri in 1833, they were entertained at Cabanné's post. The German prince reported, "We spent a very pleasant evening with Mr. Cabanné; sitting in the balcony of his house, we enjoyed the delightful temperature and the fine scene around us." [20]

Meanwhile, in 1831, while at Council Bluff, Cabanné became involved in an episode over the illegal seizure, under his orders, of 250 gallons of alcohol and other trade goods from an independent trader, Narcisse Leclerc. As the result of the repercussions from this affair, the American Fur Company almost lost its license to trade and Cabanné ruined his career in the Indian country.[21] Following Maximilian's visit, Cabanné was relieved as superintendent of the company's post at Council Bluff by Major Joshua Pilcher.[22]

In 1834, Astor sold his interests in the Western Department to Pratte, Chouteau & Company (changed to Pierre Chouteau, Jr., and Company in 1838).[23] Although Cabanné

---

[17] Cabanné, and the post he operated near Fort Atkinson, were frequently mentioned in the "Diary of James Kennerly, 1823-1826," edited by Edgar B. Wesley, in *Missouri Historical Society Collections,* VI (October, 1928), 41-97.

[18] Morgan, *op. cit.,* 153-7.

[19] Archibald Hanna and William H. Goetzman (eds.), *The Personal Narrative of James O. Pattie* (New York, 1962); Morgan, *op. cit.,* 156.

[20] Thwaites, *Maximilian's Travels,* I, p. 273.

[21] Chittenden, *op. cit.,* I, pp. 348-50.

[22] Thwaites, *Meximilian's Travels,* I, p. 274.

[23] Chittenden, *op. cit.,* I, p. 364.

retained his partnership in the firm, his role in the firm's affairs appears to have been an inconspicuous one.[24] About 1840, there was a misunderstanding on the part of several members of the company and Cabanné and, apparently, Pratte withdrew and formed an opposition company.[25] Cabanné died June 27, 1841, at his St. Louis home.[26]

Cabanné had eleven children. One of his daughters, Adelle, married John B. Sarpy, who likewise became a well-known figure in the fur trade. His sons John Charles and John Pierre, Jr. were associated with the father in the fur business. His son Julius died while on a trip on the Missouri. The family's interests in the fur trade were continued after John, Sr.'s death in the firm Pratte, Cabanné & Company, which, during the 1840s, opposed the American Fur Company on the Upper Platte near Fort Laramie.[27]

---

[24] *Contributions to the Historical Society of Montana,* x (1940), 286.

[25] Elliott Coues, *Forty Years a Fur Trader,* I, p. 161.

[26] Billon, *op. cit.,* 473.

[27] LeRoy R. Hafen and Francis M. Young, *Fort Laramie and the Pageant of the West* (Glendale, Calif., 1938), 87.

Moses Carson

by HARVEY L. CARTER
Colorado College, Colorado Springs

Moses Bradley Carson was the fourth of five children of Lindsey Carson by his first wife, Lucy Bradley Carson.[1] He was, thus, the older half-brother of the famous Kit Carson. All of the nine sons of Lindsey Carson appear to have been engaged, at one time or another, and in various ways, in the trade over the Santa Fe Trail, but only Moses and Kit seem to have had extensive careers in the fur trade.

There is some question as to both the date and place of Moses Carson's birth; the probability is that he was born in South Carolina on September 12, 1792.[2] It is thought the family moved to Madison County, Kentucky, in 1793, and from there to Howard County, Missouri, in 1811.[3] Lindsey and his two sons, Andrew and Moses, served at Fort Kincaid during the War of 1812.[4]

Just when Moses Carson entered the fur trade is not known. The first mention of him occurs in connection with the reorganization of the Missouri Fur Company in 1819, at which time he was a minor partner, owning two out of a total of thirty shares, in this last effort of Manuel Lisa's to

---

[1] Lindsey Carson (1754-1818) had by his first wife five children – William, Sarah, Andrew, Moses, and Sophia. By his second wife, Rebecca Robinson, he fathered ten more – Elizabeth, Nancy, Robert, Matilda, Hamilton, Christopher, Hampton, Mary, Sarshall, and Lindsey. See *Carson-Bent-Boggs Genealogy* (Denver, 1962), 16-17.

[2] It is frequently stated that Moses Carson was born in Madison County, Kentucky; the date is also sometimes given as May 5, 1794. The first date seems more likely since his age at the time of his death in 1868 was reported as 76.

[3] See M. Morgan Estergren, *Kit Carson: A Portrait in Courage* (Norman, Okla., 1962), 13 and 16, on the probable times of the Carson family migrations to Kentucky and Missouri.

[4] Louis Houck, *History of Missouri*, III, p. 137.

make a going concern.[5] It seems reasonable to conclude from this fact that he probably had been employed in some of Lisa's earlier ventures and had thus earned enough to invest in the company.

When the management of this company devolved, after Lisa's death, upon Joshua Pilcher, we find that Carson continued to be in a position of trust and authority. Thomas Hempstead wrote to Pilcher in April, 1822, indicating that Carson had ordered 150 traps made, which could not be completed for lack of steel to make the springs.[6] In 1823, when the punitive expedition against the Arickarees was being prepared, Pilcher offered Colonel Leavenworth the services of forty men, captained by W. H. Vanderburgh, with Moses Carson as his first lieutenant.[7] From the standpoint of the trappers, Colonel Leavenworth's conduct of the campaign was a fiasco and, although Leavenworth specifically exempted Vanderburgh and Carson from the censure he placed on other trappers, these two wrote to Pilcher expressing their mortification at being praised by the Colonel and joining Pilcher in general condemnation of all his actions.[8] Carson undoubtedly continued with the Missouri Fur Company until its failure in 1825, but it seems that he did not continue with his old associates when they reorganized as Pilcher and Company, for he is reported to have been in Santa Fe as early as 1826.

Just how he was occupied until 1831 is not clear, but in that year he took employment with Ewing Young and accompanied him on his second trip to California.[9] Carson

5 Dale L. Morgan, *The West of William H. Ashley* (Denver, 1963), xlix. See also Richard E. Oglesby, *Manuel Lisa and the Opening of the Missouri Fur Trade* (Norman, Okla., 1963), 170, 172.

6 Morgan, *op. cit.*, 3.

7 *Ibid.*, 52.

8 Donald McKay Frost, *Notes on General Ashley, the Overland Trail, and South Pass* (Barre, Mass., 1960), 99-100; 115-16. See also David Lavender, *Bent's Fort* (Garden City, 1954), 38.

was with the second group of Young's men, who came into Los Angeles in March, 1832.[10] He left Young's employ soon after this, although he decided to remain in California.

In February or March, 1833, he turned up in company with George Yount at John Work's Hudson's Bay Company camp on the northern arm of San Francisco Bay. Yount and Carson brought in a number of horses, which they sold to Work.[11] On May 26, 1836, he applied for Mexican citizenship papers in Los Angeles, stating that he had been in Mexico ten years and in California for four years, at that time.[12] From 1836 to 1845, we lose sight of him, but there is not much doubt that he continued to trap and trade, residing for the most part in the Los Angeles area.

In 1845 he went to the Russian River district north of San Francisco Bay, where, near Sotoyome, he became foreman or overseer for Captain Henry Delano Fitch, on the great land grant which he developed as a cattle ranch.[13] He is known to have played an active part in the Bear Flag Revolt in 1846 and to have supplied Frémont with horses and munitions.[14]

---

[9] Job F. Dye, *Recollections of a Pioneer, 1830-1852* (Los Angeles, 1951), 18-29.

[10] E. L. Sabin, *Kit Carson Days* (New York, 1935), I, p. 66.

[11] Robert G. Cleland, *This Reckless Breed of Men* (New York, 1952), 335.

[12] *Carson-Bent-Boggs Genealogy,* 24. Also, in 1836, he had business dealings with Abel Stearns and J. J. Warner. See Stearns Papers, BOX 71, in the Huntington Library, San Marino, Calif.

[13] *Ibid.* See also Sabin, *op. cit.,* I, p. 406, and LeRoy R. Hafen (ed.) "W. M. Boggs Manuscript," in *Colorado Magazine,* VII (Mar., 1930), 63. The Fitch Grant was located sixteen miles above Santa Rosa, at present Healdsburg. Boggs relates that Moses Carson came and buried two Americans, who were killed and mutilated by Mexicans in 1846 at Santa Rosa. John Gantt, writing from Napa Valley on Aug. 22, 1847, to Dr. John Marsh, reported, "Even Moses Carson is on the look out for a wife, but unfortunately he blew himself up with a most tremendous explosion, in the company of some ladies; since that sad accident, which I had the misfortune to witness by hearing and smelling, our redoubtable friend Moses has made his appearance scarce in this neighborhood." See Alice B. Maloney, "Three Letters of John Gantt," in *California Historical Society Quarterly,* XX (June, 1941), 151.

[14] See *Senate Reports,* 242. 36 Cong., where he filed a claim upon the United States for $653 for such supplies.

Although well established in California, and although his half-brothers, Robert and Lindsey, were also in the Russian River area, as was a nephew Moses Carson Briggs, he returned in 1853 or 1854 to Missouri, first to Rockport and then to St. Louis. In St. Louis, he married "a young, fast or high toned widow," Mrs. Geeder (neé Buckhart) and, for a while, they attempted to run a hotel. But they quickly dissipated what Moses had made in the cattle business in California and the remnants of the widow's fortune. When everything was gone, Mose cleared out for Colorado, where he lived with Jesse Nelson, whose wife, Susan Carson, was a daughter of his half-brother Robert.[15]

"Big Mose," as Carson was commonly called, was described at this time as over sixty, rough and weather-beaten, six feet tall and weighing over 200 pounds, with only one good eye and lacking several fingers. He persuaded Kit Carson, at Taos, to outfit him with traps and horses and he and Jesse Nelson went on a trapping jaunt. They trapped from Bent's Old Fort, then partly in ruins but occupied by a couple of traders from Illinois, named Hatwood and Tibbets, up the Huerfano River to its source and over Mosca Pass to Fort Massachusetts, then back along the Cucharas. Nelson said that Mose was too old and stiff and that what beaver they caught he took himself. This was in April and May of 1855.[16] They returned to Taos and then for several months Mose lived in Santa Fe, where he charged everything to Kit's account. Kit eventually paid bills amounting to over $700, despite the fact that Mose had never helped him when he was younger, said Nelson.

---

15 Francis W. Cragin Papers in the Pioneer Museum, Colorado Springs, Notebook VIII, p. 47. It is commonly stated that Moses Carson never married, but Jesse Nelson (1825-1923) was Cragin's informant and his knowledge came directly from Moses Carson himself and soon after the event. Nelson's ranch was at Nine Mile Bottom on the Purgatoire River. Colorado Territory was as yet unformed in 1855.

16 *Ibid.*, Notebook VIII, pp. 51, 53.

It must have been at this time, in 1856, that Mose wrote to Abel Stearns in Los Angeles, describing a scheme to make Los Angeles the place of deposit for furs to be traded to the Orient.[17] At this late date, and at Carson's time of life, such a plan was visionary and nothing came of it.

It may be that Mose was the "Mike" Carson, mentioned as living in Tucson in 1858.[18] At any rate, his last years seem to have been spent in the Southwest. He died in Eagle Flat,[19] Texas, a mining camp in the mountains southeast of El Paso, on January 1, 1868, and was buried by the Masonic Lodge in their cemetery there on the following day.[20]

The career of Moses Carson, although it has points of interest, is one of anti-climax. He never attained the prominence of which his early years gave distinct promise, and is chiefly remembered because of the great fame achieved by his smaller and younger half-brother, Kit Carson, who died later in the same year.

---

[17] Cleland, op. cit., 66.

[18] W. Clement Eaton, "Frontier Life in Southern Arizona, 1858-1861" in Southwestern Historical Quarterly (January, 1933), XXXVI, p. 182. An excerpt from the diary of Phocion R. Way, dated June 12, 1858, and reprinted here, says, "An older brother of Kit Carson (Mike) also resides here. I should judge he is about 55 years of age, hair entirely gray, but a large, full chested, robust and stout looking man. He appears to have nothing to do but smoke and enjoy himself – he does not appear to possess the restless untiring disposition of his brother." The description fits Moses Carson well enough but the identification is not beyond question.

[19] F. W. Cragin Papers, Notebook VIII, p. 47. Jesse Nelson said Eagle Pass or Eagle View but Eagle Flat, about seventy miles southeast of El Paso, seems more probable.

[20] Sabin, op. cit., II, p. 911. Sabin may have been correct in believing that he died in El Paso.

Jacques Clamorgan

by A. P. NASATIR
San Diego State College

Jacques Philippe Clamorgan was a capable, aggressive, enterprising and farsighted promoter. Clamorgan, Clarmorgan, Glenmorgan, Clenmorgan, Claimorgan, Morgan (all variations of the same name, Jacques or Santiago Clamorgan) indicate the obscurity of his birth and nationality. Furthermore, the fact that he was either born or spent his early life in Guadalupe Island and the West Indies gives some credence to the belief that he was of Portuguese stock. Quite probably he was of mixed Welsh, Portuguese, and French blood. He may have carried a trace of Negro blood as well.

Of his early life, little is known. In the present documentation he emerges into history as a merchant in the West Indies. As early as 1780 he became associated with Thompson and Campbell of Kingston, Jamaica, probably in the slave trade between that island and New Orleans. He was also associated with Marmillion and Company of New Orleans.

In 1781, during war time, Clamorgan, evidently unable to obtain official permission to ascend to St. Louis, furtively left New Orleans together with some goods and outside the city boarded the vessel of Duchêne Perró, and ascended to St. Louis. Within a very short time after his arrival in the latter post, he succeeded in disposing of his goods, and asked Lieutenant Governor Francisco Cruzat for permission to descend to New Orleans. Due to the war and fear that he might fall in the hands of the Natchez rebels, Cruzat refused. But after repeated entreaties on the part of Clamorgan, Cruzat gave in and granted him a passport, and gave him some official documents to deliver to New Orleans. But the permission which Cruzat granted to Clamorgan specifically ordered him to stop at Arkansas post, and see and deliver the documents to the commandant of that post, Balthazar de Villiers. The latter was to decide whether it would be too risky to permit the descent of the documents (and presumably Clamorgan) by continuing the voyage down the river to the capital. If De Villiers decided that it was too risky then he was to forward the official dispatches and documents to New Orleans via Natchitoches. Clamorgan left St. Louis, probably late in August, 1781, but did not stop at the Arkansas post. Cruzat wrote Piernas at New Orleans about this disobedience of his orders on the part of Clamorgan and asked him not to permit such disobedience to go unpunished. Cruzat told the acting governor general that he had heard a good deal about Clamorgan, none of which was good.*

Although Cruzat seems to have heard only bad things about Clamorgan, it seems that the latter enjoyed a good reputation, for in the records of the court at New Orleans no doubt is indicated about collecting $2,500 in debts from him even though he was out of the country at the time. He was back in Spanish Louisiana by 1783, and in the latter part of that year, or very early in 1784, he ascended to Upper Louisiana in company with his friend and associate François Marmillion, merchant at St. Louis. Clamorgan himself tells us in 1793 that he had been a resident of Illinois for more than ten years.[1]

---

* Cruzat to Piernas, St. Louis, December 24, 1781, Archivo General de Indias, Sección Papeles de Cuba, legajo 114; Cruzat to Baltazar de Villiers, St. Louis, August 27, 1781, *ibid.*, 9.

[1] "Index to Spanish Judicial Record of Louisiana," *Louisiana Historical Quarterly*, XXII, *e.g.*, 298, 299, 300, 303.

That he was in St. Louis or in Spanish Illinois Country is attested to by the following, among many other documents: Cruzat to Miró, St. Louis, August 28, 1784,

Because of his business acumen, past reputation, and perhaps some money, Clamorgan quickly came to be a well-known and respected merchant in the Spanish Illinois country. His interests soon spread into many parts of the upper Mississippi valley. In 1783 he was empowered to act as proxy for, and was given power of attorney for, Gabriel Cerré,[2] of one of the best known families of Ste. Geneviève. Six years later he instituted court proceedings against Pierre La Coste of Michilimackinac for the sum of 15,947 livres and 14 sous. Many other financial transactions could be cited,[3] but Clamorgan was interested in real estate as well. He purchased some property soon after settling in Upper Louisiana. This acquisition was but the beginning of his land and real estate speculation which eventually topped the million arpent figure.[4] He early took an interest in civic affairs [5] and made donations to, and became a warden of the church in Ste. Geneviève.[6]

Archivo General de Indias, Sección, Papeles de Cuba, legajo 10, (hereinafter cited A.G.I., P. de C.); Cruzat to Navarro, St. Louis, August 28, 1784, ibid., 208A; Cruzat to Oro, St. Louis, June 1, 1785, ibid., 117A; Clamorgan to Trudeau, St. Louis, April 1, 1793, ibid., 26, printed in A. P. Nasatir, Before Lewis and Clark (2 vols., St. Louis, 1952), I, pp. 169-179. Here Clamorgan states that he has been in the Spanish Illinois Country for more than ten years. Clamorgan was witness to the will of Marmillion, St. Louis, December 4, 1784, St. Louis Archives, no. 2223 (Missouri Historical Society).

[2] Louis Houck, Spanish Regime in Missouri (2 vols., Chicago, 1909), II, p. 149.

[3] Many of these financial transactions are in the Missouri Historical Society; a few are given in Nasatir, Before Lewis and Clark. See also Houck, Spanish Regime, II, pp. 148-9.

[4] Land grants are given in American State Papers, Public Lands, especially volumes II and VIII; United States Documents, Ho. Doc. 59, 24 Cong., 1 sess., see e.g., 428-30. See also Nasatir, Before Lewis and Clark, II, pp. 560-1, where a number of his land grants are cited. Most of Clamorgan's land grants were rejected by the United States Government. His heirs later brought suit, United States Supreme Court Reports (vol. 101), XI, Otto 822. See also Houck, Spanish Regime, II, p. 149. Houck, History of Missouri (3 vols., Chicago, 1908), II, cites several real estate transactions and deals involving Clamorgan. See index.

[5] Clamorgan's name appears in most petitions drawn up by the residents and in patriotic donation lists, etc. Several of these are in the Bancroft Library. See Lawrence Kinnaird (ed.), Spain in the Mississippi Valley (3 vols., Washington, D.C., 1946), being volumes II, III, IV, of the Annual Report of the American His-

Thus we see Jacques Clamorgan as a slave dealer, fur trader, merchant, financier, land speculator; and although he never married, he was the father of four children. He was to become known in Louisiana as a statesman, an explorer, and a promoter.

Clamorgan was endowed with a tremendous imagination, together with an illusive pen and a glib tongue. His ability to put vast dreams onto paper and persuade all of their reality was envied by everyone. He was respected by all but he was not accepted socially by the aristocratic French Creoles of the province. This was less a reflection upon his charming personality than upon his well-stocked harem of colored beauties. He was known to be intriguing and at times his probity was somewhat doubted. Usually he was found to be pliant and even servile, but he was accustomed to conducting great operations.

He cultivated the friendship of the important merchants of New Orleans, Cahokia, Kaskaskia, Michilimackinac, and Montreal. He never failed to get what he wanted from the Spanish officials; if not directly, he achieved his purpose indirectly.

He was engaged in, or dreamed of engaging in, cattle raising, salt refining, lead mining, agriculture, and he envisaged a strong and populous Spanish frontier in the Mississippi Valley. He was the precursor of Lewis and Clark; he traversed Texas; and he engaged in the Santa Fe trade, long before his successors made those trails famous. This island "Creole" managed his affairs in such a way that even his enemies (and they were not few in number) could not fail to recognize his talents.

torical Association for the year 1945. See index. The petition asking that Didier be named priest in 1792 is in A.G.I., P. de C., 215A. This petition is dated July 16, 1792.

6 Clamorgan and Reilhe to Trudeau, St. Louis, July 30, 1793, A.G.I., P. de C., 208B.

In 1793 his fellow merchants unanimously chose him as syndic [7] to represent the merchants of St. Louis. Soon afterwards he became the driving force in the movement to restore commerce in the Spanish Illinois and to regain for the king of Spain sovereignty over the Spanish dominions in the Mississippi Valley.

But of all his work Clamorgan is best known for his activities in connection with the Missouri Company. This company was formed for the purpose of ousting the British from Spanish territory and trade; for capturing the trade with the Indians; for discovering a route to the Pacific and joining the Missouri with Mexico and California; to give Clamorgan a chance to get rich while at the same time it offered an opportunity of defending the Spanish against the onrush of the British and Americans, whom the Spanish lived in dread of; and to defend the Spanish empire on its long but undefended and unexplored northernmost frontier; and to protect rich Santa Fe. [8]

---

[7] Nasatir, *Before Lewis and Clark*, I, p. 190.

[8] The documentation upon which this account is based from this point until the transfer of Upper Louisiana to the United States in 1804 is far too vast to give specific citations. Nearly all of the material from the Archives of Spain, Missouri Historical Society, and the Bancroft Library has been published by this writer in his *Before Lewis and Clark*, where the documents may be found in full, in English translation and edited. Some documents from the Bancroft Library are published in Kinnaird, *Spain in the Mississippi Valley*, and in Houck, *Spanish Regime*. The above remarks refer to the Missouri Valley. The documentation relating to Clamorgan's activities in the Mississippi Valley, however, have not all been published nor indeed even used in print. Some of these will be cited as *e.g.*

Clamorgan sent to Carondelet under date of October 4, 1793, a plan for populating Illinois, saying that it was necessary to increase the population of the province in proportion to its area, especially along the important frontiers, in order to prevent an invasion. Agriculturalists were especially needed and Clamorgan urged a very generous plan to bring Germans and Hollanders, six thousand families at a cost of 174,550 piasters, which sum would be paid back in full within five years. Clamorgan's scheme was to strengthen the uninhabited parts of the Mississippi frontier and prevent the Anglo-Americans from penetrating New Mexico, since they could reach that area by land in fifteen or twenty days without trouble. He urged that the prospective settlers be brought from Europe to Philadelphia in neutral vessels and from there brought overland to the Illinois. This plan of population of Clamorgan

It was Clamorgan who suggested the formation of the renowned "Company of the Discoverers and Explorers of the Missouri."[9] In addition, he persuaded a number of merchants of Illinois to take part in the company. Although he was but one of nine members of the company, it was Clamorgan who became its director and managed the bold schemes of his fertile imagination. In carrying them out he succeeded in financially ruining not only himself but his associates.

The company sent three costly expeditions up the Missouri in an effort to drive the British from Spanish territory, develop the valuable trade of the Upper Missouri Valley, and discover a route to the Pacific Ocean. The first two efforts were complete failures. The third, headed by James Mackay and John Evans,[10] hauled down the British flag from a small fort among the Mandans. Part of this group then began the long trek to the Pacific coast. Had they continued on their planned route they might very well have been successful. This expedition, like the first two, was a financial failure. No profits accrued from any of the ventures, which fact, while not forcing Clamorgan to give up hope, melted the financial hearts of his colleagues.

Although he ruined himself in the company, Clamorgan made use of intrigue for personal gain. From the jealousies

is in the Bancroft Library and is translated in Kinnaird, *Spain in Mississippi Valley,* III, pp. 208-15.

Clamorgan presented plans to the governor to form at his own expense a fort and colony near the mouth of the Des Moines River to stop foreign commerce with the Indians, keep foreigners out of Spanish territory and establish a settlement there, in return for a six-year exclusive trade of the Des Moines, Skunk, and Iowa Rivers, and other concessions. Project of Clamorgan, St. Louis, December 15, 1795, A.G.I., P. de C., 2371. See A. P. Nasatir, "Anglo-Spanish Frontier on the Upper Mississippi 1786-1796," *Iowa Journal of History and Politics,* XXIX (1931), 207-8; 215-16.

9 See A. P. Nasatir, "Formation of the Missouri Company," in *Missouri Historical Review,* XXV (1930), 3-15.

10 See A. P. Nasatir, "John Evans: Explorer and Surveyor," *Missouri Historical Review,* XXV (1931), 219-39; 432-60; 585-608.

and envy of the merchants, his associates, and by cleverly rewriting the articles of incorporation of the company, he acquired all but one of the original shares. He petitioned, in the name of the company, for large grants of land which were conceded. Eventually these holdings came into his hands. Whenever any individual asked the government for trades which would endanger his bold schemes, Clamorgan not only successfully opposed them but usually got the concessions for the company and for himself. Those who continued to oppose the company found themselves controlled through Clamorgan's ability to advance and furnish merchandise.

He befriended and won to his side Regis Loisel,[11] and more important for a time at least, the wealthy British merchant Andrew Todd.[12] Backed by the wealth, reputation, and recognized ability of Todd, Clamorgan boldly plunged ahead with his schemes. A complete monopoly of the trades of the entire Upper Mississippi Valley as well as those of the Upper Missouri Valley would bring him wealth and most certainly would assure the Spanish sovereignty. Believing in this vast plan, he persuaded Todd to back him completely. He then persuaded the Spanish officials to accept Todd. Although in disrepute himself, he persuaded Governor General Carondelet to grant to Todd the exclusive trade of the Upper Mississippi along with reduced import and export duties and other commercial concessions.

Clamorgan got Carondelet to grant further exclusive

---

[11] See A. H. Abel, *Tabeau's Narrative of the Loisel Expedition to the Upper Missouri* (Norman, Okla., 1939), 17-32. Clamorgan, Loisel and Company is dealt with together with the documents in Nasatir, *Before Lewis and Clark.*

[12] Concerning Andrew Todd see A. P. Nasatir, "Anglo-Spanish Frontier on the Upper Mississippi 1786-1796," *Iowa Journal of History and Politics,* XXIX (April, 1931), 194-232; and Nasatir, "Anglo-Spanish Rivalry in the Iowa Country 1797-1798," *Iowa Journal of History and Politics,* XXVIII (July, 1930), 337-89; Abel, *Tabeau's Narrative,* 16-17. The documents relative to the Todd-Clamorgan relations are given and cited in Nasatir, *Before Lewis and Clark.*

grants of trade to the Missouri Company as well as a subsidy of 10,000 pesos for one hundred militiamen who were to guard forts which Clamorgan envisaged as established along a great arc reaching from the Mississippi River to the Pacific Ocean. Moreover, he persuaded Carondelet to make several important exceptions to the by-laws of the company.

As a result, Todd, who as a foreigner was specifically excluded, was given an equal share in the company. Carondelet ordered that all merchandise should be purchased through Todd, while Clamorgan revised the by-laws so that he could receive a two-and-a-half percent commission on all transactions of the company. In addition he arranged a contract with Todd whereby he received a high commission on all goods purchased by the company. Thus, despite the opposition of the other merchants of St. Louis, Clamorgan grasped into his own hands the monopoly of the Indian trade in both the Upper Missouri and Upper Mississippi Valleys. To take care of these advantages and to press for more, Clamorgan reorganized his own affairs and formed "Clamorgan, Loisel and Company" which made the arrangements and asked for concessions when not permitted to, or by, the Missouri Company – Clamorgan thus acting in a dual capacity.

Clamorgan succeeded in this enterprise, in part because he appeared to be fully supported by the resources of Todd, and because the governor was most anxious to oust the British from Spanish domain and to establish a route to the Pacific coast. Needless to say, Clamorgan made the most of Mackay's and Evans' explorations.

But these dreams toppled when Todd died during the yellow fever epidemic at New Orleans in 1796. Todd's heirs and creditors besieged St. Louis and New Orleans to get all they could. They made no effort to continue Todd's enterprise nor his contracts.[13] This was one time that Clamorgan overshot his mark. He was heavily indebted to the Briton, whose heirs and agents forced Clamorgan to the brink of bankruptcy.

Nevertheless, by sheer personality, by long, flattering, dreamy letters, and by visits to New Orleans, Clamorgan held on to all of the government concessions granted to the company. In fact, he gained more. He was bold enough to propose continuing efforts to defend the Spanish Empire and to discover a route to the Pacific, even in the face of financial ruin.

Clamorgan successfully opposed all of his opponents and kept them from taking advantage of his reverses. When any of his many opponents made claims against him, the results were meagre, as no one would ever testify against him. He took advantage of this situation, knowing that if his creditors pressed him he would have to foreclose on his debtors and thereby ruin many of the inhabitants of St. Louis.

Hence even Trudeau supported him. This, to Clamorgan, was the cue to ask for more. He again petitioned for 10,000 pesos, 2,000 pounds of gunpowder a year, and one-half million arpents of land.

At the same time, Clamorgan owed 25,000 pesos to Todd's estate,[14] and another 74,000 pesos to Daniel Clark of New

---

[13] Nasatir, "Anglo-Spanish Rivalry in the Iowa Country 1797-1798," *Iowa Journal of History and Politics,* XXVIII, (reprint pp. 44-8) ; letter of Trudeau to Carondelet, St. Louis, July 21, 1797, and enclosing letter of Isaac Todd to Trudeau, Michilimackinac, June 27, 1797. Isaac Todd, uncle of Andrew Todd, was the executor of Andrew Todd's will. He collected very little and the estate settlement was a long-drawn-out and protracted affair. Abel, *Tabeau's Narrative,* 17. Clamorgan to [Trudeau], St. Louis, June 18, 1798, in Nasatir, *Before Lewis and Clark,* II, pp. 563-6.

[14] James Swan, agent of Isaac Todd at Michilimackinac, went to St. Louis in 1798 to attempt to recover for Todd payment of debts owing by the firm of Clamorgan, Loisel and Company. M. M. Quaife (ed.) *John Askin Papers* (2 vols., Detroit, 1928), I, p. 375. Swan, however, was unsuccessful in this undertaking.

Orleans.[15] The latter brought suit but Clamorgan hurried
to the capital and effected a settlement. An agreement was
made in 1799, and Clark as well as Chouteau of St. Louis,
both of whom previously opposed Clamorgan, now aided
him, protected his property, and gave him financial support
and credit.

With the accession of weak governors in the colony, the
gains of the company were wiped out in the main. Clamorgan's opponents began to get trades which previously
had been reserved for the company. The British were
greatly strengthened on the Upper Missouri and were
descending as far as the Mahas. On the Mississippi, they
nearly usurped the trade north of St. Louis.

Again Clamorgan descended to New Orleans, this time
supported by Charles Dehault Delassus, lieutenant governor
at St. Louis. Daniel Clark, Jr., advanced credits and Clamorgan reasserted his bold schemes after a lapse of activity
for some time. In order to claim a new offer of a reward, he
sent Heney to discover the route to the Pacific. He was
thwarted by the British on the Upper Missouri.

Stripped of everything but a measly trade privilege with
the Panis Republic, Clamorgan asked for and obtained the
exclusive trade of the Otos, Mahas, and Poncas, all spec-
ulative trades on account of the British influence and in-
trusions. He also received the Kansas trade, which was sure
and profitable. Moreover, he renewed his request for 10,000
pesos, for 100 militiamen and 2,000 pounds of gunpowder.
In this he was thwarted by the Intendant of Louisiana and
the state of war between Spain and England, and the con-
sequent lack of support and the usual negligence of Spain.

15 Trudeau to Gayoso, no. 8, St. Louis, June 20, 1798, A.G.I., P. de C., 49, translated and published in Nasatir, *Before Lewis and Clark*, 567-8. There is a large
correspondence with regard to these Clamorgan debts in Missouri Historical Society,
Clamorgan Collection. See Nasatir, *Before Lewis and Clark*, II, pp. 569-70.

Soon, however, Clamorgan's competitors prevailed upon the weak-willed Governor Casa Calvo and he was again stripped of all privileges except the trade of the Panis. Again he resorted to making money by backing the efforts of others. He obtained a one-third interest in the Loisel-Heney contract and company. By this device, Clamorgan's plans for the Spanish frontier were carried on until the occupation of Louisiana by the Americans. Another thrust was made towards the Pacific and Clamorgan again descended to New Orleans to solicit the aid of the government. Conflicting exclusive grants made by favoritism of the governor, and the need of arranging his business affairs, also caused this descent to New Orleans.

Clamorgan returned to St. Louis carrying orders for aid to be given to the Missouri Company and to promote its interests for resistance to British aggression. Furthermore, the company was granted the exclusive trade of the entire Missouri Valley, beginning with the Kansas Indians, with but one exception, and that exception – to Chauvin – was probably backed by Clamorgan himself. In fact, Lieutenant Governor Delassus was ordered explicitly to support Clamorgan as director of the company.

Clamorgan backed all experienced men in the Upper Missouri. He gave nearly 38,000 pesos in goods to Jacques D'Eglise, who was to explore to the Pacific and perhaps to Santa Fe as well. Loisel and Company actually led the activities on the Upper Missouri, keeping in mind Clamorgan's schemes to establish Spanish dominion in all of that vast area; and Clamorgan, now even supported by his former enemies and competitors, used Loisel's work as a basis for acquiring more land grants from the Spanish officials.

With the advent of the American acquisition of Louisiana, Clamorgan did not stop his activities, even though he no longer possessed the advantages of his intimate friendship with the government officials. Despite his earlier hatred for the Americans and despite his many enemies, he was a respected citizen.[16] In 1804 he was appointed by Governor W. H. Harrison as one of the first judges of the Court of Common Pleas and Quarter Sessions in St. Louis,[17] and he rented his house to the government to be used for a jail.[18]

However, the life of a judge and a plain American citizen was not the life for this promoter *par excellence*. He continued as an active merchant but never again engaged in vast promotional schemes as he had done under the Spaniards. He could not, however, resist the lure of high profits and the speculation on which easy money devolved. Despite his advanced age he again entered into business. In 1807 Clamorgan requested and was granted an American license to trade with the Pawnee Republic,[19] thereby giving him a ruse to enter upon his larger scheme of trade with Santa Fe. A few days later he and Manuel Lisa formed a company and bought goods to trade on the frontiers of New Mexico. Lisa, now interested in his larger schemes of the Missouri River trade, probably declined to continue operations with Clamorgan. Clamorgan ascended to the Platte River and

16 Clamorgan signed the memorial of residents of St. Louis to the President, December 27, 1805; another memorial, March, 1806. Carter, *Territorial Papers*, XIII, pp. 329-45[334]; 455-6. On November 3, 1809, after his return from New Mexico, he signed the recommendation for Judge Coburn to succeed to the position vacated by the death of Lewis. Carter, *Territorial Papers*, XIV, p. 340. He was on jury – against Easton, *ibid.*, XIII, pp. 248-51; XIV, p. 47. Among citizens who memorialized the President in support of Wilkinson, January 6, 1806, *ibid.*, XIII, pp. 385-6. He signed the petition to Congress by the Inhabitants of the Territory concerning land claims, February 1, 1806, *ibid.*, XIII, pp. 425-30.

17 F. L. Billon, *Annals of St. Louis in its Territorial Days from 1804 to 1821* (St. Louis, 1888), 9, 12, 13; he served on a jury in 1809, *ibid.*, 15. C. E. Carter, *Territorial Papers of United States*, XIII, pp. 351, 545; see also 248-51; Houck, *History of Missouri*, II, p. 383.

18 Billon, *Annals of St. Louis*, 10; Houck, *History of Missouri*, II, p. 383; *American State Papers, Public Lands*, II, p. 629.

19 T. M. Marshall, *Life and Letters of Frederick Bates* (2 vols., St. Louis, 1926), I, p. 202.

entered the Pawnee villages under his trading license. He then set out for Santa Fe where he arrived with three others, a slave, and four cargoes of goods. He was sent to Chihuahua but in the next year returned to Missouri, traversing Texas without difficulty and bringing back maps and other materials.[20]

Thus this intriguing adventurer, who repeatedly failed to blaze the trail later made famous by Lewis and Clark, was actually the first to make a trading venture into Santa Fe and return to Missouri with his profits, however little they probably were. Old man that he was, Clamorgan did not repeat his venture. Always the promoter, he offered to the public information on the trade with Spanish New Mexico. It does not appear that he himself had any opportunity to profit from his ideas.

Clamorgan fell ill and on October 30, 1814, made out his will,[21] in which he asked first that his debts be paid and that $150 be distributed to the poor. His goods were to go to his four natural children. His principal assets had dwindled to a few accounts which amounted to perhaps only six or seven hundred dollars. Most of his land grants were later rejected by the American government. His estate was appraised on November 7, 1814, at 837 piastres and his personal goods were sold on November 14 and brought $1140.37½ and included a number of books and maps.[22]

---

[20] This is fully discussed in my edition of *Manuel Lisa,* published by Argosy-Antiquarian Press, New York, 1964. See also J. J. Hill, "An Unknown Expedition to Santa Fé in 1807," *Mississippi Valley Historical Review,* VI (1920), 560-62. Lisa and Clamorgan agreement (copy sent to Lisa by Clamorgan, February 19, 1810), and Clamorgan to Lisa and H. Egliz, July 21, 1807, Missouri Historical Society, Lisa Collection. Their reply to Clamorgan's letter dated July 22, 1807, is in *ibid.*

[21] Will of Clamorgan, Missouri Historical Society, P. Chouteau Collection. His executors were Jean Pierre Cabanné and Antoine Soulard. His principal assets were some accounts due him. There were some demands against his estate which included a note due to Manuel Lisa.

[22] Records of the Probate Court of St. Louis, file 168A. See J. F. McDermott, *Private Libraries in Creole Saint Louis* (Baltimore, 1938), 79-83.

At his death, Clamorgan was more than eighty years old. He had made and lost fortunes through his sheer business acumen, facile pen, and servile attitude. That he was an economic promoter *par excellence* is not to be doubted. Although never admitted to the social set of St. Louis, he looms large as an outstanding figure in the history of the northeastern frontier of New Spain. During the last decade of the Spanish regime in the Mississippi Valley, this obscure, visionary, island Creole earned the gratitude of the decrepit, helpless Spanish government. In the defense of her frontier, Spain in no small part owed a debt of gratitude to Jacques Clamorgan.

Auguste Clermont
(August Claymore)

by HARVEY L. CARTER
Colorado College, Colorado Springs

Clermont is a name that occurs with some frequency in the literature of the fur trade. Whether any relationship existed between Auguste Clermont and Basil Clermont, who operated chiefly on the Missouri, or Antoine Clermont, the celebrated hunter employed by Sir William Drummond Stewart, is a matter of conjecture. Nor is it known when he first came to the mountains, but the fact that he is referred to – by Dick Wootton and others – as "old Claymore" would seem to indicate that he was a fairly early participant in the fur trade.[1]

He is chiefly remembered for his almost miraculous recovery from injuries received in the fall of 1838. In company with eighteen other white free trappers and six or seven Indians, he set out on an extensive trapping and hunting expedition. While they were on the Green River, Clermont alone fell in with a party of Shoshones with whom he got into a quarrel. The Indians beat his head in with their war clubs till they thought he was dead, but were prevented from scalping him by the arrival of some of his trapping companions. They found his skull was crushed and his brain lacerated, with portions of it exposed and partially destroyed. No one thought he could possibly live and one of his friends donated a suit of clothes to bury him in. To the

---

[1] T. D. Bonner, *The Life and Adventures of James P. Beckwourth* (New York, 1856; reprint 1931), 38, refers to "Clements," who led a party of six when Ashley's men separated on the Green River in the spring of 1825. This may possibly refer to Auguste Clermont.

surprise of all, he recovered and for forty years his favorite story was how he lived to wear out the suit he was to have been buried in.[2]

Six years later, Rufus Sage heard the story and also became acquainted with Clermont. His version of the incident is as follows: "Clermont, in an affray with a Spaniard, had been prostrated by a blow that fractured his scull in the occiput. His antagonist then fell upon him and thrust the point of a knife in the brain repeatedly, and finally left him for dead." [3]

Auguste Clermont was also known in southern Colorado, in later years, as "the last of the trappers," by which is meant that he continued all his life to make his living by trapping, when others had long since abandoned it. He was frequently seen in Denver in the early days of its existence and was well known there.[4] In 1860, Albert W. Archibald saw him camped on the present site of Trinidad, Colorado, with "old Charlefoux." The two were engaged in building a double cabin on the south side of the Purgatoire River, but they only finished the walls and left without putting on the roof.[5]

Clermont died in 1879 at Nine Mile Bottom on the Purgatoire River, where he was living on Jesse Nelson's

[2] Howard Louis Conard, *"Uncle Dick" Wootton* (Chicago, 1890), 69-71. It is not clear from Wootton's account whether Clermont continued with the trapping party, which went on to Fort Vancouver and returned via California and Arizona. It is more likely that he was left at Fort Hall or with friendly Indians and that his companions learned of his recovery when they saw him once more on the Arkansas River upon their return.

[3] LeRoy R. and Ann W. Hafen (eds.), Rufus B. Sage, "Scenes in the Rocky Mountains" in *Far West and the Rockies Series* (Glendale, 1956), V, pp. 269-70. Although Sage says he knew "Augustine Clermont," the story was no doubt told to him by someone else, hence the introduction of the Spaniard and his characteristic weapon. Wootton's account is first-hand and cannot be questioned.

[4] Jerome C. Smiley, *History of Denver* (Denver, 1903), 160.

[5] "Interview of Albert W. Archibald, at his home near Trinidad, Colorado, Dec. 25, 1907," in Francis W. Cragin Papers, Notebook XI, p. 40. Archibald said that Charlefoux appeared to be older than Clermont. The first houses in Trinidad were built the following year.

ranch. He had gone out trapping, as usual, with his burro and two-wheeled cart. When he did not return after two or three days, Ben Ryder, Nelson's foreman, sent his boys out to look for him. They found him dead at his little camp about six miles above Nelson's house. His burro was tied up and the cart was nearby. There were logs in the fire, and bed was made against a willow but he had not gone to bed. They found him, still in a sitting position, dead beside the ashes of his campfire.[6] (See the accompanying illustration at page 14 of this volume.[7])

6 Cragin Papers, Notebook X, pp. 37-8.

7 The companion to this photograph is in Howard Louis Conard, *"Uncle Dick" Wootton* (Chicago, 1890), 70. The one published herewith was given to F. W. Cragin by Eliza Ann Walker, Wootton's eldest daughter. The picture is interesting in itself and it agrees very closely with the description of the scene of Clermont's death.

William Craig

by FREDERICK A. MARK
Denver, Colorado

Little is known of the early life of William Craig. Indeed, much of what is known is circumstantial, obtained from writings of others and from information pertaining to his associates.

June 4, 1855, William Craig filed an affidavit in the U.S. District Court, Clark County, Washington, as a settler on unsurveyed lands, claiming 640 acres on Lapwai Creek in present northern Idaho. The document contains three important facts of Craig's life: that he was born in Greenbriar County, Virginia (now West Virginia) in 1807, that he arrived in Oregon (meaning Old Oregon) on July 25, 1829, and that he was legally married to Isabel Craig, his wife, in Missouri Territory on July 6, 1838.

In all probability Craig was married to his Nez Perce wife at the rendezvous at the confluence of the Popo Agie and Wind Rivers, since the missionary party of Gray, Smith, Eells, and Walker rested here from June 21 to July 10.[1]

Craig's affidavit stating that he entered Oregon in July, 1829, is consistent with the record of William Sublette's brigade concerning its trek up Wind River to Togwotee Pass, which it crossed in July from the valley of Wind River and descended into Jackson's Hole. Craig, Joe Meek, and Robert Newell were in this party. Meek had crossed the plains with a supply caravan headed by William Sublette, and although some writers have assumed Craig, Newell, and Meek were all members of the caravan, there is no cer-

---

[1] Without question Craig was with his cronies at the rendezvous of 1838, and was married by one of the missionaries. He could not have been legally married elsewhere.

tainty on this point. No writer has yet produced factual proof of the actual date that William Craig entered the fur trade.[2]

Thomas J. Beall, a pioneer of Idaho, spent several years in close friendship with Craig, and in his published story states that Craig told him he left home when he was eighteen years old, because he had killed a man in self-defense, and that in St. Louis he joined up with a party of French-Canadian fur trappers and went up the Missouri to Fort Benton. There, said Beall, Craig severed his connections with the party and joined an American company.[3] One fallacy of this statement is that at that date Fort Benton did not exist. But it may indicate that Craig joined a fur-trading expedition soon after he arrived at St. Louis, or about 1825, which is four years earlier than historians have assumed.

One of Craig's descendants advised the writer that Craig entered the fur trade when he was seventeen or eighteen years old.[4] The informant also stated that Craig did not leave home because he killed a man, but because he soundly threshed a schoolmate at a military school he was attending and was expelled. Feeling he had disgraced his family, he ran away from the school and went to St. Louis and entered the fur trade. The informant's uncle, Fitzhugh Phinney, who was a grandson of Craig, was the last of Craig's descendants to talk to him. When Phinney was a boy, Craig told him numerous stories of his early life.

It seems quite probable that Craig attended some kind of military school, because his writing was exceptionally good for a man of his time, and his later service with Governor

2 Dorothy O. Johansen, editor of *Robert Newell's Memoranda* (Portland, Ore., 1959), p. 13, says that Newell, Craig, and Meek were all in the caravan. But Newell himself does not say so.

3 "Recollections of William Craig," an article by Thomas Beall, in the *Lewiston Morning Tribune*, March 3, 1918.

4 Information given the writer by Mrs. Helen Peterson (Helen Phinney), great-granddaughter of William Craig.

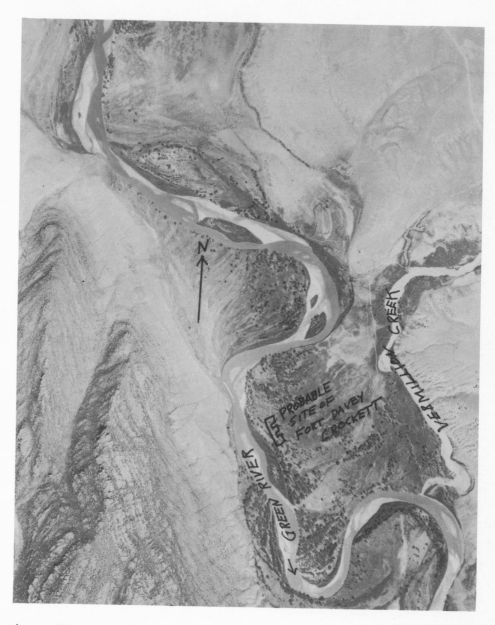

AERIAL VIEW OF BROWN'S HOLE AND PROBABLE SITE OF FORT DAVY CROCKETT
William Craig was one of the owners of the fort.

Stevens during the Indian Wars strongly indicates knowledge and ability to handle military affairs.

With great activity in the fur trade during 1825 to 1829 there was ample opportunity for men to engage in the pursuit of furs; but as indicated above, we have found no positive record of Craig's involvement before 1829.

William Sublette took a fur-trade caravan out of St. Louis in March, 1829, and the vocal Joe Meek is known to have accompanied it. No one has produced a firm record that William Craig was in this caravan, and there is some probability that he was not.

But the close association of Craig, Meek, and Newell, beginning in 1829, as given in Victor's *River of the West,* seems to be the basis for the assumption that these three men entered the fur trade in the Rocky Mountains at the same time. And the fact that Craig, in his affidavit above referred to, states that he arrived in old Oregon in July, 1829, bolsters this view.

What kind of a man was William Craig? All evidence indicates that he was a kind, generous, resourceful, compromising, and reticent man. Beall pointed out that Craig never used the pronoun "I" when describing an accomplishment, but always said "we." When he died in 1869, after a lifetime in the West, the *Walla Walla Union* said of him: "But for his liberality he would have been rich, but he has given away enough to make several fortunes."

Craig was a man of medium stature. One of his descendants told the writer that he had a ruddy complexion, steel-blue eyes, and reddish hair. Only one picture of him is known to exist. It is very likely due to his reticent nature that so little is known of him. A principal reason for the Indians' great respect for him was his devotion to his wife.[5] She, too, was a woman demanding respect. One Oregon

---

[5] *Ibid.* See portrait of Craig at page 15 of this volume.

pioneer said of her: "She had the confidence of both Indian and white and was a superior woman – when estimated in her environment."

Joe Meek and Robert Newell have provided the main sources of information concerning Craig during the fur-trade era. Others with whom we know he had close association on the trail and in rendezvous, including Zenas Leonard, Osborne Russell, Kit Carson, James Clyman, and Warren Angus Ferris, wrote or dictated events of their lives, but failed to mention Craig's name. The missionaries of early Idaho and Washington mention Craig in their writings, but not always in a favorable light. From the writings of statesmen and military men such as Governor Isaac Stevens, his son Hazard, and William Kip, Craig's ability to negotiate with Indians, to accept responsibility of great trust, to answer any call for need, are well demonstrated.

It is fortunate that Joe Meek described his early adventures in the mountains to the writer of *River of the West,* for Meek can be credited with bringing to the public's attention Craig's life in the mountains as far back as 1829. As a new recruit, Meek accompanied William Sublette to his meeting with Robert Campbell on the Sweetwater in the spring of 1829. Campbell's seasoned trappers accompanied Sublette up Wind River to a place where now stands Dubois, Wyoming, where the trappers turned west and crossed into Jackson's Hole, named after one of the partners in the firm. Jackson was somewhere in the northern mountains and Smith was returning from his fateful expedition to California. Sublette's party finally met Smith in Pierre's Hole, where rendezvous was held. Here Craig associated with nearly two hundred other trappers.

Smith took command of the brigade which included William Craig. After the Madison River country was swept for fur, the brigade moved eastward to the Gallatin River. Following the divide between the Gallatin and the Yellowstone rivers, near the present northern boundary of Yellowstone National Park, Blackfeet Indians attacked the trappers in force, killed two, and dispersed the remainder into small bands. The brigade finally united on Shoshone River and moved into the Green River Valley late in December.

April 1, 1830, saw the trappers' firm split into two brigades. The one led by David Jackson headed west for the Snake River country; the other under Jed Smith included in its membership Meek and Newell, and we can assume that Craig was with this division, for these three stalwarts of the trade seemed almost inseparable.

The brigade moved north into the wild domain of the Three Forks country where the Blackfeet reigned supreme. No white trappers had invaded this country since the Indians drove out Major Henry some ten years before. After a successful hunt, the trappers returned east to Wind River where rendezvous was held. William Sublette had returned from St. Louis with a year's supply of simple necessities of the trapper, which for the most part comprised whiskey, ball, powder, and knives.

This was the last rendezvous conducted by Smith, Sublette, and Jackson. They dissolved their partnership and sold the company to five of their leading men. The new partners called their organization the Rocky Mountain Fur Company. These resourceful Mountain Men maintained the company until 1834. While Craig is not mentioned in *Newell's Memoranda* covering the year 1830, he is in events of 1831, and it can be assumed Craig was with his mountain friends during 1830 also.

The spring hunt of 1831 began in the Crow country, and soon the Crows stole some three hundred horses, of which only fifty-seven were recovered.

As the season advanced, the company moved to Bear River, and later in the fall to the wild Salmon River country in present central Idaho, and north into present

Montana. The company was now hounded by the American
Fur Company, which had already squeezed many small
trapping companies out of business.

There is no evidence that William Craig was not an
active member in the Rocky Mountain Fur Company in
1832, when the spring hunt began on the headwaters of the
Salmon and Snake rivers. The rendezvous, held in Pierre's
Hole in the summer of 1832, was followed by the famous
Battle of Pierre's Hole, discussed elsewhere in this Series.

After the rendezvous and battle, Milton Sublette took a
brigade into the Snake River country, then south on the
Humboldt and back northeastward into the Blackfoot
country of Three Forks. We know that William Craig was
with Sublette's brigade, because Robert Newell states in his
Memoranda that his brigade, led by Fitzpatrick, met Craig
and Sublette that fall in the Three Forks country. Fitzpatrick had been dogged all season by brigades of the
American Fur Company, led by Drips and Vanderburgh.
In desperation to shake the shackles of the competing company, Fitzpatrick led his competitors directly into a band of
hostile Blackfeet. In the ensuing battle, Vanderburgh was
killed. Such were the rules of free enterprise in the days of
the fur trade.

If 1832 was an exciting year for Craig, 1833 was even
more so. Craig may have met Bonneville when Bonneville
was in winter encampment on Salmon River about four
miles west of present Salmon, Idaho. During the early
winter the Rocky Mountain Fur Company, the American
Fur Company, and Captain Bonneville were all camped in
or near the Salmon River Valley. Later, all the companies
moved south across the Snake River plains to the river
bottoms, near where Wyeth was to construct Fort Hall.

Craig, Meek, and Newell all joined up with Bonneville
following the spring hunt and rendezvous on Green River.
Bonneville appointed Joseph Walker to lead an expedition

into California. In July, Craig was among the party of fifty trappers that struck out across the Nevada desert.

On the lower Humboldt, the expedition came upon a group of dirty, destitute Indians, probably Piutes. That night the Indians camped nearby, and although they were armed only with bows and arrows, Walker was suspicious of their movements. In the morning the Indians were in a formation that Walker interpreted as an encirclement of his camp, so he ordered his men to fire on the savages. Some thirty were killed. The remainder fled in terror.

Some days later Walker led his expedition across the Sierras, then descended into the San Joaquin Valley, and on to the Pacific Coast. After spending several months in the Spanish country, the expedition headed eastward. After crossing "Walker's Pass," the expedition took a northeasterly course into northern Nevada, where, due to lack of water, Walker was forced to head north for the Humboldt.

After a hot day, Craig was sitting in the shallow, murky waters of this stream when Walker came up and asked him how the water was. Craig answered, "Fine, jump in." Walker doffed his clothes and sprang in head-first, to find the water only about two feet deep and his head in the mud. Walker threatened to shoot Craig, and it is reported Craig stayed in the brush without his buckskins until nightfall, awaiting the subsidence of Walker's wrath.

The company continued eastward, and on Bear River joined Captain Bonneville. There is little evidence of William Craig's actions during the next two years. In all probability he remained in the mountains, trapping the headwaters of the Missouri with Walker. The smaller fur-trapping organizations fell apart in the middle 1830s. Bonneville and Wyeth left the mountains, leaving their mark as gentlemen and adventurers, but financial failures. Nevertheless, their years in the western wilderness left some of the most vivid and factual reporting on the fur trade.

During the summer or fall of 1836, William Craig set-
tled down in Brown's Hole, a sheltered valley on Green
River in the extreme northwest corner of present Colorado.[6]
Philip Thompson and Pruett [Prewitt] Sinclair, Mountain
Men, formed a partnership with Craig, and established
there a post known as Fort Davy Crockett.[7]

Fort Davy Crockett was a social center of the Rocky
Mountains during its brief existence. The fort is reported
to have been constructed of logs, with three wings and a
dirt roof, and having no stockade. The Ute and Shoshone
Indians were frequent visitors for wintering and trade.
Even today the site is a lush valley with many groves of
great cottonwoods adding to its beauty. The fort was located
on a bend of Green River. Only two major bends exist in
the valley: one near the confluence of Vermilion Creek in
sections 5 and 6, Range 102 West, Township 10 North; the
other in section 26, Range 103 West, Township 10 North.[8]
Early ranchers found no evidence of the establishment, and
the writer's diligent search has found none. The first-de-
scribed location is believed by the writer to be the most
likely location, because large stands of cottonwoods still
remain, and the area is almost completely encircled by
Green River and Vermilion Creek, along which is a high,
rough escarpment providing a natural barrier to hold livestock in close proximity to the establishment.

General William Ashley visited the valley in 1825 during
his first trip to the mountains, and it is possible William
Craig was with him. The valley was visited by Colonel
Bean's party of Arkansas trappers during the winter of
1831-32, and some form of shelters may have been built.

---

[6] Kit Carson is said to have been a hunter for the fort during the winter of 1837-
38, so it is likely the fort was built sometime in 1836, probably during the summer
months when trapping could not be carried on.

[7] LeRoy R. Hafen, "Fort Davy Crockett, its Fur Men and Visitors," in *Colorado
Magazine,* XXIX, pp. 17-33. Also see illustration at page 101 herein.

[8] Lodore School Quadrangle, U.S. Geological Survey, 1954.

In all probability, Craig and his partners built the log-mud structure for their own operations. In the spring of 1839 Thompson went down to Missouri and returned with trade goods during the summer. Craig met him at Fort Vasquez on the east side of the mountains, leaving Sinclair in charge of the fort. Thompson and Craig with their families set out in September with packs for Fort Davy Crockett. During Craig's absence, a hunting party from the fort of seven white men and two squaws was attacked on Little Snake River by a band of Sioux. One of the white men was wounded, but the Sioux chief was killed, which resulted in a later attack on the fort.

With the rapid decline of the fur trade in 1839, the trappers were in need of both a livelihood and excitement. Forays into California for the purpose of stealing horses from the Spaniards became popular and lucrative. Philip Thompson joined one of these. Thompson's first horse-stealing enterprise relieved the Hudson's Bay Company post at Fort Hall of fourteen horses. Enroute to Fort Davy Crockett he and his party latched on to some thirty horses of the Snake Indians. When Craig, Meek, Newell, and Walker heard of the theft they condemned the action and intercepted Thompson and his gang and returned the horses to the Snakes. Craig may have already decided to pursue a new life, but soon after this incident the partnership broke up and Craig was headed toward the Oregon country.

Much of the life at Fort Davy Crockett was described by the travelers that passed by it going east and west.[9] Thomas Farnham, leader of an overland Oregon-bound party from Illinois, reached the post on August 12, 1839. A few days later an eastbound party returning from Fort Hall reached the post. Among the new arrivals was Doctor F. A. Wislizenus, from St. Louis. Owens and Carson, engaged in trade for Bent and St. Vrain, arrived on September 23, and

[9] See Hafen, "Fort Davy Crockett," *loc. cit.*, 17-33.

Biggs arrived to trade for Vasquez on the 25th. E. Willard Smith, who left a vivid account of his western travels, visited the fort on October 1, 1839.

The rendezvous of 1840, held on Green River, was the last to be held in the American West. General Ashley's inception of the mountain rendezvous may have saved the Oregon country for America.

At rendezvous Craig met the missionary party of Rev. Harvey Clark and agreed to escort it to Fort Hall. From there Robert Newell took the party and its wagons to Oregon. At Whitman's mission on the Walla Walla River, Craig and his old friend John Larison, with their families, headed north to Lapwai in the Nez Perce country, where Craig's wife's father, Chief James, resided.

Craig established a farm near Rev. Spalding's mission, but later moved about ten miles south on Sweetwater Creek where he developed the first cultivated farm in Idaho. He took this action because Rev. Spalding objected to him settling near the mission. In 1855, as noted previously, Craig filed an affidavit as a settler on unsurveyed land for title under the Act of September 27, 1850, for his 640 acres. Five years after his death, his heirs were apparently having difficulty in getting title to the land.

Spalding attempted to make immediate Christians out of the Indians, forbidding them to hunt buffalo, race horses, and smoke tobacco. He dealt out physical punishment and refused religious services to the Indians when his every whim was not followed. He was always at cross-purposes with the missionary board. He was quick to blame Craig for his troubles. Yet, in his diary he noted: ". . . this man is remarkably friendly, have daily intercourse. Is one of the most faithful expeditious workmen we can employ, very accommodating as a neighbor." No doubt Spalding was greatly incensed by Craig's presence as well as his influence with Chief James, his father-in-law. Prior to Craig's arrival, Spalding had apparently eliminated the chief's authority over his Lapwai band. In the end, because of Spalding's unreasonable demands upon the Indians, he lost all control over them, and they, all respect for him.

In the meantime the great westward expansion had begun. In 1843 about one thousand immigrants arrived in Oregon. In 1846 Spalding noted in his diary that six hundred wagons loaded with immigrants passed by Whitman's mission at Walla Walla.

There is little doubt that the Nez Perces at Lapwai were as uneasy as the Cayuse Indians in the vicinity of Whitman's mission at Walla Walla, as the hordes of immigrants came flowing into the Oregon country. There was no reason for the Indians to dislike Whitman, while they had every reason to dislike Spalding. When the Indians struck their brutal blow in November, 1847, and murdered Doctor Whitman and others at his mission, it was only by a miracle that Spalding escaped the same fate, and it was Craig along with his friendly Nez Perce followers that saved the lives of Spalding and his dutiful wife and got them safely out of the country.

When the news of the Whitman massacre reached George Abernethy, governor of the provisional territory of Oregon, he sent a regiment of volunteers against the Cayuse Indians who were responsible for the murders. Many whites, including Craig, Peter Skene Ogden, and others, recommended against force, fearing such action would result in a confederation among all the tribes whose combined strength could drive the whites out of Oregon.

The campaign led by Colonel Gilliam was a fizzle, with the troops capturing only some Cayuse cattle and killing four Indians. During the campaign Craig was constantly working with Old Joseph of the Nez Perces and other chiefs to keep them from joining with the hostile Cayuse and Palouse tribes. The Nez Perces were the most powerful

tribe west of the mountains, and if they had turned against
the whites there is little doubt that all the tribes would have
formed a war federation, and the whites would have been
driven from the Oregon country. It is reasonable to believe
that the influence of William Craig with the Nez Perces
was the primary reason why this did not happen.

In March, 1848, Joel Palmer, Indian Agent for Oregon,
appointed Craig Indian Agent at Lapwai. Palmer promised
the Nez Perces that no white man would be permitted to
settle on their lands without their consent. For the next few
years the tribes along the Columbia and the lower country
caused no great concern among the whites, and William
Craig remained at Lapwai and became a prosperous farmer,
apparently respected and loved by his Indian neighbors.
Thus ended another transition period in the exploration and
development of the West, in which William Craig was one
of the principal participants.

Isaac Stevens, a graduate of West Point, was appointed
the first Territorial Governor for Washington. Enroute to
his post beyond the mountains, he was to conduct surveys
for a railroad to the Pacific and to lay the groundwork for
negotiation of treaties with the Indian tribes. These activities delayed Stevens' arrival in the territory until September, 1853.

The first council to be attended by several tribes residing
within the Columbia River Basin was set for May, 1855. At
Stevens' invitation some five thousand Indians assembled in
the Walla Walla Valley, including the Yakima, Walla
Walla, Cayuse, and Nez Perce tribes. William Craig rode
to the council grounds with the Nez Perces and was appointed by Governor Stevens to be one of the four official
interpreters. After a very stormy council, the Nez Perce
chiefs suddenly agreed to the terms of reservation boundaries. Some believe this was due to personal gain and
treachery of Chief Lawyer, but it is more likely that Wil-

liam Craig convinced the Indians of the destiny of the West and the futility of the desire to hold it all as Indian country.

When the tribes consented to the reservation boundaries at the Council, the Nez Perces requested that a special provision be included in the treaty to the effect that the homestead of William Craig not be considered part of the reservation. This indicates the great esteem the Nez Perces had for Craig.

At the close of the council Craig was sent to Lapwai by Governor Stevens to organize a delegation of the Nez Perce tribe to go to the plains of Montana to attend a council with the Blackfeet. The combined group met with Governor Stevens and held a council at Hell Gate with the Salish tribes. Then the group moved on, accompanied by Craig and Nez Perce chiefs, Looking Glass, Spotted Eagle, and Eagle, from the Light, to the mouth of the Judith, where the council with the Blackfeet, after considerable delay, took place.

When the council was over, it was late October, and Stevens turned his face toward the West and began the long trek to the Spokane country for a council with the Coeur d'alenes. Enroute Stevens learned that the tribes of the upper Columbia had started warfare against the whites. Fearing attack from the hostiles if he took the low route along the Clark Fork River, Stevens crossed the snow-covered Bitterroot Range, and with Craig and a Nez Perce escort descended swiftly into the valley and entered the camp of the Coeur d'alenes by surprise. Stevens sent Craig and a party of Nez Perce to Lapwai to contact Chief Lawyer for a heavy escort to the lower country. Chief Pu-pu-mox-mox of the Walla Wallas had made the threat he would take Stevens' scalp. Stevens was conducted safely through the country by the friendly Nez Perce escort. On the last day of the year Governor Stevens appointed William Craig to Lieutenant Colonel and departed for Olympia.

As the spring grass rose on the Columbia plains, it was accompanied by the war whoops of Chief Kam-i-ah-kan's braves and neighboring tribes. The Middle Columbia was seething with an Indian war. One of Governor Stevens' first acts was to call William Craig back into service. With a party of seventy-five Nez Perces under Spotted Eagle, Craig joined forces with Colonel Shaw of the Oregon Volunteers. Shaw's three columns and Craig's Nez Perces soundly threshed a hostile force of Walla Wallas and Cayuses in the Grande Ronde Valley, which turned the tide to the whites. General Wool, commanding the Department of the Pacific, had ordered Colonel Wright to give no aid to Stevens and to keep the whites out of the country east of the Cascades. He even ordered Wright to disarm the Volunteers if he had force enough to accomplish it.

Governor Stevens finally arranged a council in late summer with most of the principal tribes at Walla Walla. The council was a failure, but after an expenditure of six million dollars and the loss of many lives, the war ended in the fall of 1856.

Craig was appointed temporary Indian Agent at Fort Walla Walla for the Cayuse tribe. Records indicate Craig was still at Fort Walla Walla in 1859 when the town of that name had its beginning. He became its first postmaster. In the fall of that year Doctor Agustus J. Tribodo arrived in Walla Walla from St. Paul via the Canadian prairies. Doctor Tribodo had no place to stay and no money, but Craig took him in, providing board and room at ten dollars a week, payable later. Of Craig, Doctor Tribodo wrote in his journal: "He appears to be a bluff jolly good fellow, had an excellent supper of beef, coffee, and corn bread. Craig's wife is a Nez Perce squaw, rather good looking. He has some fine looking half-breed daughters."

When Captain E. D. Pierce found gold on the Clearwater in the heart of the Nez Perce country in 1860, a new fever struck the country. During the fall Craig moved back to his farm at Sweetwater Creek. When the town of Lewiston was located at the junction of the Clearwater with Snake River, Craig assisted the whites in negotiating for the land from the Indians.

In the meanwhile the Bannock Indians were harrassing and killing many immigrants on the Oregon Trail. One late party bound for Oregon under the leadership of Robert Otter was attacked by the Bannocks on Bruneau River. Following the attack the survivors were left without horses or food and resorted to cannibalism before they were rescued by a military detachment from The Dalles led by William Craig as guide and scout.

In 1861 Craig established the first ferry on the Clearwater River at the mouth of Lapwai Creek. Robert Newell became the Indian Agent for the Nez Perces at Lapwai, and he and Craig are credited with preventing bloodshed when efforts of the military failed in keeping the hordes of gold seekers off of the Nez Perce reservation.

Joaquin Miller credited Craig with the origin of the name "Idaho." According to Miller, he and Craig were riding one morning facing the east, and the sun was just rising over the mountains. Miller remarked to Craig what a beautiful sight this made. Craig explained the Indians had a term for this sight – "e-dah-hoe," meaning light coming over the mountains.

Numerous landmarks bear Craig's name. In Walla Walla, a street bears his name. The Craig Mountains in Idaho were officially given that name when Lieutenant Robert H. Fletcher, under command of O. O. Howard during the Nez Perce Campaign, placed the name on his official maps. It is noteworthy that at the foot of these mountains, east of Lewiston, Idaho, Henry Plummer, later hanged by the vigilantes at Bannock, Montana, operated out of one of his secret "she-bans." Another point bearing Craig's name is

Craig Crossing, also known as Billie Crossing, where an old Indian trail crosses the Salmon River about fifteen miles below the mouth of White Bird Creek.

In 1863 the first political conventions in the new Territory of Idaho were organized. The Republicans met at Mount Idaho, and the Democrats at Idaho City. Robert Newell and Craig rode together to the Republican convention. After Newell had retired for the night at the roadhouse at Durkeeville, Craig took the speech Newell proposed to give at the convention and which he hoped would get him the office of Delegate to Congress, and read it to the other travelers downstairs. When Newell came downstairs for breakfast, he was awarded cheers and cigars. Even in late maturity the Mountain Men never overlooked the opportunity for a good joke on a comrade.

In 1869 William Craig suffered a stroke that took his life. He was survived by his wife, Isabel, one son and three daughters: Joseph William Craig, Adeline Phinney, Annie Fairfield Woodward, and Martha Robie Vaughn. Several of his descendants still live in Idaho, Washington, and Oregon. One of his great grandsons became superintendent of the Nez Perce Reservation at Lapwai and was known as a man of great brilliance and ability. In the 1930s a chapter of the Sons of the American Revolution was organized in Lewiston as the William Craig Chapter No. 2. This organization placed a monument at Craig's grave, which is located at Jacques Spur, near the mouth of Mission Creek.

While many Mountain Men witnessed the raw savagery of the early West and its transition from a wilderness to a civilized and developed country, few personally took the active and influential part in each phase of change as did Colonel William Craig. How strange that this Mountain Man of great and benevolent deeds is so little known.

John Day

by KENNETH L. HOLMES
Linfield College, Oregon

When the name of John Day is raised in a conversation of folks in the Pacific Northwest, there is apt to be a remark such as "Oh, mad John Day!" or "Oh, yes, he was the first man to go crazy in the Oregon Country." This stereotype was pinned on the trapper because of one short time in his life when he is known to have gone berserk, but it does little really to describe this ubiquitous man of the fur trade, whose name appears on two rivers in Oregon, on a county and a town in central Oregon, on some of the most remarkable fossil beds on the Pacific Slope in the "John Day Country," and now on a massive dam and reservoir being built on the Columbia River.

Washington Irving described John Day with soaring words, as the frontiersman might have looked in 1810, in his book, *Astoria:*

> He was about forty years of age, six feet two inches high, straight as an Indian; with an elastic step as if he trod on springs, and a handsome, open, manly countenance. It was his boast that, in his younger days, nothing could hurt or daunt him; but he had 'lived too fast,' and injured his constitution by his excesses. Still he was strong of hand, bold of heart, a prime woodsman, and an almost unerring shot. He had the frank spirit of a Virginian, and the rough heroism of a pioneer of the west.

John Day, son of Ambrose Day, was born in Culpepper County, Virginia.[1] His date of birth is unknown. There was a John Day from that county who fought in the American Revolution in the Fifth Virginia Regiment, but it is not certain that this soldier was the future trapper. There were

---

[1] T. C. Elliott, "Last Will and Testament of John Day," *Quarterly of the Oregon Historical Society,* XVII (December, 1916), 373-7.

several John Days from the Old Dominion who fought in the Revolution, and there is some confusion as to their identification. One of them, who may or may not have been the trapper, was granted 200 acres of Kentucky land on February 11, 1784, as a Virginia veteran.[2] John Day, the biographee, did have a brother, Lewis, who owned a plantation at Limestone (now Maysville), Kentucky, in 1797. If our John Day fought in the Revolution, he would have had to be considerably older than the forty years assigned to him by Irving for the year 1810.

In 1798 Day showed up in Missouri, where the records indicate that he petitioned the Spanish lieutenant-governor of Upper Missouri for "two hundred and forty arpens of land on a river south of the Missouri." [3] A few years later he acquired more land to the extent of 700 arpens on the "Waters of Point Labaddie Creek," in what became Franklin County. In 1804 he engaged an Asa Musick to cultivate the land and let him live in his cabin. Musick planted peach trees, built a new house, and improved the estate considerably.[4] The next year Day sold or mortgaged some of the land to Musick. He was evidently not a farmer and was more interested in hunting and trapping, for in April, 1809, he let his last interest in this land go to John Withinton for fifteen dollars.[5]

Along with hunting and trapping, he tried his hand at a very common business in pioneer Missouri, gunpowder-making. In 1809 he went into partnership with Benjamin Cooper and John Ferrell in a powder-making project.[6] Powder made from saltpeter in caves, and lead, extracted from rich galena ores, would make many Missourians wealthy in the years to come. Ben Cooper later became one

---

[2] Stella M. Drumm, "More About Astorians," *Quarterly of the Oregon Historical Society,* XXIV (December, 1923), 335-60. The section on John Day is on pp. 352-7.
[3] *Ibid.,* 353.   [4] *Ibid.,* 354.   [5] *Ibid.,* 354.
[6] Elliott, *op. cit.,* 377.

of the pioneers in the opening of the Santa Fe Trade.[7] John Ferrell was to become a partner of William Becknell and Ewing Young in a powder-making venture with the first wagon train to Santa Fe in 1822.[8] Either John Day lost interest in the gunpowder business, or the enterprise did not pan out, for in November, 1810, he showed up at the headquarters of the John Jacob Astor overland expedition on the Nodoway River, near present-day St. Joseph, Missouri. The party leader, Wilson P. Hunt, hired Day as a hunter.

This group made one of the most difficult trips of any expedition to cross the continent. In what is now southern Idaho they broke up into small parties which straggled on to the mouth of the Columbia, there to make contact with the Astor representatives who had arrived aboard the *Tonquin,* and had already established Astoria.

John Day was with one of these small groups that suffered untold hardships, living on the verge of starvation for days at a time. He and Ramsay Crooks were left behind by the others and wandered about the Snake River country during the winter of 1811-12. They finally dragged their way through the snow of the Blue Mountains and fell in with friendly Walla Walla Indians who gave them help on their way down the valley of the great Columbia. Near where the river now named for John Day enters the Columbia, the men were robbed of their guns and other possessions, and even of their clothes, by other Indians.

The story is told by Alexander Ross in *Adventures of the First Settlers on the Oregon or Columbia River.*[9] David Stuart and a party of men who had gone out from Astoria to trap the upper Columbia and search for stragglers were returning downriver by dugout in early May, 1812:

[7] Kenneth L. Holmes, "The Benjamin Cooper Expeditions to Santa Fe in 1822 and 1823," *New Mexico Historical Review,* XXXVIII (April, 1963), 139-50.

[8] Kenneth L. Holmes, "Ewing Young, Enterprising Trapper," doctoral thesis, University of Oregon, Eugene, 1963, p. 25.

[9] (Chicago, 1923), 202ff.

On their way down, one morning a little after sunrise, while near the Umatallow River, where a crowd of Indians were assembled together, they were hailed loudly in English to "come on shore." The canoes instantly closed together, and listened with some anxiety to hear the words repeated. They had no sooner done so than the voice again called out to "come on shore." To shore the canoes instantly steered, when to the surprise of all, who should be there, standing like two specters, but Mr. Crooks and John Day, who it will be remembered had been left by Mr. Hunt among the Snake Indians the preceding autumn; but so changed and emaciated were they, that our people for some time could scarcely recognize them to be white men. . .[10]

The rescued men were taken downriver to Astoria, where they were allowed to rest and recover strength. They arrived at the fort on May 12, 1812. Soon after this there was a meeting of partners at Fort Astoria at which it was decided that three parties would set out for the interior: David Stuart to the post on the Okanagan; Donald McKenzie to winter in the Snake country; Robert Stuart to travel with a party all the way to St. Louis with dispatches for Astor. They would all travel as a unit for the first part of the trip.[11]

John Day was a member of this large party when it started upstream on June 20, 1812. He seems not to have completely recovered from his terrible ordeal of the winter, for on July 1 Robert Stuart wrote in his journal that "evident symptoms of mental derangement made their appearance in John Day one of my hunters who for a day or two previous seemed as if restless and unwell but now uttered the most incoherent absurd and unconnected sentences – several spoke to him, but little satisfaction was obtained, and he went to bed gloomy and churlish – ."[12] On the next day John Day's condition became even more alarming, and he threatened suicide, but was prevented from doing this. Stuart noted that "he at length feigned great

---

[10] *Ibid.,* 202. [11] *Ibid.,* 209.
[12] Philip Ashton Rollins (ed.), *The Discovery of the Oregon Trail: Robert Stuart's Narratives* (New York, 1935), 29, entry for Wednesday, July 1, 1812.

remorse, & appeared to be quite sensible of the enormity of the crime he intended to perpetrate, this entirely lulled our suspicions, which enabled him (a little before daylight) to get possession of a pair of loaded pistols, both of which he put to his head & fired, but fortunately too high to take effect, but was instantly Secured & placed under guard, in one of the boats." [13]

On July 3 John Day's insanity "amounted to real madness," and Robert Stuart decided it would be imprudent for the Virginian to accompany the party farther. Stuart was able, by offering a few articles as gifts, to persuade some Indians of the Cathlapootle tribe to take Day back to Astoria.[14]

Washington Irving stated erroneously in *Astoria* that John Day died within a year of this incident. The trapper lived on, however, and transferred his allegiance to the North West Company when the Astorians sold out to the Canadian fur company during the War of 1812.[15]

Day's name comes up in the Alexander Henry-David Thompson journals under date of March 29, 1814, where it is stated that "arrangements were made with John Day, [Alexander] Carson and other freemen, on halves for the Spanish river." [16] This would be the Green River of today. On April 4, 1814, his name is listed among the passengers up the Columbia in a large fleet of canoes leaving Fort George (Astoria).

The Virginia trapper seems to have spent the remaining years of his life trapping for the North West Company, much of the time in the Snake River country. His will, made out in the Snake River country of central Idaho, probably on the Little Lost River, was published in the *Quarterly*

[13] *Ibid.,* 31, entry for Thursday, July 2, 1812.
[14] *Ibid.,* entry for Friday, July 3, 1812.
[15] Elliott, *op. cit.,* 374.
[16] Rollins, *op. cit.,* xcix.

of the Oregon Historical Society for December, 1916.[17]
This remarkable document was "signed and sealed" by John
Day's fellow-trapper, Donald McKenzie, on February 15,
1820. Day died on the sixteenth.

The attention the Virginian has received and the geographical features named for him are no doubt out of proportion to the importance of the man in the over-all history of
the fur trade and of the Pacific Northwest. It has been his
peculiar fortune to be memorialized in such a spectacular
way. Nevertheless, though "Mad John Day" is remembered
beyond his deserts, by a miracle of nomenclature, his career
will always be of interest beyond its intrinsic significance.

17 Elliott, *op. cit.*

Jacques D'Eglise

by A. P. NASATIR
San Diego State College

The decisive Treaty of Paris of 1763 changed the international rivalry for North America from a three- to a two-cornered struggle. Before that time Spanish claims to the regions north and east of New Mexico, based on papal decree, discovery, exploration, trade, and treaty relations with the Indians, conflicted with similar and opposing French claims. The treaty of 1763 eliminated France from continental North America, and thus the Spanish frontier moved in one fell swoop up to the Mississippi River where the Spaniards now encountered the British who were pushing their frontier to the great river.

From 1763 to 1803 the whole country from the Mississippi to the Pacific Ocean was Spanish in fact, and, except for the British to the north, there was no boundary question other than those between Louisiana, Texas, New Mexico, and California, which were Spanish provinces. The retrocession of 1800 had no practical effect on boundaries.

Geographically, in the area of the Upper Missouri and above the Sangre de Cristo, there lay a vast territory, unknown, unexplored, and uncharted on extant maps. Yet, late in the eighteenth century this huge extent of land became the center of an intense international rivalry, keynoted by Spanish fear of Anglo-American aggression as well as the competitive desire of both Spain and Britain for economic gain. Trade and loyalty of the Indian were the principal ingredients of that rivalry. Thus international rivalry and opportunity for economic gain spurred both nations to greater activity.

A description of this area drawn by the Governor-General of Louisiana in the first half of the eighth decade of the eighteenth century proved that the geography of the Upper Missouri and the Rocky Mountains was still unknown,[1] still a mystery, and that knowledge of the territory had not progressed since the French era. As the geography remained unknown, maps of the period conjectured a much smaller area than actually existed; it was surmised that the Missouri, or perhaps its branches, turned into the mountains a slight distance above the Sangre de Cristo range of New Mexico. Moreover, it was inferred that there might be a possibility of easy passageway via lakes and rivers, with only a few portages, by means of which the aggressive Indian traders of the British companies of Canada could penetrate the valuable Spanish Santa Fe area and the mines of Mexico. Perhaps, too, a way could be found via the Missouri to reach the Pacific Coast, also a center of Spanish settlement and international rivalry. An expanding and continuing frontier line on the part of the Spanish could provide a protective fence for their continuous frontier line from the Mississippi to the Pacific Coast.

Keynote to all were Spanish Illinois and the Missouri. Rivalry reached its climax in the last decade of the eighteenth century. The Spaniards had been licensing their traders to trade with tribes on the Missouri up as far as the Mahas; they knew the Missouri River up to the Sioux.

---

1 [Miró] to Rengel, New Orleans, December 12, 1785. It was drawn up at the request of Felipe de Neve and Antonio Rengel, who requested the information from Miró in a letter dated December 18, 1783. Both of these letters are printed in English translation in A. P. Nasatir, "A Spanish Account of Louisiana, 1785," in *Missouri Historical Review,* XXIV (1929-1930), 521-6. Miró's account is also published with some changes in the translation in A. P. Nasatir, *Before Lewis and Clark* (2 vols., St. Louis, 1952), I, pp. 119-27, and summarized in *ibid.,* I, pp. 73-4.

Stray, unlicensed, loyal, and foreign independent traders, perhaps vagabonds, had gone beyond that limit. From Canada Britishers, and before them Frenchmen, had traversed the territory overland to the vicinity of modern Dakota, and British traders had swarmed into the Iowa-Minnesota-Dakota area.[2]

The Mandan Indians had been seen by the La Vérendryes while Canada was still under French rule. Menard had certainly been living among these same Indians before definite contact was made with them by the Spaniards, and perhaps others. In any event it was Jacques D'Eglise who made the Mandans known to the Spaniards; thus he deserves the title of discoverer of the Mandans for them.

Santiago or Jacques D'Eglise, Santiago de la Iglesia, Iglis, or Santiago D'Yglise are among the variations in which his name appears in the documents. Little is known about this man who styled himself as a citizen residing in the city of St. Louis; he was of French or French-Canadian stock. Lieutenant Governor Zenon Trudeau states that the Missouri trader was an ignorant man "who hardly knows how to speak his own French language." D'Eglise represented the beginning of a Spanish movement up the Missouri, the intent of which was to regain the loyalty and trade of the Indian tribes, to clear the territory of the British, to hold the river as a frontier defense for New Mexico, and to discover a route to the Pacific.

---

[2] For a fuller account see A. P. Nasatir, "Anglo-Spanish Rivalry in the Upper Missouri," in *Mississippi Valley Historical Review,* XVI (1929-30), 359-82; 507-30, and additional material in Nasatir, *Before Lewis and Clark,* I, pp. 75-115. This should be supplemented by A. P. Nasatir, "Anglo-Spanish Frontier on the Upper Mississippi 1786-1796," in *Iowa Journal of History and Politics,* XXIX (1931), 155-232; A. P. Nasatir, "Anglo-Spanish Rivalry in the Iowa Country 1797-1798," in *ibid.,* XXVIII (1930), 337-89; and A. P. Nasatir and E. Liljegren, "Materials Relating to the History of the Mississippi Valley from the Minutes of the Spanish Supreme Councils of State 1787-1797," in *Louisiana Historical Quarterly,* XXI (1938), 3-73.

D'Eglise must have been an experienced trader and hunter even before he received a license to hunt on the Missouri in August, 1790. It is known that twenty-three-year-old Joseph Garreau was outfitted by Don Andrés Fagot la Garcinière of St. Louis to hunt and trap on the Upper Missouri, but what occurred on that trip remains a mystery.[3] There must have been others of the same type. But it was D'Eglise who first reached the Mandan Indians via the Missouri from St. Louis. How old he was at the time has not been ascertained. Records indicate that a Jacques Egliz obtained the grant of a lot on the Rivière des Pères from St. Ange. Later a Jacques D'Eglise received a grant of land near St. Louis.[4] Louis Houck, historian of Missouri, suggests that one Hyacinthe Egliz and Jacques D'Eglise were the same person, but such is not the case.[5]

Zenon Trudeau said of D'Eglise that he was "so simple and from a province in France of such a peculiar language [dialect] that nobody can understand it."[6] He was unable to write and marked documents with an "X." J. B. Truteau commends D'Eglise for his business ability and methods although condemning him for his morals.

In August, 1790, Jacques D'Eglise received a license to hunt on the Missouri. Just when he left St. Louis and how long he remained on the trip is not known. It is known, however, that he provided himself with some merchandise for trading with the Indians, that he returned to St. Louis in October, 1792, and made a report on his journey to Lieutenant-Governor Trudeau. Stopping at the Mahas he met

3 John C. Luttig, *Journal of a Fur Trading Expedition on the Upper Missouri 1812-1813* (ed. by Stella M. Drumm, St. Louis, 1920; new edition with additional material by A. P. Nasatir, New York, 1964), 64.

4 L. Houck, *History of Missouri* (3 vols., Chicago, 1908), II, p. 101.

5 *Ibid.,* II, p. 356.

6 Trudeau to Carondelet, no. 74, St. Louis, May 20, 1793, *Archivo General de Indias, Sección, Papeles de Cuba, legajo* 26, printed in Nasatir, *Before Lewis and Clark,* I, p. 181.

Pedro Montardy from whom he purchased some additional goods. He then ascended the Missouri until he reached the Mandans. He found that these Indians had been in constant communication with the British in Canada and had had British traders among them. The latters' base was a fortified trading post on the Assiniboine. The Mandans were also in touch with New Mexico, D'Eglise said, for they boasted Mexican saddles and bridles for their horses. Possibly the connection with New Mexico was an indirect one through the Navaho, Kiowa, and Pawnees. D'Eglise did not carry sufficient goods with him for profitable trade, but he disposed of all he had. He promised to return to the Mandans the following year and to report on them to the Spanish Commandant. He told them of the advantages they would gain from commerce with the Spaniards, and he told them of the greatness of the Spanish government. D'Eglise returned to St. Louis in October, 1792, and reported to Zenon Trudeau who, during his absence, had become the new Spanish Lieutenant Governor there.[7]

In 1793,[8] probably in March, having received permission from Trudeau, D'Eglise set out on his return journey to open trade relations with the Mandan villages. It is probable that he was outfitted by Joseph Roubideau (or Robidoux), and he was accompanied by Joseph Garreau, who had been outfitted by Buenaventura Collell.[9] Again D'Eglise was not completely successful from the standpoint of profit, but his business acumen and trading ability resulted in his securing

---

[7] Trudeau to Carondelet, no. 33, St. Louis, October 20, 1792; Carondelet to Trudeau, New Orleans, December 29, 1792; D'Eglise to Carondelet, June 19, 1794, in A. P. Nasatir, "Spanish Exploration of the Upper Missouri," *Mississippi Valley Historical Review*, XIV (1927), 57-60; also in Nasatir, *Before Lewis and Clark*, I, pp. 160-1, 163-4, 234-5.

[8] See Collell to Carondelet, October 20, 1794, *Mississippi Valley Historical Review*, XIV, p. 61; *Before Lewis and Clark*, I, pp. 241-2; Trudeau to Carondelet, June 8, 1794, *ibid.*, I, p. 233, extract in *Mississippi Valley Historical Review*, XIV, p. 59.

[9] Collell to Carondelet, October 20, 1794, cited in note 8.

enough furs to satisfy his creditors. The success of the traders would have been greater had they not been stopped by the Arikara and the Sioux, who not only wanted goods but also desired to prevent their enemies from obtaining arms. The Sioux had been friendly with clandestine British traders from whom they had received cheaper and better goods. However, D'Eglise blamed the lack of success in this venture on Garreau who, he said, had a "turbulent and libertine spirit," and who used his employer's goods "for indecent purposes other than those for which they had been designed." Garreau remained among the Arikara where, said D'Eglise, "he could not help but be very pernicious by his counsels." Actually Garreau remained among the Indians because he did not wish to return to St. Louis where he would have had to face his creditors.

On his return D'Eglise pointed out that he had been the first Spaniard to trade with the Mandans. To recompense him for his losses he petitioned the Lieutenant Governor to grant him the right of exclusive trade with the Mandans and Tayene Indians for a period of four years; he also asked a few special favors.[10]

D'Eglise did not receive the concessions he requested, for in the meantime and partly owing to his reports of English traders among the Indians on the Upper Missouri, a number of merchants under the leadership of Jacques Clamorgan had organized "The Company of Explorers of the Upper Missouri" (referred to hereafter as the Missouri Company)[11] and had been granted the right of exclusive trade with the Indians of the Missouri above the Poncas. This company, backed by the Lieutenant Governor, was subsi-

---

[10] D'Eglise to Carondelet, St. Louis, June 19, 1794, *Mississippi Valley Historical Rev.*, XIV, pp. 59-61; *Before Lewis and Clark,* I, pp. 234-5; Trudeau to Carondelet, June 8, 1794, *ibid.,* I, p. 233, extract in *Mississippi Valley Hist. Rev.*, XIV, p. 59.

[11] A. P. Nasatir, "Formation of the Missouri Company," in *Missouri Historical Review,* XXV (1930), 3-15. Full documentation on the activities of the Missouri Company are given in Nasatir, *Before Lewis and Clark.*

dized, though all too little, by the Spanish government which approved the venture. Governor General Baron de Carondelet, to spur trading activity and exploration, offered a $3000 prize [12] to the first person to reach the Pacific. D'Eglise refused to join the Missouri Company or be in its employ,[13] but he was interested in obtaining the prize money. In their instructions to J. B. Truteau,[14] the leader of the company's first expedition, Clamorgan and Reihle allude to D'Eglise's and Garreau's earlier activities. If Truteau were to be attacked by the Mahas nations because of their wishing revenge for the damages and injuries caused by D'Eglise and Garreau when passing through their villages, Truteau was immediately to notify the company. Truteau was also ordered to stop D'Eglise and Garreau from trading among or with the Mandans or other tribes; such action would be contrary to the passport granted the company by the Lieutenant Governor. The company's agents could buy out the goods remaining in the two hunters' hands if such merchandise would be useful for trading with the Indians.

D'Eglise, of course, did not leave with the company expedition,[15] but commenced to travel on his own. On August 6 he met Truteau [16] near the Platte where he delivered some supplementary instructions from Trudeau. Truteau pled with D'Eglise to accompany him on the journey up the Missouri River. The latter, acting as a rival trader, refused, for, having a smaller contingent of men and a lighter load,

---

[12] Carondelet to Príncipe de la Paz, no. 65 *reservada,* New Orleans, January 8, 1796, *Before Lewis and Clark,* II, p. 388; Carondelet to Clamorgan, September 18 and October 26, 1796, *ibid.,* II, pp. 450-1; *American State Papers, Public Lands,* VIII, pp. 235-6. Carondelet to Trudeau, July 12, 1794, says the prize was 2000 piastres; all others give 3000. *Before Lewis and Clark,* I, p. 236.

[13] Trudeau to Carondelet, St. Louis, July 15, 1795, *Mississippi Valley Historical Review,* XIV, p. 71; *Before Lewis and Clark,* I, pp. 341-3.

[14] *Before Lewis and Clark,* I, pp. 243-53.

[15] Truteau's Journal is printed in Nasatir, *Before Lewis and Clark,* I, pp. 259-311.

[16] *Ibid.,* I, p. 262.

he could travel more rapidly than the expedition dispatched by the company. D'Eglise believed that speed would enable him to obtain the valuable trade of the tribes of the Upper Missouri region before Truteau's arrival; and he was burning with a desire to discover the route over the mountains to the Pacific, thus capturing the prize offered by Carondelet.

With his company of only five men and little baggage D'Eglise could travel by night, whether it rained or not, thus passing the Indian villages. He agreed to carry some guns to the Arikara and promised to await Truteau at their villages. The latter feared that the Otos, Poncas, and Omahas, through whose villages he had to travel, would covet the weapons and prevent their being delivered to the Arikaras.[17]

D'Eglise gave Truteau information about the river as far as the Arikara villages,[18] and then moved on. Misfortune overtook him, for he was stopped by the Poncas and robbed of the materials he was carrying for Truteau and the company.[19] Truteau later tried to get paid for the weapons and merchandise but was unsuccessful. D'Eglise continued on his journey, hoping to reach the Mandans, but he was stopped by the Arikaras among whom he spent the winter, carrying on trade.[20] Truteau also finally arrived at the Arikara villages. On May 24 [21] D'Eglise left these Indians, taking with him the furs he had collected, as well as a few Truteau had succeeded in obtaining from the Cheyenne nation. He returned to St. Louis, together with two Canadians he had found among the Pawnee, arriving in that city on July 4, 1795.[22]

[17] *Ibid.*, I, pp. 262-3.   [18] *Ibid.*, I, p. 275.

[19] *Ibid.*, I, pp. 289-91, 294.   [21] *Ibid.*, I, p. 294.

[20] Trudeau to Carondelet, July 15, 1795, *Mississippi Valley Historical Review*, XIV, pp. 69-71; *Before Lewis and Clark*, I, pp. 341-3.

[22] Trudeau to Carondelet, July 15, 1795, *Mississippi Valley Historical Review*, XIV, p. 69; *Before Lewis and Clark*, I, p. 341. Declarations of Juan Fotman and Joncquard cited in note 23.

The two Canadians were carefully examined by Zenon Trudeau, who elicited from them a great deal of information concerning British activities on the Upper Missouri as well as some geographical knowledge. These matters, especially that concerning the extent of British activities in Spanish territory, were made known to the officials.[23]

Although D'Eglise had twice failed to reach the Mandans he was not discouraged but prepared for another expedition. He steadfastly refused to join the Missouri Company or even operate through it. He preferred to take out a hunting license, which the company forced him to renew. It was similar to the company's licenses and for a three-year period. He also proposed to establish a trading post among the Mandans. He planned to leave St. Louis in July, 1795, pass the winter among the Arikara, and then in the spring to cross the Rocky Mountains and reach the Pacific Ocean. Zenon Trudeau wrote, "He seems determined to make this discovery, and since he is full of courage and ambition, he is capable of so dangerous an undertaking, and it is a pity that he should not have instructions that would make it easy for him to secure all the benefits of a trip that might be of interest to the government." [24] Carondelet wished him success and told Clamorgan, "We shall see if D'Eglise gets the prize of three thousand dollars." [25]

Just what occurred on that journey, if D'Eglise actually made it, is not known to this writer. There may be a possibility that he ascended the Missouri with Mackay, who left late in August, or perhaps at about the same time as D'Eglise, on his own.

---

[23] Declarations of Juan Fotman and Joncquard, St. Louis, July 4, 1795, *Mississippi Valley Historical Review*, XIV, pp. 63-9; *Before Lewis and Clark*, I, pp. 330-5.

[24] Trudeau to Carondelet, St. Louis, July 15, 1795, *Mississippi Valley Historical Review*, XIV, pp. 69-71; *Before Lewis and Clark*, I, pp. 341-3. Trudeau to Carondelet, July 20, 1795, *ibid.*, I, pp. 343-5.

[25] Carondelet to Clamorgan, September 18, 1796, *ibid.*, II, p. 452; *American State Papers, Public Lands*, VIII, p. 235.

At any rate Mackay, writing to Evans from Fort Charles, February 19, 1796,[26] said that he was forwarding a sketch of the description of the Yellowstone which D'Eglise had obtained from the Indians. He also forwarded D'Eglise's compliments to Truteau and to a certain Mr. Nourrow [Joseph Garreau?] who "is at the ricarras & tell him that Jacques [D'Eglise] wants him to come down with the Company's cajons [?] in the spring to help him up with his goods next summer." [27]

Writing on May 26, 1797, Zenon Trudeau reported, "Moreover we have our former discoverer Jacque D'Eglise, who, as we know, also went to the Mandans, and who, according to his plan, should return only after having earned the three thousand piastres promised by the Government to the first one who should bring evident marks [indisputable proof] of having found the said sea." [28]

An assumption can be made that D'Eglise was active in Indian trade on the Upper Missouri, although precise information is lacking. In 1802, in order to engage in Indian trade, he obtained merchandise from Clamorgan, obligating himself to pay for it in the spring of 1803.[29] He also secured a passport from the Lieutenant Governor permitting him to trade in the Missouri; apparently he obtained more merchandise from Clamorgan, for which he gave a promissory note. This latter debt may not have been paid, for in 1804, on the strength of it, Clamorgan asked Amos Stoddard to sell some St. Charles property belonging to D'Eglise.[30] These factors seem to indicate a trading enterprise commencing in 1802.

D'Eglise certainly ascended the Missouri in late 1803 or

[26] A. P. Nasatir, "John Evans: Explorer and Surveyor," in *Missouri Historical Review,* XXV (1931), 447-9; Nasatir, *Before Lewis and Clark,* II, pp. 415-7.
[27] *Ibid.*
[28] Nasatir, *Before Lewis and Clark,* II, pp. 519-522, quotation on p. 520.
[29] *Ibid.,* II, pp. 703-4.   [30] *Ibid.,* II, p. 704.

early 1804. Charles Dehault Delassus wrote to the Governor General, August 10, 1804, that "the one named Jacques D'Eglise who for many years has been going on discovery trips without gain because of being an absolutely ignorant man," [31] had left St. Louis. Last year he was employed by J. Clamorgan "to trade with the nations of the Missouri. He has not returned this year and I have been assured that he has also gone to Mexico with the remainder of his merchandise." [32] Casa Calvo, in reporting Delassus' letter to his superior, Pedro Cevallos, said that Lorenzo Deroche and Santiago D'Eglise had gone to the Upper Missouri to facilitate communications with Santa Fe. He mentioned that they were recognized as voyageurs of the greatest knowledge and experience, and since D'Eglise "has not returned this year it is inferred that he has penetrated into New Mexico." [33]

The inference of both Delassus and Casa Calvo that D'Eglise had penetrated to New Mexico proved correct. Lorenzo Durocher (or Deroche) was in Santa Fe early in 1805.[34] Whether Durocher separated from Jacques D'Eglise on the Upper Missouri late in 1804, or whether they entered New Mexico together and then separated, is not clear. D'Eglise's name does not seem to appear in the New Mexico archives until late in 1806.[35] Sometime before November 20 of that year he was barbarously murdered, very probably

---

[31] *Ibid.*, II, p. 744n. This is from the copy in French in the Missouri Historical Society, Delassus Collection; the original in Spanish from A.G.I., P. de C., 141, differs slightly in wording and is given in Nasatir, *Before Lewis and Clark*, II, p. 744.

[32] *Ibid.*, II, p. 744.

[33] Casa Calvo to Cevallos, no. 47 *reservada*, New Orleans, September 30, 1804, in Nasatir, *Before Lewis and Clark*, II, pp. 755-6. See also Delassus to Casa Calvo, St. Louis, August 10, 1804, in *ibid.*, II, p. 744.

[34] L. B. Bloom, "The Death of Jacques D'Eglise," in *New Mexico Historical Review*, II (1927), 369-79, see p. 372, and Alencaster to Salcedo, May 22, 1805, in *ibid.*, II, pp. 374-5, which is New Mexico Archives no. 1888.

[35] *New Mexico Historical Review*, II, p. 372.

in the Villa de la Cañada; on that date the *Alcalde ordinario* of that Villa forwarded to the Royal Audiencia of Guadalajara a criminal suit filed against Antonio Carabajal and Mariano Venavides. These two men were accused of having assassinated the "Frenchman Santiago Iglis." Three years later, on August 4, 1809, they were sentenced to death, shot, "and their bodies hanged on the royal road." [36]

---

[36] *Ibid.*, 372-4, and documents given on pages 376-9, which are drawn from the New Mexico Archives.

Warren Angus Ferris

by LYMAN C. PEDERSEN, JR.
Gray's Harbor College, Aberdeen, Washington

On August 13, 1842, the Mormon newspaper, *The Wasp,* carried an article entitled "Rocky Mountain Geysers." This was a reprint of the same article appearing in the *Western Literary Messenger,* of Buffalo, New York, on July 13, 1842. In neither instance was the author listed. The Mormon article, published at Nauvoo, Illinois, was found and preserved by N. P. Langford, Superintendent of Yellowstone Park. In the fall of 1900, Olin D. Wheeler, an eager student of Yellowstone Park history, through an unnamed informant, found the source of the *Wasp* article to be the *Western Literary Messenger.* In the same year a copy of *Life in the Rocky Mountains* was uncovered. Warren A. Ferris being the author, it was soon discovered that he also had written the article on geysers. Thus sixty-five years after he had left the mountains, the life of Warren Ferris, trader, trapper, explorer, writer, and cartographer, began to be unfolded.

Ferris was born of Quaker parentage at Glens Falls, New York, December 26, 1810. On both sides of his family were Revolutionary War veterans. At the beginning of the War of 1812 the Ferris family moved to Erie, Pennsylvania. Fighting in the War of 1812, Warren's father died on September 10, 1813, the same day as Perry's victory at Lake Erie. The widow and her two children moved the next year to Buffalo, New York, where she married Joshua Lovejoy and gave birth to four more children. Warren received a reputable education, being trained as a civil engineer. At the age of nineteen, Warren's wandering spirit was inflamed when he received a severe reprimand from his mother who discovered him smoking on a public street. Leaving his home, he wandered to St. Louis, arriving there in June, 1829. Of St. Louis he observed: "It was composed principally of French who are generally absolute strangers to the social virtues and remarkable for laziness and debauchery." [1]

It was about this time that Pierre Chouteau, Jr., of the Western Department of the American Fur Company was organizing and outfitting the first expedition of his firm to be sent to the Rocky Mountains in an effort to wrest control of the fur trade from the Rocky Mountain Fur Company. Ferris, seeing an opportunity for adventure, entered Chouteau's employ as a trader and trapper. With the departure of the trapping party from St. Louis on February 16, 1830, Ferris began his detailed diary which served as a basis for his *Life in the Rocky Mountains*.

Traveling with wagons and then with pack animals, the party went northwestward across Missouri and finally reached Belle Vue, the trading house of Lucien Fontenelle and Andrew Drips, established eight miles above the mouth of the Platte. Drips and Joseph Robidoux were the leaders for the expedition. After lingering for four weeks at Belle Vue, the party moved on to the trading house of John P. Cabanné, eight miles below the Council Bluffs.[2] Here a "Code of Laws" was issued "with penalties annexed, for the preservation of harmony and safety, in our passage through the immense plains." [3] The trappers continued to the Elkhorn River where a change was made in camp procedure, the careless and random camp giving way to a martial

---

1 Warren Angus Ferris, *Life in the Rocky Mountains*, Paul C. Phillips, ed., (Denver, 1940), p. xxxviii. This is the basic source for the summary given here.

2 According to Phillips, John P. Cabanné, a partner of Pratte, Chouteau and Company, built this post for the American Fur Company shortly after 1822. He was in charge until 1833 when he was succeeded by Pilcher, who moved the post to Bellevue.

3 Ferris, *op. cit.*, 18.

appearance. Camps were formed in a square with one side, whenever possible, on the banks of a stream.

Continuing up the Platte River, Ferris passed Chimney Rock, or "Nose Mountain" and left a vivid description in his journal of the famous landmark. He also preserved an original story of the naming of Scott's Bluff. The party continued on, leaving the Platte and reaching the Sweetwater, so named, according to Ferris, because of the drowning of a mule loaded with sugar some years earlier. An evening was spent at Independence Rock, so named, explains Ferris, because an earlier party spent the Fourth of July in its shade. On June 20, Ferris and party crossed over South Pass and descended the Sandy.

After several more days of traveling, the trappers crossed the Green River in bull-hide canoes. After traveling twenty-five miles on Ham's Fork of the Green, several persons were dispatched in different directions in quest of a party of independent hunters and trappers. Although still a green-horn, Ferris rapidly absorbed information about the West from the older trappers.

Passing through the present region of Kemmerer, Wyoming, the expedition reached the heavily grassed bottom-lands of Bear River opposite the Utah-Idaho Bear Lake region. In the area of present Cokeville, Wyoming, the trappers tried to make contact with some "free men," or independent trappers, to ascertain the conditions of the present fur market. At this point Ferris correctly observed that the Bear River "rises in the Eut [Uintah] Mountains, flows northward about a hundred miles when it turns westward and after a further course of seventy-five miles, discharges itself into the Big Lake" [4] [Great Salt Lake].

Although but a youth, Ferris was chosen by leader Drips to accompany him, with three others, into Cache Valley in

[4] *Ibid.,* 42.

search of the free trappers. They reached the site of Logan, Utah. Ferris describes Cache Valley as one of the most beautiful in the West, and in full particulars relates the story of its naming.

Failing to find any free trappers, Ferris and his companions returned to their camp on the Bear, below present Cokeville. On August 16, by way of the Muddy, Ferris returned to Ham's Fork, where the party's goods were cached. Small parties were dispersed in quest of beaver, Ferris traveling with Fontenelle's group, which headed for the upper reaches of Black's Fork and Henry's Fork in the Uintah Mountains of Utah. After hearing that the free trappers were on the Yellowstone, Ferris returned with a party to trap the Bear River tributaries.

With the coming of late autumn, 1830, both the American Fur Company and the Rocky Mountain Fur Company men, together with large numbers of independent trappers and Indians, were encamped in the lush meadows of Cache Valley for the winter. The site was probably near present Hyrum, Utah. In a short time the American Fur Company men moved southward to Ogden's Hole [Huntsville, Utah] for several weeks.

In the latter part of December, Ferris crossed over to Great Salt Lake, near present Brigham City. Here Ferris discusses the proposed change of name to Lake Bonneville:

> An attempt has been recently made to change the name of this lake to Lake Bonnyville, [sic] from no other reason that I can learn, but to gratify the silly conceit of a Captain Bonnyville, [sic] whose adventures in this region at the head of a party, form the ground work of "Irving's Rocky Mountains." There is no more justice or propriety in calling the lake after that gentleman, than after any other one of the many persons who in the course of their fur hunting expeditions have passed in its vicinity. He neither discovered or explored it, nor has he done anything else to entitle him to the honor of giving it his name.[5]

[5] *Ibid.*, 87-8. J. Cecil Alter, "W. A. Ferris in Utah," in *Utah Historical Quarterly,* IX (April, 1941), 87-8.

March, 1831, found the company reassembled on the Bear
River when word reached them that most of the tributaries
of the Snake were already free from ice. A decision was
made to move north, and on April 4, after making a cache,
the trappers pressed their laborious way out of Cache Valley
to the forks of the Portneuf.

Ferris' journal records J. H. Stevens' account of the expedition of Joseph Robidoux who had departed from Drips'
party and had traveled northward, then down the Snake to
the Portneuf and on to present American Falls, where the
party was divided, one group trapping the Wind River
while the other, including Stevens, went to the Malad, or
perhaps Wood River. Jean Baptiste Charbonneau, son of
Sacajawea, and a member of Stevens' party, was lost for a
time but finally returned with several trappers belonging to
a party of forty led by John Work, a clerk of the Hudson's
Bay Company.[6] Ferris quotes Stevens as giving the reason
for the name of the Malad River [La Riviere Maladi]:
that beaver eaten from that stream induce "a singular fit,
the symptoms of which are, stiffness of the neck, pains in
the bones, and nervous contortions of the face."[7] In spite of
this discouraging knowledge, Robidoux's hungry trappers
indulged in a repast of fat beaver and according to Stevens
without exception suffered severe consequences.

On the route north to the Portneuf, Ferris and the main
party also met trappers from Work's brigade who advised
them of the terrain. Having spent nine days traveling
through heavy snow making the sixty miles from Cache
Valley to the point where the Portneuf leaves the mountains, Drips and party were relieved to again reach dry
ground. Within a day's travel down the Portneuf, the main
camp of John Work was reached and bloodshed between

---

[6] For Work's account of this meeting, see T. C. Elliott, "Journal of John Work,"
Oregon Historical Quarterly, XIII (December, 1912), 368-70.

[7] Ferris, 65.

the two parties was narrowly averted. Work was convinced that Fontenelle had persuaded one of his men to desert and join the Americans; accordingly he leveled his gun at the breast of Fontenelle but was restrained from firing by a more calm comrade. The parting of the two companies was far from affable.

The journey was again pursued, passing the forks of the Snake, and on to Henry's Fork. They found game abundant, and took from forty to seventy beaver a day. A portion of the party was sent to "Burnt Hole" on the Madison, but returned with little success. From Henry's Fork the expedition passed westward to the head of Camas Creek where on May 28 two members of the party were killed by Blackfeet Indians. On Beaver Creek a large village consisting of fifty lodges of Flatheads, Nez Perces, and Pend d'Orielles came into the white camp. Ferris credits the Flatheads with having never killed or robbed a white man.[8]

The expedition remained on Beaver Creek until June 19, when Fontenelle and Drips with thirty men departed for St. Louis. Accompanied by twenty Flatheads, the leaders departed for Cache Valley, where under agreement they were to meet Rocky Mountain Fur Company men and travel east together. The remainder of the party set out for the Salmon River country. On June 28, Ferris reached Day's Defile and, ascending the stream flowing from it, passed the junction of Medicine Lodge Creek. Leaving the head of Day's Creek, the party crossed a narrow pass and entered the beautiful valley watered by the Lemhi River, or as they called it, the Little Salmon. Through a narrow defile the trappers entered the small valley watered by the Big Lost River, where they found great numbers of buffalo. Further travel west brought disappointing catches of beaver

---

[8] Paul Wellman, in his *The Indian Wars of the West,* (New York, 1947), 169, cites the Nez Perce boast that no member of the tribe had ever taken the life of a white man.

and so on July 24, 1831, the return journey was commenced.

By the middle of August, Day's Defile was again reached. From the headwaters of the East Fork of the Salmon, Ferris descended into Horse Prairie, and leaving that rolling plain on the last day of August, crossed the mountains to the northwest and descended into Big Hole. After a ten-day camp, the trappers crossed through Deer Lodge Pass and into Deer Lodge Valley.

On September 15, the company moved southward over Deer Lodge Pass and then southeastward over Pipestone Pass to the forks of the Jefferson and Big Hole Rivers. Frasier, the Iroquois hunter, was killed by marauding Indians on September 18, his body being found in the Jefferson. With the death of Frasier, the three Indian guides who had promised to lead the party to the three forks of the Missouri demanded their release. On September 24, Ferris reached the Philanthropy [Ruby] River and camped several miles from its mouth.

In the early days of October the expedition moved southward to a small stream that flows into the Jefferson below Beaverhead Rock. The stream was followed to its junction with the Jefferson. The trappers then continued up that river to the junction where Horse Prairie Creek and Red Rock Creek join to form the Beaverhead. On October 8, several men departed for the Trois Tetons to meet Drips, who was expected to return that fall with men, horses, and merchandise. Leaving Horse Prairie on October 11, they reached the east fork of the Salmon. After descending some distance they crossed into Big Hole Valley where, on October 29, they met the Rocky Mountain Fur Company men, returning from their hunt on the waters of the Missouri. Ferris gives an account of their earlier engagement with Indians on Grey's Creek.

Several days after the arrival of the R.M.F. men, the trappers sent to meet Drips returned, reporting that Drips had not arrived, but that Fraeb had fallen in with Fitzpatrick on the Platte at the head of thirty men with pack horses. Fraeb took the men and horses and was at the time on his way to the Big Hole Valley, while Fitzpatrick returned to St. Louis for more equipment and supplies. The latter had been delayed by his long trip, via Santa Fe, discussed elsewhere in this Series.

While the trappers from both the American companies prepared to spend the winter of 1831-32 in the Big Hole, three A.F.C. men departed in a second effort to meet Drips, who was supposed to arrive that fall. On December 21, two men from Work's party of Hudson's Bay trappers arrived, stating that their main camp was two days' journey away and that they had been continually harassed by Blackfeet. On the 23rd of the month, Ferris and the A.F.C. trappers parted company with those of the R.M.F. and passed southward up the Salmon River to the western end of the Little Salmon River Valley.

On the 25th, Ferris and three companions returned down the Salmon River to reach the R.M.F. camp near Lemhi Pass and obtained some wanted goods. In several days a messenger arrived from Work's party, who at the time were camped with a large band of Pend d'Oreilles at Beaver Head. They were being hard pressed by the Blackfeet, who claimed that the white chief at the mouth of the Yellowstone River [McKenzie of the A.F.C.] had built a trading house at the mouth of the Marias [Fort Piegan] and had supplied the Blackfeet with guns and quantities of ammunition. They further stated that they were only awaiting the arrival of the Blood Indians from the north to wage a war of extermination against the whites. By February 4, 1832, Ferris was back at the main camp with a report of Indian activities and the latest news.

The winter was spent in trapping, moving generally to the vicinity of the Grand Tetons. From a wandering party of Bannocks they learned that a party of whites was at that time in Cache Valley. On March 4, the party crossed the frozen Blackfoot River and camped near its mouth. On the following day two men, John Gray and David Montgomery, departed for Cache Valley to ascertain if the white party there was Drips and company. Five days later hunters brought in the half-dead Gray, who had been found lying in the cedars near the Portneuf. He gave an account of their journey to Cache Valley, finding no traces of any white party, but many Indian signs. The pair of trappers were ambushed on their return trip, Montgomery being killed and Gray barely escaping with his life. The main camp was soon moved down the south fork of the Portneuf to the spot where Montgomery was killed. In honor of the unfortunate trapper, the pass from Cache Valley to the Portneuf was called Montgomery's Pass.

On the 20th the trappers reached Bear River in Cache Valley and three days later several hunters from W. H. Vanderburgh's company of fifty trappers arrived in camp. The latter had been outfitted from Fort Union at the mouth of the Yellowstone and had spent the winter in the southern end of Cache Valley. The fact that a party from Taos had already trapped the district that Ferris and his companions intended to hunt caused them to join Vanderburgh and proceed forty miles northward, up Bear River, to Sheep Rock, south of Soda Springs, Idaho. Ferris was not as enthusiastic about the springs as most early visitors, one such trapper even writing that the springs would become a "resort for thousands of the gay and fashionable world." [9] The zigzag course of the river was followed for seventy-five miles, and then on April 13, the party traveled twelve miles to the east over rolling hills to Talma's Fork which flows southward into Bear River. Smith's fork was reached on the 14th,

[9] Osborne Russell, *Journal of a Trapper* (Boise, Ida., 1921), 9.

Ferris explaining that the stream was so called for the late "Jerediah" [Jedediah] Smith.[10] The 16th found the trappers a few miles above the mouth of the Muddy, where they saw an abundance of buffalo, geese, and ducks.

On April 24, 1832, Bear River was again crossed and on that day the Indian called Pascal, who had traveled to St. Louis with Fontenelle and Drips, arrived in camp with news that Drips with a party of forty-eight was then camped on the Muddy. The following day a glad reunion was held, and drinks in abundance, according to Ferris, were the order of the day. After a march of five days Ferris and three companions raised a cache of furs on Rush Creek and returned to the camp on Smith's Fork.

On May 8, the journey was pursued to Sheep Rock and thence continued northwestward through Gray's Hole, named for John Gray, who had accompanied David Montgomery to Cache Valley two months earlier. In a narrow canyon of Gray's Creek, Ferris met a party under Jim Bridger and wrote:

> Their encampment was decked with hundreds of beaver skins, now drying in the sun. These valuable skins are always stretched in willow hoops, varying from eighteen inches, to three feet in diameter, according to the size of the skins, and have a reddish appearance on the flesh side, which is exposed to the sun. Our camps are always dotted with these red circles in the trapping season, when the weather is fair. There were several hundred skins folded and tied up in packs, laying about their encampment, which bore good evidence to the industry of the trappers.[11]

On May 19, 1832, Ferris with two Indian companions departed camp to seek the Flatheads and induce them to come to the forks of the Snake for trade. The trip was successful and a party of hunters met Ferris on his return trip.

---

[10] Jedediah Smith was killed by Comanches on the Cimarron Desert of Southwestern Kansas in 1831.

[11] Ferris, 144.

On June 3, camp was reached and the spring hunt was declared to be over. Horses and men rested and prepared for the annual rendezvous to be held at Pierre's Hole, in eastern Idaho, where they expected to meet Fontenelle with supplies from St. Louis. A leisurely journey was pursued up Henry's Fork, halting at the East Fork several days to dry meat. While there Ferris recorded: "We killed hundreds daily [buffalo] during our stay on Henrie's fork." Upon reaching Pierre's Hole, Drips and company found the R.M.F. company encamped, awaiting the arrival of Fitzpatrick. Vanderburgh was expecting Etienne Provost [12] with provisions from Fort Union, while Drips daily expected Fontenelle with supplies from Council Bluffs. Thus, in the summer of 1832, the rivals were encamped in Pierre's Hole, a place, according to Ferris, "selected as a pleasant place for a general rendezvous." [13]

On July 3, word reached the camps that William Sublette, at the head of one hundred men, was on his way to Pierre's Hole. This company of fifty men, a party of twenty-two from Gantt's company, thirteen men from the Rio del Norte under Alexander Sinclair, and a dozen or so men under Nathaniel J. Wyeth, were all there. Fitzpatrick had left Sublette's company at the Red Hills and traveled on alone to make better time, but was attacked by Indians. Ferris records in full detail Fitzpatrick's perilous adventure and narrow escape from death.

The famous battle of Pierre's Hole, which occurred at this rendezvous, is described in the "Brief History" preceding the biographical sketches in this Series.

---

[12] Provost, previously operating from New Mexico, had joined the Astor enterprise.

[13] The R.M.F. company had named Pierre's Hole as the area for the rendezvous. Vanderburgh went there to get as much as possible of the fur trade while Fontenelle went east to obtain needed goods. According to Joe Meek, both Vanderburgh's and Drips' parties knew nothing of the country and recklessly declared their intention to follow their rivals wherever they went and outbid them for furs.

After the battle, trading was resumed, then the men departed for their trapping grounds. Since Provost and Fontenelle had made no appearance at the rendezvous, Drips and Vanderburgh concluded to move over on to the Green River, where they found Fontenelle.

On August 12, all arrangements having been completed, Fontenelle with thirty men departed for Fort Union with the year's catch of furs, while Vanderburgh and Drips at the head of about ten men, including Ferris, took a northwesterly direction toward the Salmon River country on the trail of Bridger and Fitzpatrick, hoping to be led to the best beaver country. On the 20th, with two companions, Ferris departed with orders to find the Flatheads and induce them to meet the company in Horse Prairie. Although failing to find the tribe, he explored the headwaters of the Missouri and the Columbia and from a great height surveyed the bottom lands bordering the Salmon and the Big Hole Rivers. Ferris reported that hunger struck both man and beast so severely that "ravens were seen picking at a bone, in the mouth of a wolf." [14] The main party was rejoined on the first of September.

On the trail of the Rocky Mountain men, the A.F.C. trappers reached Deer Lodge Valley in Montana and followed the Big Blackfoot which flows into Clark's Fork near present Milltown, Montana. Hell Gate Pass was reached and then the continental divide was crossed. After passing the Great Falls of the Missouri and Pipestone Creek, east of present Butte, Montana, a division was made on September 16. Drips continued to pursue Bridger and Fitzpatrick, while Vanderburgh, with Ferris in his company, departed to search out new fur country. The latter party was soon encamped on the banks of the Jefferson about thirty miles below Beaver Head. Early in October the Ruby was

[14] Ferris, 165.

ascended, the divide being crossed between the Ruby and the Madison.

The morning of October 12 found Vanderburgh's company underway in a northwesterly direction on the Madison River. On the 14th the remains of a buffalo freshly butchered was found on the trail. Vanderburgh decided that a party of seven should further investigate the incident, and accordingly a small group, including Ferris, set out. At a grove of trees about a mile below the Lower Canyon of the Madison, about 100 savages suddenly opened fire from their hiding place in the trees. Vanderburgh's horse was immediately shot from under him, "but," records Ferris, "with unexampled firmness, he stepped calmly from the lifeless animal, presented his gun at the advancing foe, and exclaimed 'boys don't run.' " [15] The thought of each trapper was to preserve his own life and each acted accordingly. R. C. Nelson looked back to witness Vanderburgh being cut down by a volley from the Indians. A Frenchman named Pilou was also killed and Ferris was wounded by a shot striking his left shoulder. Fear of further trouble in the camp, which was soon on the march, was quieted by the discovery of a camp of 150 lodges of Flatheads, Pend d'Oreilles, and other Indians before reaching Horse Prairie. At the prairie, Andrew Drips was found awaiting Vanderburgh's company. The caches were soon raised and, on October 24, Drips set out for the Snake River, where he intended to pass the winter. Ferris with two men also departed to engage in trade with the Indians.

Traveling fifteen miles through Horse Prairie, Ferris made camp at the "Gates," where a small party of Bonneville's men in search of game soon arrived. Several days later twenty-five men under Joseph R. Walker, also of Bonneville's party, arrived in camp. Before long the camp

---

[15] *Ibid.*, 177.

was further enlarged by the arrival of trappers from the
R.M.F. company. One day after their arrival the various
parties took their leave, Ferris traveling over the mountains
to the east fork of the Salmon, then to Bonneville's post
near present Salmon, Idaho, of which Ferris observed:

> This miserable establishment, consisted entirely of several log cabins,
> low, badly constructed, and admirably situated for besiegers only, who
> would be sheltered on every side, by timber, brush etc.[16]

Leaving Bonneville's "fort," Ferris joined Walker's company intending to travel with them as far as the mouth of
the Blackfoot, and then make his way to the forks of the
Snake and join Drips in his winter camp. Traveling south
and then southwest, Ferris overtook the R.M.F. company in
the Lemhi Valley. All of that party except Fitzpatrick and
one other man stayed there to spend the winter. The latter
two traveled with Ferris, intending to transact some business with Drips, whose camp was reached in mid-Decem-
ber, 1832. After completing his business, Fitzpatrick departed for the Salmon, and Ferris for the mouth of the
Blackfoot to pick up men and baggage left there. The 24th
of December brought Ferris to the camp of Joseph R.
Walker, and Christmas day was spent with that amiable
trapper.

The winter passed with little activity, but with the dis-
appearance of snow and ice toward the end of March, 1833,
the company, now grown to sizable numbers, was divided.
The Spaniard Manuel Alvarez, later prominent in the
Southwest trade, marched at the head of about forty men,
intending to trap along Henry's Fork, the Yellowstone, and
to eventually join the main party on the Green at the end
of the spring hunt.[17] Drips and the second division of the

---

[16] *Ibid.,* 184.

[17] It appears from Ferris' writing that Alvarez visited Yellowstone Park in 1827
and may have published the first account of it. See Ferris, *op. cit.,* 259, 261.

trappers, including Ferris, traveled for a short time up the Lewis River and called a halt to wait for warmer weather. With a turn in the weather, Drips and company moved south and by April 26 reached Gray's Hole, where they remained until May 3. Shortly after this date the venturers traveled up the Salt River Valley in quest of a new store of salt.

By May 19, the Lewis [Snake] River was reached and camp established a few hundred yards from the junction of the Salt River. Toward the end of the month the old battlefield of Pierre's Hole was revisited and then Jackson's Hole. June 6th brought the company to the Green, and on the following day Ferris and one companion rode to determine whether any of their long separated friends had by now arrived at Horse Creek on the Green River, the site of Bonneville's "Fort Nonsense," and the appointed place of rendezvous for 1833. At the rude fort was found Joseph R. Walker, John Gray, Benjamin O'Fallon, and a second Vanderburgh. The main camp soon reached the fort and, on June 25, Ferris with a small group departed to meet the St. Louis company, who were expected daily.[18] Immediately following the rendezvous of 1833, Ferris and Robert Newell, a trader for the R.M.F. company and later a pioneer of Oregon, departed at the head of a company to engage in the Flathead trade. The party passed over Gibbon's Pass, along the Lolo, and into Grass Valley to the junction of the Bitterroot with Clark's Fork of the Columbia. The trade was continued until they met Drips on November 2, the latter reporting a successful fall hunt. Ferris observed that trading houses had been established at the mouth of the Marias and also at the mouth of the Bighorn.[19]

After several days Ferris concluded to return to the Flat-

---

[18] William Sublette and Robert Campbell formed this company in 1832 to buy furs from and supply goods to the Rocky Mountain Fur Company.

[19] Fort Piegan was constructed at the mouth of the Marias in 1831 by James Kipp; and Fort Cass at the mouth of the Bighorn in 1832 by Samuel Tullock.

heads with Francis Pillet, one of the many H.B.F. company traders. Late in November the two arrived at the camp of the H.B.F. company clerk, Francis Ermatinger, the majority of whose party had departed for the Flathead or Saleesh Post. Ermatinger and Ferris traveled ahead through Little Cammas Prairie to overtake the British trappers. Ferris found the Hudson's Bay men much better supplied and clad than the Americans. He relished tasting some vegetables brought in from Fort Colville at Kettle Falls. Ferris watched with amazement as the British camp was broken up and the entire store of goods loaded upon light barges and canoes for the trip to Fort Colville. After the departure of Ermatinger and his trappers, Ferris decided to spend the winter with a trader and his family in the Salish Range. A small cabin was constructed, not from necessity, but because "we had nothing else to do." An enjoyable Christmas was spent with the trader, whom Ferris calls "Mr. Montour," [20] and he recorded:

> Our bill of fare consisted of buffalo tongues, dry buffalo meat, fresh venison, wheat flour cakes, buffalo marrow, (for butter,) sugar, coffee, and rum, with which we drank a variety of appropriate toasts, suited to the occasion, and our enlarged and elevated sentiments, respecting universal benevolence and prosperity, while our hearts were warmed, our prejudices banished, and our affections refined, by the enlivening contents of the flowing bowl.[21]

On April 13, Ferris left the Flathead post in a barge for Horse Prairie. Here Ermatinger again made his appearance. By April 23, Ferris and Montour were prepared with goods purchased from the H.B.F. company for their departure to the Flatheads. Near present Missoula, Montana, a crossing of the Arrowstone River was made. On the last day of the month, while Ermatinger and Ferris were engaged

---

[20] Probably David Montour, nephew of Nicholas Montour, who was with David Thompson on the Kootenai in 1811.
[21] Ferris, 238.

in the tedious ceremony of shaking hands with a large camp of Flatheads on the Bitterroot River, a large party of trappers arrived, among whom was Robert Newell, from whom Ferris learned that Drips had wintered at the forks of the Snake, where Henry's Fork and South Fork unite.

From the Indian camp on the Bitterroot, Ferris and Montour, with some Indians, departed for the south, reaching Big Hole on May 12. Toward the end of the month Ferris visited and described the wonders of Yellowstone Park.[22] By May 21, the party was again underway, crossing Henry's Fork and reaching the vicinity of Pierre's Hole. Coming to the plains of Green River, Ferris directed his course toward Fort Nonsense and learned from two Indians that Drips was encamped in the Wind River Mountains east of Green River. The trail thence was immediately pursued and Drips' camp was soon reached. After an exchange of news, Ferris learned that Fontenelle and others were trapping in the "Eutaw" country to the south.

Late in August Ferris and his companions neared the Uintah Basin of northeastern Utah, taking with them two Ute Indian women rescued from the Snakes by Joseph R. Walker, one of whom was the wife of the Ute Chieftain Commoraweap. A halt was made south of the Uintah Mountains, possibly on Brush or Ashley Creek. By September 3, Ferris had reached the vicinity of present Thistle, Utah, and on the 4th camped near the Sanpitch River, in the vicinity of present Mount Pleasant, or Ephraim, Utah. From the 4th to the 8th, Ferris traveled southward across Sanpete and Sevier Valleys to the vicinity of present Richfield, and then northward along the west side of the Sevier, which he calls the "Savarah." Salt beds were found near present Salina, Utah. Moving northward from the Sevier,

---

[22] A marker erected in Yellowstone Park gives Ferris credit for the best early description of the park.

Ferris camped "on a small stream that flows into the Eutah lake," presumably the Santaquin.

Little mention is made of Ferris' trip from Utah Lake eastward to the Green River in the Uintah Basin, the journal jumping to October 29, 1834, when Ferris describes the "Chanion of White River" located east of present Ouray, Utah. Camp was made presumably at the junction of the White and the Green Rivers, near the location of Kit Carson's winter camp of 1833-34. At this point either Ferris or his printer again deleted a great amount of travel narrative, and Ferris is suddenly found on the present Whiterock-Altonah bench lands in Ashley Valley. To make such a journey, their path surely would have led them past Fort Robidoux on the Whiterocks River, and yet no conclusive reference appears in the narrative.[23] Apparently traders from Taos arrived while Ferris was at Fort Kit Carson, about one mile south of present Ouray, Utah, for Ferris records: "During our stay on this river, one of the log huts was occupied by those trappers from Taos, who joined us last fall." [24] Presumably this forced Ferris into shifting his winter camp to the mouth of Ashley Gorge, above Dry Fork Junction, six or eight miles north of the present Vernal, Utah. The small party remained in winter quarters until the end of March, 1835. On the 30th of that month the party attempted to penetrate the chasm of Ashley Gorge but were soon deterred by the terrors of the tortuous canyon. Retreating, Ferris made his way over the Uintahs in a northwesterly direction, by way of the headwaters of Bear River and then far into the Snake River region. He continued eastward through South Pass, down the Sweetwater, the Platte, and finally the Missouri to St. Louis.

---

[23] Scholars disagree as to the founding date of Fort Robidoux, some suggesting 1832, others 1837. See Hafens' *Old Spanish Trail* (Glendale, 1954), 101-2.

[24] Ferris, 277.

After six years of adventure in the Rockies, Ferris arrived home never again to return to his favorite mountain haunts and cool mountain valleys, except in memory. He concluded his journal of his days as a trapper by writing:

> When the weather was warm and pleasant; the demands of nature satisfied, a reliance on the good qualities of my arms and ammunition, not misplaced; the confidence of bestriding and governing a truly noble steed, in the spirit of stirring excitement of the chase, gloriously bounding over the plains, in the panoply of speed and power, before which the swiftest and mightiest denizens of the forest and prairie must yield themselves victims; then – *then* I was really, rationally happy. Many times have I experienced the sensations, generated by either condition; but these scenes have now passed away, their delights and perils no longer thrill nor alarm, and I bid them farewell forever.[25]

After his return, Ferris began preparing his journal for publication, and in 1836 sent it to Carey, Lea and Blanchard, publishers in Philadelphia. They replied that they were unable to publish it at that time. At this refusal Ferris became indifferent and the journal remained untouched in the Ferris family for six years. Meanwhile Warren and his brother Charles apparently decided to join the Texas revolution. Traveling down the Ohio, Warren met a number of old friends from the mountains at Louisville. Taking a steamboat to New Orleans, the Ferris brothers continued on to Galveston. The war was over when they arrived and Charles returned to Buffalo, where in 1842 he assumed the editorship of the *Western Literary Messenger,* in which episodes from Warren's journal began to appear.

In December, 1837, Ferris was elected county surveyor, with a land office at Nacogdoches. He held this position until 1840, when he surveyed the area of the three forks of the Trinity, or present day Dallas, near which he settled and remained the rest of his life. In 1841 he married Melinda Cook from Paris, Illinois. After giving birth to two chil-

---

[25] *Ibid.,* 289-90.

dren, who both died in their youth, Melinda died in 1844.
Ferris was married again in 1847, to Frances Moore of
Palestine, Texas, who mothered twelve children, three of
whom were still living in 1940. Not far from Dallas, Ferris
built a farm at Reinhardt, Texas, on the east bank of White
Rock Creek. To the end of his life the bullet wound in his
left shoulder, received in a Blackfoot attack, caused him
pain. Nevertheless, the mountains held a spell over him,
and his prose articles and poems, only two of which survive,
tell of this fascination. On February 8, 1873, at the age of
sixty-three, Ferris passed quietly away at the farmhouse at
Reinhardt.[26]

Along with his journal, the most important contribution
of Warren Angus Ferris is his famous "Map of the Northwest Fur Country," drawn in 1836. It covers generally the
territory from the 39th to the 48th parallel. From east to
west it covers from the 109th meridian to the 116th. Covering the same fur-trade area, no other map of the early 19th
century can compare with it in comprehensive accuracy.
Ferris had no instruments to determine exact location, and
a number of errors were made, such as making the Great
Salt Lake longer from east to west than from north to south.
The Great Salt Lake and Sevier Lake are too far north,
while Flathead Lake is nearly three degrees too far south,
and Yellowstone Lake is three degrees too far west. With
exact latitude and longitude eliminated, the Ferris map is in
excellent proportions and is a major contribution to the
knowledge of the early West. Many of Ferris' place names
persist on modern maps.

Besides the colorful and accurate descriptions of Bear
Lake, Deer Lodge on Clark's Fork, Yellowstone Park, the
sand hills of southern Idaho, Warm Springs Valley (Montana), Horse Prairie, Pierre's Hole, and Cache Valley

26 Phillips, *op. cit.*, preface, lxiv.

(Utah), various Indian tribes, and the life of a trapper, Ferris has preserved the original naming of such places as Chimney Rock, Scott's Bluff, the Sweetwater, and Independence Rock. He has also preserved excellent portraits of a long list of Mountain Men whom he knew personally, a list including Jim Bridger, Andrew Drips, Lucien Fontenelle, Thomas Fitzpatrick, Joseph R. Walker, Francis Ermatinger, William H. Vanderburgh, Robert Newell, Joseph Robidoux, John Work, and many others.

In all probability the importance of the life of Warren A. Ferris in the annals of western history will increase with the passage of years.

Johnson Gardner

by AUBREY L. HAINES
Yellowstone National Park

The second oldest place name appearing on current maps of Yellowstone National Park immortalizes an American trapper who was one of the harder characters engaged in that rough business, the fur trade.

Nothing is known of Johnson Gardner's life before the year 1824, when he appeared on Bear River with a band of free trappers accompanying Captain John Weber's party;[1] yet his presence there is strong evidence he came up the Missouri River in 1822 or 1823 with one of the expeditions of the Ashley-Henry enterprise. If so, he was a comrade of such latter-day notables as Jedediah Smith, Thomas Fitzpatrick, Jim Bridger and the legendary Hugh Glass, whose avenger he was to be. But the Arikara and Blackfoot Indians managed to make trapping and trading unprofitable in the upper country, and Major Henry was finally forced to abandon his fort at the mouth of the Big Horn River. Even so, he tried one last gamble by launching a trapping party south and west, and the men of that "forlorn hope," unfettered by ties to a base of operations, found their way across the Rocky Mountains into the beaver-rich littoral of the Great Salt Lake. There they were at last successful.

It was also there, and but a year later, that Gardner achieved notoriety through his success in despoiling Peter Skene Ogden, leader of a Hudson's Bay Company brigade also operating in that area. Actually, the transaction was but a thinly-veiled robbery, accomplished by inducing

---

[1] Dale Morgan, *Jedediah Smith and the Opening of the West* (Indianapolis, 1953), 143.

Ogden's Iroquois trappers to desert through promises of
high prices for furs already owed the British company.
When Ogden attempted to restrain his men, Gardner used
both threats and a show of arms to get his way.[2] That was
considered rather unsporting – even among competitors – a
view shared by some outside the ranks of the "Honorable
Company."

The meager record indicates that Johnson Gardner remained in the northern Rocky Mountains for six years. He
is mentioned by Governor Simpson, of the Hudson's Bay
Company, as being Major Pilcher's clerk at an American
trading post on Flathead Lake during the winter of 1828-
29, and his name became attached for a time to the Idaho
stream now known as Tincup Creek, a tributary of Salt
River,[3] but for what reason is entirely lost to our generation.

When Smith, Jackson and Sublette retired from the fur
trade, Gardner took the Company's note for $1,321.48 owed
him, and removed to the Upper Missouri country. There he
soon appeared on the books of the American Fur Company's
post at the mouth of the Yellowstone River – Fort Union –
through the sale of fifty-three beaver skins and one otter for
$347 on July 12, 1831.[4] From a trapping agreement entered
into with Kenneth McKenzie at that place a year later, it is
apparent that Gardner was an illiterate, for the instrument
was signed with an "x, his mark."

Among other things, the agreement set the terms for a
sale of furs Gardner then had "en cache on the Yellowstone
River;" thus, it must have been in the fall of 1831 or the
spring of 1832 that he first trapped the beautiful mountain

2 Dale Morgan presents this affair very well in the work just cited, 148-51.

3 Aubrey L. Haines (ed.), *Osborne Russell's Journal of a Trapper* (Portland,
Ore., 1955), 158, 160.

4 Hiram M. Chittenden, *American Fur Trade of the Far West* (New York, 1902),
II, p. 943. Gardner's account with the American Fur Company is discussed on pp.
941-5. See also Johnson Gardner accounts, 1831-1832, in Chouteau-Maffitt Collection, Missouri Historical Society.

valley which came to be known among the trappers as "Gardner's Hole." The river flowing from it still carries his name.

During the winter of 1832-33, the Arikara Indians caught Gardner's old comrade, Hugh Glass, on the ice of the Missouri River, and there killed the old man and two other trappers. A short time later, those Indians came into the camp of Johnson Gardner's party on the headwaters of Powder River where it was noticed they had a rifle, knife, powder horn and other items known to belong to Glass. The trappers managed to sieze three of the Indians and mete out summary justice which was as brutal as anything a savage could have contrived.

Prince Maximilian of Wied, a German scientist who became acquainted with Gardner in the course of a long boat trip down the Missouri, says that two of the Indians were killed with a knife when they attempted to escape,[5] but another version was soon current on the frontier. According to John Sanford, who passed the information on to Indian Agent William Clark, the Arikaras were scalped and burned alive when they could give no satisfactory reason for possessing the worldly goods of a white trapper.[6]

It only remains to add the comment of a contemporary scribe, one Montgomery Flagg, who says:

> Not long afterwards Gardiner himself fell into the hands of the Erickeraws, who inflicted upon him the same dreadful death.[7]

A case of *pro pelle cutem* (skin for skin) as Peter Skene Ogden would have wryly observed.

[5] Maximilian, Prince of Wied, *Travels in the Interior of North America, 1832-1834* in Thwaites' *Early Western Travels*, XXIV, pp. 102-3.

[6] Letter, J. F. A. Sanford to William Clark, July 26, 1833 (Records of the Department of the Interior, Office of Indian Affairs, Letters Received, 1823-1840). The original letter was included with an official report forwarded to Washington on August 17, 1833, and is now in the National Archives.

[7] John Myers Myers, *Pirate, Pawnee and Mountain Man* (Boston, 1963), 226.

Hugh Glenn

by HARRY R. STEVENS
Ohio University, Athens

Hugh Glenn (leader of the Glenn-Fowler expedition from Oklahoma to Taos, 1821-22) was born January 7, 1788, near the site of Gerrardstown, Berkeley County, West Virginia, the fifth of six sons of William and Alice (Evans) Glenn. His father's family were Scotch Presbyterians who migrated to Pennsylvania and thence south into the Shenandoah valley. William Glenn was a farmer and Revolutionary War veteran who sold his Virginia plantation in the spring of 1796 and moved west with his family to a farm on Johnson's Creek near Mayslick, Mason County, Kentucky, where he died late the same year.[1]

Most of the Glenn sons became farmers in Kentucky or Ohio. Hugh moved to the village of Cincinnati, where he appeared in October, 1811, as secretary of a meeting of merchants and shippers organizing the Farmers' and Mechanics' Bank of that town. With the outbreak of war in 1812 he became an assistant to John Hopper Piatt, one of the merchants engaged to provide supplies for the troops moving north toward Canada. During the campaign of 1812-13 for the recovery of Detroit he was responsible for carrying flour, biscuit, beef, and bacon along the several routes of advance. He worked as wagon master, pack-train leader, boat and sled builder, and buyer, to the great satisfaction of deputy commissary Piatt and General William Henry Harrison. He continued this work during the next fall and again in 1814, and in the last year of the war was a

---

[1] Glenn Family Bible, George A. Glenn MSS. (Harrisonville, Mo.). G. Glenn Clift, *History of Maysville and Mason County* (Lexington, Ky., 1936), 324-6.

partner with Jacob Fowler in furnishing rations to British prisoners of war being taken from Lower Sandusky to Long Point, Ontario.[2] In doing so he established a good reputation and gained invaluable knowledge of the Ohio, Indiana, and Michigan frontiers as well as extensive business experience.

In the fall of 1813 Glenn bought a small store in Cincinnati, where he sold bar iron, plows, chains, hoes, calicoes, salt, and whiskey. He continued storekeeping after his marriage on March 17, 1816, to Mary Gibson at Greensburg, Pennsylvania. In April, 1816, he was elected a director of the Farmers' and Mechanics' Bank, the youngest member of the board in which he was closely associated with lawyer Nicholas Longworth, merchant Piatt, and cashier Samuel W. Davies. He moved his store from one location to another, increasing the variety and evidently the volume of his business, and buying pork, flour, whiskey, and tobacco for export.[3]

Early in 1817 two major changes in the western economy created divergent opportunities. Glenn seized both of them, and they foreshadow his eventual tragedy. On January 17 he got a contract to supply and issue rations at certain designated western army posts and, as the military frontier was being thrust outward in many directions, at other posts that might be established later. Bond of $45,000 for fulfillment of this contract was provided by Jacob Fowler and Thomas Davis Carneal. On January 27 he was chosen by the Bank of the United States in Philadelphia to be a director of the Cincinnati office of discount and deposit which opened April 21. Glenn was again the youngest member of the board. He was admitted to membership in the local

[2] Letter Book of John H. Piatt, Ewing MSS., Library of Congress. *Western Spy* (Cincinnati), Oct. 26, 1811.

[3] *Western Spy*, Mar. 26, Apr. 9, 1814; Apr. 20, May 24, June 14, July 19, Aug. 9, 23, Nov. 8, 1816.

Masonic lodge on April 30. On March 11 his son Gibson William was born.[4]

While Glenn continued keeping store, importing and selling textiles, hardware, and tools, and exporting agricultural produce, his chief concern was the military contract. He would be expected to provide at least 260,000 rations, amounting to over three hundred tons, to army posts in the western department. The government authorized an allowance of 19¢ per ration. Glenn could expect to make a profit or stand a loss on the difference between that amount and what it cost him to buy, package, transport, and deliver the amounts required. The contract put a high premium on his energy and ability.

In March he drew on the Treasury Department for funds to buy provisions, and requested and received detailed instructions from General Thomas A. Smith at Belle Fontaine (near St. Louis) about his duties. About the middle of May he left Cincinnati, traveled to Fort Harrison (near Terre Haute, Indiana) and Vincennes where he left supplies, and soon reached St. Louis.[5]

On June 8, 1817, Glenn started up the Mississippi by keelboat carrying supplies to Forts Edwards, Armstrong, and Crawford. On the way he met Major Stephen H. Long, army topographical engineer and explorer, traveling south by skiff. Returning to St. Louis by August 22, Glenn had completed a round trip of almost eleven hundred miles in less than ordinary keelboat travel time. During the next few weeks he supplied provisions to Fort Clark (at the site of Peoria), St. Louis, Belle Fontaine, and Ft. Osage on the Missouri River a little below the site of Kansas City, and

---

[4] United States *vs.* H. Glenn, U.S. District Court, Frankfort, Ky., Complete Record Book N (MS), 473-7 (Frankfort Docket Suit no. 1270). Nova Caesarea Harmony Lodge No. 2 Masonic Records, John Day Caldwell MSS., Cincinnati Historical Society. Glenn Family Bible.

[5] U.S. Treasury Records, 3d Auditor's Office, Auditor's Reports no. 4712, vol. 5 (1819), National Archives.

was again in the territorial capital of Missouri about the middle of September.[6]

Reports of conflicts between the Osage and Cherokee Indians settled beyond the Ozark Mountains led General Smith to decide on the establishment of a fort along the Arkansas to maintain peace. Glenn was given the new responsibility of supplying the garrison, and before leaving with the expedition (commanded by Major William Bradford and accompanied by Major Long) he obtained from Governor William Clark a license to trade with both nations.[7] The journey down the Mississippi and up the Arkansas resulted in the establishment of Ft. Smith. On his return to St. Louis, probably by an Osage trading path, Glenn began in January, 1818, to speculate in western land.

Another responsibility emerged almost at once. The federal government decided to remove the Kickapoo, Illinois, Potawatamie and other nations from Illinois and Missouri. The Indians were called to attend numerous treaty councils, and Glenn, as contractor, was obliged to supply their provisions. He returned to Cincinnati during the winter to obtain them. There he found that his business was prospering in the hands of his brother James, and that he had been reelected a director of the branch Bank of the United States. He began to invest in bank stock as well as in Illinois "soldiers' lands."[8] Concerned with the difficulties of river commerce, in May he joined a group of men working to build a canal around the falls of the Ohio River below Louisville.

A further task appeared with the decision of the Secretary of War to establish an army post at the mouth of the Yellowstone. Glenn had to supply provisions for this expedition

[6] *Ibid.* Minnesota Historical Society *Collections,* II, pp. 65-6.

[7] *Niles' Weekly Register,* XIII, p. 176. Clarence E. Carter (ed.), *Territorial Papers of the United States,* XV, p. 378.

[8] David Todd MSS., Missouri Historical Society. Records of the Cincinnati Agency, Bank of the United States, Timothy Kirby MSS., Cincinnati Historical Society.

in the spring. The creation of new and more remote lines of national defense was a continuing process, and as a military contractor Glenn was being drawn constantly farther to the west.

In July and August, 1818, Glenn was in St. Louis once more, beginning to hear complaints about flour and other rations he had supplied, receiving reports from Ft. Crawford, Wisconsin, through his agent Jacob Fowler, and buying preemption rights in the proposed town of Davidsonville (Randolph County, Arkansas).[9]

By the time Glenn returned to Cincinnati, just after the middle of August, the critical situation of the Bank of the United States in Philadelphia had prompted the directors there to require the Cincinnati branch to collect everything due to it from the state-chartered banks within five months. Directors of the three state banks in the town were alarmed. Glenn, both a merchant and a director of the branch Bank of the United States, was one of the first to feel the pinch and react. He cut his imports entirely, sold his bank stock, and tried to convert his assets into cash at once. By December 19 he announced his stock of goods was gone. At the same time he formed a partnership with his brother and Captain Levi James to build a steamboat to carry more produce to New Orleans. The three-hundred-ton *Vulcan* was built locally by John Brooks and launched on March 27, 1819. Hopefully, exports could be increased and a cash balance built up.[10]

But the financial crisis developed even more quickly. On October 16 the Bank of the United States directors in Philadelphia sent fateful orders to the West. They required the

---

[9] U.S. Treasury Records, 3d Auditor's Office, Auditor's Reports no. 4712, National Archives.

[10] *American State Papers, Finance*, III, p. 326; IV, pp. 859-61. Miami Exporting Company Stock Book (MS.), Cincinnati Historical Society. Johnston Account Book, John Johnston MSS., Cincinnati Historical Society. *Liberty Hall* (Cincinnati), Oct. 20, Dec. 22, 1818; Jan. 12, Apr. 27, 1819. *Western Spy*, Dec. 26, 1818; Jan. 23, 1819.

directors of the Cincinnati branch to collect in hard money all debts due from the state banks immediately. At the same time the Cincinnati Land Office was forbidden by the Treasury to accept any money except cash or the notes of banks which redeemed their notes in hard money. The word arrived November 3, 1818. Two days later all banks in the town stopped redeeming their notes. The bubble of prosperity had burst and a long depression followed.[11]

During the next week, through his relative Dr. Daniel Drake, Glenn met the English explorer and naturalist Thomas Nuttall, who was making a trip to the Far West. He gave Nuttall letters and much valuable information, and arranged to meet him at Ft. Smith the next year, when the Englishman hoped to travel up the Arkansas with Glenn to the Rockies.[12]

Further difficulties rising from his army contract gathered over Glenn in the fall of 1818 and darkened in the subsequent months. Pressures within the federal government to economize, apparently in part motivated by political rivalry between Secretaries Calhoun and Crawford, brought a disallowance of some of Glenn's claims and insistence on additional evidence to support others. In the winter of 1818-19 Glenn and his surety Carneal went to Washington to try to get the claims paid. They were partly successful. On February 18 Glenn got $15,000; but his remaining claims for payment were cut from $42,480 to $31,432. On that balance, after he gave additional bond, another $9,000 was paid before the end of March, when he returned home.[13]

The reexamination of claims continued in Washington during the spring. Evidence next showed that the quantity of rations issued by Glenn's subcontractor to Indians at Ft.

11 *American State Papers Finance,* IV, pp. 859-64. Newspapers cited in note 10.

12 Thomas Nuttall, *A Journal of Travels,* in R. G. Thwaites (ed.), *Early Western Travels,* XIII, pp. 61-2. Richard G. Beidleman, "The 1818-20 Arkansas Journey of Thomas Nuttall," *Arkansas Historical Quarterly,* XV (1956), 255-7.

13 U.S. Treasury Records cited in note 9.

Harrison had increased in April and May, 1818, to an astonishing amount. His claim was reduced from 26,195 rations to 17,000. Other claims were also reduced. The Treasury auditor on April 3 reported that Glenn should be charged with Treasury warrants amounting to $106,900, and other items making a total of $133,346, and that he was entitled to credit for issues totaling only $95,553. The reckoning left him in debt to the United States for $37,792.[14]

Early in the summer of 1819 Glenn found that his shipping adventure with the *Vulcan* was a disaster. His ship left April 18 for New Orleans with a cargo of pork and flour. By the time it reached the market ten days later, prices had collapsed so far that his produce could be sold only at a heavy loss, if sold at all. Problems confronting him in the branch Bank of the United States were almost as discouraging. The Cincinnati branch directors held about $780,000 in paper of the state-chartered banks, rapidly depreciating in value. They were required by Philadelphia to collect specie from the state banks for this paper, but had no instructions on how to do so. They sent a proposal to Philadelphia that they be permitted to lend the paper with land as security and asked for approval. No approval came, and the paper continued to fall in value daily. As they had received at least no veto, they decided to act. In a few months, probably between March and October, 1819, they loaned nearly the whole amount. The transaction is obscure; but Glenn was closely involved in it, and in some way held responsibility. Eventually the Philadelphia bank brought claims against him for about a quarter of a million dollars.[15]

---

[14] *Ibid.* Department of War, Bureau of Indian Affairs, Letter Book D (1816-20) (MS.), 270-71, National Archives.

[15] Correspondence of the Cincinnati Agency, Bank of the United States, Kirby MSS., Cincinnati Historical Society. "Report of Standing Committee on the state of the Office," (Cincinnati Office, Bank of the United States) Nov. 28, 1819 (MS. in the Library of the Cincinnati Historical Society). Jacob Burnet, *Notes on the Early Settlement of the North Western Territory* (Cincinnati, 1847), 407-11.

During the summer of 1819 Glenn's difficulties dragged the Farmers' and Mechanics' Bank toward catastrophe. Cashier Davies had lent $170,000 to the Johnson brothers of Kentucky to build five steamboats for the use of the Yellowstone expedition. All the money had been spent. None of the boats had been finished. Davies saw no chance to recover the loan. He had also, he maintained, lent $40,000 to Glenn, which Glenn promised to repay as soon as the Treasury met his claims. Davies made inquiry of the Secretary of the Treasury and learned that the most Glenn could expect to receive was $10,000. When the bad news was confirmed Davies was forced to suspend specie payment and close the door of his bank. Davies lost his position four months later, and the bank never reopened.[16]

Finally the investigation of Indian issues at Fort Harrison, carried on between March and July, convinced the Secretary of War by August 6 "that fraud had been practised by Mitchell Brouillet, who it seems acted as [Glenn's] agent." The investigation continued in order to determine responsibility.[17]

The Bank of the United States in Philadelphia decided early in the fall to take drastic action against the Cincinnati branch directors. They criticized the management of the branch severely and issued new restrictive orders. Glenn, as chairman of a standing committee of the Cincinnati office, prepared a report containing "a refutation of the charges." The Cincinnati board adopted a resolution that embodied Glenn's report on November 8, but the Philadelphia directors removed the branch cashier and sent a replacement who arrived before the end of the month.[18]

---

[16] *American State Papers, Finance,* IV, pp. 623, 632, 728-31. Cincinnati Office, Bank of the United States, Correspondence Book 1819-20, Kirby MSS., Cincinnati Historical Society.

[17] Department of War, Bureau of Indian Affairs, Letter Book D (1816-20), (MS.) 305-7, 323, 336-7, National Archives.

[18] See note 15 above.

The winter of 1820 brought the last blows that shattered Glenn's business career. The decision on his military contract was confirmed in Washington on February 9. He owed the government over $37,000. A court martial at Terre Haute, Indiana, opened the way to court action against Glenn himself. When the Philadelphia Bank of the United States appointed the board for the Cincinnati office in February, three directors – John H. Piatt, Daniel Drake, and Hugh Glenn – found themselves excluded. In the same month, businessmen and merchants of Cincinnati fought bitterly in the ice-bound city to maintain the credit of the various banks they were connected with. Glenn apparently tried to keep a neutral course, but he was too deeply involved. Loyal to his friend Thomas Heckewelder, he came into conflict with other friends on every side.[19]

Extremities of suffering, not merely of merchants and bankers but of men, women, and children of every class and occupation, the emergence of personal hostilities, and the break-up of long-standing political associations precipitated a crisis during the spring that was followed by growing violence, mob disturbances, and eventually riot and bloodshed.

Before the social order had disintegrated to that point, Hugh Glenn, like dozens of others in his city, had left for the west. In August 1820 he was living at a trading post near the mouth of the Verdigris River sixty miles northwest of Ft. Smith, Arkansas. With a partner, Charles Dennis, a Frenchman or two, and an occasional soldier from the garrison he spent ten months beyond the last military outpost of the United States. He came to know Nathaniel Pryor, veteran scout of the Lewis and Clark expedition, entertained members of Major Long's Yellowstone expedition, gave

---

[19] Correspondence of Ethan Allen Brown, Jan.-Feb., 1820, E. A. Brown MSS., Ohio Historical Society (Columbus, Ohio). *Liberty Hall,* Feb. 4, 25, 1820. Cincinnati City Court Docket May 3, 1819-Dec., 1821 (MS.), Cincinnati Historical Society.

assistance to members of a nearby missionary group, and worked with Governor James Miller and Major Bradford in trying to avert war between the Osage and Cherokee nations.[20]

Late in the spring of 1821 Glenn returned briefly to Cincinnati. Faced with a long account of executions of court orders against himself Glenn found little satisfaction outside his own family. Early in the summer he rode west once more, through St. Louis and along the Missouri and Osage rivers to his Verdigris house. On the way he gathered several men interested in joining him on an expedition to trade with the Indians "westward to the mountains." He got a license to trade in the area from Major Bradford on August 5, 1821, and in September was joined by Jacob Fowler and other trappers and frontiersmen, among them Baptiste Roy, Jesse Van Bibber, Isaac Slover, Nathaniel Miguel Pryor, and George Douglas. A mixed crew of twenty-one, American, French, Spanish, white and black, ranging in age from sixteen (or less – one was a boy) to fifty-seven or more, they seem to have held together chiefly through confidence in their leader. The crises of the expedition suggest as much.[21]

About September 21, 1821, Glenn, having refused an invitation a few days earlier to travel with Thomas James' expedition to the west, rode north from his trading post with one or two of the men. Another one or two followed. On September 25 Major Fowler led the remaining seventeen men along the trail. They took a course generally close to the Arkansas River, along the north side.

---

[20] Nuttall, *A Journal of Travels,* in Thwaites, *op. cit.,* XIII, pp. 234-77. James, *Account of an Expedition,* in Thwaites, *ibid.,* XVI, pp. 185, 187, 282, 290. Carter, *Territorial Papers,* XIV, p. 791, XIX, pp. 263-6, 286, 309, 448. Harlin M. Fuller and LeRoy R. Hafen (eds.), *Journal of Captain John R. Bell* (Glendale, Calif., 1957), 269-70, 275, 279.

[21] Cincinnati City Court, Executions for the Miami Exporting Company, Docket No. 1, 1821-22 (MS.), Cincinnati Historical Society. U.S. District Court Record of Pleas 1828-30 (Clerk's Office, U.S. District Court, Cincinnati), 433-56. License issued by William Bradford to Hugh Glenn and others, George A. Glenn MSS.

Occasional encounters with Indians, with whom Glenn traded and swapped horses, continued until October 13. Sometimes a hunter fell ill and was left behind for a day or two. Others, riding off to shoot buffalo or to scout, lost their way and were late in returning. Pack animals wore out and had to be turned off, and important supplies cached or abandoned. From October 6 to November 4 the expedition rode through the present state of Kansas. About October 9 some Indians advised Glenn to head directly west "to the big timber near the mountains," but he decided after consideration to stay with his planned route along the Great Bend of the Arkansas. On October 14 he discharged a hired Indian. The next day his hunters saw Indians on horseback (perhaps Pawnee) who seemed to be following them, and they made a fortification of their baggage. No encounter took place. Two days later one hunter, Findlay, rode off alone to look for buffalo cows. They saw no more Indians. But Findlay did not find his way back until five days later.

On October 27 Glenn entered Spanish territory on the south side of the Arkansas. Findlay was left near the site of Cimarron, with two exhausted horses and a mule, to rest the animals five days and rejoin the party. Week passed after week and he did not catch up.

On November 1 the men saw the first ice in their kettle and on the river. The earliest signs of beaver appeared two days later. After another five days the expedition was caught in a snowstorm. November 13 was memorable. Glenn first saw the summit of the Spanish Peaks, and on the same day he faced a significant test of courage. His men encountered a white grizzly bear near the mouth of the Purgatory River. One of them, Lewis Dawson, was attacked and terribly clawed and chewed. Glenn fired, drew the bear's attention from the wounded man, was himself pursued and climbed into a tree where the bear followed him, fired again, and shot the beast. Dawson died a few days later.

During five weeks his men had seen no human beings but themselves. On November 19, just beyond the mouth of the Apishapa River, Glenn found himself surrounded by thirty or more armed Kiowas. In the following days a great number of Indians arrived, and Glenn discovered that he was virtually their captive. A Comanche chief expecting to receive goods that his Father the President had sent grew angry when Glenn told him there were no such goods, denounced him as a liar and a thief, and signified he would kill Glenn and his party. The Indian chiefs held council, and Major Fowler wrote in the journal, "our Setuation Was not of the most plesent nature." Glenn had a good supply of trading stuff, but he did not intend to hand it over. It was another important test of his character. At sundown November 24 a tall Indian ran into camp calling out "Me Arapaho chief – white man mine! White man mine – Arapaho plenty," and thus dramatically they were rescued. On November 27 Findlay, missing thirty days, caught up with them, alone and on foot.

Other incidents, both grave and amusing (laconically described in the *Journal of Jacob Fowler*) followed in the next six weeks as Glenn slowly approached the beaver country at the foot of the Rockies. He purchased a Spanish prisoner from the Comanches (whom he was compelled to return the next day), and in other more effective ways demonstrated to his men and himself those qualities of leadership that had seemingly failed him in his business life in the East two years previously. He sent out his first trapping party, six men commanded by Isaac Slover, on December 3.[22]

On December 29, encamped near the mouth of the St. Charles River, Glenn met a company of Spanish troops headed south. He learned that a revolution in Mexico had

22 Jacob Fowler, *Journal.*

overthrown Spanish rule and that the neighboring country was now independent. He decided to visit Santa Fe and try to obtain permission to hunt and trap in the former Spanish province. On January 2, 1822, with four companions from his own party he joined the soldiers on their return along the Old Mexican Road or Taos Trail. They entered the mountains through the valley of the Huerfano River and crossed the Sangre de Cristo Range by way of La Veta Pass into the San Luis Valley. They were probably the first Americans to use this route.

Glenn spent the next few weeks principally in Taos, making three trips to Santa Fe where he obtained the desired permission from Governor Melgares and again met Thomas James. His expedition, divided into several parties, trapped in the mountains around the upper Rio Grande. Rejoined by Fowler, he began his return trip to the United States on June 1, reaching Ft. Osage on July 5 and St. Louis about July 15.

Glenn's expedition to the Rockies was economically successful. He brought back more than eleven hundred pounds of fur, and received credit for $4,499 from the American Fur Company in St. Louis.[23] Little of importance was added to the fund of geographical knowledge, since the trail Glenn pioneered was seldom used in later years; but his news that trade with the province of New Mexico was now open to Americans was a major contribution that spread quickly and provided a decisive impulse to the opening of the Santa Fe Trail. After the disasters and betrayals of the preceding three years, for Glenn himself the achievements of the trip were of great personal importance. His stories were handed down in the family through succeeding generations.

After Glenn returned to Cincinnati in the latter part of 1822 he was not, however, the brilliantly successful business

---

[23] American Fur Company Records, 1822 (MSS.), Missouri Historical Society.

man he had been during the previous decade. His ship soon wore out. His canal was never built. His land speculation brought him no wealth. His claims on the United States government for expenditures on military supplies were eventually upheld in court, but not until after Glenn had sold them to another man for a small part of their original amount. Claims against him by the Bank of the United States continued for the rest of his life. "Misfortunes cast him in the shade." And yet his love for the frontier life led him again to the West, and near the end he seems to have been at least once more an Indian trader in western Missouri, perhaps with a trading post in Kansas. He died May 28, 1833, in Cincinnati. His son, who adopted the name Hugh Gibson Glenn, moved to Harrisonville, Missouri, where some of his descendants live today.[24]

---

24 George A. Glenn MSS. David Todd MSS., Missouri Historical Society. *Cincinnati Daily Gazette,* May 30, 1833.

Antoine Godin

by AUBREY L. HAINES
Yellowstone National Park

Here, in an unprincipled and ungoverned life, is a study in treachery. It is a life which reached its climax in a breach of faith likened to "Joab with a vengeance," and then ran down to an end that would have pleased the Greek goddess of retributive justice.

Antoine Godin and his father, Thyery, were two of the band of Iroquois Indians gathered from the vicinity of Montreal, Canada, in accordance with the North West Company's decision of 1816 to recruit such men for service in the Oregon country. There, they were to serve as boatmen and trappers, for they excelled at both, but character defects made them, on the whole, unsatisfactory employees.

The Iroquois were considered civilized and Christian, yet they had not profited greatly from either influence. Alexander Ross called them "sullen, indolent, fickle, cowardly and treacherous," adding, "an Iroquois arrived at manhood is still as wayward and extravagant as a lad of other nations at the age of fifteen."[1] During most of a decade, before death and defection eliminated them from the brigades of the North West Company and its successor, the Hudson's Bay Company, the Iroquois were a trial to all who led them. They were rebellious – even openly mutinous – when held in check; when not controlled, they scattered in small groups to live with the natives, preferring gambling and Indian women to the hardships of trapping. They were unproductive, and worse yet, a frequent cause of embroilments which did their employer no good.

---

[1] Alexander Ross, *Fur Hunters of the Far West* (London, 1855), I, pp. 295-6.

Antoine Godin was one of them, but his personal history is vague. He was undoubtedly born in the East prior to 1810, for he was already an *engagé* in 1825 – the year in which he earned a not-too-favorable mention, following his father's desertion to the American trappers, by asking for a release from his obligations to the Hudson's Bay Company. On April 11, Peter Skene Ogden noted, ". . being a worthless scamp, I gave him his liberty, the Americans having advanced three beaver to make up his debt." [2]

The next event which gave direction to the life of Antoine was the death of his father. It is an event which has long been accepted on the authority of Washington Irving's statement that Godin's River was "so called after an Iroquois hunter in the service of Sublette, who was murdered there by the Blackfeet." [3] While that is undoubtedly based on what Captain Bonneville heard during his stay in the Rocky Mountains, the name was not given *in memoriam,* but had been attached to the Big Lost River of central Idaho for some years prior to the death of Thyery. In his account of the Snake River expedition of 1824, Alexander Ross says: "on reaching Goddin's River, so named after one of my men who discovered it, I sent off eight men to trap it downwards," [4] – a statement which is sufficiently positive.

Thus, Goddin's River was named for the living trapper a number of years before his demise, which is usually given as "about 1830." Yet, there is information that the year was 1828. In a casualty list submitted to William Clark to show the "Names of Persons Killed belonging to the Parties of Wm. H. Ashley and Smith, Jackson & Sublette & &," there is the entry: "Johnson, Godair – 2 – Bear River – Blackfeet." [5]

[2] T. C. Elliot (ed.), "The Peter Skene Ogden Journals," in *Oregon Historical Quarterly,* x (Dec., 1909), 360.

[3] Washington Irving, "Bonneville's Adventures," in *Works of Washington Irving* (New York, 1882), III, p. 301.

[4] Ross, *op. cit.,* 69, 72.

But, whether Thyery Godin died by the hand of a Black-foot in 1830 along the stream he had discovered earlier, or in 1828 "near the Great Salt Lake, while attempting to pass from one American camp to another, but a few miles distant," [6] is really unimportant; more to the point here is the fact that, thereafter, Antoine harbored a vindictive hatred for the Blackfoot people.

The opportunity to exact a reparation of blood came in the summer of 1832. Antoine Godin arrived at the great rendezvous held near the present town of Victor, Idaho, in the role of the good Samaritan, bringing in the emaciated Thomas Fitzpatrick riding double behind him;[7] and he left that boisterous gathering soon afterward with a party of forty-two men – including Nathaniel Wyeth, his eleven Easterners, and some free trappers – under the leadership of Milton Sublette. While yet in Pierre's Hole and just as they were readying for the second day's march (July 18), Indians estimated to number two hundred were discovered approaching. The camp was hurriedly prepared for defense and some of the more experienced men rode forward to investigate.

The Indians were of the Blackfoot confederacy and probably Gros Ventres on one of their frequent migrations. War was not their intention at that time, for the entire village approached openly and a scarlet-blanketed chief stood forth seeking a parley. Antoine Godin rode forward with Baptiste Dorian, a fellow of similar character, and together they murdered the chief for revenge and his bright blanket.

Such was the origin of the battle of Pierre's Hole, a brief struggle of little importance to the fur trade except as it has come to typify the trapper-Blackfoot animosity. As for

[5] Dale Morgan, *Jedediah Smith and the Opening of the West* (Indianapolis, 1953), 345. See also Morgan's *West of Ashley* (Denver, 1964), 186, 293, 314.

[6] *Ibid.,* 295.

[7] Stanley Vestal, *Mountain Men* (Boston, 1937), 108.

Antoine, subsequent events would indicate his treachery made him a marked man.

Nathaniel Wyeth returned to the Rocky Mountains in 1834, establishing Fort Hall as a trading post on the bank of the Snake River. Among the names which appear on the first page of the account book kept there is Godin's,[8] with the hint that he was not particularly reliable and should have only limited credit. The entries from October 3, 1834, to mid-1836, indicate he established himself as a meat hunter for the fort.

The account book contains evidence which fixes rather closely the time of Godin's death. On May 19, 1836, the last credit was placed to his account for meat brought to the fort, and two days later he made his last draw from the store – one pound of balls. Entries beginning on the 23rd are credits from the sale of his personal effects (blanket, rifle, saddle, camp axe, powder horn, and knife).[9] Thus, there is little doubt it was on or about May 22, 1836, that Antoine Godin answered the hail of the half-breed James Bird by crossing Snake River to bargain for furs, and to unknowingly deliver himself to his enemies.

Arriving alone, Godin sat down with Bird and his Blackfoot companions for a smoke before trading; and there, in full view of the fort, he was shot as the pipe came around to him.[10] A ledger entry is not the only way to close an account; Bird took care of that formality by carving "NJW" on the forehead of the dying Antoine Godin.

---

[8] "Account Books of Fort Hall," in the collection of the Oregon Historical Society, Portland, Ledger no. 1, pp. 1-2 (account of "Antwine Goda").

[9] *Ibid.*, 444-5.

[10] The story of Antoine Godin's death is told in a colorful manner in several places, particularly the following: H. M. Chittenden, *American Fur Trade of the Far West* (New York, 1902), II, p. 663; Eva Emery Dye, *McLoughlin and Old Oregon* (Garden City, N.Y., 1926), 99-100; and in Bernard DeVoto, *Across the Wide Missouri* (Boston, 1947), 261. James Bird reappeared as an interpreter for Isaac I. Stevens at the time of the treaty negotiations with the Blackfoot nation (1855), and his likeness may be seen in the *Life of Isaac Ingalls Stevens*, by Hazard Stevens (Boston, 1901), II, p. 118.

Miles Morris Goodyear

by EUGENE E. CAMPBELL
Brigham Young University

When the famous Whitman-Spalding missionary party arrived at Fort Hall in 1836, they were accompanied by nineteen-year-old Miles Goodyear, who was to gain a certain fame as a Mountain Man and trader even though he came West almost at the end of the fur-trading era. Thirteen years later he was dead, but in that relatively short period he established himself as a trader and guide; built Fort Buenaventura at the location of present-day Ogden, Utah; and figured in many important events in western history. These included the pursuit of the Arapahoes and Cheyennes after their attack on Fort Bridger in 1843; Sir William Drummond Stewart's famed pleasure rendezvous in the Green River Valley; the entrance of the Mormon pioneers into Utah; and the California Gold Rush of 1849. His participation in the Gold Rush was preceded by one of the longest horse drives in western history.

Born at Hamden, Connecticut, February 24, 1817, Miles Goodyear, along with five brothers and sisters, was orphaned when his father died in 1819 and his mother passed away in 1821. The eldest son, William, was unable to keep the family together and with the exception of infant Andrew, the Goodyear children were "bound out" to anyone who would "assume" the responsibility of their "keep" in exchange for such labor as they were able to perform.[1] It is not known who cared for Miles until he was ten, but at that

---

[1] Charles Kelly and Maurice L. Howe, *Miles Goodyear: First Citizen of Utah* (Salt Lake City, 1937), 14-15.

Unfortunately, Kelly and Howe failed to document their work with footnotes, but their bibliography indicates use of the basic sources available. They do not hesitate to use their imagination when such sources are unavailable, however.

age he was "bound out" to a Squire Peck of North Haven for a period of six years.[2] During this time he learned to read and write and "doubtless to cipher" and gained a liking for poetry.[3] He also gained a hearty dislike for farm work and a great desire for absolute freedom. He dreamed of establishing a home in some "beautiful valley of the Rocky Mountains far from the scene of his servitude."[4]

The first step in making this dream a reality came in 1834 when he began moving westward, stopping to earn the necessities of life. It was over a year before he reached Detroit in June, 1835, and almost another year before he set out for Chicago on foot in the spring of 1836.[5] Continuing on to the Missouri in an apparent attempt to contact agents of the American Fur Company he met the Oregon-bound missionaries "some 40 miles from Fort Leavenworth."[6]

This meeting proved to be a fortunate one for both Goodyear and the Whitman party. It gave young Miles a source of food, supplies, and transportation while traveling West, and contact with Thomas Fitzpatrick and other Mountain Men with whom the Whitman party was traveling; and it provided the missionaries with an able-bodied worker who could care for stock, cook over the open fire, and scout for roads and camping sites.

Mr. Gray, lay assistant to Whitman and Spalding, was favorably impressed with young Goodyear, whom he described as being "about 16 year old . . . light flaxen hair, blue eyes, thin and spare."[7] He underestimated his age by three years, and apparently his hair was more auburn

[2] Ibid.

[3] Dale Morgan, "Miles Goodyear and the Founding of Ogden," Utah Historical Quarterly, XXI (July, 1953), 196.

[4] Kelly and Howe, op. cit., 17.

[5] Grace Goodyear Kirkman, Genealogy of the Goodyear Family (San Francisco, 1899), 182, 189-90, as quoted in Morgan. Mrs. Kirkman's work is undoubtedly the source for much of Kelly and Howe's information of Goodyear's early years.

[6] William H. Gray, History of Oregon (Portland, 1870), 113-14.

[7] Ibid.

than flaxen, being later known as "red head" or "red deer."[8]

Young Goodyear unwittingly played an important part in the development of the Oregon Trail as an avenue for bringing wheeled vehicles into the West, for Dr. Whitman insisted on taking one of his wagons across the Green River and Horse Creek, beyond which point "no wheel had ever made a track."[9] Miles was required to do much of the back-breaking labor in bringing the wagon through to Fort Hall. Gray believed Whitman's determination to take the wagon beyond Fort Hall was the primary reason for Goodyear's separation from the missionary company.[10] He may have been apprehensive also about the restrictive policies of the Hudson's Bay Company in the Columbia River area.[11]

He seems to have parted with the missionaries on good terms, for he "was furnished with a couple of horses and the best outfit the missionaries could give him and allowed to remain or go as he might choose."[12]

Little is known of Goodyear's activities between this time and 1842. Gray heard that he had "joined a party that went with the Bannock Indians and became a member of that tribe."[13] Matt Field, who talked with Goodyear in 1843, learned that he had spent the winter of 1836-37 at Blackfoot Creek, some forty miles from Fort Hall.[14] In a letter written by Miles Goodyear to his brother Andrew, dated November 1, 1842, he indicated that he "had employed his time trapping, trading and hunting for the past three years . . ." with equipment derived from the Hudson's Bay Company.[15] Since Fort Hall was controlled by Hudson's Bay Company after 1837 it seems quite likely he was operating out of Fort Hall. His travels certainly took him into Utah, because he

---

[8] Matthew Field, *Prairie and Mountain Sketches* (Norman, Okla., 1955), 148.

[9] Kelly and Howe, *op. cit.*, 29. A wheeled cannon had been taken to the rendezvous at Bear Lake in 1827.

[10] Gray, *op. cit.*, 114. [11] *Ibid.*

[12] *Ibid.* [13] *Ibid.*

[14] Field, *op. cit.*, 148. [15] Kelly and Howe, *op. cit.*, 43.

acquired a wife, Pamona, the daughter of Chief Pe-teet-neet who lived in the vicinity of present-day Payson sometime during this period. Since she had borne him two children by 1843 when Matt Field contacted him, Morgan presumes that he must have taken Pamona "into his lodge" by 1839.[16] Shoshone "women and horses" had a reputation of being the best in the West,[17] but apparently Goodyear found this Ute squaw more to his liking. Field described her in 1843 as "a fat squaw with a broad, glazed leather St. Louis fireman's belt around her waist, marked 'Central' in large gold letters." [18] Three years later a young Swiss immigrant, Heinrich Lienhard, pictured her as "a beautiful Indian woman not above doing the family wash." [19] One is left to wonder whether she went on a reducing diet during those three years or whether young Lienhard had a different concept of physical beauty than that possessed by Field.[20]

It seems reasonable to surmise that Goodyear traveled in many parts of the Rocky Mountain area, learning the trade from older trappers, traders, and Indians during those years.

Goodyear apparently shifted his operations from Fort Hall to the Uintah Mountains by 1842, for he was at Fort Wintey (Uinta) in October when Marcus Whitman stopped there during his famous ride from Oregon to the States. Miles used the opportunity to write his family for the first time in eight years. His letter reveals an excellent ability to express himself in writing, and indicates his fondness for poetic expression, which he used effectively. It suggests a

---

[16] Morgan, op. cit., 200.   [17] Kelly and Howe, op. cit., 36.

[18] Field, op. cit., 156.

[19] J. Roderic Korns, "West from Fort Bridger," Utah Historical Quarterly, XIX (1951), 194-5.

[20] The Manti Home Sentinel, August 15, 1889, carried an article by an undesignated author which described Goodyear's wife as "a handsome Ute squaw whose native grace, beauty, and amiability won the admiration of all who knew her." See Utah Historical Quarterly, VI (July, 1933).

sense of pride in his possessions and a determination to "gain his fortune" before returning to his family in the East.[21]

Apparently Goodyear shifted his operations to Fort Bridger at this time, since those whose journals mention meeting him were in the vicinity of that post. He was there in July of 1843 when a band of Arapaho and Cheyenne Indians made a raid on the horse herd there. Miles led in the pursuit of the raiders and gained a reputation for his courage and daring in this episode.[22] Talbot reported that he had heard "from all accounts that he (Goodyear) had run the gauntlet with great bravery," and that his man, Le Meuse, had "got the scalp of the Cheyenne that was killed, and sold it to Sir William Stewart."[23]

In August, 1843, Goodyear accepted the invitation of Sir William Drummond Stewart to join his party in a pleasure excursion in the Green River Valley not far from Fort Bridger. Sir William had been part of the same company that Goodyear had come West with, and doubtless had become acquainted with young Miles in 1836. Now, seven years later, Stewart had returned from Scotland with a title and considerable wealth. He wanted one last fling in the West and invited some of the Mountain Men to share his pleasures. Goodyear and Jack Robertson are mentioned specifically along with "other trappers" who accepted Sir William's invitation and joined his party at present-day Fremont Lake, a few miles northwest of South Pass. Here they spent "great days of exploring and fishing and story-telling and drinking, culminating in three days of Rocky Mountain Racing." Goodyear placed second in a dramatic horse race described in detail by Matt Field.[24]

The first indication that Goodyear intended to establish a trading post of his own is found in a news item in the

---

[21] Kelly and Howe, *op. cit.*, 43-4 (Quotes the Goodyear Genealogy).
[22] Field, *op. cit.*, 138-9, 144.   [24] Field, *op. cit.*, 150.
[23] *Journals of Theodore Talbot* (Portland, Ore., 1931), 43.

Independence *Western Expositor* in September, 1845. He
had traveled to St. Louis and was returning west to the
mountains to build a "kind of a fort . . . and if possible make it a sort of half-way house between this and
Oregon and California, where the companies may stop and
refresh themselves and obtain supplies. . ." [25] He indicated that he intended to raise vegetables and grains as
part of these supplies. He was ready to leave Fort Bridger
to establish this post just at the time the Donner Party was
preparing to venture over the newly-established Hastings
cut-off, according to a letter written by James F. Reed,
which Morgan believes clearly establishes the date of the
founding of Ft. Buenaventura. [26] This discredits legends that
date the founding of the post as early as 1841 and also
McBride's reminiscent account of having visited the fort
in the summer of 1846. [27] Reed's letter indicated that Goodyear had a partner in his new venture, an "Englishman by
the name of Wills," but both Bryant and Egan give his name
as "Wells." Bryant adds the title Captain to his name and
states that he "once held a commission in the British army.
He was in the battles of Waterloo and New Orleans. He was
a man of about sixty, vigorous and athletic, and his manners,
address, and general intelligence, although clothed in the
rude buckskin costume of the wilderness, confirmed the
statements in regard to him, made by himself and others." [28]
Morgan wonders if this first meeting would justify such a
partnership, but leaves the question unanswered.

Fort Buenaventura, apparently named after the legendary
river of the Utah area, was

> located on the Weber River about two miles above its junction with
> the Ogden, a little south of what is now 28th Street, east and slightly

25 Dale Morgan, *Overland in 1846* (Georgetown, Calif., 1963) I, p. 280.
26 Morgan, *Utah Historical Quarterly*, XXI (July, 1953), 210-11.
27 *Ibid.,* 212-13.
28 *Ibid.,* 214. See also *Ruxton of the Rockies* (Norman, Okla., 1950), 210.

north of a large sand mound. The site was magnificent, the rugged scarp of the Wasatch rising immediately to the east, and the broad Weber Valley sloping gently west to the distant band of shining water that was the Great Salt Lake. The fort consisted of about half an acre enclosed with pickets; as usual with the forts of the West, a log house stood at each corner of the enclosure, with adjoining corrals for the horses, cattle, sheep, and goats. This at any rate describes the fort as it existed in the fall of 1847, though some of the improvements may have been the product of a full year's labor.[29]

Leaving his Ute wife and children together with his flocks, herds and Indian retainers with Captain Wells, Goodyear set out for California by the southern route and arrived in Los Angeles in January, 1847, just in time to sell his supply of dressed deer and elk skins to Frémont's ragged Battalion. Their quartermaster agreed to purchase Goodyear's entire supply, issuing vouchers in the amount of $1,225.50 in favor of Miles Goodyear.[30] Putting his capital to work, Miles purchased horses, perhaps several hundred, and with the aid of three Indians and four other companions, began a drive that was to take him to Sutter's Fort, through the Sierras to the Great Salt Lake and his post near Ogden, and on to Fort Bridger. It was while he was on his way to Fort Bridger that he made contact with the Pioneer Company of the Mormon westward migration which was to bring thousands of settlers into the Great Salt Lake Valley, and was to force Miles Goodyear to make an abrupt change in his plans.

The Mormon leaders had heard that a man was "living and making a farm" [31] in Bear River Valley and were both pleased and displeased with the news. They were happy to know that food could be grown in that area, but were disturbed to learn that they would not be the first settlers in

[29] Morgan, *op. cit.*, 215, based on a letter from Andrew Goodyear printed in Kelly and Howe, *op. cit.*, 42.

[30] Edwin Bryant, *What I Saw in California* (New York, 1848), 413.

[31] *William Clayton's Journal* (Salt Lake City, 1921), 229.

the valley. They learned of his identity unexpectedly two days after they passed Fort Bridger when they came upon his camp on Sulphur Creek near the Bear River.[32] Goodyear visited with the Mormons and told them about his post and of the area in general, and the following day, July 11, led several of the Mormons over the road that he thought was the best of two routes that had been used by the California immigrants of 1846. Leaving the Mormons, he continued on down the Bear River hoping to intercept travelers along the Oregon Trail in order to sell his horses.[33]

Brigham Young, the Mormon leader, after spending a month aiding his pioneers to establish a settlement in Salt Lake Valley, returned to the Missouri River encampment of the Mormons at Winter Quarters. Before leaving, he counseled Henry Sherwood to try to find the means to "buy out" Goodyear. This advice seemed especially urgent when some "saints" became dissatisfied with life in Salt Lake and headed north for Goodyear's post. Fearful that the Fort might be a gathering point for the dissatisfied and apostate Mormons in the area, the Mormon leaders determined to follow Brigham Young's advice. They found the means to do so when Captain James Brown of the sick detachment of the Mormon Battalion rode into Salt Lake with $5,000 in gold, the back pay of the Battalion he had been sent to collect.[34]

In the meantime, Miles Goodyear had been pleasantly surprised by a visit from his brother Andrew, who arrived at Fort Buenaventura on November 13, 1847. He was carrying some letters sent by Brigham Young's party, which was returning to Winter Quarters, and so felt obliged to visit Salt Lake City as soon as possible. He and Miles rode into Salt Lake on the same day that Captain Brown returned with the back pay of the Mormon Battalion and apparently

---

[32] Journal of Orson Pratt, *L.D.S. Millenial Star,* XII (June 1, 1850), 163-4.
[33] Morgan, *op. cit.,* 314.   [34] *Ibid.,* 316-17.

they began to negotiate for the sale of Fort Buenaventura. The deal was concluded on November 25, 1847, just a week after the initial contact, and Miles Goodyear disposed of his land (to which he held no legal title), improvements and stock, with the exception of his horses, for $1950 in gold.[35] Goodyear's post was soon occupied by members of Brown's family, followed by other settlers, thus giving Ogden the right to claim to be the oldest settlement in Utah, since Goodyear's fort was established in September of 1846, some ten months before the founding of Salt Lake City.

Miles Goodyear has been called "Utah's First Citizen," but his "citizenship" was short-lived, for after selling out to the Mormons he made another horse-buying trip to California and then became involved in one of the longest stock drives in U.S. history, driving some 230 horses all the way from the California ranchos to St. Joseph, Missouri, where he spent the winter of 1848-49.[36]

It was here that Goodyear heard the first sensational reports of the discovery of gold in California, and having failed to sell his horses on his trip east, he decided to add to his herd and drive them back across the continent as soon as the weather permitted in the spring of 1849. He announced his intentions publicly in an interview which was printed in the *Missouri Republican* on March 30, 1849, in which he suggested the route "by the way of Kearny as the most practicable route." [37]

Miles reached Ft. Kearny by May 17, 1849, and sent a letter to the *Missouri Republican* in which he described the "variety of conveyance" used by those heading for the gold fields and gave some practical advice concerning routes to follow after leaving South Pass. He signed the letter M.M.G. (A resident of the Prairie and Mountains, but now bound for Sierra Nevada's snowy fountains.)[38]

[35] *Ibid.,* 318.
[36] *Ibid.,* 320-21.
[37] *Missouri Republican,* March 30, 1849.
[38] Morgan, *op. cit.,* 324-5.

He was at Ft. Laramie during the early part of June, and arrived at his former headquarters, Ft. Buenaventura, about July 1. He apparently decided to remain there and celebrate the 4th of July with old friends and, presumably, his wife and children.[39]

William Kelly, an Irishman from Liverpool, happened to stop off at Ft. Buenaventura at this time, and gained the impression that Goodyear was a wealthy Mormon, who was "preparing to drive a large caballada of horses and mules to the California market. . ."[40] He later recorded in his journal that Goodyear had arrived with the "horses in a wretched state in spite of the early season."[41]

Although Miles Goodyear had come to California as a horse trader, he later disposed of his horses and became infected with gold fever, eventually locating a bar in the Yuba River which proved to be a rich strike and became known as Goodyear's Bar. He erected a fine cabin for Andrew and himself, and then in anticipation of the rainy season, made a trip for supplies. The labor and exposure of the trip brought on a fever and he died on November 12, 1849, at the age of thirty-two. His brother Andrew carried out his last wish and buried his remains at Benicia, where he erected a monument bearing the following inscription:[42]

THE MOUNTAINEER'S GRAVE
Here sleeps, near the Western Ocean's Wave
MILES M. GOODYEAR

---

39 Kelly and Howe, *op. cit.,* 104-5. According to their account Miles "split his herd here, leaving sixty head of good animals in charge of Hector Haight, a Mormon, to be sold and the proceeds used for the support of his wife and children, as needed." The ultimate fate of Goodyear's wife and children is discussed at length by Kelly and Howe, *op. cit.,* 122-9.

40 Wm. Kelly, *Across the Rocky Mountains* (London, 1852), 170.

41 Kelly and Howe, *op. cit.,* 107-8.

42 *Ibid.,* 112-13, 120.

Mathew Kinkead

by JANET LECOMPTE
Colorado Springs, Colorado

An early Santa Fe trader, one of Taos' first distillers, Colorado's first cattleman, a founder of Fort Pueblo – all these interesting titles belong to Mathew Kinkead, but because he took into his Taos home a boy he had known in Missouri, he lost his identity in the legend of Kit Carson, and has since been famous only for his hospitality.

Mathew Kinkead was born in Madison County, Kentucky, in 1795.[1] His father was David Kinkead; his mother may have died after Mathew's birth, for on December 9, 1796, David married Isbel Rogers.[2] Seven years after their marriage they moved with their eight children from Kentucky to the Femme Osage River in Missouri. In the spring of 1804 they moved again, to the forks of the Charette in present Warren County, Missouri, on land they had been granted by Governor Delassus on January 14, 1803. In 1809 their claim to the land was denied by the local board of commissioners because it had inexplicably been omitted from a list of claims.[3]

Doubtless outraged by this piece of red tape, David Kinkead moved his family still farther away from civilization, to the lush Missouri River bottom in central Missouri known as Boone's Lick because Daniel Boone's sons mined salt there in 1807. When the War of 1812 broke out the five or six hundred Boone's Lick settlers crowded together in four

---

[1] "Mexico – Naturalization, 1829-1831," Ritch papers, Henry E. Huntington Library, San Marino, Calif.

[2] Annie Walker Burns, *Record of Marriages of Madison County, Kentucky, 1785-1851* (Washington, D.C., 1936).

[3] *House Report 234*, 23 Cong., 1 sess. (ser. 261).

forts for protection against the Indians. These forts saved many a young man for a career in the West, among them Stephen Cooper who opened the trade with Santa Fe in 1821, Josiah Gregg who wrote the best book about the Santa Fe trade, William Wolfskill, Kit Carson, James Cockerell, Reuben Gentry and a host of Santa Fe traders.

One of these forts was built by David Kinkead on the north side of the Missouri, about a mile north of the present Boonville railroad bridge. It was a log stockade with houses built around the inside walls and a strong gate for corralling stock at night. In this fort were twenty-nine men and boys capable of bearing arms; among them were David, Mathew and John Kinkead.[4] Mathew (but not David or John) was a private in Capt. Sarshall Cooper's company, which had frequent skirmishes with the Indians.[5] Many men were lost from Boone's Lick in the three-year war, and much property was destroyed. David Kinkead was fortunate indeed to lose only a dark bay mare and her colt, stolen by the Sacs in June, 1814, and valued at $80.[6]

After the war the settlers came out of their forts and again built their cabins about the countryside. David Kinkead and three other men were appointed to organize Howard County and to establish the county seat, which they located near Kinkead's fort and called Franklin.[7] On March 4, 1816, David Kinkead sold the land around his fort but retained the fort for himself. In the coming years his children grew up and moved, some to various places in Howard and Boone counties, and their names – John Kinkead, William

---

[4] *History of Howard and Cooper Counties, Missouri,* (St. Louis, 1883), 98, 159, 162.

[5] Louis Houck, *A History of Missouri* (Chicago, 1908), III, p. 115.

[6] "Record of Claims, 1807-1830," U.S. Superintendency of Indian Affairs, St. Louis, Mo., vol. XI, p. 13, William Clark Papers, Kansas State Historical Society, Topeka.

[7] *Missouri Gazette,* Sept. 14, 1816, p. 1, c. 2; Howard County (Mo.) Records, B-103.

Kinkead, and Jane Kinkead Neely – appear in the county records of deeds and mortgages.[8]

Mathew Kinkead apparently owned no land in Howard county, nor in Boone, Cooper, St. Louis, or St. Charles counties. In the records of those counties Mathew is shown to have owned only one piece of property, a Negro girl named Jane whom he and his father mortgaged to Robert Hood on May 1, 1824, for the sum of $325. Mathew and David gave Hood their note, due December 24, 1824, but only David signed it.[9] Had Mathew already bought $325 worth of goods and gone to Santa Fe, hoping to return by Christmas and redeem his father's slave girl?

The company of Santa Fe traders that left Franklin in 1824 consisted of 81 men, 156 horses and mules, 23 wagons and a little piece of artillery, which was never used. From Fort Osage, west of Boone's Lick, they traveled to the Arkansas and over the Cimarron desert to Santa Fe, the round trip taking four months and ten days. The traders took out cotton goods, shawls, handkerchiefs, some light articles of cutlery, looking-glasses, and other articles; they brought back Spanish milled dollars, gold and silver bullion, beaver pelts and mules. Their profits, despite high Mexican tariffs, were immense,[10] and David Kinkead undoubtedly got his Negro girl Jane back by Christmas.

There is no direct evidence that Mathew Kinkead went to Santa Fe with the 1824 caravan, although in 1848 he said that he first came west in 1824. There is no doubt, however, that not only Mathew but his brother John went to Santa Fe with the 1825 caravan. Fifty-odd traders left Franklin about the first of May, rendezvoused at Fort Osage, where

---

[8] Howard County Records (Fayette, Mo.) Book B, 229.

[9] Howard County Records, Book H, 345.

[10] "Answers of Augustus Storrs to Queries Addressed to Him by the Hon. Thomas H. Benton. . ." (dated Franklin, Mo., Nov., 1824) quoted in A. B. Hulbert, *Southwest on the Turquoise Trail* (Denver, 1933), 77-98.

they doubled their number, and arrived at Santa Fe in July.[11] A Mexican public officer listed all the traders, including Mathew and John Kinkead, as foreigners, and sent their names to the Supreme Government in Mexico City.[12] On July 9, Mathew "Quinque," as the custom officer spelled this difficult name – there is no letter "k" in Spanish – presented six bales (three mule-loads) of goods at the customs house, worth $1,123.76, to which the customs officer added 25% and then charged Kinkead 18% on the total, or $252.56 in duties.[13]

If Kinkead returned to Missouri with the caravan that fall, he did not remain long. More likely he went to Taos either with his goods or the proceeds therefrom, and made plans with William Workman to start a distillery. On February 13, 1826, William Workman wrote his brother David at Franklin that he had bought up a large quantity of corn and wheat that he meant to turn into whiskey, if David would buy him two eighty-gallon stills and other necessary articles and send them out by Abraham Barnes. Workman added that he and Kinkead would together pay half the cost, and Samuel Chambers would pay the other half.[14]

In the winter of 1826-7 Kinkead took into his Taos home the young Kit Carson, runaway apprentice to David Workman of Franklin.[15] Carson described the incident simply:

> We arrived in Santa Fe in November, and I proceeded to Fernandez de Taos, my present place of residence, the same month, and remained during the winter with an old mountaineer by the name of Kincade.[16]

---

[11] *Missouri Intelligencer,* May 14, 1825 and June 4, 1825, quoted by Kate L. Gregg, *The Road to Santa Fe* (Albuquerque, 1952), 254n.

[12] "1825 Jan. 1-July 15 Santa Fe [Mexican Custom House] Libro donde constan copiadas por menor las cuentas sequidas á los estrangeros. . ." Ritch papers, Henry E. Huntington Library, San Marino, Calif.

[13] "1825, July 9. Santa Fe [Mexican Custom House] Declaration of Mathew Kinkead." Ritch papers.

[14] Letter of William Workman to David Workman, Taos, Feb. 13, 1826, copy kindness of Conrad Krebs, Albuquerque.

[15] Jacob Beard to F. W. Cragin, Oct. 29, 1904, Cragin Collection, Pioneers' Museum, Colorado Springs, Colo.

Carson's biographers, with little or no more to go on than the above, have turned the "old mountaineer" into a variety of characters, including an ancient ex-trapper who "sat in his mud-roofed hovel in Taos that winter, telling tall tales of his prowess to Kit, drinking raw Taos whiskey . . ." [17] and a "renowned explorer" who drew maps with a stick on the mud floor of his "solitary hut" in a mountainous dell, and who served "no intoxicating drinks." [18] Many of the later biographers declare that Kinkead died in 1827, an assumption based perhaps on E. L. Sabin's statement (1914) that "Kincaid makes an unrecorded exit from the scene. His name scarcely breaks the surface of the activities of that period." [19]

Most confusing is Carson's own description of Kinkead; by no stretch of the imagination could "old mountaineer" be made to fit Mathew Kinkead who was thirty-one years old in 1826. Later it would fit, and perhaps when he dictated his autobiography in 1856, Carson was thinking of what Kinkead finally became.

Kinkead was living in Taos in December, 1830, and had become a naturalized citizen of Mexico. In this month, on behalf of two citizenship petitions, he certified that he knew "Juan Caequindo" (John Kuykendall), merchant of Kentucky, and "Admon Con" (Edmond Conn), carpenter of Missouri. As on his 1825 customs declaration, he signed both certificates "Mathew Kinkead" in plain schoolboy handwriting, and followed it with a modest rubric.[20]

In the winter of 1830-31 the traveler George Nidever

---

[16] *Kit Carson's Own Story*, ed. by Blanche C. Grant (Taos, 1926), 10.

[17] Stanley Vestal, *Kit Carson, the Happy Warrior of the Old West* (Boston, 1928), 28f.

[18] John S. C. Abbott, *Christopher Carson known as Kit Carson* (New York, 1873), 33-4.

[19] Edwin L. Sabin, *Kit Carson Days* (New York, 1935), 32.

[20] "1830, Dec. 4. Certificate concerning Juan Caequindo"; "1830, Dec. 6, Certificate concerning Admon Con." Ritch papers.

listed the men he knew in Taos: Rowland, who had a flour
mill, and Workman, who had a store. "Besides these foreigners, there were the two brothers Kincaid and an old man
by the name of Chambers. . ." [21] In the winter of 1831-2
Kinkead was again seen in Taos, along with Conn and Long
and "old Chambers." [22] Perhaps he was then operating the
distillery with Rowland and Workman, who we know operated it later, but contemporary reference to it is lacking.

In October, 1835, Mathew Kinkead and seventy-five other
men received grants of land in the valley of the Mora River
on the eastern slope of the New Mexico mountains. "Mateo
Ringinel" (as his name is transcribed in the government
documents; in the original papers it is probably "Mateo
Quinqued") was granted two hundred varas of land in the
valley of Santa Gertrudes, later the town of Mora, N.M. [23]

Kinkead's neighbor in Santa Gertrudes de Mora was
Manuel Suhazo, or Suaso, his wife Maria Teresa Sandoval
Suaso and their four small children, Tomas, Juana, Rufina
and Maria de la Cruz, all of Taos. [24] Sometime in the next
four or five years, Maria Teresa – or Teresita, as she was
called – began living with Kinkead and bore him two children, Rafaela and Andres. Teresita was "pretty as a peach;"
she was also strong-willed and jealous. Unlike most women
of her era and her race, she was willing to share the work
and worry of a frontier life with her man – that is, until a
man she liked better came along.

In 1841 or 1842 Kinkead moved from the Mora River to
the Arkansas River, near the mouth of Fountain Creek at
the present site of Pueblo, Colorado. In the spring of 1841
Dick Wootton drove a flock of Kinkead's sheep from north-

21 *The Life and Adventures of George Nidever* (Berkeley, 1937), 21.

22 Albert Pike, *Prose Sketches & Poems, Written in the Western Country* (Boston,
1834), 32.

23 "Private Land Claims in New Mexico," *House Exec. doc. 14,* 36 Cong., 1 sess.
(ser. 1047), 180f.

24 Document 1353, Blackmore papers, Museum of New Mexico, Santa Fe, N.M.

ern New Mexico to Westport (Kansas City) where he sold them.[25] With the proceeds he bought a herd of forty milch cows and drove them to the mouth of the Fountain. After fitting up a corral, Wootton caught forty-four newborn buffalo calves and turned them in with the milch cows, an arrangement agreeable to both cows and calves. When the calves were three years old, Wootton drove them back to Westport and sold them to a dealer who disposed of them to zoos and curiosity shows.[26] Wootton did not spend the winters on the Arkansas taking care of his cows; every winter, he stated, he worked for Bent's Fort, smuggling goods into Taos.[27]

Was it Kinkead, then, who remained on the Arkansas during the winter of 1841-42 guarding the cattle? Wootton does not mention a partnership with Kinkead in his operation on the Fountain, but he does mention that the sheep that financed the venture were Kinkead's. There is another source that confirms the fact that Kinkead was engaged in the buffalo-calf business: according to Tom Autobees, in April or May Kinkead and Teresita would drive some milch cows onto the plains, pick up the newborn buffalo calves and put them to suck on the cows. In the fall the half-grown buffalo calves would be taken east and sold.[28]

No traveler in the winter of 1841-2 tells us whether or not Kinkead and Teresita, or anyone else, spent the winter at the mouth of the Fountain, but by next spring someone had discovered that domestic cattle not only survived on Arkansas valley grasses through the winter, but actually became fat on them. How much this discovery had to do with the founding of Fort Pueblo in the spring of 1842 no one

[25] *Transcript of Record,* U.S. *vs.* Maxwell Land-Grant Company . . . , Sup. Ct. Oct. Term, 1886, no. 974, testimony of Richens L. Wootton, May 20, 1885.

[26] Frank Hall, *History of the State of Colorado* (Chicago, 1890), II, p. 235; H. L. Conard, *"Uncle Dick" Wootton* (Chicago, 1890), 88ff.

[27] Testimony of Richens L. Wootton, *loc. cit.*

[28] Tom Autobees to F. W. Cragin, Nov. 8, 1907, Cragin Collection.

knows, but there is no doubt that stock raising, along with farming and Indian trading, was a major occupation from the very beginning. The post was built of adobe on the north side of the Arkansas just above the mouth of the Fountain. One of the builders, according to Dick Wootton, was "Kincaid." [29]

In the summer of 1842 Alexander Barclay, former book-keeper at Bent's fort, proposed entering into partnership for the raising of buffalo calves, with "some men who are making a business of catching and rearing them beneath the mountains," but on this occasion his intended partners – probably Kinkead and Wootton – defaulted. In the spring of 1843 Barclay bought eight buffalo calves, tried and failed to sell them in St. Louis, and returned to Pueblo in February of 1844 to live.[30] By this time the buffalo-calf business was undoubtedly dead; the last we hear of it is in the summer of 1843, when Fremont passed Maurice LeDuc, later and perhaps at this time an employee of Mathew Kinkead, who was camped on Fountain Creek engaged in catching buffalo calves.[31]

In the latter part of 1843 Kinkead left Pueblo and started a cattle ranch on the Hardscrabble, a southern tributary of the Arkansas thirty miles above or west of Pueblo. The ranch was located at the mouth of the Hardscrabble cañon, where the little river rushes onto the plains from its sources in the Wet Mountains. At this spot Kinkead built a house of upright logs for his family and jacal cabins for his hired hands, among whom were Maurice LeDuc, Calvin Briggs, John Burroughs, Tom Wells, LaFontaine, and Gagnez.[32]

---

[29] Frank Hall, *op. cit.*, II, p. 256.

[30] Letters of Alexander Barclay dated Sept. 1, 1842, Nov. 27, 1842, June 30, 1843, and February, 1844. Microfilm, Colorado State Historical Society, Denver.

[31] J. C. Fremont, *Report of the Exploring Expedition to the Rocky Mountains in the Year 1842, and to Oregon and North California in the Years 1843-'44* (Washington, 1845), 115.

[32] Mrs. George Simpson, Oct. 21, 1904, to F. W. Cragin. Cragin Collection.

Kinkead's little settlement was perhaps no more than a cattle ranch, but to Andrew Drips, U.S. agent with the special mission of preventing the importation of liquor into the Indian country, it smelled like whiskey. As Drips wrote on December 1, 1843:

> There is at present two towns of them sort of [whiskey] traders one on a fork of the Arkansas & one other lately built on the Spanish line the setlers is generaly French Americans & Spanards I am informd that a man by the name of Kincaid is the principle person in the new village in the Spanish Territory.[33]

In February or March, 1844, George Simpson, Joseph B. Doyle and Alexander Barclay started another settlement on the Hardscrabble, six miles below or north of Kinkead's ranch.[34] To this settlement moved some seventy people, including George Simpson and his bride, Teresita's daughter Juana, whom he married at Bent's Fort by common law, for the nearest priest was at Taos. In June, 1844, a daughter Isabel was born to George and Juana Simpson at the Hardscrabble settlement, and in October the Simpsons took their new baby to Taos where Father Martinez baptized Isabel and married her parents. Accompanying the Simpsons were Cruz Suaso (aged thirteen) and Joseph B. Doyle, whom Father Martinez also married.[35]

About the same time that her daughters were being married in Taos, Teresita left her aging husband and moved six miles north to the Hardscrabble settlement, to begin a new life with Alexander Barclay. Teresita's life with Barclay was far from serene, as agonized entries in Barclay's diary show, but she never went back to Kinkead, who appears to have kept very much to himself after her desertion. Two

---

[33] Account book, Drips papers, Missouri Historical Society library, St. Louis.

[34] Janet S. Lecompte, "The Hardscrabble Settlement, 1844-1848," *The Colorado Magazine,* xxxi (April, 1954).

[35] Taos Matrimonial Records, Sept. 30, 1833-Dec. 15, 1845, p. 270; Taos Baptismal Records, 1844-1847, p. 10; both in Chancery, Santa Fe.

years later, on October 2, 1846, Barclay "went up to Kin-
kades and met the old man face to face for the first time in
two years."[36]

When Teresita left Kinkead she did not take Rafaela and
Andres with her. Andres remained with his father, and
there is no record of Rafaela on the Arkansas at all. She
may have lived with relatives in Taos or Mora until her
marriage to William Kroenig in 1856. She died in 1858 at
Kroenig's ranch near Watrous, N.M., after the birth of her
second child.[37] There were other Kinkeads on the Arkansas
– a John Kinkead and his father, and a Louie Kinkead –
but Barclay's diary gives no hint of their relationship to
Mathew.[38]

Kinkead continued to live on the Hardscrabble until at
least the end of 1847. On April 27, 1847, he did $24 worth
of business at Lancaster P. Lupton's store at Hardscrabble;
he bought domestic calico and thread, two brass kettles and
four shirts, paying for them with one steer, half a bushel of
beans and two pigs.[39] On October 23, 1847, Barclay's diary
records that the "Kinkeads and Andreas" arrived at Barclay's and Doyle's trading house two miles above Pueblo,
and Andres slept at Barclay's with his mother. The next
day "Mr. Kincade" himself visited at Barclay's and Doyle's.
On November 23, Kinkead was still at Pueblo. On January
29, 1848, Barclay records that "Jim" was at his house and
bought Kinkead's pigs, which Kinkead had apparently left
there for Barclay to sell.[40]

In the middle of July, 1848, an emigrant on the Oregon
trail met Kinkead on the Big Sandy, west of South Pass,
and wrote:

36 Diary of Alexander Barclay, Colorado State Historical Society.
37 *History of New Mexico* (Los Angeles, 1907), II, p. 956.
38 Diary of Alexander Barclay.
39 Lupton papers, Colorado State Historical Society, Denver.
40 Barclay Diary.

a Mr. Kincaid is now in camp trading with our men, he having some 200 head of cattle which we need in some measure. This gentleman (Kincaid) removed to these mountains from Boone County, Missouri in the year 1824. He is quite an old man, yet active, although he has been injured in .... by being lame.[41]

Although "quite an old man" in 1848 (he was then fifty-three) Kinkead appears to have lived well into the 1850s or even later, and to have prospered in his old age. He took Andres and moved to California (one source says in the spring of 1849, with John Brown, Jim Waters and others [42]) and lived at Sacramento, where he became very wealthy and owned ships and haciendas. Jacob Beard, son-in-law of George Simpson, was with Kinkead when he died, but Beard himself does not say when, where or how this happened.[43] In 1878 Andres, now known as Andrew J. Kinkead of Tulare County, California, returned to New Mexico to sell his father's interest in the Mora grant, in some lots in Taos, and some city property in Salt Lake City.[44] In 1892 Andrew paid his mother, now ninety-one years old, a visit at the late Joseph B. Doyle's ranch at Undercliffe, Colorado, and a year later Teresita died.[45]

[41] Richard Martin May, "Sketch of a Migrating Family to California," Bancroft Library, cited in Appendix F, Charles L. Camp, *James Clyman Frontiersman,* (Portland, 1960), 290.

[42] Tom Autobees to F. W. Cragin, July 29, 1908; Nov. 10, 1907; Cragin Collection.

[43] Fanny Kroenig Jones to F. W. Cragin, June 26, 1908; Jacob Beard, Oct. 29, 1904, Cragin Collection.

[44] Mora County (N.M.) records, Book IV, p. 351; Book V, p. 23. Charles A. Kinkead was a pioneer Salt Lake merchant (1849) and is not to be confused with Mathew, although he might well be a relative.

[45] Tom Autobees, Nov. 7, 1907, Cragin Collection.

James Kipp

by RAY H. MATTISON
National Park Service

One of the original members of the Columbia Fur Company, James Kipp, was born near Montreal, Quebec, Canada, in 1788.[1] When about twenty, he entered the fur trade as a hunter and trapper in the Red River region. By 1818, he was on the Upper Missouri. A "Canadian of German descent," [2] he was, according to Henry A. Boller, an educated man who was reported to be the only white man who mastered the Mandan language.[3] Kipp became an agent of the Columbia Fur Company about 1822 and in the following year went to the Mandan villages on the Missouri in that capacity.

Kipp early established a reputation as a builder of fur-trading posts. In May, 1823, he commenced building a fort near the Mandans. After the Arikara moved near the post, following their chastisement by the Leavenworth Expedition in that year, the situation of the six white men stationed there became so dangerous that they were afraid to venture outside the fort's walls. However, in the following year, conditions improved when the Arikara moved down the river. In November, 1826, Tilton took charge of the post and Kipp moved up to the mouth of the White Earth River where he built another post.[4] After the merger of the Columbia Fur Company with the American Fur Company, Kipp, in 1828, was commissioned by the company to build Fort

[1] Henry A. Boller, *Among the Indians* (Chicago, 1959), 41.

[2] Reuben G. Thwaites (ed.), *Travels in the Interior of North America by Maximilian, Prince of Wied* (Cleveland, 1905), II, p. 223.

[3] Boller, *op. cit.*, 41.

[4] Dale L. Morgan (ed.), *The West of William Ashley* (Denver, 1964), 59-60.

Floyd, later known as Fort Union,[5] where he was still located early in 1831.[6] In the spring of that year, he built Fort Clark near the Mandan villages and in the following winter erected Fort Piegan, above the mouth of the Marias River among the Blackfeet.[7]

Kipp's chief responsibility, however, according to the Irish adventurer, John Palliser, was as the purveyor of furs and skins obtained from the Indian trade, from the Yellowstone down the river to St. Louis. Each year in the summer he brought down the Indian goods by barges and mackinaws to the Mississippi River city, from which place he returned to the Indian country.[8] When not occupied in this work, he was usually in charge of one of the several trading posts of the Company.

Kipp was a familiar figure on the Missouri for over four decades. Nearly all of the well-known travelers on the river met him on their journeys. When George Catlin, the Indian artist, stopped at Fort Clark in 1832, Kipp, who was in charge of that post, took him to his quarters, treated him with "genuine politeness" and entertained him with "the pleasures of his amusing and interesting society." [9] Kipp accompanied Catlin to the Mandan, Hidatsa and Arikara villages and assisted the artist in every way possible in making his sketches and in making observations of these three tribes.[10]

He was also in charge of Fort Clark when the two distinguished German visitors, Maximilian, Prince of Wied, and Charles Bodmer, the artist, spent the winter of 1833-4

[5] Doane Robinson, *South Dakota Historical Collections,* IX (1918), 155.

[6] Annie Heloise Abel (ed.), *Chardon's Journal at Fort Clark, 1834-1839* (Pierre, So. Dak., 1932), 228.

[7] *Ibid.,* 225-7.

[8] John Palliser, *The Solitary Hunter* (London, 1956), 59-60.

[9] George Catlin, *Letters and Notes on the Manners, Customs and Condition of the North American Indians* (London, 1841), I, p. 79.

[10] *Ibid.,* I, pp. 149, 155, 177, 205.

there. For a short time, the two Germans were forced to share "the small apartment" in which the trader lived with his Indian wife and half-breed family.[11]

The visitors accompanied Kipp on his trading expeditions to the various tribes in the vicinity of Fort Clark. As the result of his many years of residence in the region, the trader was able to supply Maximilian much information on the manners and customs of the Indians and did much to allay their suspicions toward the German artist.[12]

Kipp appears to have been stationed at a number of posts for brief periods. Father Pierre-Jean de Smet, the missionary, met him at Fort Union in 1841. The priest stated that Kipp was the principal administrator of the company's post and characterized him as "a gentleman well worthy of his station."[13] The naturalists, John Audubon, who described him as "one of the partners of the Upper Missouri Outfit," and Edward Harris met the trader on their trip up the Missouri in 1843. Kipp boarded the company's steamboat, on which they were traveling, near Fort Clark and accompanied them to Fort Union. He provided Audubon with many specimens for his collections. While at Fort Union, Kipp ascended the Yellowstone to take charge of Fort Alexander.[14] In 1846, Kipp was in charge of Fort Union when Charles Larpenteur was out of employment there.[15] Describing him as "a hardy old veteran" who was "upwards of sixty years of age," Palliser met the old trader

[11] *Maximilian's Travels,* III, p. 13.

[12] *Maximilian's Travels,* II, pp. 222-395; III, pp. 11-83.

[13] Hiram M. Chittenden and Alfred T. Richardson, *Life, Letters and Travels of Father Pierre-Jean De Smet, 1801-1873* (New York, 1905), I, p. 269.

[14] John Francis McDermott (ed.), *Up the Missouri with Audubon: The Journal of Edward Harris* (Norman, Okla., 1951), 88, 89n, 93, 117, 163; Maria R. Audubon (ed.), *Audubon and His Journals* (London, 1898), 9, 10, 19, 26, 36, 50, 52, 65, 69, 113, 146.

[15] Elliott Coues (ed.), *Forty Years a Fur Trader on the Upper Missouri: The Personal Narrative of Charles Larpenteur, 1833-1872* (Minneapolis, 1962), I, pp. 243-6.

in 1847 at his farm near Independence, Missouri, where his
white wife and family lived. Palliser accompanied Kipp
and his party up the river to Fort Union on one of Kipp's
annual trips.[16] Thaddeus Culbertson, the scientist, met Kipp
while the trader was in charge of Fort Berthold in 1850.[17]

One of the most intimate descriptions of the aging Kipp
was made by the Swiss artist, Rudolph Friederich Kurz,
who spent a brief period in 1851 at Fort Berthold. At that
time cholera was sweeping through the post among the
tribes. Kipp was using what medical knowledge he possessed
in administering to their needs, doling out small doses of
whiskey to the sick Indians. Kurz characterized the trader
as "approaching old age," "unhappy, dissatisfied with himself and morose," having "lost a good fortune on account of
his addiction to strong drink." [18] Despite his bitterness, however, Kipp and his Mandan wife, who were the only two
persons purportedly at that time who could speak both
Mandan and English,[19] unstintingly gave Kurz, who was
compiling a dictionary of the Mandan language, a great
deal of assistance, in part, "to be answerable, under his
[Kipp's] own name, to scholars." [20]

Despite his advancing age, Kipp remained in the fur
trade for over another decade. When Boller made his first
trip up the Missouri in 1858, he visited Fort Union. There
Kipp was the "Bourgeois in Charge," who welcomed the
party "with true mountain hospitality." [21]

Kipp retired from the Indian trade to his farm in Missouri about 1865. After his retirement, he made occasional

---

16 Palliser, loc. cit.

17 John Francis McDermott (ed.), Journal of an Expedition to the Mauvaises
Terres and the Upper Missouri in 1850, B.A.E. Bulletin 147 (Washington, 1952),
100.

18 J. N. B. Hewitt (ed.), Journal of Rudolph Friederich Kurz, B.A.E. Bulletin
115 (Washington, 1937), 123. See Kipp's portrait at page 15 of this volume.

19 Lewis Henry Morgan, The Indian Journals (Ann Arbor, 1959), 166.

20 Kurz Journal, 364.   21 Boller, op. cit., 41.

visits to his friends at Fort Benton. On July 2, 1880, he died
at his home in Missouri and was buried at Parkville.[22]

Unlike many of his contemporaries, Kipp seems to have
been highly regarded among the trading fraternity. In 1848,
he was made one of the partners of the Upper Missouri
Outfit and appears to have continued in that capacity for
over a decade.[23] Palliser wrote that Kipp was "a great
favourite" at Fort Union.[24] Joseph La Barge, the steamboat
captain and fur trader, held him in high esteem.[25] Charles
Larpenteur, on the other hand, felt Kipp discriminated
unfairly in favor of Kipp's nephew who worked for the
company.[26]

Kipp had one son, Joseph, born November 29, 1849, by
his wife Earth Woman, the daughter of Four Bears, Mandan chief.[27] When Lewis Henry Morgan, the anthropol-
ogist, made his trip up the Missouri in 1862, Joseph Kipp
provided him with a Mandan vocabulary and other information about the Mandans.[28]

---

[22] *Ibid.,* 41, fn. 30.

[23] LeRoy R. Hafen and Francis M. Young, *Fort Laramie and the Pageant of the
West, 1834-1890* (Glendale, 1938), 131; *Montana Historical Society Contributions,*
x (1910), 234-5. John E. Sunder gives 1842 as the date at which Kipp was made
partner. (John E. Sunder *The Fur Trade on the Upper Missouri, 1840-1865* [Nor-
man, 1965], 106.)

[24] Palliser, *op. cit.,* 79.

[25] H. M. Chittenden, *History of Early Steamboat Navigation on the Missouri
River* (New York, 1903), ii, p. 60.

[26] *Forty Years a Fur Trader,* ii, p. 254.

[27] *Montana Historical Society Contributions,* x, p. 270.

[28] Morgan, *op. cit.,* 166-7.

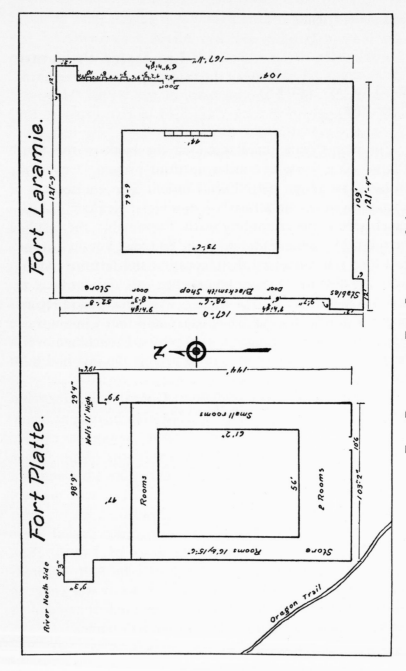

FORT PLATTE AND FORT LARAMIE, 1846

See text page 212. From drawings in Thomas Bullock's Journal, Mormon Church Archives.

Lancaster P. Lupton

by ANN W. HAFEN
Provo, Utah

For many years there stood on the bank of the South Platte, some thirty-five miles north of present Denver, the ruins of an adobe post, Fort Lupton. The goldseekers of 1859 noticed it, and an early Colorado settler established a ranch around the crumbling walls. Presumably, the fort had been built by some trader with the Indians; but the fur men had long since deserted their vocation and left the country.

In the absence of exact knowledge, speculations were offered as facts. Mythical characters were created and legends began to form. One published story said that Lupton was a Spaniard, who had fought a duel with a Frenchman over a beautiful Indian princess, and to protect the girl had built the adobe-walled fortress.[1]

But the name given – Madero Gonzales Lupton – impressed the new Colorado State Historian in 1924 as incongruous. He traced this story to a Denver newspaper of 1890 and found that the pioneer quoted was still living. When confronted with the story the old-timer swore a bit, and said he never told the fantastic tale. Who, then was the real Lupton?

Contemporary records of the fur trade period were searched. Col. John C. Fremont's diary of July 6, 1843, stated: "We reached, in 10 miles, Fort Lancaster, the trading establishment of Mr. Lupton."[2] Since it was common practice for a fur-trade post to be given the first name of its founder, Lancaster was likely the founder's name.

[1] Warren E. Boyer, *Vanishing Trails of Romance* (Denver, 1923).

[2] J. C. Fremont, *Report of Exploring Expedition to the Rocky Mountains,* etc. (Washington, 1845), 111.

A government journal revealed that with Col. Henry Dodge and his dragoons, in a peace-promoting expedition to the Rocky Mountains in 1835, was a Lieutenant Lupton in charge of one of the companies. Eagerly the historian turned to army records. He read: "Lancaster P. Lupton, West Point graduate. Resigned from the army in 1836. Became a fur trader on the South Platte River."[3] A later edition of the *Register* said Lupton moved to California in 1849, and died at Arcata in 1885.

The historian dispatched a letter to the postmaster of Arcata, California, inquiring about descendants of Lieutenant Lupton. A Lupton granddaughter responded. Anxious for an interview, the historian routed his vacation trip to the northern California coast. Imagine his delight when the granddaughter presented him with a yellowed package of Lieutenant Lupton's papers. It contained a diary, accounts kept at his trading post, letters, names of his children, and his photograph.[4] Here was proof conclusive. Lupton had indeed married a Cheyenne Indian girl. Several children were born to them at the fort. In 1849 he went west with the California gold rush, and later settled on a ranch with his admirable family near Arcata. The historian embodied this new-found information in a bronze plaque and placed it on a historic marker by the roadside.

Other pieces of biographical data have since come to light, and now a fairly complete story of the founder of the fort can be presented.

Lancaster P. Lupton was born in New York State in 1807, a son of William and Julia Lupton. With a brother and two sisters, the family lived in moderate circumstances.

---

3 G. W. Cullum, *Biographical Register of Officers and Graduates of the United States Military Academy* (2nd ed., 1868), I, p. 348.

4 These, now in the library of the State Historical Society of Colorado, are the basis of much of the material presented in this story. See also, LeRoy R. Hafen, "Old Fort Lupton and its Founder," in the *Colorado Magazine*, VI (1929), 220-26.

See Lupton's portrait at page 16 of this volume.

On July 1, 1825, he entered the United States Military Academy at West Point, and graduated four years later. Robert E. Lee and Joseph E. Johnston were classmates. He was placed in the Third Infantry, and stationed at Jefferson Barracks, near St. Louis. In the fall of 1830 he embarked with his company and went to Natchitoches, Louisiana. The following spring he ascended the Red River in a keelboat to Fort Towson and assisted in the rebuilding of this post.[5] In June, 1833, he left Fort Towson and journeyed on horseback to Little Rock, and thence floated down the Arkansas in a pirogue.

At the recommendation of Colonel S. W. Kearny, Lupton was appointed a lieutenant in the newly-created First Dragoons and was ordered to Nashville on recruiting service for his regiment.[6] In 1835 he saw service on the Santa Fe Trail and at Fort Gibson in present Oklahoma. Lupton's own journal gives some details of these early activities.

In the spring of 1835 when Colonel Henry Dodge was ordered to lead a detachment of dragoons on a peace-promoting expedition to the Rocky Mountains, Lieutenant Lupton accompanied him in command of Company A.[7] This was Lupton's first journey up the Platte River trail and his first visit to the central Rockies. His impression of the country was no doubt favorable. He noted that the region of the upper Platte would be a suitable place for a fur-trade post with the Arapaho and Cheyenne Indians of the region. As a result of superior service on the expedition, Lupton was given a brace of pistols by Dodge.

However, difficulties arose when Lupton got into a political argument with some of his military companions. In an

---

[5] Affidavit of Lieut. Henry Bainbridge, dated Nov. 7, 1835 (in the library of the State Historical Society of Colorado).

[6] Letter of Kearny to Lupton, dated at Fort Des Moines, Oct. 26, 1835.

[7] See "Colonel Dodge's Journal" in *House Exec. Doc. 181*, 24 Cong., 1 sess. The journals of Capt. Ford and of Hugh Evans were published in the *Mississippi Valley Historical Review*, XII, p. 550, and XIV, p. 192.

unguarded moment he criticized the policies of the president of the United States, using disrespectful language. Jealous officers trumped up a case against him "for abuse of a superior officer." Fearing that he might be cashiered from the army, he decided to resign and avoid the disgrace of a court-martial trial.[8]

By March 1836, he had resigned from the army and set out on a new career. He would go west and try his fortune in the fur-trade field. He journeyed to Fort Laramie, then followed the trappers' trail southward to the South Platte and decided upon a location for his trading establishment. Already a post had been constructed by Louis Vasquez and Andrew Sublette on the banks of this South Platte River for trade with the Indians of the region. Lupton decided that this favorable locality called for another such post.

About thirty-five miles north of the point where Cherry Creek flows into the Platte, Lupton chose a level spot close enough to the river for convenience, but distant enough to be safe from floods that race down from the Rockies. He hired Mexicans to help him build his post. With hewn timbers from the cottonwoods along the stream and with adobes molded of gray clay from the river banks, Lupton erected his fort. Like other fur-trade posts of the period, it was a thick-walled structure, about one hundred feet square and ten to twelve feet high. It had bastions, or watch towers, at diagonal corners, provided with loopholes for defense. Within the enclosure were rooms for living quarters and storage.

From all the country around the Indians came to the new post. They brought buffalo robes, deer skins, bear skins, and beaver pelts, as well as handmade moccasins and buckskin clothes. These they bartered for white man's goods which

---

8 This explanation is given by Rufus B. Sage, who traveled with Lupton in 1841. See reprint of his work edited by LeRoy R. and Ann W. Hafen, in *The Far West and the Rockies* (Glendale, 1956), IV, pp. 130-131.

had been brought out from the states in large ox-drawn wagons or pack-mule trains. Besides ammunition, tobacco, and whiskey, the Indians eagerly sought the more unusual goods which the young trader carried in his stores: vermilion, combs, beads, rings, and looking glasses; battle axes, squaw axes, lead, powder, brass kettles, bells, sugar and coffee. All these items were bartered for furs – money was seldom or never used. But a buffalo robe or a beaver skin was valued at $3 or $4 in St. Louis money.

No sooner had young Lupton established himself on the Platte, than jealous Fort Laramie and Fort Bent saw much was being taken from their Indian trade. So each decided to have a branch post on the South Platte. Within three years after Lupton built his fort, a string of four posts dotted a twenty-mile stretch along the South Platte River. The other posts were Fort St. Vrain, Fort Vasquez, and Fort Jackson.[9] Real rivalry developed.

Lupton, however, was well liked by the Indians, and his trade did not suffer overmuch from the competition. He augmented his business by planting a garden, and then developed a livestock farm. Travelers paused to enjoy its hospitality. They found him a genial, well-informed young gentleman, and went away marvelling that such as he should be master of a fur-trade post far out in the wilds. He spoke seldom of his past, and jumped into his new life with abandon. Several travelers and explorers came by and left a record of what they saw.

E. Willard Smith, in the summer of 1839 traveled up the Arkansas River with the competing traders, Vasquez and Sublette. Smith tells of overtaking Lupton, who with a train of six ox-drawn wagons was hauling supplies to his post.[10]

Later the same year, Dr. Frederick Adolphus Wislizenus,

---

[9] LeRoy R. Hafen, "Early Fur Trade Posts on the South Platte," in the *Mississippi Valley Historical Review*, XII, p. 334.

[10] Smith's "Journal," in *The Far West and the Rockies*, III, pp. 161, 167.

a German traveler, visited this region and wrote of the South Platte forts: "The construction is the customary one; the outer walls are of half-baked brick. There is much rivalry and enmity between the three forts." [11]

Lupton married Thomasina, daughter of a Cheyenne chief. The date or circumstances of the marriage are not known, but the first child, a son named John, was born in 1842. Three other children were to be born to them on the South Platte or upper Arkansas.[12]

In view of the importance of the Fort Laramie region for trade with the Sioux Indians, Lupton decided to establish a trading post at that favorable location. His Fort Platte was built in 1840 or 1841, on the right bank of the North Platte, about three-fourths of a mile above the mouth of Laramie Fork. Rufus B. Sage, who accompanied Lupton to the post in the fall of 1841, described it as an adobe-walled structure with a store, warehouse, and other rooms backed against the outer wall and facing an interior court.[13]

Whiskey was a major part of the trade items brought to the fort by the supply wagons in early November, 1841. Soon employees and Indians were "most gloriously drunk" and all engaged in "screeching, firing, and fighting." Lupton sent some of his trade goods north to the White River branch of the Missouri and took other supplies to his fort on the South Platte.

In the spring of 1842 two boats loaded with sixty packs of buffalo robes from Fort Platte were launched on the North Platte, but the spring rise enabled them to get only two hundred miles down stream. Then the furs had to be

---

[11] F. A. Wislizenus, *A Journey to the Rocky Mountains in the year 1839* (St. Louis, 1912), 137.

[12] Data obtained in 1929 from Mrs. Julia Lupton Skinner, only daughter of L. P. Lupton then living.

[13] *The Far West and the Rockies*, IV, pp. 219-20. The exact dimensions were taken by the Mormons who in 1847 passed the fort (then deserted). See the ground plan, with measurements in this volume, page 206.

piled on the bank to await wagon-hauling the remaining distance to the Missouri River.[14]

Lupton's fur-trade venture on the North Platte was short-lived. By the summer of 1842 Fort Platte was in the hands of Sybille, Adams, & Company.[15] It was to be operated three more years before being abandoned.[16]

When Captain J. C. Fremont came by Fort Lupton in 1843 he reported that this "post was beginning to assume the appearance of a comfortable farm; stock, hogs, and cattle were ranging about on the prairie; there were different kinds of poultry; and there was the wreck of a promising garden, in which a considerable variety of vegetables had been in a flourishing condition, but it had been almost entirely ruined by the recent high water." [17]

Some indication of prices at Fort Lupton in 1844 are given by the post records: cows, $12; steers, $10; calves, $4; flour, $12 a fanega (about 1.6 bushels); whisky, $4 per gallon; corn, $14 per sack.[18]

By the middle 'forties the palmy days of the western fur trade had passed. Beaver skins, once the principal resource of the region, had dropped surprisingly in price, due in some measure to the introduction in the East of the silk hat. In addition, the unrestrained competition among the fur gatherers and the unregulated exploitation of furs which was reducing so greatly the number of fur-bearing animals, helped to make the fur trade unprofitable. As the business declined, trappers and fur men deserted their pursuits and forsook their old-time haunts. Lupton was faced by this discouraging turn of events.

In the summer of 1844 he paid a short visit – the first in

[14] *Ibid.,* v, pp. 19-32.   [15] Fremont, *op. cit.,* 35.

[16] L. R. Hafen and F. M. Young, *Fort Laramie and the Pageant of the West* (Glendale, 1938), 92.

[17] Fremont, *op. cit.,* 111.

[18] Lupton papers in the library of the State Historical Society of Colorado.

eight years – to his parents, then living in Milton, Wisconsin, but returned west again in the fall. With the decline of the fur trade his post had become practically valueless.

He now sought re-establishment in the army, but Colonel Kearny could give him no assurance of immediate success.[19] He journeyed to Washington to seek a commission but failed of his goal. So he came west again. At Westport he joined a Bent and St. Vrain caravan and traveled up the Arkansas to Bent's Fort.[20] From this point, on November 8, 1846, he addressed a letter to the president of the United States requesting an appointment as "Indian Agent at some of the agencies that will probably be formed in Oregon or California." [21] The appointment did not come.

A letter written by Lupton's parents on April 5, 1847, gives an indication of their attitude towards their son. The father wrote: "I have received two letters from you since you left us. . . You have indeed been a wanderer too long, I fear, for your benefit." On the margin of the letter the mother pleaded: "I do hope you *will* come home again soon. I feel as if I could not be so long separated from those I love, and you are very dear to me, Sonny." [22]

Lupton must at last explain what had kept him so long in the West; tell what he had heretofore kept a secret from his family in the East. So he wrote to his father, in French (doubtless to keep the contents from other members of the family), and told of his marriage to the Indian girl, of his children, and asked his father's advice. The father responded:

---

[19] Kearny's letter to Lupton of Oct. 5, 1845, *ibid.*

[20] This was the train that young Lewis Garrard accompanied. Garrard mentions Lupton in his *Wah-To-Yah, and the Taos Trail* (Cincinnati, 1850), 17, 22.

[21] The letter and accompanying letters of recommendation by A. C. Dodge, W. B. Ogden, and John Pettit were found in the archives of the Indian Affairs Office in Washington, D.C.

[22] Letter in the State Historical Society of Colorado collection.

Dear Lancaster: Why have you kept this truth from us thru all these years? Had you but told us of your marriage, then we should have understood much. Nothing could have been more disappointing to us than for you to desert your wife and family. The knowledge that you have acted like a man in accepting your parental obligation is a great satisfaction to us. We are so grateful now for understanding. Our one hope is that you can rear your children as you would had you married a white woman, that you will give to them all the advantages a father can bring. That is our dearest wish. God bless you, my son, and the blessings of His generous hand be ever over your wife and children.[23]

Lancaster, doubtless, was greatly relieved and sustained.

In the winter of 1846-47 Lupton moved to Hardscrabble, a settlement of ex-fur men on a branch of the upper Arkansas River. Here he ran a farm and opened a store. One by one the other settlers moved away, but Lupton was still there in November 1848, when Fremont came by, seeking a railroad route to the Pacific Coast. Fremont stopped to purchase supplies, obtaining 130 bushels of shelled corn to sustain his mules in a crossing of the San Juan Mountains.

After Fremont had passed, Lupton wrote a letter, on November 28, 1848, to Senator Thomas Hart Benton (Fremont's father-in-law), giving him the latest news and an appraisal of prospects: ". . . The snow is unusually deep in the mountains, and many old mountainmen here have expressed a doubt whether he can get over with so large a cavalcade – about one hundred horses and mules and thirty-odd men; but I think he will do it. He has experience himself, with energy, patience and perserverance, and many of his old comrades." [24]

The report was too optimistic. Fremont got stalled in the deep snows of the high San Juans; lost all of his mules and

---

[23] *Ibid.*

[24] Published in L. R. Hafen and A. W. Hafen, *Fremont's Fourth Expedition* (Glendale, 1960), [*The Far West and the Rockies,* XI], 284.

ten of his men, and had to turn back to New Mexico for succor. There he reorganized and then took a more southern route to California.[25]

Although Lupton had for some years intended to move to California, it was not until news of the gold discoveries spurred him on that he finally made the journey. Packing his belongings, he took his family and joined the gold rush of 1849, going by the northern, or Humboldt route, to the coast. He worked first in the gold fields and subsequently settled in northern California. There, at Arcata, he made a home, and there four additional children were born.[26] The fine family became a substantial part of the community. Lancaster died near Arcata on August 2, 1885.

---

25 *Ibid.*

26 Data from Mrs. Margaret Richert, Lupton's granddaughter, of Bayside, California. Dr. Hafen and this writer obtained, in 1929, a list of Lupton's children, with dates of birth and death: John, 1842-1927; Lancaster, 1844-46; Elizabeth, 1846-50; Platt, 1848-1912; George, 1850-1912; Julia, 1852-still living 1929; Eliza, 1854-1928; and William, 1856-1920.

Kenneth McKenzie

by RAY H. MATTISON
National Park Service

Described by Hiram M. Chittenden "as the ablest trader that the American Fur Company ever possessed,"[1] Kenneth McKenzie was born at Bradlack in Rosshire, Scotland, April 15, 1797, of purported distinguished parentage.[2] According to his own statement, which appeared in the *St. Louis Inquirer* in 1824, McKenzie left Scotland and arrived in America in 1816 when he was not more than twenty years of age. He served as a clerk with the North West Company. Leaving its employ, he migrated to the United States. Immediately after his arrival in this country, he went to St. Louis where, in February, 1822, he took initial steps to become an American citizen.[3]

When McKenzie came to St. Louis, four firms were competing to control the fur trade on the Missouri. One of these, which was later to develop into the Rocky Mountain Fur Company, was led by General William H. Ashley; the second, the Missouri Fur Company, was headed by Joshua Pilcher; the third, commonly known as "the French Com-

---

[1] Hiram M. Chittenden, *The American Fur Trade of the Far West* (New York, 1936), I, p. 383. See portrait of McKenzie at page 16 of this volume.

[2] Compare Annie H. Abel (ed.), *Chardon's Journal at Fort Clark, 1834-1839* (Pierre, So. Dak., 1932), note 65, with Chittenden, *op. cit.,* I, p. 383. Chittenden and Abel are in disagreement on the date of McKenzie's birth as well as his relationship with Sir Alexander Mackenzie, the noted explorer. In view of her more recent and greater depth of research, the author believes Miss Abel's information to be more accurate.

[3] Dale L. Morgan (ed.), *The West of William H. Ashley* (Denver, 1964), 85. According to Abel, there is some cloud on his record in Canada. Why and when he left the service of the North West Company is unknown. There is evidence that McKenzie may have gone over to the service of the Hudson's Bay Company before its absorption of the North West Company in 1821, since an order for the apprehension of a former employee, "Kenneth McKenzie," was issued by Canadian authorities June 10, 1825. Abel, *op. cit.,* 217, note 65.

pany," was dominated by a close-knit group of French families in St. Louis, of whom Pierre Chouteau, Jr., Bernard Pratte and John P. Cabanné were prominent members. The fourth, the American Fur Company, was backed by the powerful John Jacob Astor, who established a branch, the Western Department, in St. Louis in 1822.[4]

The new organization, which McKenzie was increasingly to dominate and which was to concentrate its major efforts on the Upper Missouri (above the Big Sioux River), became known as the Columbia Fur Company. The partners were largely from the Hudson's Bay and North West companies, with which were associated at least two Americans, William P. Tilton and S. S. Dudley. The principal figure at the outset was Joseph Renville, a British subject, who, following his services in the English army during the War of 1812, returned to the United States and operated a post on Red River. Other Canadian partners – in addition to McKenzie – who were to become prominent figures were Daniel Lamont, Honoré Picotte, James Kipp, and William Laidlaw. In view of the fact that an Act of Congress of May 6, 1822, debarred foreigners from entering the Indian trade, the new company's license was issued to Tilton and Dudley. Granted by William Clark on June 17, 1822, for three years, it authorized the firm to trade with the Sioux on the St. Peters, the Minnetarees (Hidatsa) and Mandan and Crow Indians at their villages. The capital employed by the new outfit was stated to be $9,907.78.[5]

Within a short time the company entered the Missouri region. From its base established on Lake Traverse, the source of the Red River, Thomas Jeffries in the winter of 1822-1823 made his way overland and established a post near the Mandan villages. There, on the prairie, in the following May, James Kipp began building a fort. After

4 Paul C. Phillips, *The Fur Trade* (Norman, Okla., 1961), II, pp. 401-6.
5 Morgan, *op. cit.,* 59.

encountering considerable difficulty with the Arikaras, the company became firmly established in that vicinity, and in 1826 Kipp moved up river to build another company post near the mouth of the White Earth River for the Assiniboin.[6]

A short time later, the company constructed a post at Prairie du Chien, on the Mississippi, and a third as far east as Green Bay on the west shore of Lake Michigan. However, the company's principal posts were built on the Missouri River. From its principal post, Fort Tecumseh (later to be replaced by Fort Pierre a few miles distant), erected about 1822 or 1823, the company pushed its operations southward and erected Fort Lookout, and also strategically located other posts at the mouths of the Niobrara and James Rivers. Near the mouth of the Platte it established another post. In an attempt to drive out their new rivals, the American Fur Company built competing posts adjacent to all the Columbia Fur company trading establishments above Council Bluffs.[7]

While the American Fur Company was first able to compete successfully with McKenzie and his associates on the lower regions of the Missouri and on the Upper Mississippi, it was unable to hold its own against them on the upper portions of the Missouri. On the Yellowstone and to the far Northwest, the Columbia Fur Company pushed its business, through independent traders and trappers among the Crows and Blackfeet where there was no competition. In addition to beaver, the new company did a large business in buffalo robes and muskrats, in which the profits were large, and in which trade the American Fur Company was not particularly interested. As a result the gross income of the Columbia Fur Company, of which McKenzie was now president, from 1825 to 1827 was $150,000 to $200,000, half of which was from buffalo robes.[8]

[6] *Ibid.*, 59-61.   [7] Phillips, *op. cit.*, II, p. 410.
[8] Phillips, *op. cit.*, II, pp. 412-17; Chittenden, *op. cit.*, I, p. 327.

With the exception of McKenzie's aggressive outfit, the American Fur Company by 1827 had either absorbed or driven out all serious competitors in fur business on the Missouri River. Unable to crush its remaining rival, the Astor interests decided to attempt to divide the trade. Early in 1826, Ramsey Crooks, acting for the American Fur Company, made overtures to McKenzie. Unable to reach an understanding, negotiations were not renewed until the spring of the following year. Finally, a compromise was reached about July. According to the terms, the Columbia Fur Company was to withdraw from the Great Lakes and the Upper Mississippi regions, which reverted to the Northern Department of the American Fur Company. A sub-department, called the Upper Missouri Outfit and comprising the three partners, McKenzie, Laidlaw and Lamont, was created under the Western Department and given the Missouri Valley above the Big Sioux River. The Upper Missouri Outfit was generally to operate as an independent organization. Late in the year, the transfer of the property resulting from the merger was effected.[9]

Through the remainder of 1827, following the agreement, McKenzie devoted his attention to the details of the new organization. He proposed to the company that he lead a trading expedition to the Rocky Mountains, where Ashley had turned his attention following his disaster of 1823 at the Arikara villages. The company, however, dissuaded McKenzie, suggesting that he first establish a permanent base at the mouth of the Yellowstone for operations in the upper country.[10]

Remaining as the head of the Upper Missouri Outfit and with Kipp as his assistant, McKenzie in 1828 initiated his plan to bring the entire Upper Missouri region under his control. With Laidlaw and Lamont directing the general operations of the company from Fort Tecumseh, McKenzie,

---

[9] Chittenden, *op. cit.,* I, pp. 327-8.   [10] Morgan, *op. cit.,* 174-5.

with Kipp implementing the building, established Fort
Floyd (later re-named Fort Union) on the north bank of
the Missouri a short distance above the Yellowstone.

Within the next several years McKenzie, using Fort
Union as his headquarters, extended the operations of his
company toward the West. Through the assistance of Henry
Vanderburgh, he brought the free trappers and traders
operating on the Yellowstone, the Missouri River to the
west, and their tributaries into the mountains, under his
control. He also sent emissaries to the heretofore hostile
Blackfeet and opened trade relations with that tribe. After
building Fort Clark in early 1831 near the Mandan villages,
Kipp, acting under McKenzie's direction during the winter
of 1831-1832, established Fort Piegan, to be supplanted
soon by Fort McKenzie, near the mouth of the Marias in
Blackfeet country. In 1832, Samuel Tullock built a post on
the Yellowstone, at the mouth of the Big Horn, in the heart
of the Crow country. Forts Union, McKenzie, and Cass
became the primary bases of the company's operations in
the Northwest. Through both McKenzie's and Pierre Chouteau, Jr.'s influence, steamboat navigation was opened in
1832 from St. Louis to Fort Union, enabling the company
to exercise a closer control over its giant trade empire.[11]

Meanwhile, the company had succeeded in crushing all
serious competition on the river. If competition failed, it
tried force. If strong-arm methods proved ineffective, the
company then endeavored to buy out the opposition, which
seldom proved necessary. Only the high-handed dealing by
the company of the independent trader, Narcisse Leclerc,
had aroused strong public sentiment against its methods.
By 1833, five years after McKenzie had taken over the
Upper Missouri Outfit, the control by the American Fur
Company of the entire Missouri River seemed assured.[12]

[11] Chittenden, *op. cit.,* I, pp. 329-39; Phillips, *op. cit.,* II, pp. 420-2.

[12] Chittenden, *op. cit.,* I, pp. 346-50; Ray H. Mattison, "The Upper Missouri Fur
Trade: Its Method of Operations," *Nebraska History* (March, 1961), 14-17.

At that time, McKenzie was the recognized ruler of a far-flung empire. Called "King of the Missouri" and also "Emperor of the West," he was both respected and feared by the hundreds under him. Chittenden summarizes:

> . . . His [McKenzie's] outposts were hundreds of miles away. His parties of trappers roamed far and wide through the fastness of the mountains. From every direction tribes of roving Indians came to his post to trade. Altogether it was a remarkable business that he followed, and one which only a man of great ability could have handled so successfully. . .[13]

McKenzie lived in a style befitting his position. Far removed from white civilization, he presided over his table, spread with a white table cloth; his clerks, wearing coats, were seated according to their rank. On his table were served fresh buffalo meat, butter, cream and milk, and vegetables from the company's garden.[14] He was a gracious and lavish host. When the distinguished artist, George Catlin, and the aristocratic Pierre Chouteau, Jr., visited Fort Union in 1832, McKenzie served his guests Madeira and port wines, from bottles set in a pail of ice, every day.[15]

When it appeared that the Western Department and McKenzie's domination of the fur trade on the Missouri were complete, the company met its strongest competition. In 1832 the firm of Sublette and Campbell organized to oppose the company. During the following year, the new outfit established rival trading establishments all along the upper river adjacent to those of the Upper Missouri Outfit. Well supplied with liquor, Sublette and Campbell were able to keep up a strong competition during the winter of 1833-34. Federal law forbade the use of liquor in the Indian

13 Chittenden, *op. cit.,* I, p. 385. See also Ray H. Mattison, "Fort Union: Its Role in the Upper Missouri Fur Trade," *North Dakota History* (Jan.-Apr., 1962), 14-15.

14 Elliott Coues (ed.), *Forty Years a Fur Trader on the Upper Missouri* (Minneapolis, 1962), I, pp. 70-71.

15 George Catlin, *Letters and Notes on the Manners, Customs and Condition of the North American Indian* (London, 1841), I, p. 21.

trade. Somehow, Sublette and Campbell were able to smuggle it through to their posts. McKenzie believed it essential to compete on even terms with his rival. Unable to ship liquor up the river by the company's steamboats or to convince officials to relax the law, he decided to take matters into his own hands. He, therefore, purchased a still and shipped it to Fort Union where he began making whiskey for the Indian trade from corn raised by the Mandan Indians. The existence of the still was reported to William Clark, Superintendent of Indian Affairs, in St. Louis. When the public learned of the still, it aroused such an outcry of indignation against the methods of the company that Astor almost lost his license to trade. Despite the fact that company officials knew of the still, McKenzie was made the scapegoat of the affair and was rebuked by the company.[16]

Several events, in addition to the distillery affair, contributed in 1834 to McKenzie's retirement from the fur trade. Early in that year, Astor himself withdrew from the American Fur Company. Pratte, Chouteau and Company of St. Louis purchased the Western Department, which continued to operate in the name of the company. Pratte, Chouteau and Company at once decided to make peace with the opposition so it arrived at an understanding with Sublette and Campbell. In return for the rival outfit's agreement to retire from the Missouri River trade, the company agreed to abandon its mountain business. In the same year, the company's contract with the Upper Missouri Outfit was not renewed, so to Pratte, Chouteau and Company alone was left the domination of the trade of the entire Missouri Valley. As a result, McKenzie was no longer head of the Upper Missouri Outfit. Pratte, Chouteau and Company and its successors henceforth operated under that name.[17]

In the closing months of 1834, following his retirement

---

[16] Chittenden, op. cit., I, pp. 355-62; Phillips, op. cit., II, pp. 426-8.
[17] Phillips, op. cit., 428-9.

from the fur business, McKenzie went to Europe and while
in Germany was a guest of Maximilian, Prince of Wied,
who had visited Fort Union the previous year. While
abroad, also, he learned wine-making, and returned to St.
Louis the following spring. In 1840, he bought out Pierre
Chouteau, Jr.'s, interest in a commission firm which the two
of them had established as a subsidiary to the American Fur
Company. Later he had a wholesale grocer and commission
firm. In 1848, he became an importer of fine wines and
liquors. Meanwhile, according to Charles Larpenteur, he
was active to a limited degree in the fur trade on the Upper
Missouri as Larpenteur saw him on several occasions at
company posts in the mid-1840s.[18]

John Palliser, in 1848, visited with McKenzie at St.
Louis following the Irish adventurer's journeys in the
Upper Missouri region:

> . . . [I] proceeded to Mr. Mackenzie's [*sic*] where I enjoyed the
> best of dinners and wines. Over the latter we sat up together, com-
> paring notes and impressions to a late hour, I frequently reminding
> him of brilliant hunts, and many other of his achievements and adven-
> tures, related to me by Indians and trappers of the country . . .[19]

At the time of McKenzie's death, April 26, 1861, he was
operating a wholesale liquor business and had amassed a
fortune. He had, meanwhile, invested heavily in lands in
Illinois, Missouri, and Minnesota, as well as in railroads
and other industries. He was survived by his wife, Mary
Marshall of Tennessee, whom he married June 26, 1842,
and their five children. His half-breed son, Owen, prominent in the Missouri fur trade, was killed by Malcolm
Clark in 1863 as the result of a quarrel.[20]

18 Abel, *op. cit.*, note 65, p. 218; *Forty Years a Trader*, I, p. 225; II, p. 237;
Maximilian's Travels, I, p. 18.

19 John Palliser, *The Solitary Hunter or Sporting Adventures in the Prairies*
(London, 1856), 210.

20 Abel, *op. cit.*, note 65, p. 218; Stella M. Drumm, "Kenneth McKenzie," *Dictionary of American Biography* (New York, 1946), XII, pp. 95-6.

Stephen Hall Meek

by HARVEY E. TOBIE
Portland, Oregon

Stephen Meek is more aptly describable as a Mountain Man than is his more famous younger brother Joseph. Although the latter devoted eleven years to mountain operations, he should be remembered essentially as a politician. Steve, on the other hand, never achieved lasting prominence in any public or private career. Though his activity was tremendous, his struggles brought him full circle into the mountains again; and there he died.

Stephen Hall L. Meek, son of James and Spicy Walker Meek, was born near Abingdon, Virginia, July 4, 1805.[1] After Steve's mother died in 1821, James soon married a widow, Nancy Yearsley, with children of her own. Late in his teens, probably, Stephen left an overcrowded home into which a new discipline had been introduced, sought relatives to the westward, and in so doing entered the magnetic field of the fur trade. Concerning his St. Louis employment by William Sublette in the fall of 1828 – rubbing furs with rum to keep out the moths – Steve joked in later years about the intoxicating effects of the alcoholic odor. He quoted Captain Billy's antidote: "Be sure you rum yourselves before you rum the beaver." Later, in 1829, he worked in brother Hiram's steam mill at Lexington, Missouri. In 1830, according to Steve's autobiography, he enlisted with William Sublette and left for the Rocky Mountains.[2] The

---

[1] Date of birth is based mostly on an entry in Steve's Uncle Joseph's family Bible. An 1807 birth date which appears on Meek's tombstone and elsewhere sometimes harmonizes better with reminiscent statements that slip a cog of a year or two. See a forthcoming book by this writer, *Steve's Hard Luck, The Adventures and Times of Stephen Hall L. Meek,* for detailed notes and references.

brigade halted its wagons on July 16 at the appointed site on Wind River. Steve, the wagonmaster of later years, should have remembered gratefully, as training, any part which he had in accomplishing this first in mountain transportation.

Enlarged by the new recruits, trapping expeditions covered a large area centering (1) on Snake River and (2) on the three forks of the Missouri. The Snake country party wintered in the area around the Blackfoot and Bear rivers — at Blackfoot Lake as Steve remembered. The other group selected quarters on the Yellowstone River. Blizzard conditions prevented communication between Henry Fraeb and Jean Baptiste Gervais, the partners in charge of the western operation, and Milton Sublette, Thomas Fitzpatrick and James Bridger, who conducted business among the Blackfoot and Crow Indians. In his septuagenarian autobiography, either Meek's memory failed somewhat, or he did manage, through an exchange of men, to serve with both groups. Apparently Steve was a member of Milton's party in the spring of 1831 when that affable, brave and uninhibited leader moved to the "Park on the Platte." There groups of trappers reunited before returning to Cache Valley, "near the big lake," to wait in vain for Fitzpatrick with the annual supply train.

Joe Meek was with Fraeb when that leader and his party sought the missing supplier. If Steve was with Milton, as he remembered, he went with that "booshway" and Jim Bridger by way of Gray's River, north to Salmon River and beyond into Flathead country before returning to Salmon

---

2 Meek's autobiography says he left home when "scarcely twenty." Some time, however, must be allowed because of a reference to a "youth in Kentucky." Although the date of Steve's entry into Rocky Mountain fur operations has been set variously from 1827 on, his autobiography (San Francisco *Golden Era*, April, 1885) has not been disproved on this point. See *Steve's Hard Luck*, Chap. II, note 1 and Chap. IV, note 1. For verification of subsequent facts, see the manuscript of this forthcoming book.

River to meet Fraeb with the delayed supplies. Already it was October, and the trappers went into winter quarters with the "Flatheds and Napercies."

Again, in the spring of 1832, Steve and his companions trapped over a wide area. Meek's assignments during that time are not clearly a matter of record. Was he with Milton when that adventurer was stabbed in a quarrel with Iroquois Indian leader John Gray? Why did Steve fail to mention the great battle of Pierre's Hole which was made famous through the writings of nine or more witnesses? After that point in the story, the mists of Meek's memory cleared sufficiently to provide facts that agree with what is known from other sources. "I went," he said, "to the Blackfoot country with Bridger's brigade." The search for furs led them along Big Hole and Deer Lodge rivers, Clark's Fork and across the divide to Dearborn River and the Missouri, returning to Three Forks. They moved across tributaries of the Missouri to streams emptying into the Yellowstone, including the Greybull River, from headwaters of which they proceeded to Green River, then made their way to winter quarters on the Salmon River. By January, 1833, the trappers had re-located at the junction of the Snake and Portneuf rivers.

It was a very cold winter, and spring hunting for all groups was delayed by lingering snow. Fraternization among waiting trappers paved the way for shifts in employment. During the shortened season Steve remembered trapping along the Snake, Salmon and Portneuf rivers. Rendezvous was at Green River near the site of Daniel, Wyoming. There Steve signed with Captain Bonneville to accompany Captain Joseph R. Walker to the Great Salt Lake and into the little-known country to the westward. As it turned out, or perhaps by design, much more than lake and desert exploration was attempted.

The original party of thirty-five or forty, including Stephen Meek, was augmented by free trapper additions, among them brother Joe, until nearly sixty men were making their way in the direction of the Sierras. By the time the last buffalo killed near Salt Lake had been jerked, each man accountable to Clerk Zenas Leonard had sixty pounds of meat, four horses and everything necessary for comfort — everything, that is, except a hospitable terrain. The food supply could not be adequately replenished and all too soon neared exhaustion. Meager results from trapping were made more discouraging by Indian thieving. The number of natives crowding in upon the party became, or seemed to become, too formidable and definitely menacing. Near Humboldt Sink, showdowns with arms seemed to be called for, and a few dozen Indians were slaughtered at what were named "Battle Lakes." Survivors of the concentrated fire, Steve said, "scattered like partridges from the hawk." Now, indeed, in hostile country the explorers had reached the point of no return.

In a wetter than usual year, the terminal marshes of the Barren (Humboldt) River, were unfordable. It was October 10 (Leonard's figure) before the mountaineers were able, by building rafts of rushes, to escape from the boggy trap. "We got too far West," Steve reported, "and finally started . . . for California. . ." Almost as if in flight, they drove toward the mountains rather than southward as Jedediah Smith and Peter Skene Ogden had done in earlier years. According to Steve, four days' travel across salt plains brought the party to the mountains, where, according to Leonard, the first summit was reached on October 16. The four day interval suggests the West Walker River as the southern-most acceptable route to a pass.

Whatever the path of entry, a most trying time followed. Steve remembered that the crossing required fifteen days. Fourteen more days, he reported, brought them to a tule-bordered stream. The waters were flowing toward the Pacific Ocean, eleven days' journey away. The return to the atmosphere of the Leonid meteors on the night of November 12, 1933, fixes the date of arrival at San Francisco Bay as November 13.

Within a fortnight, the party set out for the capital, following the shores of San Pablo and San Francisco bays and crossing the Santa Cruz mountains to Santa Clara Valley. First stop at a settlement was at the Gilroy rancho; then the aliens were given temporary asylum at San Juan Bautista Mission. Captain Walker set out for Monterey, where, armed with passports given him by Bonneville, he was granted permission to winter in California. In disposing of accumulated furs and acquiring supplies for the return trip, the captain and some of his men returned several times to Monterey. In January, camp was moved three days' journey farther east where horses would be safer. Recovery of stolen animals furnished some excitement. Bull baiting, bull-bear fights and "balls and parties given by the Spanish ladies," on which Steve reported, made the winter unusually enjoyable, for some of the men at least.

On February 14, 1834, according to Leonard, the party began its foothill journey toward a pass and a return. Proceeding southeasterly as pasturage indicated, ten days, according to Steve, were required to reach the "snow bank on the south side of the Salt or California mountain." Before crossing what came to be known thereafter as Walker Pass, cattle which they had been driving had to be left behind, and deep snow in the gap was responsible for loss of thirty horses and nine mules. Though the exit was not easy, no further setbacks are recorded. On the other side, avoiding the Mohave Desert and skirting foothills that provided pasturage for horses and mules more numerous than the number with which they had left the Salt Lake area the preceding summer, progress was without important incident until crossing desert lands was finally attempted. Walker's decision to try the detour narrowly missed becoming a tragic error. Bitter dissension ensued, and Leonard reported the loss of sixty-four horses and other animals during the attempted shortcut. Intersection of the return route with that of the previous fall was featured by another clash with Battle Lakes Indians.

Years after the events, both Meek brothers told stories of more extensive wanderings than the Leonard account indicates. The clerk's startlingly large inventory of animal losses may tend to confirm Steve's story of a trip ". . . south to the Colorado, thence north again, passing West of Great Salt Lake to Bear River, where we met Bonneville." Of course, if the party intercepted its 1833 path *west* of Salt Lake, any river reached on the unfortunate eastward swing would not have been the Colorado. Joe's odyssey as reported in *River of the West* is proved by the time element alone to have been, in large part at least, a misplaced occurrence.

Reaching Snake River, the returnees met a party under Jean Baptiste Gervais which was impressed by the remaining horses. In mid-June the Walker party reached the appointed rendezvous site on Bear River. After the fair was over, Steve had another opportunity to reach the West Coast, but he was disappointed. He remembered trapping Snake River and "all its tributaries" with a party of twenty-two under Bonneville, going ". . . to Walla Walla; then up John Day River, over to Lake Harney, then to Malheur, Owyhee and Powder rivers. . ." Bonneville was forced to return to winter camp with a Snake village on upper Bear River where buffalo meat was plentiful.

Having been tempted by Hudson's Bay Co. offers in the fall of 1834, and apparently anticipating Bonneville's inevitable withdrawal from the fur trade, Steve again started for the lower Columbia in the spring of 1835. He became an employe of Tom McKay, stepson of Dr. John McLoughlin, Hudson's Bay Company chief factor. After wintering at and near Fort Vancouver, the new employer in 1836 took Steve with him to California with a special spring brigade which trapped its way beyond Fort Umpqua, along Klamath River, Scott River and the Sacramento, returning by way of the American, Yuba, Pit, McLeod and Shasta rivers.

Part of McKay's outfit was represented at the American rendezvous at Horse Creek on Green River. With brother Joe and trapper friends, Steve may have been among those who rode on with a whooping welcome to escort the Whitman party across the divide. When higher Hudson's Bay Co. authorities forbade McKay's semi-independent operations, Steve was free to travel back to the settlements with good friends. He ". . . proceeded to St. Louis, Mo. with their furs."

As Steve arrived in the United States, land speculation, crises in banking and government policies were among the factors leading the people of the States into the days of catastrophe known as the Panic of 1837. By returning in the spring to the mountains with associates, trapping on the way, Steve was able to escape from a common peril. Before leaving, he gave an interview to the Jonesborough (Tenn.) *Sentinel* which stated all too concisely the most conservative account in existence of the Walker expedition to California in 1833-4.

From July 5 to about July 20, 1837, rendezvous was again at Green River near Horse Creek. Afterward, Steve and his companions did their fall trapping in the Black Hills area, ". . . on the Sweetwater and Platte, and wintered at Fort Larmie [*sic*]." "In the spring of 1838," the autobiography stated, "I went south to Pike's Peak; then to Taos, New Mexico, then to the Arkansas and to the north fork of the Platte. . ." He spent part of the winter a few miles from the site of Denver, possibly at the old "Fort Convenience" of Louis Vasquez and Andrew Sublette; but he went to Independence on horseback with the annual express. At Lexington, Missouri, he had time to visit brother Hiram, sister Lusannah Meek Allison and some lady friends. His expert story-telling so impressed the mother of the girls that she exclaimed:

"Law sakes! Mr. Meek, didn't you never get killed by none of them Indians and Bears?"

"Oh, yes, madam," said I gravely, "I was frequently killed."

After riding back to Laramie with the express and waiting for spring, Steve joined the brigade that had normally been led by Henry Fraeb, then, ". . . in July went as wagon master of the train of ox-teams taking furs to Independence." In the spring of 1840, Steve accepted employment as wagonmaster of a Magoffin brothers freight train bound for Santa Fe and Chihuahua. He spent two winters in the Mexican province. While there he served for a time as a mercenary in a joint government and private war against the Apaches. James Kirker, an old trapper, led a horse recovery campaign that brought in, Steve reported, fifteen thousand animals at $2.50 per head. There is no record that Meek took part in earlier disgraceful scalp hunting for subsidy which Kirker had masterminded. Return of Santa Anna to power changed government policy and ended such private campaigns.

Steve returned to Independence ready to start all over again. The opportunity came to join the emigration of 1842. When the going got rough, he served as guide for those members of the train who had not yet abandoned their wagons. By taking a detour which he called "Meek's and Sublette's cut-off," his party arrived at Fort Hall on the same day as the packers piloted by "Bad Hand" Fitzpatrick. Taking another shortcut from Sandy River, the party arrived at Willamette Falls early in October.

The newly-arrived immigrants soon found themselves in

the midst of a land and power controversy between the Methodist missionaries and Dr. McLoughlin and the company he served. Rev. Alvan Waller, carpenter and preacher, had staked out a claim a mile square on the Clackamas River; the Hudson's Bay Co. had long occupied and used advantageous sites along the Willamette River. Eighteen-forty-two immigrants L. W. Hastings, J. M. Hudspeth, and Stephen Meek were employed by Dr. McLoughlin in surveying and selling lots at Willamette Falls. Steve secured the first lot. When he started to make improvements, Waller stopped him, remarking bitterly that he was much obliged to the doctor for giving away lots on *his* claim. Thus prevented from building, Steve wintered near Joe on Tualatin Plains and also on French Prairie.

In the spring of 1843, subsidized by the Hudson's Bay Co., led by Hastings and guided by Meek, fifty-three men, women and children left for California. However, about a third of the party returned after meeting a northbound group bearing unfavorable reports.

The 1843 emigrants from Oregon arrived safely at Sutter's Fort near the junction of the Sacramento and American rivers. Meek, however, went on to Monterey where he found acquaintances of 1833-4. California was a doctorless country, grateful for anyone who could cope with medical emergencies. When a Mexican boy cut off a toe, Steve stuck it back on, secured it with a mud cast and it grew. Thereafter he was Dr. Meek, even Governor Micheltorena's surgeon.

In 1844, a year before the overthrow of the governor in the civil war, Meek suddenly abandoned his brief professional career and associated himself with Captain Stephen Smith who, having become naturalized, was proceeding with his plans to build and operate a steam flour mill, saw mill, shingle mill and distillery near Bodega. Suddenly the two Steves left by ship, intending to take a trading trip covering much of the world. At Valparaiso, Smith found a message requiring his return to Baltimore. Meek went along, delayed at Quayaquil by a nearly fatal attack of yellow fever. From Panama they went by ship to New York, arriving in July, 1844, too late for the Democratic Convention in Baltimore which nominated James K. Polk, husband of Steve's cousin Sarah. "Cousin Jeems" was later elected President.

Meek soon went to Pittsburgh, then to his old home in Virginia where, he said, "I found an absence of seventeen years had made me almost a stranger." In March he went by sea to New Orleans, then upriver to St. Louis, where he started pulling wires which would help him to qualify for the greatest opportunity of his career. What Steve called "the immense emigrant train" was assembling in western Missouri, two main points of departure being Independence and St. Joseph. Stephen Meek, because of obviously better qualifications and a cut-price offer, was elected guide for the train of nearly five hundred wagons. An even happier day was about to dawn. On May 11, 1845, Steve first met Elizabeth Schoonover, a seventeen-year-old, Canadian-born lassie. On May 18 they were married, celebrating with a dance on the green.

Meek guided the enormous, clumsy cavalcade on an exceptionally smooth and successful trek to the vicinity of Fort Hall. Unfortunately, in that area counterparts of present day Chambers of Commerce were very active in arguing the advantages of California or Oregon. Steve's mountain acquaintance, Caleb Greenwood, was on hand to express Captain Sutter's offer of free land. "Well stocked with falsehoods," as one immigrant expressed it, the old Mountain Man emphasized the danger of Indian attack on the regular route to Oregon. The rumor spread and became influential.

Nathan Olney, an 1843 immigrant with interests at The Dalles, and Stephen Meek conceived a plan to bypass possible danger. They made a rough map of the area through which Steve had trapped with Bonneville in 1834 and, for fifty dollars and provisions for Olney and Mr. and Mrs. Meek, offered to pilot those interested over the alternate route. Some wagon companies, as well as the packers first contacted, chose to take the left-hand trail along the Malheur River across central Oregon to The Dalles.

At first all went well – ". . . plenty of grass, fuel and water . . .," wrote one traveler. Within five days, however, another diarist commented: "Rock all day pore gras more swaring than you ever heard." The animals cringed as they hobbled over "black, hard, nine-cornered stones," and often lay down in the road. Two weeks' travel brought the immigrants to the "digers lakes," which could not be forded. Meek wanted to go around the stagnant waters and head for streams he knew beyond, but no one would follow him further south. It was futile for him to warn of scarcity of water on the northerly swing chosen by the rebellious travelers. It was a dry year. Steve's apprehensions would have been even greater had he been aware of the difference between 1845 and 1834, when streams were full.

Results of the popular decision to cross the "dry ridge" were much worse than anyone could have foreseen. The time came when day and night search failed to locate water. For four and, in some cases, five days wagons piled up and waited until Steve finally located a spring. The opposite of quarantine conditions existed. While passing along Snake River, the travelers had not only been exposed to contagious California gossip, but to "camp fever," the incubation period for which timed badly the day when a number of people "tuck sick." Some died. Scapegoat for all misfortunes was the luckless guide. He was forced to hide, and finally to flee with his wife. When warned, he replied, "I have brought you here and I will take you off if you will go." "Diligently and persistently," he did his best for his hostile followers until the very end of the ordeal.

With mostly undeserved curses still ringing in their ears, Steve and Elizabeth Meek settled down to live until 1848, and part of the time thereafter, at Oregon City and at Linn City just across the Willamette River. From the first, the "Hard Luck Pioneer" never was able to get much closer than the door to legislative halls, nor could he escape from the political doghouse. Even with the help of popular and influential brother Joe, he failed of election as sergeant-at-arms of the legislative assembly of 1847; and an act to authorize him to construct a road over the Cascades failed of passage.

For a short time in 1846, the Meeks operated a hotel in Linn City; then, soon after the birth of Spicy Jane Meek on October 16, 1846, Steve established his famous "TELEGRAPH LINE EIGHT OX POWER" freight and passenger line to Tualatin Plains. That enterprise was also short-lived. He staked out a 320-acre claim west of the river, but this he soon abandoned. He did, however, for a time hang onto two exceptionally well situated lots, now occupied by Publishers' Paper Company. Steve served briefly as a commissary agent in the Cayuse War that followed the Whitman Massacre of November 29, 1847.

In the spring of 1848, before news of the discovery of gold in California would have reached him, Steve took his wife and daughter by sea to California. By October he was at work in the Coloma mines. After opening a butcher shop at that place in January, Steve returned to Oregon in time to be elected sergeant-at-arms for the last provisional legislature which met at Oregon City, February 5, 1849. Within less than a month, a new territorial government was established with Joe Meek as Marshal. Borrowing forty-five dollars on April 16, Steve returned to California. Elizabeth, with two babies, returned to Oregon when summer weather permitted, and Steve followed at the end of the 1849 mining season.

In the summer of 1850, Oregon politics were still seething over recriminations concerning the Whitman Massacre. Marshal Meek, in the absence of prospecting Governor Lane, was for a time the real acting governor. With Steve as a member of his posse, the Marshal arrested Indians surrendered as murder suspects and confined them for trial. After their conviction, Joe proceeded with the execution in defiance of acting-governor, Secretary Kintzing Pritchett. Steve also was in disagreement with Joe because he felt that Kiamasumpkin, one of the suspects, was innocent. The brothers almost came to blows. On October 1, 1850, Steve was awarded a contract for an Oregon City street clearing project.

In the spring of 1851, Meek left overland for mines in northern California where, by working very hard, he made a good strike near Yreka. He was back in time to be named doorkeeper *pro tem* for the rump territorial council scheduled to meet at Oregon City, December 1, 1851. The following spring he took his family with him by sea to San Francisco. This time he took a stock of goods to Coloma, sold them and resumed mining. "The mine caved in," he said, "and I sold out and went to Santa Cruz and opened a butcher shop."

Having again improved his fortunes, Meek also purchased a valuable Pajaro Valley estate. Unfortunately, heirs got the property away from him in the courts. In the spring of 1858, the Fraser River mining excitement ended forever Steve's pleasant and prominent life as a Santa Cruz business man. Selling property and collecting debts, he steamed away to the mines. He returned poorer than before, sold the rest of his holdings and moved to Amador County.

Near Jackson, where his brother Hiram now lived – most of the time at Volcano and briefly at China Gulch – Steve Meek sweated out the Civil War. Inflation took the profits out of mining and caused shutdowns. Incendiary fires, prev-

alent drunkenness, heat and dust, disease and political antagonisms were other aggravations that had to be borne. By
1863, had he been able to afford transportation for a sizable
family, Steve was desperate enough to consider a move to
new diggings back in Oregon. The return of peace came too
late to improve the family fortunes. Disease struck down
members of the family, the marriage of the oldest daughter
removed a housekeeper, and Elizabeth died of "consump-
tion" in 1865. After arranging for care of his remaining
children, Steve resumed a vagabond existence.

The nadir of Meek's material prosperity almost coincided
in time with the zenith of the development of his personality. Listeners to his stories and professorial pronounce-
ments were amazed at this ". . . sagacious, shrewd and
intelligent old man." His age in the sixties was emphasized
by a beard, but belied by undiminished energy and characteristic industry.[3] In 1867 he ". . . took a train of
twenty-two wagons, loaded with quartz machinery from
Sacramento to South Boise, Idaho." That year, like 1834,
was troubled by lingering high water – lakes where there
had been none in dry 1845. Sometimes Steve had to build
his own road. After arrival he visited the editor of the Idaho
Statesman, whose expressed admiration was worded in
superlatives. "He talks like a book, and what he don't know
. . . is not worth knowing . . . He is a walking
geography . . . and . . . we would rather dive
into the depths of his extraordinary memory than to trust to
the finest bound book or the highest colored map. . ." –
thus wrote the enthusiastic editor.

Steve spent the winter swapping stories and reminiscences
with his younger brother Joe, who looked much older than
he. Steve's most famous yarn was his description of an
Indian maiden whose hair, eighteen feet long, was arranged
in folds by an attendant. Already, the writing of the life of

---

[3] See his portrait at page 17 of this volume.

Colonel Joe Meek was in progress. Steve was proud to lend a hand, a service for which he never received any credit.

Spring found Steve at The Dalles, preparing to haul freight to government camps. From Canyon City he led a group of prospectors in search of the semi-mythical Blue Bucket mine, hypothesized by surviving 1845 immigrants – a "wild-goose chase," Steve admitted. Before returning to California, he served briefly as wagonmaster and scout in the Shoshone Indian War, then in its final weeks.

Back in Amador County, Steve visited Hiram and re-established a home in Volcano with his younger surviving children. For a time he acted as salesman for *River of the West,* life of Joe Meek which he claimed was written, as part of it doubtless was, by his educated niece Olive. Pressed for funds and unwilling to disappoint creditors or sponge too heavily on relatives, Steve resumed his trapping. This decision greatly impressed the correspondent of the Trinity *Journal* who raved about ". . . a good honest man . . . who . . . if broke [will] get something to do and stick to it. . ."

In the late seventies Steve was in demand, not only as a guide for hunting parties, but as a consultant for historians Harry L. Wells and H. H. Bancroft. He was preparing his own life story, the first version of which was published in 1881 by Wells and associates in the *History of Siskiyou County.* Later he broke the silence of his isolation to pen defenses of William G. Rae and Captain John Sutter.

There is a sadness in the last words of the autobiography: "Being now advanced in years and having lost all the money my good fortune and hard labor had brought me, I was compelled to take to the mountains to secure a livelihood." Yet it is not the loss of wealth that slipped through his luckless fingers that constitutes the tragedy of Stephen H. L. Meek. Lack of formal education was the unfortunate cir-cumstance, for, with his native endowments and industrious energy, he could have been a great physician, geographer, scientist or humorist. He traveled full circle around life's mountain, ending his career as he began it, with gun and traps. Nevertheless, at the end, which came near Etna, California, January 11, 1889, more than a record of tread-mill existence remained. He is remembered as outstanding for industry, honesty, ". . . courage, persistence and hardihood as well as kindliness and good will toward his fellowman." He was a "true pioneer" who ". . . positively refused to let hardship and bad luck get him down."

David Dawson Mitchell

by RAY H. MATTISON
National Park Service

David Dawson Mitchell, one "of the most successful traders on the upper Missouri," [1] later achieved distinction both as a soldier and as a government official. Born July 31, 1806, in Louisa County, Virginia, he was one of the more cultured of the traders. Little is known about where he spent his youth. In the early days of the fur trade, he migrated west and was connected in 1828 with the Ioway Outfit of the Western Department. Apparently he early earned a high reputation as a trader, for when he was transferred to the Upper Missouri Outfit in 1830, he was given the generous salary of $700 per annum. [2]

For several years, Mitchell was placed in charge of several posts. During the winter of 1830-1831, he was at the Yanktonnais establishment. [3] When James Kipp, after building Fort Clark, was called away early in 1831 to build Fort Piegan near the mouth of the Marias in the heart of the Blackfeet country, Mitchell was placed in charge of the former. [4] After Kipp returned to Fort Union in 1832, Fort Piegan was destroyed. Mitchell was then sent to build a new post, which he named Fort McKenzie, in honor of Kenneth McKenzie, head of the Upper Missouri Outfit.

When Mitchell arrived near the mouth of the Marias to rebuild the fort, he selected a new site seven miles above the old one on the west bank of the Missouri. Awaiting them

---

[1] Paul C. Phillips, *The Fur Trade* (Norman, Okla., 1961), II, p. 420. For a portrait of Mitchell see page 17 of the present volume.

[2] Annie Heloise Abel (ed.), *Chardon's Journal at Fort Clark, 1834-1839* (Pierre, So. Dak., 1932), 233-4, 99 fn.

[3] *Ibid.; South Dakota Historical Collections*, IX (1918), 139.

[4] *South Dakota Historical Collections*, IX, p. 148; Abel, *loc. cit.*

on the bank were several thousand Indians, many of whom were hostile. While the fort was being built, the white men lived on the keelboat where the trade goods were kept. As soon as the post was completed, the traders moved into the new structure where they were more secure from the Indians. For several months, the situation of the white men was dangerous and only "the decision and resolute conduct" of Mitchell saved them.[5]

In 1833, Maximilian, Prince of Wied, and the artist, Bodmer, accompanied Mitchell and his party up the Missouri by keelboat from Fort Union to McKenzie. Mitchell was still in charge of the Blackfeet post. At that time, the position of the white traders was still very precarious and delicate. While at Fort McKenzie, numerous parties of Blackfeet, as well as those of their enemy, the Assiniboin, came to the post to trade. Maximilian had an opportunity to witness firsthand how the American Fur Company conducted its business. He was very much impressed with the skill with which Mitchell, Alexander Culbertson and their subordinates dealt with the warlike tribes. A man of resolute courage, Mitchell was a master of the art of Indian diplomacy and psychology. He knew when to be firm and when to be conciliatory. Bernard de Voto described Mitchell as a distinguished "master of his specialty," "a great man of the fur trade," who had risen to "eminence in the American Fur Company by proved merit." [6]

While Maximilian and Bodmer were at Fort McKenzie, the white men continued to feel their lives in danger. On one occasion, a white trader was killed by a Blood Indian who went unpunished for his crime. The two Germans were witnesses to an attack, adjacent to the fort, on a party of

[5] Reuben G. Thwaites (ed.), *Travels in the Interior of North America by Maximilian, Prince of Wied* (Cleveland, 1905), II, pp. 91-2.

[6] Bernard De Voto, *Across the Wide Missouri* (Boston, 1947), 138; *Maximilian's Travels*, II, p. 11-133.

Blackfeet who were sleeping off a drunk, by a party of six hundred Assiniboin and Crees. This attack, recorded by Bodmer, is one of the best-known works painted by the German artist while on the Upper Missouri.[7]

Mitchell assisted both the prince and artist in every way possible while at the fort. Maximilian accompanied the trader on his visits to the Indians. Mitchell also provided guards for both the prince and the artist when they went outside the fort. Maximilian had desired to take a trip to the Rocky Mountains. Fearing for their safety, Mitchell dissuaded the prince and the artist from making such a journey. As a result, the two Germans departed from the fort, after a stay of over a month, down the Missouri to Fort Clark, where they spent the winter.[8]

Mitchell remained in charge of Fort McKenzie, until 1834 or 1835,[9] when Alexander Culbertson succeeded him. Rather than permit Mitchell to leave the company, the Upper Missouri Outfit made him a partner in 1835.[10] When Francis Chardon, who superintended Fort Clark, went on a vacation in 1836, Mitchell was placed in temporary charge of that post.[11] According to Charles Larpenteur, Mitchell served as superintendent of Fort Union in 1838.[12]

In 1841, Mitchell was appointed Superintendent of Indian Affairs in St. Louis and served intermittently in that capacity until 1852. Soon after he occupied that position, the government made a more determined attempt to enforce the liquor laws in the Indian country. In 1842, the army

[7] *Maximilian's Travels,* II, pp. 134, 146-53.

[8] *Ibid.,* II, pp. 164-7.

[9] According to Abel, Mitchell was in charge of Fort McKenzie until his contract with the Upper Missouri Outfit had expired and he resolved to retire from the services of the company. (Abel, *op. cit.,* 234, 99fn.) Hiram M. Chittenden states that Mitchell left Fort McKenzie in 1834. (Hiram M. Chittenden, *Early Steamboat Navigation on the Missouri River* [New York, 1903] I, p. 229).

[10] Abel, *op. cit.,* 219-20, 67fn.   [11] *Ibid.*

[12] Elliott Coues (ed.), *Forty Years a Fur Trader on the Upper Missouri* (Minneapolis, 1962), I, pp. 150, 157.

ordered a company of soldiers to the Council Bluffs sub-agency in Iowa in an abortive attempt to put an end to the liquor traffic among the Potawatomi.[13]

During the same year, the government re-established the Upper Missouri Agency. Mitchell succeeded in getting his friend Andrew Drips, who had likewise been an employee of the Upper Missouri Outfit, appointed Indian Agent. In a feeble effort to enforce the liquor laws, Drips visited a number of the company's posts but was unable to find any liquor. Finally, an opposition trader accused Drips of conflict of interests in enforcing the liquor laws. As a result, Drips, in 1846, was removed as Indian agent, and despite the efforts of the government to prevent it, the liquor traffic continued unabated in the Missouri River fur trade.[14]

After the outbreak of the Mexican War, Mitchell, in 1846, was made Lt. Colonel of the 2nd Regiment Missouri Volunteers, of which Colonel Sterling Price was in command. When the regiment reached Santa Fe, Mitchell was given command of a detachment that was transferred to Doniphan's 1st Missouri. When in that Mexican town, Mitchell formed a connection with Gertrudes Barcelo, better known as "La Tules." A beauty, she operated a "sporting emporium" where thousands of dollars were exchanged. Needing a thousand dollars to purchase supplies for his men, Mitchell purportedly got in good graces with the senora and obtained a loan for that amount from her by escorting her to a ball.[15] Mitchell distinguished himself in the Battle of Sacramento, February 28, 1847, and led the American army into the capital city of Chihuahua.[16]

---

13 Ray H. Mattison, "The Indian Frontier on the Upper Missouri to 1865," *Nebraska History* (September, 1958), 259-60.

14 *Ibid.*, 260-61.

15 Stella M. Drumm, *Down the Santa Fe Trail: The Diary of Susan Shelby Magoffin, 1846-1847* (New Haven, 1962), 119-20, 44fn.

16 William E. Connelly (ed.), *Doniphan's Expedition and the Conquest of New Mexico and California* (Kansas City, 1907), 423-43.

When Mitchell arrived in Chihuahua, he was directed to make a search of all the principal houses for contraband of war. Reaching the residence of Governor Trias, who had fled the city, he was denied entrance by John Potts, the acting British consul of that town, who stated that the governor had left the house in his charge; hence, it was under English protection and he would not open it. It was only when Mitchell advanced on the door with two lit howitzers that the Englishman surrendered the key to him. An examination of the house was made, but no contraband was found.[17]

In 1851, Mitchell was again appointed Superintendent of Indian Affairs at St. Louis. It was while serving in this capacity that he promoted the Fort Laramie Peace Council at which was consummated the famous Fort Laramie Treaty, a landmark in Indian-white relations in the Trans-Mississippi West. For a number of years, the increasing traffic along the Oregon-California Trails had made the plains tribes more and more restive. With the view of arriving at an understanding with them, Congress in February, 1851, appropriated $100,000 for holding a treaty council. Mitchell and Thomas Fitzpatrick, famous trader and now Indian agent, were appointed by the President as commissioners for the government. The two men designated Fort Laramie as the place of meeting and set the date for September 1. Runners were sent out in all directions to notify the various bands of the proposed meeting. Father Pierre-Jean De Smet, the famous missionary, traveled almost 5,500 miles in gathering various Indian delegations for the council.[18]

The historic council was begun September 8 at the mouth

[17] *Down the Santa Fe Trail,* 229-30, 92 fn.

[18] Hiram M. Chittenden and Alfred T. Richardson (eds.), *Life, Letters and Travels of Father Pierre-Jean De Smet, S.J., 1801-1873* (New York, 1905), II, pp. 614-16; LeRoy R. Hafen and Francis M. Young, *Fort Laramie and the Pageant of the West, 1834-1890* (Glendale, Calif., 1938), 178-9.

of Horse Creek, in present-day Nebraska, about thirty-six miles below Fort Laramie. About 270 soldiers were present to have a quieting effect on the ten thousand Indians who attended. After smoking the calumet with the leading chiefs, Mitchell addressed them and expressed the views of the government. He asked that chiefs be chosen to accompany Fitzpatrick to Washington. For nine days the Indians feasted and danced, during which time they continued their negotiations. The treaty, granting emigrants passage along the established Oregon-California Trail, after being fully discussed, was signed by the chiefs on September 17. Goods were distributed by the government several days later. The council was a great success and the treaty gave promise to an enduring peace which, unfortunately, did not materialize. Following the council, Fitzpatrick took eleven of the head men, selected at the council, back to Washington to meet the President.[19]

After leaving the Indian service, Mitchell, in 1855, promoted an organization of the Missouri and California Overland Mail and Transportation Company which he served for several years as president. After the outbreak of the Mormon difficulties, he supplied the government with a large number of mules for the Utah Expedition.[20] According to Larpenteur, Mitchell, while at Fort McKenzie, "married" one of the notorious Deschamp sisters at Fort Union.[21] In 1840, he legally married Martha Eliza Berry, daughter of Major James Berry, of Kentucky. Mitchell died in St. Louis, May 31, 1861.[22]

[19] *Ibid.*, 179-96; Charles J. Kappler (comp.), *Indian Affairs, Laws and Treaties*, II (Washington, 1904), 594-6.

[20] Stella M. Drumm, "David Dawson Mitchell," *Dictionary of American Biography* (New York, 1946), XIII, p. 41.

[21] *Forty Years a Fur Trader*, I, pp. 97, 5 fn.

[22] *Down the Santa Fe Trail*, 174, 73 fn.

Antonio Montero

by EDGELEY W. TODD
Colorado State University, Fort Collins

One of the most enigmatic minor figures in the Rocky Mountain fur era, Antonio Montero,[1] seemingly comes out of nowhere, occupies an obscure place in history for about thirteen years, and then disappears. Comparatively little is known about him, and the little that is known has often been confused with other figures. It has even been said of him that he was entirely fictitious, the product of Washington Irving's imagination. Antonio Montero becomes an individual of some interest, consequently, largely because of this very enigma.[2]

---

[1] His name appears in a number of forms: Matéo, Montano, Matara, Montaro, etc.

[2] So many errors have been perpetuated concerning Montero that an effort must be made here to point them out. The first is that of Captain William F. Raynolds, who in his *Journal* (1859-60) refers to him as "a Portuguese trader named Antonio Matéo" (U.S., 40 Cong., 1 sess., *Senate, Exec. doc. no. 77*, p. 65). Chittenden, *History of the American Fur Trade* (Stanford, 1954), II, pp. 966-7, quoted from Raynolds and thereby helped perpetuate this mistaken form of Montero's name. It appears also in Struthers Burt, *Powder River* (New York, 1938), 53, where the date 1828 is erroneously assigned to the erection of Portuguese Houses; see text, below. Both errors are repeated in *Wyoming Pageant* (Casper, 1940), 103, by Virginia Trenholm and Maurine Carley. This same book states without supporting evidence that Portuguese Houses served the Hudson's Bay Company. I have been unable to verify this assertion. As will be shown later, Chittenden and later Aubrey Haines in his edition of Osborne Russell's *Journal of a Trapper* confused Montero with David Adams, an employee of Captain Benjamin Bonneville.

More serious is the confusion of Antonio Montero with Joseph Reddeford Walker, who was employed by Bonneville during the whole of the latter's stay in the mountain West (1832-35). This error originated with W. F. Wagner in his edition of the *Adventures of Zenas Leonard* (Cleveland, 1904), 249. Here, noting Leonard's statement that Bonneville sent Walker into the Crow country in the autumn of 1834, Wagner further observed the absence of Walker's name in Washington Irving's account. Since Montero's name appears in connection with what Wagner assumed to be the same events as those involving Walker, Wagner concluded that Irving "substituted Montero for Walker" and explained the substitution on the basis of

Much of what we would like to know about Montero has escaped detection. He was born in Oporto, Portugal – the year is unknown – the son of José Soarez Montero and Ana María Manuela Montero.[3] Other than this, his origin and background, and time of coming to America are blank.

Equally obscure are the circumstances of his entering the fur trade. The first tangible evidence in this connection shows him to have been employed by the American Fur Company in the early 1830s. It consists of a letter of credit from Lucien Fontenelle to William Laidlow, agent for the American Fur Company at Fort Pierre.[4] Written at the Green River rendezvous near Horse Creek on July 20, 1833, the letter directed Laidlow to pay Montero a balance due him of $260.25, which was probably Montero's wages for

Bonneville's anger with Walker over his alleged failure on the California expedition.

Acting on Wagner's supposition, Walker's biographer, Douglas Watson in *West Wind* (Los Angeles, 1934), 75-6, declared categorically: "Suddenly and out of nowhere a new character appears, a certain Montero, and strange to relate this Montero follows the trail set for Walker for the year between July, 1834 and June, 1835. . . Irving makes the mythical Montero do all that [Zenas] Leonard saw Walker do. We are confronted with a queer situation. Did Bonneville substitute the name Montero for Walker? There seems to be little doubt but that he did. Did Bonneville refer to Walker slurringly when talking with Irving as the man from Monterey, using the Spanish – Montereyño, or did he simply call him the hunter, translating the latter likewise into Spanish, which would then be exactly the name Irving employs – Montero? . . . All search for a real Montero as captain in the fur trade heading a band of Bonneville's men during the year 1834-35 has been fruitless." Wagner's and Watson's theory as to the fictitious Montero has been most recently repeated by John C. Ewers in his edition of Leonard's *Adventures* (Norman, Okla., 1959), xxiii, where, following a line of reasoning parallel to Watson's, he declares: "There can be little doubt that Walker and Montero were one and the same man."

It is the purpose of this biographical sketch to distinguish between fact and fiction where Montero is concerned by basing every factual statement upon verifiable evidence and to attribute to Montero what definitely belongs to him. As one of Bonneville's men, Montero had a very real existence with a clear and distinct career quite apart from Walker's, and it is possible to follow him with reasonable thoroughness from 1832 to 1845.

3 Fray Angélico Chávez, "New Names in New Mexico, 1820-1850," *El Palacio,* LXIV (1957), 376.

4 Chouteau-Maffitt Collections, Missouri Historical Society.

the preceding year. This document suggests that he may have entered the fur trade in 1832 or earlier as an employee of that company.

On the same day, July 20, Montero endorsed this letter of credit over to Michel Sylvestre Cerré, who was at this time in the employ of Captain Benjamin L. E. Bonneville.[5] It is not clear why Montero should have done so, but it was probably for personal goods and equipment needed for the coming trapping season. Montero may now, also, have transferred his allegiance from the American Fur Company to Bonneville. He had come to the rendezvous of 1833 as one of 160 men led by Fontenelle;[6] and since it is known that Bonneville offered high wages, Montero may have been induced to join him for this reason.[7] Eventually he became the leader of one of Bonneville's brigades. His literacy, though limited, may have been a point in his favor because the several trapping brigades kept in touch partly through written communication. As will be shown later, an exchange of letters subsequently took place between Montero and Zenas Leonard, another of Bonneville's employees, working with Joseph R. Walker.

Exactly what Montero's actions were that season (1833-34) are solely conjectural. He could, for example, have been one of the forty men whom Walker led to California that

[5] Washington Irving, *The Adventures of Captain Bonneville,* ed. by Edgeley W. Todd (Norman, 1961), 16-17.

[6] *Ibid.,* 154.

[7] Competition for men was as keen as that for beaver. Bonneville had the year before (1832) lost several Delaware Indians to Fontenelle, whereupon he set about to capture some of Fontenelle's men in return. Near Fort Bonneville, Irving tells us, Bonneville associated with Fontenelle's men camped nearby and "profited by the opportunity to collect from them information concerning the different parts of the country about which they had been accustomed to range. . . He also succeeded in securing the service of several to guide and aid him . . . and to trap for him during the ensuing season. Having strengthened his party with such valuable recruits, he felt in some measure consoled for the loss of the Delaware Indians, decoyed from him by Mr. Fontenelle" (*ibid.,* 49, 71). In light of these circumstances, Montero may have entered Bonneville's services at this time, but the letter of credit argues strongly for 1833 rather than 1832.

year; or he could have aided Michel Cerré in transporting
Bonneville's furs back to St. Louis via the Bighorn, Yellowstone, and Missouri rivers. Another possibility is that Montero was among those whom Bonneville sent out to trap
along the west side of the Bighorn River in August of that
year, or one of the few whom Bonneville kept with himself
in his various movements in the Wind River Mountains
area. Eventually Bonneville established his winter camp of
1833-34 on the Portneuf River north of Soda Springs, and
from here set out on his first expedition along the Snake
River into Hudson's Bay Company territory and to the
Columbia. Montero could well have been with Bonneville
on this venture. Indeed, he might have been in any one of
these undertakings. Unfortunately, no record shows which.

At this point, it is advisable to go back to the year 1832-33
to correct an error concerning Montero that has been kept
alive in Chittenden's *History of the American Fur Trade.*
Washington Irving relates that Bonneville had in 1832-33
sent a party of twenty men into the Crow country to trap
along the Yellowstone River and its tributaries. This group
was under a leader whom Irving chose to leave unnamed.
One disaster after another plagued them. Men, furs, horses,
and equipment were lost to overpowering rivals and to the
Crows; later, near the headwaters of Powder River, the
remaining horses were stolen by Arikara Indians. The few
Arikara prisoners held as hostages were burned to death as
the frightful penalty for their thefts. These affairs are told
in chapter 19 of the *Adventures of Captain Bonneville.*

Chittenden advanced the theory that the leader of this
trapping party was Antonio Montero. "A trader (probably
Montero by name)," he wrote, "had been sent the year
before to make a fall hunt in the Crow country with instructions to come to the Salmon river wintering ground upon its
completion." [8] Chittenden then gives a synopsis of Irving's
recital of these events.

The trader whom Chittenden believed to be Montero was actually David Adams,[9] another employee of Bonneville. His name was omitted from Irving's text because at the time that the *Adventures of Captain Bonneville* was published (1837), Adams was still operating in the mountains, and though Irving condemned the fiery deaths of the Arikara hostages, prudence led him to conceal the name of the person responsible for this outrage. The omission of Adams' name made it possible for later writers like Chittenden to assume incorrectly that Montero was the figure intended.[10] If Montero did not join Bonneville until July, 1833, as Fontenelle's letter of credit suggests, then he was still in the service of the American Fur Company at the time that Adams was running into trouble in the Crow country.

We must now rejoin Bonneville upon his return from his first expedition to the Columbia. He kept a rendezvous with his men on Bear Lake, which he reached on June 13, 1834, and here, about June 16, was joined by the Walker party returning from the seemingly fruitless journey to California. If Montero had not been trapping during the preceding months east of the continental divide, we may assume that he was now sent to the Bighorn Mountains area at the head of a trapping brigade.

Bonneville, between July and mid-November of that year (1834), made his second unsuccessful venture to the Columbia. When he returned, he established his winter headquarters on Bear Lake and remained here until April 1,

---

[8] Chittenden, *op. cit.,* I, p. 404.

[9] Aubrey L. Haines, editor of Osborne Russell's *Journal of a Trapper* (Portland, 1955), 167n, errs in following Chittenden's identification of Montero with David Adams.

[10] The evidence for David Adams is unmistakable. See Todd (ed.), *Adventures of Captain Bonneville,* pp. xxix-xxx, where Bonneville's letter of instructions to Adams for this fall hunt is reprinted; see also *ibid.,* 150n. James P. Beckwourth's *Life and Adventures* (New York, 1931), 163-6, gives Beckwourth's account of Adams' losses to the Crows and the defection of some of his men. Beckwourth specifically names Adams as the leader.

1835. Montero, meanwhile, during the fall of 1834 followed Bonneville's instructions to trap in the Crow country, after which he was to winter on the Arkansas. That autumn, as Bonneville was moving south toward Bear River, he spent three days hunting buffalo along the Portneuf River. While he was thus engaged, two messengers arrived from Montero's group. They made known that Montero and his party "had not been able to accomplish the whole of their mission" [11] – that is, had not gone to the Arkansas to winter. Montero had decided to remain where he was for the winter and spring, when Bonneville would meet him again. Bonneville kept these two men with him until November 17, 1834, and then furnishing them with the supplies they had been sent to obtain, dispatched them on their return to Montero, "appointing," in Irving's words, "a rendezvous toward the last of June following [1835], on the forks of Wind River valley [junction of Wind River and the Popo Agie], in the Crow country." [12] This rendezvous took place near the end of June, 1835, when Montero again met Bonneville. [13]

It was during the previous autumn of 1834 that Montero constructed Portuguese Houses on the Powder River. This is evident from Irving's statement:

> Montero had followed the early part of his instructions [i.e., to trap in the Crow country]; after trapping upon some of the upper streams, he proceeded to Powder River. Here he fell in with the Crow villages or bands, who treated him with unusual kindness, and prevailed upon him to take up his winter quarters among them. [14]

Their "unusual kindness" may have been motivated by a desire to have an ally in repelling the inroads of their traditional enemies, the Blackfeet, who had during the past year dealt particularly severe blows, including the death of one of their important chiefs, Arapooish. Irving recounts at

---

[11] *Adventures of Captain Bonneville,* 350.
[12] *Ibid.*   [13] *Ibid.,* 365.   [14] *Ibid.,* 365-6.

some length one of these engagements between the Blackfeet and the Crows shortly after Montero encamped near
them on Powder River.

In order to avoid trouble with the Blackfeet, as well as to
be out of the immediate vicinity of the Crows, whose proximity was a nuisance, Montero moved some miles from them
and on Powder River built what Irving refers to as "a
winter cantonment of huts." [15] This post was named Portuguese Houses, or at least came to be known by that designation. Here Montero maintained close vigilance, guarding
the horses during the daytime and returning them to a stout
stockade of cottonwood logs at night. The post was evidently
not intended as a temporary winter shelter, and Irving's
reference to the camp as being composed of "huts" very
possibly gives the wrong connotation. Montero built, indeed,
with some thought of permanence, for when Captain W. F.
Raynolds and James Bridger visited the site twenty-five
years later, in September, 1859, they found the remains of
a strongly-built structure. Raynolds, making at that time an
exploration of the Yellowstone and Missouri rivers, had
camped on Powder River. In his journal he wrote:

> Bridger and myself turned our faces down stream . . . [and]
> after a ride of about 15 miles we came to the ruins of some old trading
> posts [sic], known as the "Portuguese Houses," from the fact that
> many years ago they were erected by a Portuguese trader named An-
> tonio Matéo [sic]. They are now badly dilapidated, and only one side
> of the pickets remains standing. These, however, are of hewn logs, and
> from their character it is evident that the structures were originally
> very strongly built. Bridger recounted a tradition that at one time this
> post was besieged by the Sioux for forty days, resisting successfully to
> the last alike the strength and the ingenuity of their assaults, and the
> appearance of the ruins renders the story not only credible but prob-
> able.[16]

[15] *Adventures of Captain Bonneville,* 368. For their location, see Russell, *Journal
of a Trapper* (1955), plate VII and p. 168.

[16] U.S. 40 Cong., 1 sess., *Senate Exec. doc. no. 77* (Washington, 1868), 65-6.

Irving makes no mention of such a siege by the Sioux, although something of the sort may have occurred after Bonneville left the mountains. But Montero was not free of trouble from the Blackfeet:

Montero had not long removed his camp from the vicinity of the Crows, and fixed himself in his new quarters [writes Irving], when the Blackfeet marauders discovered his cantonment, and began to haunt the vicinity. He kept up a vigilant watch, however, and foiled every attempt of the enemy, who, at length, seemed to have given up in despair, and abandoned the neighborhood. The trappers relaxed their vigilance, therefore, and one night, after a day of severe labor, no guards were posted, and the whole camp was soon asleep. Toward midnight, however, the lightest sleepers were roused by the trampling of hoofs; and, giving the alarm, the whole party were immediately on their legs, and hastened to the pens. The bars were down; but no enemy was to be seen or heard, and the horses being all found hard by, it was supposed the bars had been left down through negligence. All were once more asleep, when, in about an hour, there was a second alarm, and it was discovered that several horses were missing. The rest were mounted, and so spirited a pursuit took place, that eighteen of the number carried off were regained, and but three remained in possession of the enemy. Traps, for wolves, had been set about the camp the preceding day. In the morning, it was discovered that a Blackfoot was entrapped by one of them, but had succeeded in dragging it off. His trail was followed for a long distance, which he must have limped alone. At length, he appeared to have fallen in with some of his comrades, who had relieved him from his painful encumbrance.[17]

At Portuguese Houses Montero was in charge of fifty men, and from this place he sent trappers into the field. What some of them endured by way of winter hardships that drove at least one man to desert can be inferred from the following letter of James A. Hamilton, writing from Fort Union on the Upper Missouri. The letter, addressed to Pratte, Chouteau and Company, July 18, 1835, mentions several boatloads of furs being sent down, and among other matters alludes to one of Montero's men: "B. Bourdalone

---

17 *Adventures of Captain Bonneville*, 369-70.

No. 21. on the List, who works his passage down, came in here half dead, from a Division of Captain Bonnevilles party under Montero, who has been for the last year with 50 Men trapping & trading in the Crow Country he tells a wofull tale the leading features whereof Mr Tulloch had previously heard from other quarters. . ." [18]

By messenger and letter Montero remained in close communication that winter of 1834-35 with another of Bonneville's detachments located about 150 miles west and somewhat south of Portuguese Houses. Joseph R. Walker and his men had in November gone into winter quarters "sixty or seventy miles east of the main chain of the Rocky Mountains, on the headwaters of Wind River," [19] where in a broad valley northwest of modern Riverton, Wyoming, Walker built, according to Zenas Leonard (who joined him on December 4) "a temporary trading house for the winter season." [20]

Two letters survive from the correspondence between Walker's and Montero's camps during that winter season. Both are from Leonard. The first, dated January 11, 1835, is in reply to a letter from Montero written only five days earlier, on January 6. In view of the season and the mode of travel, the short interval between is remarkable.

The content of Montero's letter can only roughly be inferred from Leonard's reply. What is evident is that Montero had had some beaver pelts stolen, perhaps by some of his own men; Leonard advised caution in solving the theft and thought that questioning certain unnamed individuals would result in the discovery of "who took the beaver with-

---

[18] *Fort Union Letter Book*, 1833-1835, pp. 83-5; quoted in Annie Heloise Abel (ed.), *Chardon's Journal at Fort Clark, 1834-1839* (Pierre, 1932), 300. Hamilton's casual reference to Montero without identifying him implies that Montero's former association with the American Fur Company rendered such identification unnecessary.

[19] Leonard, *Adventures*, ed. by John C. Ewers (Norman, 1959), 156.

[20] *Ibid.*, 138.

out making any disturbance with the men. . ." Montero
had also requested that a mule be sent him, probably to
replace an animal lost to Indians, but Leonard refused to
send the mule because it was lame. Montero had also asked
for an additional man, but Leonard advised him that he
could not be sent because this would deprive the camp of a
needed hunter. And it also appears that Montero himself
would travel to the Wind River post within two weeks.[21]

Leonard's second letter, dated January 20, 1835, confirms
that Montero had indeed visited Walker's post in the interim
and had since returned, apparently, to Portuguese Houses.
The letter shows that Leonard was sending some men to
Montero and that nothing new was known about the theft
of the beaver pelts. "There has one horse died since You
left here," Leonard wrote. "I would be glad if you would
Send Manning to me as Soon as possible as I am troubled
getting meat Since the Indians have passed here and our
horses [are] very poor."[22]

The next June 22, or thereabouts, found all of Bonneville's brigades, Montero's among them, assembled at the
junction of the Popo Agie and Wind River. Bonneville
within a few days had everything in readiness for his return
to the East; but from what Zenas Leonard recorded, it was
Bonneville's intention to return from the States the next
summer (1836). With this in mind, he left two trapping
parties behind. One of them, with fifty-five men, was under
Joseph Walker.[23] The other, according to Bonneville's own
record, as given by Irving, was headed by Montero.[24]
Bonneville actually did carry out part of his intention of
returning to the mountains, for in the spring of 1836, while
proceedings for his reinstatement in the army were still

[21] Leonard's letter is at the Missouri Historical Society.

[22] Missouri Historical Society. Other matters in the letter, much of which has
become illegible, are not clearly relevant to the present discussion.

[23] Leonard, *op. cit.*, 160.

[24] *Adventures of Captain Bonneville*, 370.

in the hands of his superiors in Washington, D.C., he set out on May 8 "to make a final close of my interests there," as he wrote later to the Adjutant General.[25] His destination was in all likelihood Portuguese Houses and the Popo Agie, there to meet Montero and Walker and to arrange to terminate his affairs with them after one more year.[26]

Montero was hard-pressed during the winter of 1836-37. One exasperating problem was related by Joe Meek to his biographer, Mrs. Frances F. Victor. In *River of the West* she reports this occurrence as taking place that year:

> About Christmas all the company [Bridger's] went into winter-quarters on Powder River, in the neighborhood of a company of Bonneville's men, left under the command of Antoine Montero, who had established a trading-post and fort at this place, hoping, no doubt, that here they should be comparatively safe from the injurious competition of the older companies. The appearance of three hundred men, who had the winter before them in which to do mischief, was therefore as unpleasant as it was unexpected; and the result proved that even Montero, who was Bonneville's experienced trader, could not hold his own against so numerous and expert a band of marauders as Bridger's men, assisted by the Crows, proved themselves to be; for by the return of spring Montero had very little remaining of the property belonging to the fort, nor anything to show for it. This mischievous war upon Bonneville was prompted partly by the usual desire to cripple a rival trader, which the leaders encouraged in their men; but in some individual instances far more by the desire for revenge upon Bonneville personally, on account of his censures passed upon the members of the Monterey expedition [Walker's], and on the ways of mountain-men generally.[27]

It may have been the onslaught of this horde of men that led

---

[25] *Ibid.*, p. xxxviii.

[26] Before setting out, Bonneville secured a one-year's license at St. Louis, granted on April 19, 1836, by William Clark. The record shows that his capital was a modest $1,122, that he employed fifteen men, and that he was to trade "at a point of timber on the south side of the Grand river Platte, called Laramais' [*sic*] point, – with the Arapahoes." *Letters Received by the Office of Indian Affairs,* 1836-1838. St. Louis Superintendency. Microfilm roll 751. National Archives and Records Service. Washington: 1956.

[27] *River of the West* (Hartford, 1870), 223-4.

Montero in December, 1836, to offer to barter seven packs of beaver pelts for goods with Milton Sublette at Fort Laramie, but Sublette was unable to supply him.[28]

Another incident involving Montero is provided by Osborne Russell, who was robbed by the Crows in 1837. Russell recorded in his *Journal* a conversation between himself and Lucien Fontenelle at Fort Laramie. Since Fontenelle had recovered from Montero some of Russell's furs by a show of force, this conversation deserves to be given in full. Russell quotes Fontenelle as saying:

> . . . I have met with that Village of Crows and recovered all your property that could be identified. I told them when I heard the circumstances that if they did not produce your property forthwith their heads would pay for it within 24 hours. On hearing this they immediately gave up as they repeatedly affirmed all except the Beaver skins which they had traded to a Portugese by the name of Antonio Montaro who had built some log cabins on Powder River for the purpose of trading with the Crows. I immediately[,] continued he[,] went to the Cabins and asked Mr. Montaro what right he had to trade Beaver skins from Indians with white mens names marked upon them knowing them to be stolen or taken by force from the Whites?" [*sic*] and asked him to deliver them to me which he refused to do. I then ordered him to give me the key of his warehouse which he reluctantly did I then ordered my clerk to go in and take all the Beaver skins he could find with your names marked upon them and have them carried to my camp which was done without further ceremony.[29]

Montero did not long remain in the fur country after this. By the following summer (1838) he had left Portuguese Houses and returned to Missouri. There, from Independence on August 5, he wrote to David Adams, Bonneville's former employee, and explained his present circumstances:

> I hope that you will not thinck hard for my desapintment to you about

---

28 See letter of M. G. Sublette, Fort William (i.e., Fort Laramie), to Pratte, Chouteau and Co., December 13, 1836. Part of this letter reads: "Antoin Montaro has [sent] seven pack of Beaver hear for goods but I cannot supply him. . ." Missouri Historical Society.

29 *Journal of a Trapper* (1955), 80-1.

coming up this year [one word illegible] for my aferes [affairs] with my Partners it was so that I am obliged to go up this year without aney goods: nothing more then for to get my own propertees [from Portuguese Houses] down from the Rock Montains that they have left ther indestrest [*sic*] and all so I could not get no settlement from them whatever.

But I hope that we will see each other next year and then I will be in beter fixt for to do my beseness.

Sir I am well and I hope you the same[.]

Antonio S [?] Montero
Your Best friend [30]

Almost immediately Montero must have started on a return journey to Powder River to recover the disputed property cached at Portuguese Houses. What may have given rise to the conflicting claims alluded to in his letter to Adams is unknown. Some light may be shed upon this matter, however, by an event that took place within a few weeks.

This event was an order, dated September 2, 1838, issued by Joshua Pilcher, newly appointed Superintendent of Indian Affairs in St. Louis, less than a month after Montero wrote to Adams. Pilcher's order, addressed to Papin, Picotte and Chardon, and couched in legalistic phraseology, is nothing less than a command that Montero be denied the right to remain in the Indian country. It may have been that the "cache or deposit of Furs & Peltries belonging to one of our citizens," to which Pilcher refers, was the property left at Portuguese Houses which Montero wished to recover. Pilcher's order reads:

Whereas Antonio J. Montero a man notoriously of bad character, and one capable of inciting the Indians to acts of mischief, and embarassing Such of our citizens as are lawfully ingaged in the trade or otherwise in the Indian country — has gone into the country without permit or

---

[30] Adams Papers, Missouri Historical Society. The outside of the letter is addressed in a different hand to "Mr. David Adams, Care of Jos. Lespagnols, St. Louis, Mo."

licence and that too with the *avowed* intention of breaking upon a cache or deposit of Furs & Peltries belonging to one of our citizen[s] lawfully engaged in the Indian Trade and appropriating the Same to his own use – and complaints having been made against the Said Montero for various malpractices in the Indian country heretofore. Now therefore I, Joshua Pilcher Indian Agent for the Upper Missouri River do command the Said Montero to leave the country, and to the end that this order may be fulfiled, all persons lawfully in the country are forbidden to empl[o]y Said offender in any way aid or incourage him in remaining in the Indian country, but on the countrary it is requested that they will use all reasonable measures to Send Said Montero out of the country.[31]

By some means, however, Montero succeeded in reinstating himself in the good graces of the St. Louis Superintendency the following year, for on July 27, 1839, Pilcher granted him a one-year license to trade, as the record reads, "with the Crows at Fort Antonio [Portuguese Houses] on Powder River; with the Sioux at Larames [*sic*] Fork of the River Platte, with the Cheyennes at the foot of the mountains on the South fork of the River Platte, or with any other Indians that may visit either of those posts." [32] Montero, whose capital was a meager $469.05 (his bond was $500, guaranteed by one R. Taylor), took twelve men with him on what may have been his final trading venture. This license is the last bit of evidence that has come to light concerning Antonio Montero and his career in the fur trade.

With the decline of the fur trade and the termination of Montero's operations as a trader in 1839-40, he seems to have associated himself briefly in some way with Bent's Fort, for on April 30, 1841, Charles Bent, writing from Fort William (as Bent's Fort was originally named [33]) to

---

[31] Chouteau Collections, Missouri Historical Society.

[32] *Letters Received by the Office of Indian Affairs,* 1839-41. St. Louis Superintendency. Microfilm roll 752. National Archives and Records Service. Washington: 1956.

[33] David Lavender, *Bent's Fort* (Garden City, 1954), 139.

Manuel Alvarez, United States consul at Santa Fe,[34] stated that "Montaro [*sic*] takes your rifle to Taos, I have had it put in order." [35] If Montaro is indeed Antonio Montero (and this seems to be a reasonable assumption), his activities for the next few years center in northern New Mexico. Here he married María Francisca Vigil on August 9, 1841. Two children were born to them – Maria Paula on February 6, 1843, and Antonio on May 25, 1845.[36]

Of greater interest are at least two lawsuits involving himself and Charles Bent. There is some evidence, however sparse, that he was also involved in legal entanglements with Lucien Maxwell. Of these various cases, the ones with Bent are the more prominent, even though most of the details are lacking, and numerous allusions to them appear in letters which Bent wrote to Alvarez between 1843 and 1846 [37] as well as in other documents of the time.

The first suit was apparently instigated by Montero, for Alvarez stated in a letter to Daniel Webster that "The Prefect of the First District [Juan Andrés Archuleta] . . . in the name of an insignificant individual [Montero], caused a suit to be presented, most outrageous and unjust, against Bent." [38] The hearing took place on February 16, 1843, so Bent himself stated, at "the Rancho" (probably Ranchos de Taos, a few miles below Taos proper). Montero's counsel was Louis Robidoux, who succeeded in winning his client's case. A few days later, February 29, Bent confided to Alvarez that he had paid "the

[34] *Ibid.,* 191.

[35] *New Mexico Historical Review,* XXX (1955), 159. For information leading to a knowledge of Montero's affairs in New Mexico, I gratefully acknowledge suggestions from Mrs. Janet Lecompte.

[36] Chávez, *op. cit.,* LXIV, p. 376.

[37] These letters have been published in the *New Mexico Historical Review,* XXX (1955), 165-253, *passim.* Lavender, *op. cit.,* 218-19, 401, alludes to the litigation but sheds little light upon it.

[38] Quoted in Lavender, *op. cit.,* 218.

mone I was centenced to pay" in order that he might avoid "more difficulty." [39]

Another document bearing upon Montero's litigation against Bent, which shows that the general sentiment was against the American, is a letter written by Archuleta two days after the trial to General Don Manuel Armijo, governor of New Mexico. The suit obviously aroused widespread interest. A translation of Archuleta's letter follows:

> On this same date [February 18, 1843], I advise Your Excellency through the appropriate channels regarding the matter of Bent and Montero, a matter that is getting a good deal of attention. It can undoubtedly lead to results inimical to the good order and tranquillity which the Department enjoys today, for the majority of the people in my District are apprehensive, and I am afraid the authorities of the Nation will become involved, for our inhabitants, tired of suffering the evils originated by Bent, are calling for revenge against him, and although I realize my personal limitations compared to yours, I humbly make the following suggestions: and much more when the enemies of peace insist that the said Bent be given protection in this Prefecture and in that government. . . There is no doubt that they are trying to defraud Montero of his personal effort, and it is also true that he can prove the accusations against Bent, and all there is lacking is a judge with knowledge and conscience to have it verified, for which Your Grace will take the steps you deem necessary in the case. . .[40]

That this was but the first suit involving Montero and Charles Bent is evident from another letter to Alvarez which Bent wrote nearly two years later on November 12, 1844. A postscript reads in part: "I have written to Eugen [Eugene Leitensdorfer] to get Juan Vigil, to send an order heare for Montano, to be called to Santafe, for the purpos of having his trial. I am informed he is preparing to leave, and it is absolutely nessary, that this sute should commence." [41]

---

[39] *New Mexico Historical Review,* xxx, p. 166. The money Bent was "centenced to pay," so Alvarez stated, was $800, forced upon "him on the most frivolous pretext . . . without the shadow of justice." Quoted in Lavender, *op. cit.,* 219.

[40] The original, in Spanish, is in the Ritch Collection, Huntington Library.

This suit, for which the circumstances are also unknown, must have been decided in Bent's favor, for another letter to Alvarez contains the statement: ". . . the justice has in a maner done nothing as yet, except proving that Montano is a *falsidore* [falsifier] he has had him in detention for three days and I supose will put him in prison to day, but light is so scarce with him I doubt wether he ever will be able to see through the mist that envellops him. . ." [42]

A week later Bent again wrote to Alvarez and once more alluded to what he now called "the Criminal Trial of Montano," which he believed would "last some time, he has been proved gilty of the charges, he [is] in formal prison." [43] The last letter to Alvarez, February 23, 1845, containing the final reference to Montero's affairs, indicates that he "has run off God knowes where, but J. M. Vigil [Jose Manuel Vigil] says he has gone to joine the Texians" [44] – an allusion to the struggles that led that year to the annexation of Texas by the United States.

In this last recorded bit of information concerning Antonio Montero, the obscure circumstances of his life in the West seem fittingly to close. That he was a shadowy figure so far as history records is clearly apparent. But while it would be a mistake to overemphasize his importance in the history of the fur trade, it is equally apparent that he stood somewhere above its many nameless participants. The information about him sheds some light, however dim, upon the part that one man played in the history of the early West.

[41] *New Mexico Historical Review*, xxx, p. 167.

[42] *Ibid.*, xxx, p. 252. The letter is dated Rio Arriba, January 17, 1845.

[43] January 24, 1845. *Ibid.*, xxx, p. 252.

[44] *Ibid.*, xxx, p. 253. Additional references to Montero appear in Archive No. 1169, "Official Proceedings of Mariano Martinez de Lajanza," New Mexico Archives, Museum of New Mexico, Santa Fe, N.M. These documents relate to the litigation between Montero and Bent and suggest that their difficulties involved financial matters. They also reveal that Montero had a claim against Lucien Maxwell.

Albert Pike

by HARVEY L. CARTER
Colorado College, Colorado Springs

Brief as it was, Albert Pike's association with the fur trade of the Far West was of importance in various ways. His is the only published record of the activities in which he and others engaged during 1831 and 1832; it is the record of one of the few trapping expeditions operating eastward into Texas from a New Mexican base. His adventures provided the occasion for the composition of some poetry of very good quality, for some of the most vivid word pictures of the high plains country, and one of the earliest and best characterizations of the Mountain Man as a type and of Bill Williams, in particular. It is not too much to say that to Albert Pike must be credited the discovery of the literary possibilities of the Southwest.

Albert Pike, son of Benjamin and Sarah (Andrews) Pike, was born in Boston on December 29, 1809.[1] He was descended (as was Zebulon Montgomery Pike, the explorer) from the English emigrant, John Pike, who came to Massachusetts Bay Colony in 1635. Albert Pike grew up in Byfield and Newburyport, where his father was a shoemaker. He may have attended a session at Harvard College in 1822 before teaching school, and in 1823 he qualified by examination for the junior class at Harvard but could not afford to pay the tuition for the first two years, as was required.[2]

---

[1] *Appleton's Cyclopaedia of American Biography* (New York, 1888) v, p. 18. This sketch was published before Pike's death. There is a longer sketch in the *Dictionary of American Biography* (New York, 1934) XIV, pp. 593-5.

[2] The records of Harvard College do not list Pike as a student although he stated that he was in attendance there for one term. Harvard awarded him an honorary Master of Arts degree in 1859.

Thereafter, he taught school at various places in Massachusetts from 1824 to 1831.

In March, 1831, he set out for the West, accompanied by his friend, Rufus Titcomb. They traveled, by various means, via Albany, Buffalo, Cleveland, Cincinnati, Nashville, and Cairo to St. Louis, walking about five hundred miles of the way.[3] On August 10, 1831, they joined a train of ten wagons and thirty or forty men commanded by Charles Bent and headed for Taos.

This was the memorable year in which Josiah Gregg had taken his first caravan to Santa Fe, and in which Jedediah Smith had been killed on the Cimarron cut-off. The Bent train, although later and smaller, was notable for being the first in which the wagons were pulled entirely by oxen.[4] Pike's horse ran away during a thunderstorm and he walked about five hundred miles of the journey. Details of the trip are sparse but we know that they reached the Cimarron on October 22; that on November 18, at the Point of Rocks, before they reached the Canadian River, they encountered a severe snowstorm, which delayed them for a week; that some horses and oxen froze to death and that many of the men, including Pike, suffered from frostbitten feet; that they crossed the Sangre de Cristos, amid further hardships from cold weather, and reached the still-house in the valley, three miles from Taos, on November 29, 1831.[5]

---

3 Fred W. Allsopp, *Albert Pike: A Biography* (Little Rock, 1928), 17.

4 David Lavender, *Bent's Fort* (New York, 1954), 127-30. Allsopp states that Pike and Titcomb joined the wagon train at Independence but Pike himself in an unpublished autobiography said, "At St. Louis, I joined a trading party for Santa Fe, the captain of which was Charles Bent. The party went up to Independence, having left St. Louis on August 10." See Maurice G. Fulton and Paul Horgan, *New Mexico's Own Chronicle* (Dallas, 1937), 103-4, where a portion of this autobiography is printed.

5 Albert Pike, *Prose Sketches and Poems* (Boston, 1834), 17, 20, 21, 24. Pike's "Narrative of a Journey in the Prairie" was first published in this book, which is now exceedingly scarce. In 1835 he published the "Narrative" in his newspaper, *The Arkansas Advocate*. The "Narrative" is most accessible in *Publications of the Arkansas Historical Association* (Conway, 1917) IV, pp. 66-139. When citations are

Pike remained at Taos but one week and then proceeded to Santa Fe where he worked as a clerk until August, 1832. During this time, he made two trading trips, south to San Miguel and west to Jemez. He also found time to write several poems, his subjects being the mountain scenery, the Indian tribes, the only robin that he saw, and a girl in Massachusetts to whom his thoughts occasionally strayed.[6]

In August, 1832, Pike heard of a party organizing in Taos, under John Harris, of Missouri, for the purpose of trapping beaver in the Comanche country. Accordingly, he went to Taos, parting from his friend Titcomb at this time.[7] However, on arriving in Taos he bought his outfit, consisting of powder, lead, tobacco, six traps, one horse, and one mule, from a Mr. Campbell, and decided to join him instead of Harris. Pike and a friend went alone into the valley of the Picuris, where they hunted, got lost temporarily, and where Pike wrote more poetry. Meanwhile, Campbell's party, which consisted of about forty Mexicans, joined with that of Harris, who had enlisted about thirty Americans. The combined party entered the Picuris valley September 4, where Pike joined it. Among the Harris men were Aaron Lewis and Bill Williams, with both of whom Pike was already acquainted and who had both impressed him favorably. He mentions also an Irishman, Tom Burke, from Virginia, whom he found an entertaining but mendacious talker.[8]

On September 6, they left the Picuris, crossed the mountains to the Mora River and camped at a deserted village

---

made to the "Narrative" hereafter, the pages referring to *Prose Sketches and Poems* will be given first, and in parentheses following them will be given the corresponding pages in vol. IV, above.

[6] Pike published a sketch of one of these trading trips in *The Boston Pearl*, February 20, 1836. It is reproduced in abridged form in Fulton and Horgan, *op. cit.*, 104-8. The poems mentioned are scattered through *Prose Sketches and Poems*.

[7] Whether Pike and Titcomb quarreled is not clear. Pike dedicated his first book to another member of the Titcomb family.

[8] Pike, *"Narrative,"* 36-8 (94-5).

where they killed many rattlesnakes among the ruins. They then went down the Mora to the Santa Fe Trail but crossed to the Gallinas, under the impression that it would lead them to the headwaters of the Red River, which, like Zebulon Pike before them, they imagined arose in the mountains to the south. However, it led them to the Pecos River, which they began to descend on September 15. Harris and Campbell quarreled and encamped at some distance from each other but both reached the Bosque Redondo on September 20, and here they determined to strike across the Llano Estacado in a southeasterly direction. However, the Mexicans, of Campbell's party, became alarmed by reports of returning Mexican traders concerning outrages committed by hostile Comanches and refused to go any farther. Campbell and the Mexicans thereupon began their return to Taos but Pike, in disgust at their behavior, rode over and joined the Harris camp.[9]

They broke camp on September 21, and for several days, while crossing the Staked Plains, suffered from lack of both water and food. On several occasions the only food for the entire party was a single antelope, killed by Bill Williams. On September 27, they encountered a band of Comanches. With difficulty they restrained the hostile intentions of Williams, which would have been suicidal. Pike, Williams, and Harris had supper with the chief, who said they would find beaver in nine days. Soon they reached one of the heads of the Colorado River and met other Comanches with whom they exchanged tobacco for food. Beaver was still scarce and a plan to go to the San Saba River was proposed but rejected.[10]

---

[9] Ibid., 38-44 (96-101). The Bosque Redondo was a round grove of timber about forty miles north of present Roswell, New Mexico. It was also called the Bosque Grande.

[10] Ibid., 49-56 (106-114). There is some confusion as to whether they were upon the headwaters of the Colorado or the Brazos. The proposal to go to the San Saba, among other considerations, seems to indicate that they were on a fork of the Colorado.

During the next few days the party broke up into smaller units and continued downstream. On October 9, Pike, Aaron Lewis, and an Englishman named Irwin were together and became lost. Later they encountered a half dozen men with Bill Williams who were also lost. Still later both these groups were reunited with the main body under Harris. The poor trapping was the cause of a permanent disintegration of the venture beginning on October 13. Pike and four companions, Lewis, Irwin, Ish, and Gillette left the river and headed north. Bill Williams and six others split off a few days later and returned to Taos. Harris and the remainder of the party spent the winter on the Canadian River.[11]

Pike has left an interesting account of the small group which he headed and a fine description of the country which they now traversed. Ish and Gillette were from Missouri, the latter characterized by the twenty-three-year-old Pike as "a mere boy." Irwin, the Englishman, had made his way to Santa Fe from California. Lewis had come to New Mexico with two companions about the time that Pike had arrived there. He was from Arkansas Territory. All were well supplied with ammunition. In addition to their rifles, they all had pistols except Irwin, who had a double-barreled English fowling piece. Their clothing was showing wear, especially their moccasins, but they had blankets with them.

Their course was in a northeasterly direction and they crossed several streams, some of which were dry or nearly so. They suffered from thirst as the water they found was salty. Game was scarce during the first few days, except for wild horses, of which they saw great numbers. Pike found their meat good eating, especially the part of the neck lying just under the mane. Horse tongue, which he tried, he did not find very palatable. They also killed deer and wild turkeys. After traveling about 140 miles they reached the

[11] *Ibid.,* 59-60; 79-80 (117; 137).

Red River. Here they found the prairie more open and saw immense herds of buffalo, of which they easily killed all they needed for food. It was on October 21 that they crossed the Red River and they continued their course until they reached the Washita River on November 8. It was running strongly and, as they were unable to make a crossing, they turned down the stream.[12]

As they proceeded they met a large Osage hunting party led by their chief, Young Claremore [Clermont]. They did some trading with these Indians. On November 14 they left the Washita and a week later reached the Red River at the mouth of the Blue. They had passed through the Cross Timbers and during this week they encountered both snow and a prairie fire. On December 1, they reached the road leading to Fort Smith. Along this road, Pike traded his gun to some Choctaw Indians for twelve pounds of meat. They reached Fort Smith, Arkansas Territory, on December 10, 1832, and Pike, in commenting on their condition, tersely said, "Falstaff's ragged regiment was nothing to us." [13]

This was not quite the end of their Western adventures. On September 26, 1832, a party under Captain John Dade, an old Kentucky frontiersman, had been attacked, while returning from Taos laden with furs, by Chief Capote and fifteen hundred Comanches. After killing Dade and many of his men and taking their furs, this large warlike band attacked Fort Towson on the Red River on December 19. Word of their intentions had spread and a hundred Texans under Colonel James Bowie came to help defend the fort. At Fort Smith, Colonel Arbuckle raised a company of volunteers, which included Pike and his four companions.

---

12 *Ibid.,* 64-72 (122-29). They were in some doubt as to the identity of the rivers. When they reached the Red River, they were surprised, as they thought they had passed it. When they reached the Washita, they thought that, because of its size, it might be the Red.

13 *Ibid.,* 74-8 (132-6).

The combined forces drove off the Indians from Fort Towson with great loss.[14]

Soon after this Pike learned of the fact that his friend and tentmate, while with the Bent wagon train, had been wounded by Comanches and abandoned along the Canadian River to die. He wrote a moving poem to the memory of his friend.[15]

This episode brought to an end the career of Albert Pike as a trapper and closed his connection with the Far West. Had he continued longer in this activity, it is probable that his literary output would have been larger, both in prose and poetry. The larger and better part of his poetry was written early in life. He was a master of many forms of versification. A close examination of his poems reveals a style more approximating that of Lord Byron than any other writer. Pike was a typical, if minor, representative of the romantic school of verse. His "Hymns to the Gods," written in 1831 and published in *Blackwood's Magazine* in 1839, received high praise. A collection of his poems was published in 1854 under the title of *"Nugae."*

Pike's long and varied subsequent career is of considerable interest but will only be outlined here. He taught school and published a newspaper in Arkansas during the years 1833 to 1835. On October 10, 1834, he was married to Mary Ann Hamilton at Arkansas Post.[16] Arkansas was admitted to the Union in 1836 and Pike, admitted to the bar in that same year, decided to cast his lot with the new state. He rose rapidly in the legal profession and prospered in a financial way. In 1849, he was admitted to practice before the Supreme Court of the United States and handled many important and lucrative cases. He did not finally discontinue his legal practice until 1879. For a few years in the

---

[14] Allsopp, 46-8.
[15] Pike, *"Narrative,"* 80 (165).   [16] Allsopp, 69-75.

1850s he lived in New Orleans and published a book on the Civil Code of Louisiana. He later compiled an extensive work on Roman and French law, which was never published. One of his most famous cases involved the successful handling of claims of the Choctaw Indians against the Federal Government. He served as a Judge in Arkansas, was a Whig in politics, and a notable orator, but had an aversion to holding public office.[17]

Another phase of his life embraces his military career and incidents growing out of it. When the Mexican War was declared in 1846 he promptly raised a squadron of cavalry. He served as a Captain and participated in the battle of Buena Vista. After the war, his uncomplimentary references to the behavior of certain Arkansas troops drew him into a duel with Colonel John S. Roane which was witnessed by over two hundred people. Pike calmly enjoyed his cigar up to the moment of action. After two exchanges in which neither party was touched, the participants were persuaded to let the matter rest.[18]

When Arkansas seceded from the Union, Pike saw no alternative but to go with his adopted state, although he did not approve either slavery or secession. By appointment of Jefferson Davis, he became Commissioner of the Confederate Government to all the Indian tribes south of Kansas and west of Arkansas and was given a military commission as Brigadier General. Pike's intention was merely to enable the Indians to defend themselves against possible inroads from the North but he was drawn into participation in the battle of Pea Ridge. This produced much criticism from the North and it also involved him in an unhappy controversy with General Thomas C. Hindman, which resulted in Pike's resigning his commission. Although an unwilling rather than a zealous Confederate, he was the author of one of the best versions of the Southern patriotic song, *Dixie*.

[17] *Ibid.*, 76-101.　　　　[18] *Ibid.*, 121-35.

After the end of the war, it was some time before he obtained a pardon for his Confederate activities. During this time he was for a time a recluse in Arkansas and also spent some time in Canada.[19]

In 1868 he removed to Washington, D.C., which was his home for the rest of his life. For a time he continued the practice of law but increasingly he became absorbed in Masonry, which he had entered in 1850. In 1859, he became Grand Commander of the Scottish Rite, Southern Jurisdiction, and this position he held until his death. He also became an honorary member of the Grand Councils of many foreign countries. Pike became the greatest scholar of the Masonic order. He studied and revised the Rituals, casting them in their present form and vastly improving them in the process. He was a self-taught student of many languages and had a working knowledge of Sanskrit, Greek, Latin, French, Italian, and Spanish. He occupied himself much with studies of ancient alphabets, oriental philosophy and poetry, and left many works which have never been published. Yet his published work was both enormous and varied. His writing was done always with a quill pen prepared by himself and his chirography was small and regular. He was undoubtedly the best known and best loved Mason in the world and he probably did more for the fraternity than any other single person.[20]

Pike's appearance was patriarchal. From the time of his western adventures, he wore his hair at shoulder length and his beard long.[21] He was a tall man and portly, of jovial disposition and Jovian countenance and, as his hair and beard became silvery white, presented a most distinguished appearance. His wife died in 1876; his poem "Love Blooms but Once" expressed his thoughts on this occasion. Two sons and a daughter had preceded her in death. Another son and

[19] *Ibid.,* 175-235.   [20] *Ibid.,* 136-51; 235-58.
[21] See page 18 of this volume for his portrait.

daughter, who left issue, died before their father. His son, Yvon, survived him when he died, full of years and honors, on April 2, 1891.[22]

Albert Pike was one of the most versatile of men, in whom the qualities of the introvert and the extrovert were fully blended and balanced. What his life might have been, if his excursion to New Mexico had been productive of enough beaver to induce him to remain a trapper and trader, is impossible to say. Even his short career in the fur trade enriched the literature of the subject. The mountains, the woods, and the prairies left a permanent impression on his vigorous mind which he, in turn, was able to convey to posterity through his gift for literary expression.

[22] *Ibid.,* 309-22. Pike left directions that his body should be cremated but this was not done. He was buried in Oak Hill Cemetery, Washington, D.C.

William Pope

by ANDREW F. ROLLE
Occidental College, Los Angeles

Little is known concerning the origins of William Pope except that he was born in Kentucky. He first appears as a member of the party of trapping adventurers led by James Ohio Pattie and his father Sylvester in 1828 and is mentioned in the former's *Personal Narrative* (1831). After leaving New Mexico and trapping the sloughs near the Gulf of California, the Pattie party was apprehended by Mexican authorities at Mission Santa Catalina in Lower California on March 12, 1828. Accused of espionage, Pope and other members of the group were marched northward under guard after March 27. At San Diego, in Upper California, Governor José María Echeandía imprisoned the Pattie party as foreign interlopers. During November of that year, however, Pope and a trapping companion, Isaac Slover, were released and allowed to proceed eastward via Sonora, Mexico. The motive for this leniency by the California authorities was obviously to repatriate them.[1]

Pope, like Slover, returned to New Mexico. At Taos he began a family and was naturalized as a Mexican citizen. Probably in 1837, Pope came back to California, settling at Los Angeles with eight members of his family and a company of twelve men. His name appears at various times in that city's municipal records. In 1838 he petitioned for and received a land grant for a lot "whereon to build a house east of the city and on the other side of the Los Angeles River." During the next year Pope received permission to

---

[1] Hubert Howe Bancroft, *History of California* (San Francisco, 1884), III, pp. 163, 166-7, 178; IV, pp. 280, 671, 782; VI, p. 19.

erect a grist mill on the bank of the Los Angeles River, stating that he had lived in the area for three years.[2]

The historian Hubert Howe Bancroft records that Pope
was known in California as Julian Pope, "that being," states
Bancroft, "the baptismal name he received in New Mexico."
In 1841 Pope obtained a land grant six miles in length and
three in width on which he began the Locoallomi Rancho.
Located in Napa County far to the north, near the ranch of
the trapper George C. Yount, the area lay just below Mt. St.
Helena and to the east of the Russian fur-trading post at
Fort Ross. This northeastern portion of the Napa Basin is
today known as the Pope Valley and comprises some 20,000
acres of land. Through it runs Pope Creek. He settled there
under a Mexican passport dated March 2, 1841. The expenses for Pope's journey from Los Angeles to the site were
paid for by the Mexican government which was, obviously,
eager to see this northernmost area settled by trustworthy
residents.[3]

Pope did not live long at Locoallomi. In the fall of 1842,
he accidentally killed himself by severing an artery with an
axe and hemorrhaged to death. His widow married Elias
Barnett, who had been with the Bidwell-Bartleson overland
party of 1841 and who had settled in Pope Valley. Pope's
son Joseph became the claimant of the rancho. Among
Pope's other four children, one daughter was a Mrs. Juan
Burton and she lived, appropriately, in the Pope Valley.[4]

---

2 LeRoy R. and Ann W. Hafen, *Old Spanish Trail* (Glendale, Calif., 1954), 181,
198.

3 *History of Napa and Lake Counties, California* (San Francisco, 1881), 55.

4 C. A. Menefee, *Historical and Descriptive Sketch Book of Napa, Sonoma, Lake
and Mendocino* (Napa, Calif., 1879), 170-1.

Nathaniel Pryor

by RAYMOND W. SETTLE
Monte Vista, Colorado

Nathaniel Pryor was a member of the Lewis and Clark expedition, 1804-1806; soldier in the United States Army;[1] Indian trader at Arkansas Post;[2] and sub-agent for the Osage Indians on the Arkansas, Neosho, and Verdigris rivers in northeastern Oklahoma.[3] He was born in Virginia, probably Amherst County,[4] but the date is unknown.

His mother was a daughter of William Floyd and Obadiah Davis of that county, and his grandmother, wife of Nathaniel Davis, was the daughter of Nicketti, daughter of Chief Powhatan and a sister of Pocahontas. On his mother's side he was connected with the Shelbys, the Lewises, the Cabells, and President Thomas Jefferson. His paternal ancestry is as yet untraced.[5]

He probably moved to Kentucky with Charles Floyd, an uncle, whose son Charles was about Pryor's age, and located at the Falls of the Ohio (Louisville). When Captains Meriwether Lewis and William Clark of the United States Army stopped there on their way to St. Louis in 1803 to make arrangements for their great exploring expedition to the Pacific, young Pryor and Floyd volunteered their services, were accepted, and appointed to the rank of sergeant in the organization.[6] John Ordway, another volunteer, was also

---

[1] Grant Foreman, "Nathaniel Pryor," in *Chronicles of Oklahoma*, VII, pp. 152-62; F. B. Heitman, *Historical Register and Dictionary of the United States Army* (Washington, 1903), 808; Elliot Coues, "Letters of William Clark and Nathaniel Pryor," in *Annals of Iowa*, I, pp. 613-20.

[2] Foreman, *op. cit.*, 152.   [3] *Ibid.*, 155.

[4] Elliot Coues, "Biographical Sketch of Nathaniel Pryor," in *Mississippi Valley Historical Review*, VI, pp. 249-50.

[5] *Ibid.*, 249.   [6] *Ibid.*, 249.

given that rank. After spending the winter at Wood River, on the east bank of the Mississippi opposite the mouth of the Missouri, they embarked upon their unprecedented enterprise on May 14, 1804.

After a successful journey, on which they suffered much hardship and encountered many dangers, they returned to St. Louis, September 23, 1806, having been away two years, four months, and six days, during which time they traveled, according to their own estimate, 7,545 miles through an unknown, Indian-infested wilderness. Only one man was lost, Sergeant Charles Floyd, who died on August 20, 1804, of illness diagnosed by Captain William Clark as "a Bilicose Chorlick." [7]

The results of this almost incredible journey are so numerous and far-reaching that only bare mention of the major ones can be made. It extended the United States western boundary from the continental divide to the Pacific Ocean and conclusively proved there was no navigable water route to it. It established the fact that the far western country was rich in natural resources, especially in beaver; gave both impetus and direction to the infant fur trade; and thrust such men as Manuel Lisa (1807), John Jacob Astor (1808) and the great, and near-great trading and trapping companies upon the broad stage of action. It bolstered the claim of the United States to Oregon, and blazed the trail for the conquest of the entire Far West.

Although Nathaniel Pryor served in a humble capacity on the expedition, he earned the unqualified praise of his superior officers. In assigning credit for the achievement of vast results, a generous portion must go to him and others like him. The value President Jefferson set upon their serv-

---

[7] Bernard DeVoto, *The Journals of Lewis and Clark* (New York, 1953), 21. Although this volume is a condensation, it perhaps is better suited to the average reader than the eight-volume R. G. Thwaites, *Original Journals of the Lewis and Clark Expedition* (1904-1905).

ices is seen in the fact that he asked Congress to double the pay of the soldiers in the expedition, gave each enlisted man 320 acres of land, and Lewis and Clark 1,600 acres each in the Louisiana Purchase.

To what Pryor devoted his time for the next five months after the return of the expedition is not known. The Mandan Chief, Sha-ha-ka (Gros Blanc, or Big White), and his family came downriver to St. Louis with the expedition and were taken on to Washington to visit President Jefferson. Upon their return to that city Pryor was appointed ensign in the First Infantry, United States Army, on February 27, 1807, and given command of twenty soldiers to escort the Indians back to their own country. Ex-Lieutenant Auguste Pierre Chouteau, with a trading expedition of thirty men on their way to the Mandans, and William Dorion with ten men serving as escort for a homeward-bound band of Sioux Indians who had come down to St. Louis for a visit early that spring, made up the party. All told, the expedition under Pryor's command consisted of sixty-seven men.[8]

The combined parties set out in the latter part of May, 1807, and by September 9 had reached an Aricara village on the Upper Missouri when the Indians fired upon them and ordered them to land and trade with them. In a short time about 650 warriors, mostly armed with guns, were congregated at the water's edge. Pryor refused to land as they demanded and moved on upstream, with the hostile Indians following along the bank. Again they demanded that he land and trade, and again Pryor refused. Seeing that the white men would not place themselves in their hands, the Indians collected in a willow thicket and fired upon the boats. Pryor opened upon them with two swivels, with which the boats were equipped, and small arms. After

---

[8] Coues, "Letters," *op. cit.,* 614; *Missouri Historical Review,* XXIX, pp. 116, 118.

about a quarter-hour of heavy firing on both sides he ordered a retreat downriver. Three of his own men and seven of Chouteau's were wounded, one mortally, and three killed. On October 16, 1807, Pryor reported to General William Clark, Governor of Missouri Territory, that the expedition had failed.[9]

Pryor was promoted to second lieutenant May 3, 1808, but after about two years of service on the western frontier resigned his commission. On April 1, 1810, he secured a license from Governor Clark to trade with the Winnebagos or Puans at a place called DeBuque's Mines, where Dubuque, Iowa, now stands. He erected a suitable trading post, a lead-smelting furnace, and soon developed a promising business. About six months before the outbreak of the War of 1812 Governor Clark requested him to secure information concerning the activities of Tecumseh and his brother, the Prophet, who were endeavoring to consolidate the northern and southern Indian tribes into a confederation against the encroaching white settlers. He complied with the request, which, together with the influence of British agents and the loss of friends and relatives in the battle of Tippecanoe, November 7, 1811, turned his former Winnebago friends against him.[10]

On January 1, 1813, eight of the tribes came to the trading post with guns and offered violence. About sundown of that day sixty more came, shot down his oxen, and killed two of his men. They seized him and were about to kill him also when a woman in the post restrained them for the moment. They then shut him up in the building, intending to burn it with him inside. While they were plundering the place he made his escape, crossed the Mississippi River on the ice,

---

[9] *Ibid.*, 614. See also Jacob Fowler, *Journal* (New York, 1898), 5; and Walter B. Douglas, "Manuel Lisa," in Missouri Historical Society *Collections* (St. Louis, 1911), III, pp. 252-3.

[10] Foreman, *op. cit.*, 156-7.

and was safe. Later he presented a claim for $5,216.25 to the United States government for losses incurred in the attack.[11]

Pryor's whereabouts and activities for a year and a half after the catastrophe at DeBuque's Mines are not known. On August 30, 1813, he was commissioned first lieutenant in the Forty-Fourth Infantry, and on October 1, 1814, promoted to captain. He served under General Andrew Jackson, and fought in the battle of New Orleans on January 8, 1815. On June 15 of that year he was honorably discharged,[12] thus ending his military career. As happened in his previous separation from the Army, he again turned to trading with the Indians as a means of livelihood. Consequently, not long after his discharge he formed a partnership with Samuel B. Richards and opened a trading house at Arkansas Post on the lower Arkansas River, under the name of Pryor & Richards, to trade with the Arkansas Osages. Samuel M. Rutherford was employed as clerk.[13]

Early in 1817, the partners bought a five-acre tract of land at Arkansas Post from Alexis Jordelias and wife. In March, 1819, Thomas Nuttall met Pryor and Richards descending the Arkansas River to New Orleans with cargoes of furs and peltries gotten in trade with the Osages.[14] On November 28, 1819, he secured a license from acting Governor Robert Crittenden of Arkansas Territory to trade with the Osages at Arkansas Post and to ascend the Arkansas River with one boatload of goods to the mouth of "Six Bull" (Neosho) or the Verdigris.

On January 1, 1820, Harold Stilwell, having bought Richards' interest in the tract of land, served notice in the *Arkansas Gazette* on Pryor and George R. Sampson that he

[11] *Ibid.*, 157.

[12] *Ibid.*, 162; Thomas James, *Three Years among the Indians* (Chicago, 1953), 5-6.

[13] Foreman, *op cit.*, 153.   [14] *Ibid.*, 154.

would petition the court to appoint commissioners to make partition of the five-acre tract of land. In the same issue was a notice that Samuel M. Rutherford had sued Pryor, the surviving partner in Pryor & Richards, for $630 in wages and $1,000 damages. In the January, 1821, term of the Arkansas County Court, Alexis Jordelias sued him and Sampson to recover $92.90 on a note given by them and Samuel B. Richards on April 23, 1817, probably in connection with the land they bought from him and his wife. Judgement of $300 was asked and an attachment issued upon the property of Pryor and Sampson.[15]

Evidently the operation of the business at Arkansas Post, like every one in which Pryor engaged, was not successful. After the death of Richards he exercised his rights under his license from acting Governor Crittenden, moved up the Arkansas and built a small trading post a mile and a half above the mouth of the Verdigris River. Here Thomas Nuttall found him in May, 1821. He was also there in August when General Thomas James arrived by water from St. Louis to make final preparations for his journey to Santa Fe.[16] When the General discovered the Arkansas River was not navigable to a point sixty miles from Taos, New Mexico, as he had been told, Pryor assisted him in buying twenty-three horses from the Osages to carry his goods. Then, accompanied by forty Osage hunters on their way to buffalo country, he traveled two days with the General.[17]

From September 20, 1821, when Pryor went out with the hunters, until December 10 of the same year, when he returned, he was with the Osages, possibly somewhere along the Canadian River. About this time he married an Osage woman, installed her in his trading post, and frequently represented the Osages in adjusting numerous difficulties

[15] *Ibid.,* 153.   [16] *Ibid.,* 155.

[17] James, *op. cit.,* 115-16, 119; "Union Mission Journal," in *American Missionary Register,* II, Sept. 12, 20, 28, 1821; July 6, 1822.

between them and other tribes and white people. In this capacity he worked intimately with Clermont, "Builder of Towns," and made many trips to Fort Smith, to the Cherokees in present Pope County, Arkansas, and to Fort Gibson after it was built in 1824. After Union Mission was established in 1820 he rendered the missionaries valuable assistance on many occasions. For about a decade, at his own expense, and at considerable inconvenience to himself, he served both Indians and government as unofficial, unpaid Osage sub-agent. Even after another had been appointed to that post he cheerfully continued to serve his adopted people.[18]

Pryor, perhaps more than any other white man, had the complete confidence and respect of Indians, military authorities, government representatives, and other white people.[19] At length, in 1830, owing to his great influence with his savage friends in general, and his command of the Osage language, Governor Clark, who was Superintendent of Indian Affairs at St. Louis, gave him a temporary appointment as sub-agent for Clermont's band of Arkansas Osages at $500 per year.[20] When the post became vacant through the death of the regular sub-agent, Pryor's friends unsuccessfully undertook to secure his appointment to that position.

On June 6, 1827, Governor George Izard of Arkansas wrote a strong letter of recommendation, urging Pryor's appointment as sub-agent to live with Clermont's band.[21] Colonel Matthew Arbuckle, commandant at Fort Gibson, on July 3, 1827, wrote to Governor Clark saying that Pryor would be of great service in making and preserving peace between the Osages and their enemies the Choctaws, Cher-

---

[18] Foreman, *op. cit.*, 155; W. Julian Fessler, "Jacob Fowler Journal," in *Chronicles of Oklahoma*, VIII.

[19] Foreman, *op. cit.*, 155.   [20] *Ibid.*, 159.   [21] *Ibid.*, 160.

okees, Kickapoos, Delawares, Shawnees, and other bands.[22]
He said he had been making efforts to bring them all together at Fort Towson in a peace conference, and believed
Pryor could render valuable service in promoting such a
desirable meeting. He further said that if he were permanently located at Clermont's village as sub-agent he had
it in his power to do more good than any man he knew.
Nothing came of these recommendations and Pryor had the
disappointment of seeing another and less able man installed
in his stead.

In 1830, as mentioned above, the sub-agency at Clermont's village having again become vacant, Pryor was
appointed to it. He did not serve long, however, for he died
at his post of duty about June 1, 1831.[23] The town of Pryor,
Oklahoma, and nearby Pryor Creek, perpetuate his name.

22 *Ibid.*, 161; John Joseph Mathews, *The Osages, Children of the Middle Waters* (Oklahoma City, 1961), 431, 434, 478, 506, 508.

23 Foreman, *op. cit.*, 155; James, *op. cit.*, 117; "United States Indian Agencies Affecting Kansas," in Kansas Historical *Collections* (Topeka, 1925), XVI, p. 724.

Nathaniel Miguel Pryor

by RAYMOND W. SETTLE
Monte Vista, Colorado

Nathaniel Miguel Pryor (1798-1850), silversmith, clock-maker and trapper, was born in Kentucky near the falls of the Ohio (Louisville).[1] He moved to Missouri in 1820,[2] but where he located is not known. Nothing concerning his parentage, family, early childhood or young manhood has been found. What his relation to ex-sergeant Nathaniel Pryor was is not known. The next authentic information we have of him is that in the early fall of 1821 he was in the Fort Smith country, in the vicinity of the Hugh Glenn, Joseph Bougie (Bogy?), and Nathaniel Pryor trading posts.[3]

When Jacob Fowler, second in command of the Glenn-Fowler expedition of that year, made up the official roster of members he included "Nat Pryer," whose name he mentioned three times in his *Journal* and misspelled a different way each time.[4] When Elliot Coues edited Fowler's document in 1898 he erroneously identified this man as ex-sergeant Nathaniel Pryor of the Lewis and Clark expedition, 1804-1806, and formerly captain in the United States Army, possibly on the basis of the similarity of names. The Glenn-Fowler expedition set out from Glenn's trading post on September 25, 1821, ascended the Arkansas River and

---

[1] Kate L. Gregg, *The Road to Santa Fe* (Albuquerque, 1952), 255.

[2] *Ibid.*, 255; H. H. Bancroft, *History of California* (San Francisco, 1886), IV, p. 785.

[3] Jacob Fowler, *Journal of* (New York, 1898), 5.

[4] *Ibid.*, 5, 61, 155-6. W. B. Douglas, editor of Thomas James, *Three Years among the Indians and Mexicans* (Chicago, 1953), makes no mention whatever of Nathaniel Miguel Pryor, and follows Coues in identifying Fowler's "Nat Pryer or Priar" as the ex-sergeant of the Lewis and Clark Expedition. Fowler, *op. cit.*, 4.

reached the site of present Nepesta, Colorado, on November 20.[5]

From that camp, on December 3, 1821, a trapping party of five men under Isaac Slover was sent upstream to the Sangre de Cristo Mountains to trap beaver. One of these was Nathaniel Miguel Pryor, Fowler's "Nat Pryer." At that time, and since September 20, Captain Pryor had been with the Osage Indians on their annual fall hunt, perhaps on the Canadian River some five hundred miles to the southeast. The Slover trapping party returned on January 11[6] after almost a month and a half of unsuccessful work, and on January 30 the expedition set out for Taos,[7] where it was divided into three parties, one of which was again under command of Isaac Slover. Pryor was very likely a member of it. All of them followed the Rio Grande upstream to the San Luis Valley, where they remained until the latter part of April, 1822, when they returned to Taos to make preparations for their homeward journey.[8]

On June 1, 1822, the Glenn-Fowler expedition, accompanied by that of General Thomas James, set out for Missouri.[9] While in camp in the vicinity of present Syracuse, Kansas, Fowler wrote that Nathaniel Miguel Pryor and George Douglas left the expedition and joined that of James. Two days later they returned to their own party.[10] This was the last time Fowler mentions Pryor in his *Journal*. Nothing is known of his activities for about three years.

In the summer of 1825 he was again in the Fort Smith-Verdigris area, possibly at ex-captain Pryor's trading post, where he and three unnamed trappers outfitted themselves to go to New Mexico along the route of the Glenn-Fowler expedition of 1821.[11] On August 27, near the mouth of

---

5 Fowler, *op. cit.*, 61. This could not have been ex-sergeant Nathaniel Pryor, for on this date he was nearing Union Mission on his return from the Osages' fall hunt. "Union Mission Journal" in *American Missionary Register*, II, Dec. 10, 1821.

6 Fowler, *op. cit.*, 83.   7 *Ibid.*, 95.   8 *Ibid.*, 136-7.

9 *Ibid.*, 142-3.   10 *Ibid.*, 155-6.   11 Gregg, *op. cit.*, 70.

Walnut Creek, at the top of the big bend in the Arkansas River, they found the camp of Commissioners George C. Sibley, Benjamin Reeves, and Thomas Mather who were engaged in surveying and marking the Santa Fe Trail.[12]

Since both parties were following the same route, Pryor and his companions traveled with Sibley's party for almost a week. The Sibley expedition halted at the Caches, and Pryor went on to Santa Fe, his party enlarged to six by the addition of two of Sibley's men, Dudley Dedmon and George West.[13] If he took his small party out on a trapping expedition that fall, nothing is known of it. Bancroft says he spent four years in New Mexico,[14] but unfortunately does not say which years they were.

In September, 1827, a party of thirty trappers, to operate on the Gila and Colorado Rivers, was formed in Santa Fe. Among them were Sylvester Pattie and his fifteen-year-old son, James Ohio, William Pope, James Puter, Richard Laughlin, Isaac Slover, and Nathaniel Miguel Pryor. Sylvester Pattie was elected captain. They set out on September 23 and reached the Gila on October 6. On November 27 the party divided. The seven above-named men remained with the Patties and continued trapping down the Gila with several horses to carry their furs. On a December night, 1827, Indians stampeded their animals and drove them all off.[15]

With no means of transportation they buried their furs and set out on foot across a heat-tormented desert for California. After twenty-four days of indescribable suffering from heat, thirst, starvation, and exhaustion they arrived at Santa Catalina Mission on March 12, 1828. Ten days later they were arrested, taken to Los Angeles and thrown into solitary confinement. Sylvester Pattie died, and James

12 *Ibid.*, 8.   13 *Ibid.*, 81.   14 Bancroft, *op. cit.*, 185.
15 James Ohio Pattie, *Personal Narrative* (New York, 1962: ed. by William H. Goetzman), 120-21, 125-6; Bancroft, *op. cit.*, III, p. 163.

said he effected the release of the others by vaccinating twenty-two thousand Indians and Spaniards at the request of the governor.[16]

Upon gaining his freedom, Nathaniel Miguel Pryor worked for a time at San Luis Rey Mission, north of San Diego. In 1829 he received a carta (letter of recommendation) from the governor. From 1830 he lived in Los Angeles, where he practiced the trades of silversmith and clockmaking, and hunted otter along the coast.[17] The Californians called him Miguel, and he sometimes wrote his name Miguel N. Pryor.

In 1836 he received a certificate of long residence and good character from the *ayuntimento,* and a few years later married a Señorita Sepulveda, who died in 1840. He served against Micheltorena in 1845, commanded a company of artillery in 1846, and the following year he was arrested for aiding the Americans in the Flores revolt. In 1847 he was an alderman in Los Angeles. He died in 1850.[18]

---

16 Pattie, *op. cit.,* 139-51, 155, 167, 198; Bancroft, *op. cit.,* 163, 168-70, 393.

17 In the Stearns Papers, Box 71 (Huntington Library) is a receipt dated Aug. 31, 1833, from Abel Stearns for $160, payment in full to Pryor for ten otter skins.

18 Bancroft, *op. cit.,* 785; Gregg, *op. cit.,* 255.

John Baptiste Richard

by JOHN DISHON McDERMOTT
National Park Service

John Baptiste Richard * was born in St. Charles, Missouri, in 1810, the first son of John Baptiste and Rosalie Cote Richard. Two brothers followed him, Peter in 1820 and Joseph in 1823.[1] Of French descent, Richard's ancestors evidently migrated to the New World in the first decades of the eighteenth century. Moving into the Mississippi River Valley, they settled in Kaskaskia, Cohokia, and Vincennes; in 1791, a John Baptiste Richard, probably Richard's grandfather, crossed the river and settled at New Madrid in what is now the state of Missouri.[2]

---

* I wish to acknowledge the great contribution of Mr. Frank Aplan of Rushville, Nebraska, to this article. Without him it could not have been written. My knowledge of the Richard family structure is based on interviews of the direct descendants of both John and Joseph Richard by Mr. Aplan. Generous with the materials he has collected on the family, Mr. Aplan has also provided advice and insights that cannot be emphasized too much.

[1] The name is pronounced "Reshaw," and is a corruption of the original French pronunciation. The uvular "r" apparently proved too difficult for the American-born Richards, and they settled for the "w" which comes fairly close to the correct sound. There is some question concerning the correct date of Richard's birth. His age is given as fifty in the 1860 Denver Census and sixty in the 1870 Fort Laramie Census, but his parents were married in the Catholic Church in St. Charles on January 7, 1812, according to O. W. Collet's *Index to St. Charles Marriages*. Richard's direct descendants – Mrs. William McGaa, Mrs. William Tibbits, and Mrs. William Swallow – contend that John, Peter, and Joseph were full brothers. The birth dates of Peter and Joseph are recorded in Collet's *Index to St. Charles Baptisms,* but no mention is made of John. Richard may have been born out of wedlock, or more probably, his parents, following the custom of the time, lived as man and wife under common law until they could have the marriage sanctioned by the church.

[2] The first recorded mention of the family in the Mississippi River Valley occurs in 1738. In that year, Jean Baptiste Richard, a Kaskaskia merchant, killed Henri Cotan in a drunken brawl. Tried for murder, the court acquitted him on grounds of self defense. Referred to as "La Parisien," he undoubtedly migrated from Paris or vicinity. See Natalia Maree Belting, *Kaskaskia Under the French Regime* (Urbana,

Richard came to the fur trade naturally. While he was growing to manhood, his relatives roamed the wild regions from Mexico to Canada in search of beaver. In February, 1819, Cabanne and Company designated one of the Richards to share the responsibility of the command of its Upper Missouri River operations, and in March of the same year, Thomas Nuttall met another Richard in central Arkansas, loaded with furs obtained by trade with the Osages.[3] In the early 1830s, Noel Richard worked for the American Fur Company near Fort Tecumseh, and in 1832, Richard's father seriously considered a trip west for William Sublette.[4]

Leaving St. Charles, Richard went west in the late 1830s. In 1840, he formed a partnership with A. M. Metcalf and bartered for furs in the Rocky Mountains.[5] In early 1842 he became an employee of Sybille and Adams, owners of

Ill., 1948), 94. Cahokia records contain a number of references to a Pierre Richard during the period 1778 to 1790. See Clarence W. Alvord (ed.), "Cahokia Records, 1778-1790," *Collections of the Illinois Historical Society*, v [The Virginia Series, II] (Springfield, 1907), 347 ff. The John Baptiste Richard who settled in New Madrid came from Vincennes. Since he brought his wife with him, it is unlikely that he was Richard's father, but he may very well have been his grandfather. See Louis Houck, *The Spanish Regime in Missouri* (Chicago, 1909), I, p. 328.

[3] Letter from Cabanne and Company to John Dougherty, *et. al.,* February, 1819, Charles Gratiot Letterbook, Charles Gratiot Collection, Missouri Historical Society, cited in Richard E. Oglesby, *Manuel Lisa and the Opening of the Missouri Fur Trade* (Norman, Okla., 1963), 171; Thomas Nuttall, "Journal of Travels into the Arkansas Territory During the Year 1819," in *Early Western Travels, 1748-1849,* ed. by Ruben G. Thwaites (Cleveland, 1905), XIII, pp. 138-9.

[4] Charles E. Deland and Doane Robinson (eds.), "Fort Tecumseh and Fort Pierre Journal and Letter Books," *South Dakota Historical Collections*, IX (Pierre, 1918), 144. (Hereafter cited as *SDHC,* IX.) Letter from William Sublette to William Ashley, April, 1832, Sublette Papers, Missouri Historical Society, courtesy of LeRoy R. Hafen. Sublette ordered Ashley to give Madam Richard $10 three months from the date of the letter, if John Richard kept an agreement, apparently to go to the mountains.

[5] *Missouri Argus,* July 9, 1840, cited in Louise Barry (comp.), "Kansas Before 1854: A Revised Annals," *Kansas Historical Quarterly,* XXIX (Autumn, 1963), 334. Metcalf proved undesirable to Indian agents on the Upper Missouri, and in 1843 they refused him permission to trade with the Sioux near Fort Laramie. See *SDHC,* IX, pp. 186-7.

Fort Platte, an adobe-walled trading post built in 1841 on the south bank of the North Platte River about a mile from the mouth of the Laramie. Richard soon became the firm's most trusted employee, and in the spring of 1842 he accompanied Sybille and Adams to St. Louis to sell their buffalo robes.[6] The next year, he commanded the expeditions taking robes east. Leaving Fort Platte on May 7 with five or six wagons, he reached Missouri in two months.[7]

Not far from Fort Platte stood Fort John, commonly referred to as Fort Laramie. Owned by the powerful American Fur Company, Fort John engaged in a deadly struggle with its neighbor post for trade in robes, skins, and furs.[8] Intense competition led to the excessive use of alcohol in the Indian trade.[9] Richard seems to have been assigned to the purchase of liquor for Fort Platte, and he rapidly gained a reputation for smuggling alcohol in from the New Mexican settlements.

In 1842 the American Fur Company succeeded in having one of its men, Andrew Drips, appointed Indian Agent for

[6] Two heavily loaded boats left Fort Platte pointed for St. Louis on May 7. The traders hoped to float their cargo down the Platte on the spring rise to the Missouri, and then on to the fur trading capital. The Platte, however, proved impossible, and after two hundred agonizing miles of dragging the boats over the shallow stream, the boat crews cached the robes on the river bank and sent word back to the post of their failure. Obtaining wagons, Adams, Sybille, and Richard collected the robes and personally escorted them to St. Louis. See LeRoy R. and Ann W. Hafen (eds.), *Rufus B. Sage, His Letters and . . . reprint of "Scenes in the Rocky Mountains,"* [*Far West and the Rockies Historical Series,* v] (Glendale, Calif., 1956), II, pp. 19-34; Letter from William Sublette to William Drummond Stewart, September, 1842, Sublette Papers, cited in LeRoy R. Hafen and Francis M. Young, *Fort Laramie and the Pageant of the West, 1834-1890* (Glendale, 1938), 80.

[7] *New York Spectator,* July 19, 1843, courtesy of LeRoy R. Hafen; Harrison C. Dale (ed.), "A Fragmentary Journal of William Sublette," *Mississippi Valley Historical Review,* VI (June, 1919), 110.

[8] During the first few years of its existence, Fort Platte competed very successfully with Fort John. In August of 1843, Theodore Talbot wrote that the smaller post was more active and that Indians were continually about. Charles C. Carey (ed.), *The Journals of Theodore Talbot, 1843 and 1849-1852.* (Portland, 1931), 34.

[9] Rufus Sage ably chronicles the quarrels, brawls, and deaths resulting from the liquor trade. For a particularly vivid description see Hafen, *Sage,* I, pp. 224-7.

the Upper Missouri.[10] Drips, in turn, selected another
American Fur Company employee, Joseph Hamilton, as
sub-agent for the Laramie region.[11] During the winter of
1842-1843, Richard used liberal quantities of alcohol in his
trade with the Sioux on the north forks of the Cheyenne
River, and the loss of life in consequence stirred Drips to
action. He ordered his sub-agent to make an autumnal raid
on Fort Platte, hoping to catch the bootleggers with a fresh
supply of liquor brought in for the winter trade.[12]

During the summer of 1843, Bernard Pratte and John
Cabanne became the owners of Fort Platte, and Richard,
Hamilton's main target, became unemployed.[13] The raid,
however, occurred as scheduled. In early September Hamilton made his move, but the Fort Platte traders, learning of
his mission, moved the liquor cached in the post and hid it
elsewhere, escaping detection.[14] When Richard returned to
the Laramie region shortly thereafter, he reached an agreement with Pratte and Cabanne. On November 5 they requested permission from Drips to include Richard under
their trading license and apparently received it.[15]

---

[10] Drips (1789-1860) was thoroughly acquainted with the country and the mechanics of the fur trade. While not deliberately using his official position to aid his
old company, he did grant the firm every opportunity to compete equally with rival
companies. Shortly after his appointment Drips received a letter from D. D. Mitchell,
Superintendent of Indian Affairs, instructing him to make the liquor trade one of
his main concerns. Hiram M. Chittenden, *The American Fur Trade of the Far West*
(Stanford, Calif., 1954), I, p. 368; Mitchell to Drips, St. Louis, October 6, 1842,
SDHC, IX, pp. 173-4.

[11] Joseph V. Hamilton (1811-1867) after his appointment as sub-agent still continued in the service of the American Fur Company and found it impossible not to
look out for the interests of the firm. *SDHC,* IX, fn. 189, p. 177.

[12] Letter from Honore Picotte to Hamilton, Fort Pierre, April 30, 1843, *SDHC,* IX,
p. 181; Chittenden, *Fur Trade,* I, p. 369.

[13] Letter from John Hill to Drips, Fort John, September 17, 1843, and letter from
Drips to Mitchell, Fort Pierre, September 7, 1843, Drips Papers, Missouri Historical
Society, cited in Hafen and Young, *Fort Laramie,* 85.

[14] Letter from Hamilton to Drips, Fort John, October 7, 1843, *SDHC,* IX, pp. 196-
7; Chittenden, *Fur Trade,* I, p. 369; affidavit of John Hill, Fort John, September 17,
1843; letter from O. Sarpy, September 7, 1843; letter from A. R. Bouis, Fort Pierre,
October 4, 1843, Missouri Historical Society Papers, cited in Hafen and Young, *Fort
Laramie,* 87.

About this time, Richard married Mary Gardiner, a half-blood living with the Northern Ogalalas or Smoke People, and cemented an alliance with that tribe that was to last until his death. They were to have six children: John, Jr., Louis, Peter, Charles, Josephine, and Rosalie.[16]

The Fort Platte traders did well during the winter of 1843-1844, utilizing the liquor brought in by Richard from Taos and that which escaped Hamilton, but the next winter

---

[15] Most scholars follow Chittenden in assuming that Richard was in the employ of Pratte and Cabanné in September and October of 1843. This interpretation of the facts, however, is subject to serious questioning. The fact that Pratte and Cabanné asked for permission to include Richard under their license on November 5, is difficult to explain unless one accepts their statement that they had actually "engaged" him that very day. It seems illogical to assume that Richard would not have been included under the license from the very beginning if he were truly an employee, since he was a trader by profession and a trader that got results. It is even more difficult to assume it when one learns that Cabanné reached Fort Platte in early October with twenty licensed traders. On November 4, Drips wrote Hamilton and told him that he had every reason to believe that Richard recently brought a good supply of liquor into the area, and mentioned the activities of Richard, Sybille, and Pratte and Cabanné as if they were three different concerns. A more logical explanation would be that Richard was in Missouri selling robes for Sybille and Adams when he learned that Pratte and Cabanné would become the operators of Fort Platte, that he took his pay and used it to buy liquor in New Mexico, that he returned to the Laramie region in mid-October and began operating independently and without a license on the north forks of the Cheyenne, that because of the raid on Fort Platte he realized Hamilton meant business, and that he made a deal with Pratte and Cabanné for legitimacy. Chittenden, *Fur Trade*, I, pp. 368-9; letter from Hamilton to Drips, October 7; Drips to Hamilton, Fort Pierre, November 4; and Pratte and Cabanné to Drips, Abbott's Wintering Ground, November 5, 1843, *SDHC*, IX, pp. 196-7, 177-9, 175.

In Hamilton's letter of October 7, he described the places authorized to Pratte and Cabanné for trading under the license: "Cheyenne River, the forks of Cheyenne and Old Woman's Fork, Bute Range on the north fork of the Platte the Platte river, on Laramie Fork at the mouth of the Chug Water, at Yibeles Hile [Sibille's Hole], on the headwaters on the Chug on Horse creek, on Cannon Ball river, Hot River, Apple River and Beaver river, on the Arkansas river, on White River, and at such other points as the mutual interest of the Indians and traders Messrs. Pratte & Cabanne may render necessary which shall be designated [by] the upper Missouri agent."

[16] The Writings of Alice Brown, MS, in the possession of her daughter, Mrs. Ben Swallow, Chadron, Nebraska. Alice Brown was the oldest girl of Josephine Richard and Big Bat Pourier. Interviews by Frank Aplan with the surviving Pourier girls, Mrs. William McGaa, Mrs. William Tibbits, and Mrs. William Swallow.

Fort John began to emerge triumphant in the contest.[17] The pressure applied by the sub-agent and the greater financial resources of the American Fur Company were probably factors in the victory. Whatever the reasons, Pratte and Cabanne abandoned their post during the summer of 1845. Acting for the company, Joseph Bissonette took the goods left over from the spring trade and moved down the North Platte to a point about eight miles east of Fort John where he established another post, named Fort Bernard after Pratte.[18] In December, Honore Picotte of the American Fur Company post, Fort Pierre, reported that he had succeeded in buying out the Pratte and Cabanne interest at Fort Bernard and that the two traders were glad to be out of the business.[19]

The American Fur Company found Richard less cooperative. Occupying the half-finished log fort, he carried on a brisk winter trade much to the annoyance of Picotte. The Fort Pierre manager declared that Richard and the other Taos peddlers obtained many of the good robes by trading corn for them and recommended that five hundred bushels be sent to Fort John.[20] Richard's partners in the enterprise were his brother Peter, Joseph Bissonette, a Mr. Branham of Kentucky, and one of the Bordeaux. On June 11, 1846, Edwin Bryant met some of Richard's partners near Grand Island, Nebraska, navigating two mackinaw boats loaded with buffalo robes, bound for the nearest port on the Missouri.[21]

---

17 Cabanné reported trading successful on the North Platte during the winter of 1843-44, and on June 21, 1844, six mackinaw boats loaded with pelts reached St. Louis from the post. *Niles Register*, May 4, 1844, p. 160 and *St. Louis Reveille*, June 22, 1844, cited in Hafen and Young, *Fort Laramie*, 88-9.

18 Letter from A. R. Bouis to Honore Picotte, Fort Pierre, August 31, 1845, *SDHC*, IX, p. 206.

19 Letter from Honore Picotte to James Kipp, Fort Pierre, December 18, 1845; Fort Pierre Letter Books, 1845-1846, Missouri Historical Society.

20 Letter from Honore Picotte to Pierre Chouteau, Jr., Fort Pierre, March 11, 1846; Fort Pierre Letter Books.

In the spring of 1846, the Indian trade having been completed, Richard and his partners concentrated on the emigrant trade. Here, too, they competed successfully with Fort John, using another technique. They simply undersold the powerful rival, at times by thirty or forty per cent.[22]

Francis Parkman reached Fort Bernard on June 15 and found Richard a typical mountain man. He wore a shirt, leggings, and moccasins made of deer skin, gaily ornamented with dyed porcupine quills. Although small, he possessed an athletic form, lean but well-muscled. His hair, which fell down below his shoulders, was black, curly, and parted in the middle. His eyes were black and his complexion swarthy.[23]

In late June, the main party of emigrants swept by Fort Bernard and Fort John,[24] and on July 10, Richard left his post to make his annual pilgrimage to New Mexico for liquor.[25] Several days before, he met the Crosby-Brown party of Mississippi Mormons who planned to winter on the east side of the mountains. Richard recommended Pueblo and became their guide, proving a faithful and able pilot according to Brown.[26]

[21] Edwin Bryant, *What I Saw in California*, etc. (London, 1849), 65-7. For Bryant's description of Fort Bernard and its inhabitants see pp. 88, 93-4. In his journal, Parkman indicates that Joseph Bissonette was one of the main partners. See Mason Wade (ed.), *Journals of Francis Parkman* (N.Y., 1947), II, p. 494.

[22] Richard charged ten cents less a pound for flour and three and one half cents less a pound for bacon. Wade (ed.), *Parkman Journals*, 494, 617-18, 627.

[23] Francis Parkman, *The Oregon Trail* (New York, 1949), 89. For Parkman's description of Fort Bernard and its inhabitants see pp. 88-91 and 120-3.

[24] For other accounts of the activities of emigrants at Fort Bernard see Bernard DeVoto, *The Year of Decision, 1846* (Boston, 1943), 178-86; letter from George L. Curry to the *St. Louis Reveille*, Fort Bernard, June 25, 1846, reproduced in Charles L. Camp, *James Clyman Frontiersman, 1792-1881* (Portland, 1960), 232-4.

[25] Parkman, *Oregon Trail*, 283. Santa Fe and Taos were the great centers for the barter of alcohol by traders. See letter from Drips to Thomas H. Harvey, Superintendent of Indian Affairs, Fort Pierre, April 11, 1845, reproduced in Chittenden, *Fur Trade*, I, p. 369.

[26] John Brown's journal, quoted in LeRoy R. Hafen and Francis M. Young, "The Mormon Settlement at Pueblo, Colorado, During the Mexican War," *The Colorado Magazine*, IX (July, 1932), 124.

On August 20, Parkman found Richard in Pueblo quartered in the trappers' stockade. Prevented from reaching Taos because of the Mexican War, Richard stayed in Pueblo to await the cessation of hostilities.[27] During his absence, Fort Bernard burned to the ground.[28] The reasons for its destruction are not known, but Richard must have suspected the American Fur Company.

During the next six years, Richard continued to trade on a small scale at various sites along the North Platte and the Laramie. In 1848, Joseph Robidoux supplied the backing for his trade in buffalo robes, and, as in the past, Richard obtained corn from Kansas to supplement regular trade items.[29] In 1850 he apparently had a trading post at Ash Point about twenty miles below Fort Laramie,[30] but sold his interest to Seth Ward and William Guerrier early in 1851.[31]

In the early 1850s, Richard branched out into other business activities. Forming a partnership with a French-Canadian named Monterevier, Richard began farming above Fort Laramie. Prince Paul Wilhelm of Wurttenberg visited the farm in October, 1851, and viewed the entrepreneurs' corn field, vegetable garden, and orchard.[32] At

27 Parkman, *Oregon Trail*, 283-5.

28 Journal of Thomas Bullock, cited in Hafen and Young, *Fort Laramie*, 123.

29 Letters of Benjamin Harding to Joseph Ribidoux, Great Nemahaw Sub Agency, Kansas, May 2, May 31, and June 6, 1848, reproduced in Hoover H. Jordan (ed.), "The Letter Books of Benjamin Harding (Part II)," *Nebraska History*, XXXVI (December, 1955), 264, 267-8.

30 Howard Stansbury, *Exploration and Survey of the Valley of the Great Salt Lake of Utah* (Philadelphia, 1852), 288; Robert W. Richmond, "Developments Along the Overland Trail From the Missouri River to Fort Laramie, Before 1854," *Nebraska History*, XXXIII (September, 1952), fn. 75, p. 174; Merrill J. Mattes, "Robidoux's Trading Post at Scott's Bluff and the California Gold Rush," *Nebraska History*, XXX (June, 1949), 120-1.

31 Letter from John S. Tutt to John Dougherty, Fort Laramie, May 21, 1851, Dougherty Papers, Missouri Historical Society.

32 Louis C. Butscher, "A Brief Biography of Prince Paul Wilhelm of Wurttenberg (1797-1860)," *New Mexico Historical Review*, XVII (July, 1942), 209-10; Paul C. Phillips and J. W. Smurr, *The Fur Trade* (Norman, Okla., 1961), II, p. 544.

the same time, Richard entered the ferrying and bridge building business with Langdon, Steele, Miller, and Randall.[33]

Early in 1851 the partners raised eight thousand dollars and built two bridges, one over the Laramie near Fort Laramie, now a military post, and one over the North Platte near the mouth of Deer Creek one hundred miles west.[34] Post trader John Tutt of Fort Laramie declared that both bridges were poorly built, and when his wagons crossed the one over the Platte in early May, it sank four feet. James Frear reached the Platte bridge during high water on June 2, 1852, and decided not to cross it, fearing that it was unsafe. In July diarists mentioned only the remains of a bridge.[35]

Because the Laramie bridge was inside the military reservation, the Post Council of Administration probably regulated the toll. The price for wagons fluctuated between two and three dollars. In 1853 the spring flood swept the structure away, and since Richard and his partners had done little to keep it in good repair, Fort Laramie's commanding officer recommended that another company be given the contract for a new bridge.[36]

Early in 1853 Richard and his companions built another

[33] Tutt to Dougherty, May 21, 1851.

[34] The Fort Laramie Council of Administration authorized the construction of the bridge on December 28, 1850, and the traders built it about one hundred yards down river from the post. See Merrill J. Mattes and Thor Borresen, "The Historic Approaches to Fort Laramie (Fort Laramie National Historic Site, 1947)," MS, 30. On March 22, 1851, the *Missouri Republican* announced that, "a fine and substantial bridge has been built over the Platte 100 miles above Laramie." See Albert Watkins (ed.), "Notes of the Early History of the Nebraska Country," *Nebraska State Historical Society Publications,* xx (Lincoln, 1922), 232. Hereafter cited as *NSHS,* xx.

[35] Tutt to Dougherty, May 21, 1851; Paul Henderson, "The River Crossings on the North Platte (Emigrant Trail Trek No. 10)," *Annals of Wyoming,* xxxii (October, 1960), 225.

[36] Mattes and Borresen, "Historic Approaches," 30; letter from Richard B. Garnett to Adjutant General Samuel Cooper, Fort Laramie, July 24, 1853, Records of the Office of the Quartermaster General, Consolidated Correspondence File, Fort Laramie, Record Group 92, National Archives.

bridge over the North Platte near the present town of
Evansville, Wyoming. This time the men built a more
substantial bridge; at least those who crossed it in 1853
applauded its strength. Count Leonetto Cipriani crossed
the bridge in June and stated that it consisted of twelve
arches made from cedar and had piers formed of huge tree
trunks filled with gravel.[37] During the next few years,
Richard evidently bought out his partners, for travelers
make no mention of them.

After 1853 Richard lived near the bridge with his half-
breed family. He constructed a log cabin, a blacksmith
shop, and a few other buildings on the south side of the
river. He named his own price for crossing the bridge, and
during high water travelers had little choice but to pay it.
The standard fee for wagons was five dollars, and he
usually charged four dollars for every hundred head of
stock. If the water level was so low that emigrants might
take a chance in fording the stream, he would reduce the
price for wagons to three dollars and sometimes to two
dollars.

Richard normally received payment in cash, but he was
willing to accept goods for the toll, and he had no difficulty
in securing all the furniture and household implements
that he needed from emigrants. He traded fresh stock for
lame animals and sometimes made a profit of one hundred

<hr>

[37] Olaf T. Hagen, "Platte Bridge Station and Fort Caspar," *Annals of Wyoming,*
XXVII (April, 1955), 7; Ernest Falbo (ed.), *California and Overland Diaries of
Count Leonetto Cipriani From 1853 Through 1871* (Portland, 1962), 89; Thomas
Flint, *Diary* (Los Angeles, 1923), 38; *Daily Missouri Republican,* November 2,
1843 in *NSHS,* XX, p. 252; Dale L. Morgan (ed.), "The Mormon Ferry on the
North Platte: The Journal of William A. Empey, May 7-August 4," *Annals of
Wyoming,* XXI (July-October, 1949), 117. In his history of Natrona County, Wyo-
ming, Alfred J. Mokler made the statement that Richard built the bridge in 1854-
1855, and historians continue to perpetuate the error. See Mokler, *History of Natrona
County, Wyoming, 1888-1922* (Chicago, 1923), 109. For a recent example of the error
see J. W. Vaughn, *The Battle of Platte Bridge* (Norman, 1963), 9.

per cent in a single transaction. During the off season he continued to trade for robes and skins with Red Cloud's band.[38]

Richard prospered at his new business. Traveler William Sloan claimed that Richard had pocketed over forty thousand dollars in tolls by June 11, 1853.[39] He made enough money, at least, to provide Ward and Guerrier with trade goods for the year.[40] The following year was also a profitable one. On June 11, for example, Richard made five hundred dollars by exacting his high water fee from Sarah Sutton's party.[41]

Richard was less fortunate in 1855. In April he lost seventy-five head of horses to pillaging Sioux. After the Battle of Ash Hollow in September, white traders were not safe in Indian country, and Richard fled to Fort Laramie for protection. Major William Hoffman recommended that twenty-five soldiers guard the bridge from harm during the winter, and General Harney agreed. Soldiers dubbed the site Camp Payne. Hoffman told Richard that he could return to his bridge if he promised not to trade with the Indians until peace had been made. Richard refused and spent the winter at the post in a quiet rage,

---

[38] Ward G. and Florence S. DeWitt, *Prairie Schooner Lady: The Journal of Harriet Sherrill Ward, 1853* (Los Angeles, 1959), 87; Mokler, *Natrona County,* 109-10; Sarah Sutton, Diary, MS. in possession of Mrs. Frances T. McBeth, Oakland, Calif. Also pertinent are the following diaries found in the Newberry Library and available in typewritten form at Fort Laramie National Historic Site: Phoebe G. Judson, *A Pioneer's Search,* 41; Helen M. Carpenter, *Overland Journey;* Emily M. Horton, *Our Family,* 27-8; T. J. Ables, *Trip Across the Plains,* 5; and J. A. Wilkinson, *Journal,* 72-3. Occasionally, emigrants rebelled against the high toll and ferried across the river. See C. G. Coutant, *The History of Wyoming* (Laramie, Wyo., 1899), I, pp. 365-7.

[39] William Sloan, "Autobiography of William K. Sloan," *Annals of Wyoming,* IV (July, 1926), 245-6.

[40] Promissory Note, May 20, 1853, John Hunton Papers, Wyoming State Archives and Historical Department, Cheyenne.

[41] Sarah Sutton, Diary, June 11, 1854.

contemplating the profits lost from inactivity.[42] The spring of 1856, however, found him back at the bridge doing a booming business.[43]

During the winter of 1857, Richard again quarreled with the military. In December, General Johnston, commander of the Utah Expedition, ordered thirty rifles seized from his stock of goods. Apparently Richard was keeping the rifles for a Mormon party who planned to return for them in the spring. When Richard appeared at Camp Scott, he declared that the weapons were his private property, and demanded three thousand dollars for them. He was informed that the necessity for their retention had passed and that he might have them again.[44] Richard, however, did make some money because of the Utah Expedition; on May 8, 1858, he sold one hundred head of cattle to the commissary at Camp Scott.[45]

In late June or early July of 1858, Richard learned of the presence of gold near Pike's Peak, apparently through his Indian connections. With some other traders from the Fort Laramie region, he made a trip to the gold fields and took some samples near Cherry Creek. Reaching the Kansas-Nebraska border settlements in late August, he was one of the first men to spread the word of the discovery.[46]

[42] Letter from Major William Hoffman to Assistant Adjutant General of the Sioux Expedition, Fort Laramie, October 15, 1855; letter from Hoffman to Lieutenant James Deshler, Fort Laramie, October 27, 1855; and letters from Lieutenant A. E. Latimer to John Richard, Fort Laramie, December 29 and December 31, Records of the United States Army Commands, Letters Sent, Fort Laramie, Record Group 98, National Archives; Robert Ellison, "The Platte Bridge Fight," *Winners of the West*, III (March 15, 1926), 6-7.

[43] J. Robert Brown, *A Journal of a Trip Across the Plains of the U.S. From Missouri to California, in the Year 1856* (Columbus, Ohio, 1860), 51-2. Brown wrote: "The brothers Richards own the post and bridge here, and are coining money from it; they have made over $200,000 apiece, but that demon, gambling, keeps them down."

[44] Otis G. Hammond (ed.), *The Utah Expedition, 1857-1858: Letters of Capt. Jesse A. Gove*, etc. (Concord, N.H., 1928), 312-13; Records of the Office of the Adjutant General, Fort Laramie Post Returns, July, 1858, Record Group 94, National Archives.

Richard and his brother Joseph returned to Cherry Creek later in the year and built a trading house near the stream, becoming the proprietors of one of the first business establishments in what is now the city of Denver. General William Larimer reported that the Richards had a fine stock of Indian goods and a large herd of beautifully marked ponies. By 1860 the brothers had both a store and saloon on Blake Street.[47]

Joseph ran the store while Richard supervised business operations on the North Platte and made occasional trips to Denver. The brothers suffered heavy losses in the Denver fire of April, 1863, and when Joseph died the following year as the result of a drinking bout, Richard sold what property and stock he may have had left.[48]

At the same time, the bridge business declined because of competition. During the late 1850s Louis Guinard built a new bridge across the North Platte about seven miles above Richard's, and in a few years drew most of the emigrant travel.[49] In addition to tending his bridge during the high

[45] Hammond (ed.), *The Utah Expedition,* 276-7.

[46] Contemporary newspapers carrying stories that mentioned Richard were the *Kansas City Journal of Commerce,* August 26; the *Missouri Republican,* August 29, August 31, and September 1; the *Missouri Democrat,* September 25; the *Boston Journal,* August 31; the *Boston Evening Transcript,* September 1; and the *Omaha Times,* September 8. See *NSHS,* xx, p. 309; James F. Willard, "Spreading the News of the Early Discoveries of Gold in Colorado," *The Colorado Magazine,* vi (May, 1929), 102-3; LeRoy Hafen (ed.), *Colorado Gold Rush: Contemporary Letters and Reports, 1858-1859* [Southwest Historical Series x] (Glendale, 1941), 30-31, 64; LeRoy Hafen (ed.), *Pike's Peak Gold Rush Guidebooks of 1859* [Southwest Historical Series ix] (Glendale, 1941), 72.

[47] J. E. Wharton and D. O. Wilhelm, *History of the City of Denver,* etc. (Denver, 1866), 53-5; *Denver City and Auraria, The Commercial Emporium of the Pike's Gold Regions, in 1859* (n.p., 1859), 26-7, 38; William H. H. Larimer, *Reminiscences of General William Larimer and of His Son,* ed. by Herman S. Davis (Lancaster, Pa., 1918), 154-5; Writings of Alice Brown; interview of Mrs. William McGaa, Mrs. William Tibbits, and Mrs. William Swallow by Frank Aplan, December 1, 1963; interview of Baptiste Pourier by Eli S. Ricker, January 7, 1906, Ricker Collection, Nebraska Historical Society, Lincoln.

[48] Wharton and Wilhelm, *History of Denver,* 109-113; interview of Magloire Alexis Mosseau by Eli S. Ricker, October 30, 1906, Ricker Collection; writings of Alice Brown.

water season, Richard moved from place to place during
the off-season, trading with the Sioux at their camps. When
the army established a sub-post near Guinard's bridge in
May, 1862, Richard supplemented his income by selling
hay to the small garrison and to others nearby.[50]

Richard's last recorded brush with the military occurred
in August, 1864. Soldiers arrested Richard, his family, and
a number of Ogalalas and sent them to Fort Laramie under
guard. The reasons for the arrest are lost to history, but
apparently troops at Platte Bridge Station had engaged
some Ogalalas in a skirmish, and the army hoped to force
the Indians to surrender by holding some of their people
hostage.[51]

In a short time, Richard was free, but the incident evidently drained the last bit of enthusiasm he held for the
Platte Bridge site. In the spring of 1865, he sold his trading
post near the bridge and established a camp on Rock Creek,
about twenty miles west of present-day Laramie. In 1869
he settled near Bordeaux, Wyoming, on the creek that now
bears his name and busied himself raising horses and cattle.[52]

After 1865 Richard took a less active part in the Indian
trade, but financed the operations of his half-breed son,
John, Jr., who traded with the Crows and the Sioux. Like
his father, young Richard sought success in diversity. He

49 Richard Burton, *The Look of the West, 1860: Across the Plains to California*
(Lincoln, 1963), 147; Mokler, *History of Natrona County*, 111; Coutant, *History of
Wyoming*, 367; Ellison, "The Platte Bridge Fight," 6.

50 Telegram from William O. Collins to Lieutenant Glenn, Fort Laramie, November 18, 1862, Telegram Book of the Eleventh Ohio Volunteer Cavalry, October 27,
1862, to April 8, 1863, Colorado State Agricultural College, Fort Collins. For detailed accounts of the military camp at Platte Bridge, see Agnes Wright Spring,
Caspar Collins: The Life and Exploits of an Indian Fighter of the Sixties (New
York, 1928); Alfred J. Mokler, *Fort Caspar: Platte Bridge Station* (Casper, Wyo.,
1939); and Vaughn, *The Battle of Platte Bridge*.

51 Will G. Robinson, "Digest of the Commissioner of Indian Affairs – 1853-1869,"
South Dakota Historical Collections and Report, XXVII, 370-1; George Hyde, *Red
Cloud's Folk: A History of the Oglala Sioux Indians* (Norman, Okla., 1956), 114.

52 Pourier Interview, Ricker Collection; John Hunton, "Reminiscences," *Annals of
Wyoming*, VI (March, 1926), 262.

carted trade goods to Virginia City, Montana, during the gold rush, held the haying contract for Fort Phil Kearney shortly after the Wagon Box Fight, and supplied Fort Fetterman with both wood and hay.[53]

Born to violence, John, Jr., killed a soldier at Fort Fetterman in September of 1869, but through influence escaped prosecution, and by 1871 he had so ingratiated himself with the Indian Bureau that he owned a trading store at Red Cloud Agency.[54] On May 17, 1872, when young Richard murdered Yellow Bear, the brother of two of his former wives, the chief's friends killed him on the spot.[55]

The losses engendered by John, Jr., as the result of his many escapades, left Richard a relatively poor man, and once again he personally led the trading expeditions into Sioux country. During the winter of 1875, Richard and Alfred Palladay started north with a wagon load of trade goods, but death ended the trip on the upper crossing of the Niobrara River. Marauding Cheyennes were evidently the perpetrators of the crime, but several white men were accused, including the famous scout, California Joe.[56]

[53] Pourier Interview, Ricker Collection; Virginia Cole Trenholm, *Footprints on the Frontier* (Douglas, Wyo., 1945), 248; Bickford, "Bickford's Reminiscenses," MS, typewritten copy found in Fort Fetterman Miscellaneous File, Wyoming Archives and Historical Department; letter from W. G. Bullock to Robert Campbell Company, Fort Laramie, April 1, 1869, in Agnes Wright Spring (ed.), "Old Letter Book: Discloses Economic History of Fort Laramie, 1858-1871," *Annals of Wyoming*, XXVII (October, 1941), 292.

[54] Journal of Ada Vogdes, 129, MS., Huntington Library, San Marino, Calif.; Trenholm, *Footprints*, 128; Harry Young, *Hard Knocks: A Life Story of the Vanishing West* (Chicago, 1915), 118. The trading store is shown on a map included by Colonel John Smith, Special Agent, in a letter to Francis Walker, Commissioner of Indian Affairs, November 21, 1871, Red Cloud Agency, Records of the Bureau of Indian Affairs, Red Cloud Agency, Record Group 75, National Archives. Vouchers for everything from cabbage to cattle can be found in the above cited records.

[55] Telegram from D. R. Risley to Francis Walker, May 18, 1872, Red Cloud Agency Records; interview of William Garnett by Eli S. Ricker, January 10, 1907, Ricker Collection.

[56] Interviews of George W. Colhoff, November 22, 1906; Frank Salaway, November 4, 1906; and W. R. Jones, January 23, 1907, by Eli S. Ricker, Ricker Collection; Joe E. Milner and Earle R. Forrest, *California Joe* (Caldwell, Ida., 1935), 278.

Osborne Russell

by AUBREY L. HAINES
Yellowstone National Park

The expedition which left Independence, Missouri, April 28, 1834, bound for the Rocky Mountains and mouth of the Columbia River under command of Nathaniel J. Wyeth, introduced a young New Englander, Osborne Russell, to the fur trade of the northern Rocky Mountains. The journal he kept during his nine years as a trapper was later published,[1] and it remains one of the best accounts of that life to come from the men who waded icy beaver streams in the quest for furs. And yet, had he never written that manuscript, which Archer Butler Hulbert has called "one of the priceless documents of the early West," his subsequent career as a frontier jurist, politician, merchant, and miner would be reason enough to remember him.

Osborne was born at Bowdoinham, Maine, June 12, 1814,[2] to George G. and Eleanor (Power) Russell. He was one of nine children in that family of New Hampshire origin, and his boyhood probably included more farming than schooling. Family tradition says that he, like many New England boys, wanted to go to sea, but that he did not have his father's approval; so he ran away at the age of 16 to be a sailor. Soon discovering he had chosen a harsh career, he deserted the ship with the rest of the crew at New York, and then entered the service of a "Northwest Fur

---

[1] First published for limited private distribution by L. A. York (ed.) as *Journal of a Trapper, or, Nine Years in the Rocky Mountains, 1834-1843* (Boise, Ida., 1914). A second edition (1921) was placed on sale.

Russell's narrative was republished verbatim from the original manuscript by A. L. Haines (ed.) as *Osborne Russell's Journal of a Trapper* (Portland, Ore., 1955).

[2] "Hallowell, Maine, Vital Records," vol. 1 (births), 255.

Trapping and Trading Company," operating at that time
in what is now Wisconsin and Minnesota.[3]

Whatever Russell's employment was during the three
years prior to joining Wyeth's enterprise, the experience
was no particular qualification for the life of a trapper, for
he signed up with the Columbia River Fishing and Trading
Company as an inexperienced hand at a wage of $250 for
eighteen months.[4] From the diary so fortunately begun at
that time, we know that he and his comrades started the
westward march "with joyous hearts enlivened by antic-
ipated prospects," unaware they were embarking upon an
enterprise the scientist, John Townsend, could only describe
as "devoted to destruction."

The touch of springtime was on the Kansas prairies as
Wyeth's expedition passed along the route later made famous
as the Oregon Trail, and all went well until the grand rendezvous of traders, trappers, and Indians was reached on
Ham's Fork of Green River. There the men of the Rocky
Mountain Fur Company refused to take all the merchandise
Wyeth had agreed to bring out to them; as a result, he was
forced to establish a fort on Snake River as a place to dispose
of his surplus goods.

Russell was one of the eleven men left under Robert Evans
to garrison Fort Hall. He languished through a hot summer and a sultry fall at that mismanaged cottonwood stockade he so aptly characterized as "the most lonely and dreary
place I think I ever saw." The occasional meat hunts to
supply the fort's larder broke the boredom and gave a
trapper-in-the-making his first experience with a rifle. A
practical education was also advanced importantly when a
band of Snake Indians came to the fort to trade and pro-

---

[3] L. A. York (ed.), *Journal of a Trapper* . . . (1914), 101.

[4] Although Russell says he joined on April 4, 1834, his wage was computed as
beginning on April 19. See "John Russell in acct Current with C.R.F. & Trading
Co.," pp. 13-14 in Ledger No. 1, Account-books of Fort Hall, 1834-1837 (now in the
collection of the Oregon Historical Society).

vided Russell with a working knowledge of their language in the course of that business.

With the coming of winter, activity increased in the vicinity of Fort Hall. Captain Thing brought men and supplies from the post on the lower Columbia, and many Indians and white trappers established winter quarters in the cottonwood groves of the Fort Hall bottom. Among the latter were some of Jim Bridger's men who came seeking employment in Wyeth's venture, and they brought the experience so sadly lacking in the Columbia River Fishing and Trading Company's ranks.

The direct result was a "spring hunt" fielded in late March, 1835, under the leadership of Joseph Gale.[5] Russell was one of seven camp keepers who accompanied the trappers on the brief circuit which took them through Cache Valley, over the mountains to Bear Lake, northward onto Salt River, and back to the fort by way of the Blackfoot. It was but a brief prelude to a more ambitious "fall hunt" intended to tap the fur resources of the Yellowstone plateau and the headwaters of the Missouri.

Bad luck dogged this latter venture from the beginning. One man was drowned while attempting to cross Snake River near present Swan Valley, Idaho, and another was so seriously wounded in a battle with Blackfoot Indians at Pierre's Hole that the party's progress was greatly impeded. Regardless of that, the hunt was continued: across Teton Pass to a second dangerous crossing of Snake River in Jackson's Hole, and into the mountains southeast of present Yellowstone Park. There Gale became confused and veered eastward onto the headwaters of Wind River, where he lost three men who denied they had reached the Yellowstone.

---

[5] Gale came to Oregon in October, 1834, with a party which included Ewing Young and Hall Kelley. Entering Wyeth's service, he arrived at Fort Hall on December 24, 1834, with the party Captain Thing brought up from Fort William. He was soon trusted with command of trapping parties, though Russell considered him "an arbitrary Rocky Mountain Chieftain."

Much difficult mountain-hopping finally brought the party to their objective, but only after the loss of another trapper while passing down the Lamar River. That, with the desertion of five others three weeks later, so crippled the expedition that Gale should have retreated to Fort Hall; instead he pushed out into acknowledged Blackfoot country on the upper Madison and was again in warfare.

Fortunately for the subject of this sketch, Gale's party met fourteen of Jim Bridger's trappers on the afternoon of September 8, 1835, and that chance reinforcement, which included Kit Carson and Joe Meek,[6] enabled them to fend off an attack by eighty Blackfoot Indians on the following day. But it was a Pyrrhic victory for the men from Fort Hall, for their losses in horses and mules left them unable to move camp except by the kindness of Jim Bridger.

In an attempt to gain an earlier release from that embarrassing predicament, Gale ordered Russell to make the dangerous journey, alone, to Fort Hall for the needed horses. Jim Bridger advised against such foolhardy venturing but Russell went rather than be accused of cowardice. He promptly lost himself among the lava flows and sinks of the Snake River plain, and twenty days in that desolate land completed the hardening of his heart against Joseph Gale and the Columbia River Fishing and Trading Company.

Russell's enlistment had expired by the time he reached Fort Hall,[7] and, as he had determined not to be "kicked over hill and dale" any longer, he took his discharge from Wyeth and departed for "Mutton Hill" on Portneuf River to winter with fifteen of his comrades who had likewise abandoned a discouraging employment. Bad weather drove

---

[6] Meek's vivid description of the battle has been published by Francis Fuller Victor in *River of the West* (Hartford, Conn., 1871), 167-9.

[7] According to an entry in the Account-books of Fort Hall (Ledger No. 1, pp. 119-20), Russell's term of service ended on October 20, 1835, but he did not receive his discharge until December 20, when Nathaniel Wyeth arrived from Fort William on the lower Columbia River.

them out of the mountains the following February, and the group broke up, some returning to Fort Hall and others joining Bridger's company then wintering on Blackfoot River. Russell was among the latter and he was accepted as a full-fledged trapper among those experienced Rocky Mountain hands. His apprenticeship was over.

The following eight years were spent as a trapper in the northern Rocky Mountains. He was associated with the partnership of Fitzpatrick, Sublette and Bridger until that remnant of the old Rocky Mountain Fur Company merged with the American Fur Company; and he was with the latter until after the rendezvous of 1838. Then, as the approaching end of organized American enterprise in the mountains was rumored about, Russell turned to the life of a free-trapper with Fort Hall as his base.

His movements during those years are recorded in detail in *Journal of a Trapper* and so can be passed over briefly. Beginning with a spring hunt which worked the country upon the headwaters of Gray's Creek and Blackfoot River, Bridger's trappers drifted eastward along Bear River to the valley of the Green, reaching the appointed rendezvous on Horse Creek on June 28, 1836. That gathering of hunters and Indians was treated to some sights which were novel in the Rocky Mountains: for the first time the supplies from the "States" were conveyed to that wilderness fair in wheeled vehicles – mule carts – and with the caravan came the wives of the Oregon missionaries, Marcus Whitman and Henry Spaulding. Russell remarks that the two ladies were "gazed upon with wonder and astonishment by the rude savages they being the first white women ever seen by these Indians and the first that had ever penetrated into these wild and rocky regions." [8]

Two weeks later Russell left the rendezvous with a party

---

[8] Russell, *Journal of a Trapper* (1955), 41.

of trappers who were to join Jim Bridger at the Yellowstone Lake for a fall hunt in the Blackfoot country. Passing
northward through Jackson's Hole, the trappers crossed
Two-Ocean Pass and moved down the valley of the upper
Yellowstone River to its great, blue lake. Bridger appeared
with the camp on August 16, and, three days later, Russell
and six companions veered off into the mountains which
parallel the north boundary of present Yellowstone National Park.

Rejoining the camp in Gardner's Hole, they moved cau-
tiously down the Yellowstone River with it, into Blackfoot
country and trouble. The skulking attacks to which the
trappers were subjected soon took the lives of three men and
left several others wounded. But, everything considered,
Bridger's men came out better than they might have, for a
fine display of northern lights was all that saved them from
a showdown fight with a considerable portion of the Blackfoot nation toward the end of February, 1837.

Starting the spring hunt April 1, the brigade worked its
way south between the Bighorn River and the Yellowstone
mountains until the Wind River Plain was reached; then a
swing south and west around the Wind River Mountains
brought them to Horse Creek, the designated rendezvous
for 1837. The annual supply train was not expected for
nearly a month, so the assembled trappers and Indians idled
away the time by gambling, yarning, horse-racing, and in
thoroughly chastising a village of Bannock Indians. The
latter activity was made necessary when a misunderstanding
about some horses led to open hostilities. The trappers followed and fought those Indians for three days before granting them peace, thereby demonstrating their conviction that
the rifle was "the only pen that can write a treaty which they
will not forget." [9]

The carts arrived from the States on July 5; then the

_____
[9] *Ibid.*, 60.

trappers had two weeks to enjoy a few dearly-bought luxuries and indebt themselves for a new "outfit" before the fall hunt began. Russell and five others started for the Yellowstone country ahead of the brigade led by Bridger and Lucien Fontenelle, but they were stopped by a Blackfoot hunting party which killed Russell's horse from ambush and compelled a retreat to the safety of the main party. A second start was more successful.

After arranging to meet the camp in the fall at the mouth of Clark's Fork of the Yellowstone, Russell's little party departed from Jackson's Hole, following the route of the previous year to the Yellowstone Lake. From there, he and his comrades hunted the mountains east and north of the present park before moving down the Yellowstone River.

But Fontenelle was late arriving at the place agreed upon and such a small party could not remain there, exposed as they were to Blackfoot mischief; so they moved south into Crow Indian country and were robbed by some rascals of that nation. An escape from their predicament was managed by making a terrible march afoot to Fort William (Laramie), where they arrived destitute and sick on November 18, 1837. The callous treatment accorded Russell by the proprietor of that post caused him to vent his feelings – in his diary – in a manner reminiscent of his thoughts on Joseph Gale.

Russell was rescued by Thomas Biggs and re-equipped, so that he was able to reach the winter encampment of the trappers on Powder River, near the "Portugese Houses" of Antonio Montero. Schemes for the ruination of that trusted lieutenant of Captain Bonneville were the principal sport of the trappers during the winter of 1837-8, and they put an end to the forlorn venture he represented.

The spring hunt, which began at the end of February, took Bridger's trappers northward toward the Yellowstone River, then westward up that stream and over the moun-

tains to the Gallatin Valley and the Madison River, which
was reached on June 1. Along that stream they found a trail
recently made by the passage of a Blackfoot village. It was
a trail marked by evidences of the terrible toll smallpox
was then taking of that tribe. On coming up with the village
soon afterward, the whites precipitated a battle which
further reduced the stricken Indians.

Continuing on to Henry's Lake, the trappers came upon
another Blackfoot village and were preparing to administer
more of the treatment which comes from smoking gun
muzzles when those Indians sent emissaries to seek peace
and trade. Russell says the trappers "were ashamed to think
of fighting a few poor Indians nearly dwindled to skeletons
by the small pox,"[10] so they traded and passed on to the
Snake River Valley.

The camp crossed the mountains by the Teton Pass, and
from there Russell made his way to the rendezvous on
Wind River, arriving with one companion on July 5, 1838.
But that gathering of the trappers was not the carefree affair
it had formerly been. The caravan which brought the supplies also introduced a rumor that the American Fur Company was abandoning its trade in the mountains. Actually,
there were two more rendezvous, but not for Russell.

During a summer spent trapping on both sides of the
Teton Mountains, the discontent sowed at the rendezvous
of 1838 corroded Russell's loyalty. September found him at
Fort Hall, which was to be his locus thereafter.

The following summer – 1839, Russell went into the
Yellowstone country for the last time. It was a hunt which
went well enough until August 28, at which time his small
party was encamped on a prominent bench on the east side
of Pelican Creek, about a half mile from the shore of
Yellowstone Lake. While Russell and a companion were
lounging in camp, they discovered it was surrounded by

---

[10] *Ibid.*, 89.

Blackfoot Indians. Though escape seemed all but impossible, they passed through a shower of arrows and gained the shelter of the adjoining forest with nothing worse than flesh wounds.

The Indians held a revel over their booty – within hearing of the suffering trappers – and left the following day. After foraging the wreckage of their outfit, with a comrade who had been out hunting at the time of the attack, the three men "left the place heaping curses on the Blackfoot nation," though Russell admits that "neither injured them or alleviated our distress." [11] The return of the little party around the shore of Yellowstone Lake, down Snake River and over the Teton Mountains to Fort Hall was an epic journey for men in their condition.

Russell hunted and trapped in the vicinity of Fort Hall until November 23, 1840, when he moved to Cache Valley to winter there, and on the shore of the Great Salt Lake, in the company of some half-breed trappers. That was followed by a trading junket to a village of Ute Indians near Utah Lake; then back to Fort Hall.

Again Russell hunted and trapped in the vicinity of the fort, reluctant to leave a familiar way of life, yet recognizing "that it was time for the white man to leave the mountains as Beaver and game had nearly disappeared." Always studious and seldom without books, Russell used much of his enforced leisure for a careful study of the Bible. Out of that came a firm conviction of its truth, and a feeling that he had not lived according to its principles;[12] it was a conversion which led him to abandon the life of a Mountain Man. So, on August 23, 1842, Russell joined the Oregon-bound wagon train headed by Elijah White and arrived at Willamette Falls a little over a month later.

[11] *Ibid.*, 105.

[12] "Diary of Rev. George H. Atkinson, 1847-58," edited by E. Ruth Rockwood, in *Oregon Historical Quarterly*, vol. 40 (December, 1939), 350.

After passing nearly unscathed through nine years of the most dangerous sort of life, Russell had every reason to consider himself delivered from peril, yet it was not so. Less than a year after his arrival at the falls, where Oregon City was then taking form, Russell was injured by a premature explosion while blasting rock in a millrace. That accident destroyed his right eye and changed his life completely.

During his convalescence, Russell studied law and thus prepared himself to play an important role in Oregon's first civil government. Efforts to organize the settlers in the Willamette Valley began in 1841, and, on July 5, 1843, they matured into a Provisional Government with a constitution, code of laws, and elected officials. However, the chosen judge refused to serve, so that the Executive Committee found it necessary to fill the position by appointment on October 2. The man selected was Osborne Russell.

It was that service on the bench of Oregon's Supreme Court which earned Russell the title of "Judge" by which he was known thereafter, and his popularity is attested by his success in the election of May 14, 1844. In the contest for the Executive Committee positions (Oregon then had a committee of three men to handle the functions of the governorship), Russell ran first among fourteen candidates, receiving over forty-two percent of the total votes cast.

The second Executive Committee guided the embryonic community of Oregon through a perilous time. It required a spirit of tolerance, a largeness of viewpoint, and great patience to reconcile the rampant nationalism of the American immigrants – who were impatient for true territorial status under the United States – with the conservative interests of the Hudson's Bay Company and its retired servants; but those were characteristics Russell and his two colleagues had. They performed the duties of a difficult office with a statesmanship which caused Peter H. Burnett to describe them as "those intelligent, calm, and faithful American officers . . . admirable men for that position." [13]

In 1844, the Legislative Committee abolished the Executive Committee of three in favor of a single governor. Russell was a candidate for that position in the election held in 1845. He, with W. J. Bailey and George Abernethy, represented the moderates, while A. L. Lovejoy represented the rasher element of the community. Perceiving that the cause of moderation was in danger, both Russell and Bailey threw their support to Abernethy at the last moment, insuring his election.

Russell was thus left without an office and was free to further his personal affairs. On October 23, 1846, he claimed 640 acres of land on the Luckiamute River in present Polk County, and it was there that he prepared the manuscript for *Journal of a Trapper*. The inspiration to do so resulted from a perusal of James Ohio Pattie's narrative of his experiences as a trapper in the Rocky Mountains,[14] which impressed Russell as quite inaccurate. He decided to draw upon his own diary to present the American fur trade as he had known it.

His 192 closely-written pages provided a faithful record of nine years in the life of an ordinary trapper; a narration which is factual and yet very human and revealing. It also reminds us that the fur trade was not the exclusive preserve of great captains and petty scoundrels, but also had its decent middle class. Russell's work is a fitting *vale* for those men.

The manuscript for *Journal of a Trapper* was sent to an agent in the East for publication prior to April, 1848. With it went instructions to forward a copy of the published book to Russell's younger sister, Martha, in Maine. Apparently

---

[13] Peter H. Burnett, "Recollections and Opinions of an Old Pioneer," in *Oregon Historical Quarterly,* vol. v (September, 1904), 299, 302.

[14] James Ohio Pattie, *The Personal Narrative of James O. Pattie, of Kentucky,* ed. by Timothy Flint (Cincinnati, 1833).

publication could not be arranged, but the agent did comply with the spirit of his instructions by having the manuscript bound and delivered. It remained in the family until published by Martha's grandson, L. A. York, in 1914.

Continuing with Russell's personal adventures: he reentered Oregon politics as a delegate from Polk County at the Yamhill Convention in 1847, and he was elected to represent that county in the Territorial Legislature in the following year. He was also one of the original Trustees of Pacific University established at Forest Grove.

When news of the discovery of gold in California reached Oregon late in 1848, many of the men of the Territory left immediately for the mines, Russell among them. In California, Russell served as *pro tempore* judge at the vigilance trial of the men whose hanging gave Placerville its earlier names of "Gallowstown" and "Hangtown." He was also moderately successful as a miner and merchant until ruined by the duplicity of a business partner who absconded with the firm's assets.

Most of Russell's remaining years were spent in an attempt to repay creditors. He never married, and his health, always frail after the accident which destroyed his right eye, deteriorated. On May 1, 1884, he entered the county hospital at Placerville, suffering from what was termed "miner's rheumatism." He was paralyzed below the waist during those last years before his death on August 26, 1892.[15]

Though he rests in an unmarked grave, Osborne Russell will never be forgotten; his contributions as a chronicler of the fur trade and a champion of the Oregon country have assured him a remembrance more durable than most expressed in stone.

---

[15] Death notice in the *Placerville Mountain Democrat,* September 4, 1892, p. 1, col. 3: "DEATH NOTICE: Russell – At the County Hospital, August 26, 1892, Osborn Russel (Judge), a native of Maine, aged 78 years."

Isaac Sparks

by JOHN E. BAUR
Los Angeles, California

Isaac Sparks was born in Bowdoin, Maine, probably in 1804. In 1816, he and his father went by keelboat from the Allegheny River to St. Louis. Young Sparks lived in that city until April 6, 1831, when, according to Mrs. F. H. Day, who interviewed him in 1859, he joined Jedediah S. Smith's party for Santa Fe. When they reached the tributaries of the Arkansas River, J. J. Warner and two other young men joined them and they hunted antelope. The Pawnees attacked the party and one member was killed. When they had crossed the Arkansas to the Cimarron, they became lost in the sandhills of that area. Going alone, Smith discovered water, but was killed by the Comanches, and although the Indians menaced the remainder of the party, they did not attack.[1]

That fall, Sparks left with Ewing Young from Santa Fe on a beaver-trapping expedition to California. There were thirty-six men in the group.[2] They traveled by way of Zuñi and reached the headwaters of the Salt River where Indians stole their traps and animals. Now they followed the Gila to Yuma. At the Colorado River, the trappers separated and Sparks came on to California, arriving in Los Angeles on February 10, 1832. For a time he was detained by the Mexican authorities because he had no passport, but finally Sparks made his way to San Pedro.[3]

---

[1] Mrs. F. H. Day, "Sketches of the Early Settlers of California: Isaac Sparks," *The Hesperian* (San Francisco), II (July, 1859), 198. The portrait of Sparks which appeared with Mrs. Day's article is reproduced in this volume at page 18.

[2] Job Francis Dye, *Recollections of a Pioneer, 1830-1852.* (Los Angeles, 1951) *Early California Travel Series,* II, p. 18.

[3] Day, *op. cit.,* 198.

In southern California, Sparks, like several other American beaver trappers, turned to sea otter hunting. At first all he had was his rifle, but before long he was successful enough to be able to hire a swimmer to retrieve the otters he had shot. Then Sparks built a light boat to go to sea after the animals. As his business expanded, he formed a company, and so continued in his fur activities from 1832 to 1849.

Isaac Sparks' California hunting adventures were not without drama. Once he and a Negro hunter, Allen Light, were driven into the highlands of Santa Rosa Island by Northwest Coast Indian hunters who stole their supplies. In 1836 there was fighting between the Northwest Indians and the party of Sparks and his associate, George Nidever.[4]

In 1849 he went to San Francisco Bay where he hunted sea otters with a company of twenty men and four boats, sailing as far north as Cape Mendocino. On his return he learned of the gold excitement and released his men so they could mine.[5]

During the Mexican War, Sparks had hoped to remain neutral between the *Californios* and the Americans, but his attitude displeased John C. Frémont, who had marched south to Santa Barbara where Sparks lived in December of 1846. George Nidever advised Sparks to join the California Battalion, which he did.[6]

In California, Isaac Sparks had married María de los Remedios Josefa Eayrs, the daughter of Captain George Washington Eayrs, a famous American sea otter hunter. Sparks and his wife had three daughters, Flora, Rosa, and

---

4 Adele Ogden, *The California Sea Otter Trade, 1784-1848* (Berkeley and Los Angeles, 1941), 125.

5 Arthur Woodward, "Isaac Sparks – Sea Otter Hunter," Historical Society of Southern California *Quarterly* (Los Angeles), xx (June, 1938), 45-7. The William Heath Davis Collection, Boxes 9-10, Huntington Library, San Marino, Calif., contains business correspondence of Sparks and Davis, 1848-51.

6 Woodward, *op. cit.*, 47.

Sallie. In 1843 he had been granted Rancho Huasna, near Arroyo Grande in present-day San Luis Obispo County, from Governor Manuel Micheltorena. This tract contained 22,153 acres. Later, he purchased Rancho El Pismo in the same general area.[7]

In the American period, Sparks became a member of the Santa Barbara city council. His hospitality was notable. Visiting Santa Barbara in January of 1850, Augustus M. Heslep remarked:

> I found a St. Louisan at Santa Barbara in the person of a resident merchant, Mr. Sparks, a brother-in-law of R. B. Dallam. I am grateful to have it in my power to speak of the kindness of Mr. Sparks. I arrived at Santa Barbara amidst a drenching rain, and whilst there, I spent the evening with him before a cheerful fire and with our wine and cigars. . . I am also gratified to state that Mr. Sparks is in the enjoyment of excellent health and has acquired an ample fortune in this new and interesting portion of the continent.[8]

Although his health was good, Sparks had lost an eye during an encounter with a bear, supposedly while he was en route to California from New Mexico.[9] According to an observer during his last days, Santa Barbarans never wearied "of hearing the scarred and worn veteran recount the thrilling adventures and hair-breadth escapes through which his devious but always honorable path, led him to this distant coast." [10]

Isaac Sparks died in Santa Barbara on June 16, 1867.[11]

---

[7] See the Francis Ziba Branch papers, Bancroft Library, University of California, Berkeley, relating to the sale of the Huasna Ranch; nineteen items are involved, 1858-1865.

[8] "Letters and Journal of Augustus M. Heslep," in *Southern Trails to California in 1849*, ed. by Ralph P. Bieber; [*Southwest Historical Series*, v] (Glendale, Calif., 1937), 384.

[9] *The Life and Adventures of George Nidever, 1802-1883*, ed. by William Henry Ellison (Berkeley, 1937), 52.

[10] *First Steamship Pioneers*, ed. by a Committee of the Association (San Francisco, 1874), 164.

[11] Woodward, *op. cit.*, 47.

Louis Vasquez

by LeRoy R. Hafen
Brigham Young University

Youngest of the twelve children of Benito Vasquez and Julie Papin was Pierre Louis, born in St. Louis on October 3, 1798.[1] His father was born in Galicia, Spain, in 1750, and came to St. Louis with Governor Piernas in 1770. At this time St. Louis and the Louisiana country west of the Mississippi was owned and ruled by Spain. Benito Vasquez took an active part in matters affecting the life of St. Louis, being captain of militia, a farmer, and a trader. In the absence of the governor he frequently acted as commandant of the village. Julie Papin, a French girl from Canada, whom he married on November 27, 1774, became the mother of his dozen children.[2]

Of the childhood and youth of Pierre Louis – always called Louis – little is known. Considering the time and place, he had a fair education, as his letters testify. His father died when he was twelve, and young Louis appears to have been taken under the wing of his eldest brother, Benito Jr., whom he addressed in extant letters running from 1824 to 1842 as *"Chere Parin."* [3]

Louis Vasquez engaged in the fur trade of the Missouri River in his early twenties, possibly with the Ashley-Henry expeditions.[4] On September 24, 1823, he obtained a license

---

[1] Old Cathedral Church Register, St. Louis, and Collet's *Index to Instruments Affecting Real Estate, St. Louis, Missouri,* Grantors, I, pt. 3. These data were kindly supplied to the writer by Miss Stella M. Drumm, librarian of the Missouri Historical Society in 1925.

[2] *Missouri Historical Society Collections,* IV, p. 12.

[3] These letters, written in French, are in the library of the Missouri Historical Society, St. Louis.

[4] H. C. Dale, *The Ashley-Smith Explorations* (Glendale, Calif., 1941), 83.

to trade with the Pawnees,[5] and was back in St. Louis the
following June.[6] Here, on December 8, 1824, he wrote the
first of his extant letters.[7] He was in the Great Salt Lake
region with the Ashley men in the middle twenties, and was
even said to have been the discoverer of Great Salt Lake.[8]
But this claim cannot be accepted.[9]

Positive data on the activities of Vasquez in the middle
and late twenties are lacking. But in the early thirties he
comes clearly into the record, and thereafter can be followed
satisfactorily. On December 10, 1832, Vasquez, intending
"to make a voyage to the western mountains," signed a
document leaving, in case of death, all his property to his
brother Benito.[10]

The next spring he traveled west as chief assistant to
Robert Campbell in conducting the supply train to the
summer rendezvous. By now he is spoken of as "an old
mountain man." [11] Upon reaching the Laramie River, Vasquez was sent out to find the trappers and learn where the
rendezvous was to be held. The main party then continued
to the Green River, where the fair of the wilderness was
held.

After the trading and celebration were over, the furs were
transported on pack animals over South Pass and to the

---

[5] Issued by Richard Graham, *House doc. 54,* 19 Cong., 2 sess.; cited by Dale L.
Morgan in his *The West of William H. Ashley* (Denver, 1964), 303.

[6] *St. Louis Enquirer,* June 7, 1824; reprinted in D. M. Frost, *Notes on General
Ashley,* etc. (Worcester, Mass., 1945), 132.

[7] Missouri Historical Society Collections. This letter tells of difficult times, but
gives nothing on his experiences in the fur trade.

[8] A Salt Lake City correspondent of the *San Francisco Bulletin* tells in the *Bulletin*
of Oct. 29, 1858, of "meeting, during the past week, Major Vasquez, the oldest
mountaineer in this country and the discoverer of Great Salt Lake. . . This they
at first took to be an arm of the Pacific Ocean. . . The following spring, Vasquez
built a boat, and circumnavigated this sheet of brine."

[9] Dale L. Morgan presents the various conflicting claims to discovery of this
inland sea but without resolving the problem. See his *Ashley, op. cit.,* 304.

[10] Document in the Vasquez papers, Missouri Historical Society.

[11] Elliott Coues (ed.), *Forty Years a Fur Trader . . . Narrative of Charles
Larpenteur* (New York, 1899), 15.

Bighorn River. Here bullboats were made of buffalo skins sewed together and stretched over a willow framework. In these craft the furs were boated down the Bighorn and Yellowstone, Vasquez taking the mules and cattle by land.

During the winter of 1833-34 Vasquez traded with the Crows, with whom he was well acquainted, and in the spring brought in to Fort William, near the mouth of the Yellowstone, thirty packs of buffalo robes and one of beaver skins.[12]

He made his way southward to the Sweetwater, along which the 1834 supply caravan was expected to travel. When William Sublette and his train reached the vicinity of Devil's Gate, they "found a letter sticking in a twig near Fitzpatrick's 'Cach.' When Sublette read it and make known its contents," writes William M. Anderson, a member of the party, "there was a shout of joy from the whole company. It was from Lew Vasquez, a great favorite of the mountaineers who had almost been given up for lost. This letter was his resurrection. He was much talked of today and always praised. One old trapper said 'thank God he lives, and I shall hear his merry laugh again.' " [13]

With the information from Vasquez's letter the party continued on to Green River, where various parties of trappers were assembled. On June 14, according to Anderson, Vasquez, Thomas Fitzpatrick (head man of the Rocky Mountain Fur Company) and two others dashed into camp. Soon "Vasquez and Sublette are shaking hands with their right and smacking and pushing each other with the left. They both ask questions and neither answer." [14]

At the rendezvous Vasquez received a letter from his brother Benito and on July 9, 1834, wrote from Ham's Fork

---

[12] *Ibid.*, 42, 43, 44, 62.

[13] "Anderson's Narrative of a Ride to the Rocky Mountains in 1834," in J. W. Hakola (ed.), *Frontier Omnibus* (Missoula, Mont., 1962), 73.

[14] *Ibid.*, 75.

a newsy one in return. He said he had traded with Crows during the preceding fall and spring and that two of his men, Bourdon and Hebert, had been killed by the Blackfeet. He sent in a draft for 50 piastres by William Sublette. "Embrace the whole family for me. Tell them that I love them all," he wrote, and added, "If you can procure me some novels Mr. Campbell will be pleased to bring them to me." [15]

When the trader caravan, returning from the rendezvous of 1834, reached the Sweetwater they found carved on a tree a message from Andrew Sublette, who had been on the upper Missouri as an agent of his brother William.[16] Andrew was soon to become a partner of Louis Vasquez.

Louis Vasquez doubtless remained in the mountains during the fall of 1834 and spent the ensuing winter there. Here Andrew Sublette joined him and they may have formed their partnership at this time. On December 30, 1834, Vasquez wrote a letter to his brother Benito from "Fort Convenience." This temporary post was probably near the mouth of Vasquez Fork (Clear Creek), a branch of the South Platte, a few miles north of present Denver, Colorado.[17] Louis writes that he is sending the letter by Andrew Sublette, who is going down to Missouri expressly to carry news of their situation.[18] In April, 1835, Andrew returned to the mountains, traveling with Robert Campbell who came out to dispose of Fort Laramie to Thomas Fitzpatrick. Then Campbell and Andrew returned down the river, boating their furs (probably including those of Sublette and Vasquez) back to Missouri.[19]

---

[15] Letter of Louis to Benito Vasquez, original (written in French) in Vasquez Papers, Missouri Historical Society.

[16] Anderson's diary of August 16, 1834, quoted in Doyce B. Nunis, *Andrew Sublette* (Los Angeles, 1960), 35.

[17] See the discussion regarding this fort in L. R. Hafen, "Fort Vasquez," *Colorado Magazine,* XLI, p. 203.

[18] Vasquez Papers, Missouri Historical Society.

[19] *Missouri Republican,* July 18, 1835; *Niles Register,* Aug. 8, 1835.

Vasquez also returned to St. Louis in the summer of 1835 (probably with Campbell and Andrew Sublette) and while there, on August 1, 1835, leased his 77½ acres of land in St. Louis County to his brother Benito for a term of ten years for ten dollars, it being understood that the lease was "made for the sole use, benefit and behoof of the said Benito and his children, and not for the profit of others." [20]

On July 29, 1835, Louis Vasquez and Andrew Sublette obtained a trading license from William Clark, Superintendent of Indian Affairs at St. Louis.[21] Such a license was regularly renewed by the partners for several later years.

They returned to the South Platte and there built their adobe Fort Vasquez in the fall of 1835.[22] During the ensuing winter Vasquez and Sublette appear to have carried on a brisk trade with the Indians on the South Platte, which caused considerable concern among the traders on the North Platte.[23] In October, 1836, Andrew Sublette set out from the South Platte with part of Vasquez and Sublette's buffalo robes. Vasquez sent along a letter to his brother Benito, in which he says that Pike Vasquez (his nephew, who is with him) is well, and adds: "I pray you treat Sublette as you would me for my sake. He is a good youngster. . . Pike writes his mother. . . Write me by Sublette this winter." [24]

Vasquez brought his furs down to St. Louis the next spring and there packed them for shipment to New York.[25] While in St. Louis he obtained on July 15 a trading license from William Clark, issued to "Luis Vasquez and Andrew

---

[20] Vasquez Papers, Missouri Historical Society. Written in English.

[21] Letter of Supt. William Clark, listing licenses issued in 1835; National Archives, Washington, D.C.

[22] See Hafen, "Fort Vasquez," *op. cit.*

[23] *Ibid.*

[24] Louis Vasquez letter from "Platte River, Oct. 9, 1836," found in the Vasquez Papers, Missouri Historical Society. The translation from the French was made for me in Feb., 1928, by Prof. E. B. Renaud of Denver University.

[25] Louis Vasquez letter of June 18, 1837, to his brother Benito; Vasquez Papers, Missouri Historical Society.

Sublette, trading under the style of Vasquez & Sublette"
with twenty-two men. William Sublette was listed as security
for the partners. A similar license was to be issued to them
on June 30, 1838.[26]

On July 15, 1837, at St. Louis, Vasquez wrote to his
brother: "I cannot go to see you for I am alone and I am
obliged to go with the men." [27] Presumably he returned to
his fort that fall.

Already vigorous competition was developing on the
South Platte. Lieut. Lancaster P. Lupton, who had accompanied the Henry Dodge Dragoons to the mountains in the
summer of 1835, had seen the possibilities of the fur trade
with the Indians at the base of the Rockies. He resigned
from the Army in March, 1836, and came west to engage in
the Indian trade. Whether he built his fort in 1836 or 1837
is not certain.[28] The post was located about a mile north of
the present town of Fort Lupton, Colorado.

Peter A. Sarpy and Henry Fraeb, financed and backed
by Pratte, Chouteau & Co. of St. Louis, obtained goods in
April, 1837, and freighted them in wagons to the South
Platte. Here they built their Fort Jackson.[29]

Fort St. Vrain, first called Fort Lookout, was established
by Bent and St. Vrain in the summer or fall of 1837. It was
located on the east side of the South Platte River, about a
mile and a half below the mouth of St. Vrain's Fork.[30] Bent
and St. Vrain had previously sent traders from their famous
Bent's Fort on the Arkansas (established in 1833-34), but
found it advantageous to establish a trading post on the

---

26 I found these documents more than thirty years ago in the Indian Bureau
archives, Washington, D.C. in the "St. Louis Supt. Files, c 316."

27 Vasquez Papers, Missouri Historical Society.

28 LeRoy R. Hafen, "Old Fort Lupton and its Founder," in the *Colorado Magazine*,
VI (1929), 220-6.

29 LeRoy R. Hafen, "Fort Jackson and the Early Fur Trade on the South Platte,"
in the *Colorado Magazine*, V (1928), 9-17.

30 LeRoy R. Hafen, "Fort St. Vrain," in the *Colorado Magazine*, XXIX (1952),
241-55.

South Platte. In 1838 they purchased the competing Fort Jackson from Sarpy and Fraeb. The inventory of goods at the sale gives us a valued list of goods and prices.[31]

Details of the Vasquez and Sublette supply train's travel from Missouri to Fort Vasquez in the summer of 1838 are told by the noted Mountain Man, James Beckwourth. The route was along the Santa Fe Trail and the Arkansas River to Bent's Fort and then northward to the destination on the South Platte. In his usual boastful manner Beckwourth pictured himself as the leading figure at the fort. He says that Sublette and Thomas Fitzpatrick took the skins to St. Louis.[32]

On July 20, 1839, Vasquez made out a legal paper at St. Louis stating that inasmuch as he was about to leave for the upper Missouri River to remain some time, he appointed W. L. Sublette to be his attorney. A. Pike Vasquez, Louis' nephew, executed a similar legal paper.[33]

The Vasquez and Sublette westbound supply train of 1839 was accompanied by an excellent diarist, E. Willard Smith, who made an excellent record of happenings. The company left Independence, Missouri, on August 6, 1839, with four six-mule wagons and thirty-two men. It reached Bent's Fort on September 3, and arrived at Fort Vasquez on the 13th. "The Fort is quite a nice place," writes E. W. Smith, "situated on the South fork of the river Platte. It is built of *daubies* [adobes], or Spanish bricks made of clay baked in the sun." [34] Enroute the company had passed rival Lupton and his six ox-drawn wagons headed for his competing fort.[35]

[31] See the article on Fort Jackson cited above, which contains a photostatic copy of one of the original pages.

[32] T. D. Bonner, *The Life and Adventures of James P. Beckwourth* (New York, 1931), 300.

[33] These documents are in the Sublette Papers, Missouri Historical Society.

[34] "The E. Willard Smith Journal, 1839-1840," in L. R. and A. W. Hafen, *To the Rockies and Oregon, 1839-1842* (Glendale, Calif., 1958), 154-67, 168.

[35] *Ibid.*, 161-2.

During the fall of 1839 Vasquez and Sublette sent Thomas Biggs with some of their goods to trade at Brown's Hole in northwestern Colorado. E. W. Smith also went to this favorite trade center. They returned to Fort Vasquez in April, 1840.[36]

After building a flat-bottomed "Mackinaw boat," thirty-six by eight feet in size, they loaded the craft with seven hundred buffalo robes and four hundred buffalo tongues and began a voyage down the South Platte on April 26. It was a difficult undertaking, but by dint of much wading and pushing, the crew of seven men reached the mouth of the Platte on June 22 and St. Louis on July 3, 1840.[37] It was one of the very few successful voyages of the South Fork and main stream of the Platte. They had made a voyage of some two thousand miles in sixty-nine days.

Vasquez and Sublette sold their fort and business in 1840 or 1841 to Lock and Randolph. This company became bankrupt through mismanagement and various difficulties – including the loss of forty-five horses and mules stolen by the Sioux, the failure of a boatload of furs to reach the States, and other misfortunes. So they evacuated Fort Vasquez in 1842 and quit the country.[38] Vasquez and Sublette held the note of Lock and Randolph for $800, on which they were unable to collect.[39] W. L. Sublette, in writing to W. D. Stewart to borrow $12,000, says: "Vasquez and Sublette made a rather sinking business of it. Brother A. W. Sublette is now on the farm." [40]

Louis Vasquez's movements immediately after the sale of Fort Vasquez are not known. He appears to have stayed in

36 *Ibid.*, 180, 186, 187.

37 *Ibid.*, 187-91.

38 R. B. Sage, *Scenes in the Rocky Mountains,* as reprinted in Hafen and Hafen, *Far West and the Rockies,* v (Glendale, 1956), 57-8.

39 Letter of Robert Campbell to W. L. Sublette, dated May 23, 1842; Sublette Papers, Missouri Historical Society.

40 W. L. Sublette letter of September, 1842, in the Sublette Papers.

the mountains and was soon to become associated with his old friend James Bridger. Bridger and Henry Fraeb had started a trading partnership in the mountains in 1840, but in August, 1841, Fraeb was killed by the Indians while he was out from the partners' trading post on Green River. Louis Vasquez, after the dissolution of Vasquez and Sublette and the sale of their Fort Vasquez, was free to enter into partnership with Bridger. Both came down from the mountains in the early summer of 1842.

James Bridger, already or soon to become a partner of Vasquez, while coming down from the mountains was met by Charles Preuss. Bridger had "a large party of traders and trappers," according to Preuss, who was leading a detachment of Fremont's party. They met on the North Platte, a little above its junction with the South Fork, on July 8, 1842.[41] Vasquez may have been in the party or in a separate one before or behind Bridger, for William T. Hamilton says that he and the party of Old Bill Williams met Vasquez above Fort Laramie, coming down from the Sweetwater country with furs in ox-drawn wagons, and that Vasquez bought pelts from the Hamilton-Williams party.[42]

After arrival at St. Louis, Vasquez arranged with Robert Campbell to take care of his business, and then set out in August, 1842, with James Bridger to trade in the Green River country. They took a company of thirty or forty men and were fitted out by the American Fur Company.[43] Just before setting out Vasquez wrote his brother: "The company has given me good advantage and good profit. They advance me the merchandise delivered in the mountains at 50 per cent in advance on the New York price and I con-

[41] J. C. Fremont, *Report of the Exploring Expedition to the Rocky Mountains,* etc. (Washington, 1845), 37.

[42] W. T. Hamilton, *My Sixty Years on the Plains* (Columbus, Ohio, 1951), 45, 47. Hamilton says his party set out from Independence, Mo., on March 15, 1842, but he does not give the date of meeting Vasquez.

[43] Sublette Papers, Sept., 1842, Missouri Historical Society.

sider that a very good advantage considering that the expenses are very considerable from here to there . . . I have left the full power with Robert Campbell to arrange my affairs and I assure you that he is very much interested in me and you need not worry he will arrange that to your satisfaction. Embrace the whole family for me I leave to make money or to die . . . There is no mortgage on the habitation." [44]

The Vasquez and Bridger party appear to have reached the Green River Valley in the fall of 1842 and to have occupied trading houses on Black's Fork. These apparently were built on a bluff beside Black's Fork and were occupied but briefly.[45] The main establishment they erected and which became famous as Fort Bridger, was built on the grassy bottomland where Black's Fork spreads out into several branches. It was constructed by the summer of 1843 and is well recorded thereafter.

In early July, 1843, Vasquez and Joe Walker set out with furs from the Green River country for the forts on the Laramie. On July 20 they met westbound emigrants on the Sweetwater. This was the year of the so-called "Great Migration" on the Oregon Trail; in fact, the trek of emigrants and their resultant trade was one of the reasons for the establishment of Vasquez and Bridger's Fort.[46] Overton Johnson, one of the company, records:

> On the 20th [July, 1843] we met Messrs. Vasques and Walker, with a company of twenty or thirty men, coming down from the

[44] Letter to brother Benito, St. Louis, Aug. 18, 1842, in Vasquez Papers, Missouri Historical Society.

[45] Theodore Talbot, who was in the Thomas Fitzpatrick detachment of Fremont's party (some days behind their chief) in 1843, writes on Aug. 30: "Came nearly west along Black's Fork passing under the bluffs on which Vasquez and Bridger's houses are built. We found them deserted and dismantled. They are built of logs, plastered with mud." – Theodore Talbot, *The Journals of Theodore Talbot* (Portland, Ore., 1931), 41.

[46] See Bridger's letter of Dec. 10, 1843, quoted in H. M. Chittenden, *The American Fur Trade of the Far West* (New York, 1935), I, p. 475.

Mountains, where Messrs. Vasques and Bridger have a small Trading Post among the Shoshonee or Snake Indians. They were loaded with furs and skins, which they were taking to the Forts on the Platte [Forts Laramie and Platte], where they supply themselves with such articles as they want for the Indian trade.[47]

Vasquez and his party traveled with such dispatch that they delivered their furs on the Laramie and returning westward caught up with the emigrants near Devil's Gate. The parties then traveled westward together; they crossed Green River on August 10 and "arrived at the Trading House of Messrs. Vasques and Bridger" on the 13th.[48] The emigrants had expected to stay there a few days to "make Meat," but finding no buffalo, moved on. One of the groups employed Joe Walker to be their guide to California.[49]

Vasquez was soon out trading with the Indians and when Theodore Talbot's detachment of the Fremont Expedition came up on August 30, Vasquez' return was thus recorded by Talbot: "Vasquez with his gallant party of mountaineers and a band of Indians came dashing into camp at full speed." [50]

Most of the westbound emigration of 1844, comprising some fifteen hundred persons, took a shortcut from Green River toward Soda Springs and thus by-passed Fort Bridger. James Clyman, Mountain Man turned emigrant, was one who traveled by way of Vasquez and Bridger's Fort. In his diary, of August 31, 1844, he noted: ". . . early in the afternoon arived at Bridger & Vasqueses trading house [Fort Bridger] a tempory concern calculated for the trade with Shoshonees and Eutaws which trade is not

[47] Overton Johnson and W. H. Winter, *Route Across the Rocky Mountains* (Princeton, 1932), 15. P. B. Reading, in the emigrant group, reported the same meeting; *Quarterly, Society of California Pioneers*, VII, p. 168.

[48] Johnson and Winter, *op. cit.*, 23. See also Reading's journal, 170.

[49] George R. Stewart, *The California Trail* (New York, 1962), 43-4.

[50] Talbot's Journal, *op. cit.*, 41. Fremont, who passed through the valley earlier in the month, did not go to Bridger's Fort; Fremont, *op. cit.*, 130.

verry valuable   this place is likewise the general rendezvous of all the rocky mountain hunters & Trappers   that
once numerous class of adventurers are now reduced to less
than thirty men which Started out under the command of
Mr. Bredger   yestarday on an excursion through the mountains of Northern & central Mexico." [51] Bridger made a
trapping tour to California in the fall of 1844.[52]

During the summer of 1845 Vasquez was in the Green
River area. But fear of the Sioux and Cheyennes, who were
at war with the Shoshones, had driven him from his and
Bridger's trading post. Johnson and Winter, returning from
the West Coast, met Vasquez and Pegleg Smith several
miles from the emigrant road, on June 22, 1845.[53] But in
late July, Vasquez was back at Fort Bridger and there
helped J. R. Snyder and Capt. Walker pack for their westward trip.[54]

Louis Vasquez was at Fort Laramie when Francis Parkman arrived at that post on June 15, 1846. The old Mountain Man was about to set out with his wagons for Fort
Bridger.[55] He was back at his post, well-stocked, in time
to catch the emigrant trade.

When Edwin Bryant reached Fort Bridger on July 16
he found it busy with emigrants buying supplies and fresh
animals. Hastings was there, promoting his route to the
south of Great Salt Lake, and Vasquez and Bridger were
reenforcing his arguments. For these two traders travel on
the proposed route was a matter of survival for their supply
fort. Already most of the travel was bypassing them and
taking the cutoff (Sublette's, or Greenwood's) to the north.

---

[51] Charles L. Camp, *James Clyman, Frontiersman* (Portland, 1960), 99.
[52] Dale L. Morgan, *Overland in 1846* (Georgetown, Calif., 1963), I, p. 31.
[53] Johnson and Winter, *op. cit.*, 148.
[54] Diary of J. R. Snyder in *Quarterly, Society of California Pioneers*, VIII, p. 243.
[55] Francis Parkman, *Oregon Trail* (Boston, 1880), 95, 99, 103, 113. Clyman
had reached Fort Bridger on June 7, 1846, and found no one at the post; Camp,
Clyman, 220.

Bryant and his small group, traveling on horseback, were willing to chance the new trail, but he left with the fort proprietors a letter advising wagon emigrants not to risk it.[56]

J. F. Reed, of the famous Donner-Reed party, wrote from Fort Bridger on July 31:

> I have replenished my stock by purchasing from Messrs. Vasques & Bridger, two very excellent and accommodating gentlemen, who are the proprietors of this trading post. . .
>
> I want you to inform the emigration that they can be supplied with fresh cattle by Messrs. Vasques & Bridger. They have now about 200 head of oxen, cows and young cattle, with a great many horses and mules; and they can be relied on for doing business honorably and fairly.[57]

Later, Reed did not regard so highly the owners of Fort Bridger. He placed on them part of the blame for the subsequent tragedy endured by the Reed-Donner party, for they had endorsed Hasting's route and had failed to deliver to Reed, Bryant's letter of warning.[58]

While Bridger remained at the fort, Vasquez went back to the States in the fall of 1846. At St. Louis the 48-year-old Louis married a Kentucky-born widow, Mrs. Narcissa Land Ashcraft, who had two small children.[59] The next year he returned to Fort Bridger with his new family. He was in charge of the fort in early October and had employed several Mormons at the post.[60]

On May 8, 1849, Vasquez wrote a letter to Brigham Young telling him of the murder of a Bannock Indian and warning that the Indians talked of going into Salt Lake Valley to war upon the whites. Upon its receipt in Salt

---

[56] Stewart, *California Trail*, 165.

[57] Quoted in Morgan, *Overland in 1846*, 279-80.

[58] Stewart, *op. cit.*, 167.

[59] Records in the Vasquez family Bible, as cited in L. C. Bray, "Louis Vasquez, Mountain Man," in the Kansas City Westerners' *The Trail Guide*, III, no. 4, p. 10.

[60] "Journal History," Oct. 5, 1848, in the Mormon Church Historian's Office, Salt Lake City.

Lake City, President Young observed: "I believe I know that Old Bridger is death on us, . . . but Vasquez is a different sort of man."[61]

In the early summer of 1849, Vasquez left his family at Fort Bridger while he took trading supplies and animals east of South Pass to meet and trade with west-moving gold-seekers and to induce them to travel via Fort Bridger. William G. Johnson, one of these travelers, gives the following description: "Mr. Vasquez was a fine portly looking gentleman of medium height, about fifty years of age, and made an impression of being intelligent and shrewd." Johnson was conducted through the fort by Mrs. Vasquez, who invited him to sit on a chair and treated him to fresh buttermilk.[62]

William Kelly who also visited Vasquez in June, 1849, speaks of him as a Frenchman.[63] Col. A. G. Brackett wrote: "In the palmy days of 1849 and '50, Mr. Bridger had a partner named Vasquez, a Mexican, who put on a great deal of style, and used to ride about the country in a coach and four."[64] John Wilson, Indian Agent, wrote to the Secretary of the Interior from Fort Bridger on August 22, 1849: "We arrived here yesterday. Messrs. Vasques and Bridger are the proprietors, and have resided here and in these mountains for more than 25 years. They are engaged as traders, belonging to the American Fur Company. They are gentlemen of integrity and intelligence, and can be fully relied on in relation to any statement they make in regard to the different tribes, claims, etc."[65]

When the Mormons were asking for a Delegate to Con-

---

61 *Ibid.*, May 7, 1849.

62 Quoted in J. C. Alter, *James Bridger* (Salt Lake City, 1925), 207-8. See portrait of Vasquez at page 19 of the present volume.

63 *Ibid.*, 205.

64 *Collections of the Wyoming Historical Society*, I, p. 68. The parentage of Vasquez explains why one person called him a Frenchman and another a Mexican.

65 *House Exec. doc. 17*, 31 Cong., 1 sess., 184.

gress, the petition was sent to Fort Bridger and "was signed by about eighteen or twenty mountainers and old Lewis Vasquez signed his name as did also Lewis Vasques, Jr. Old Vasquez has a little child and he signed his name 'Jr.' " [66]

Not content with trading possibilities at Fort Bridger, Vasquez extended his business to Salt Lake City, opening a store there in 1849.[67] At one time he also maintained a flatboat ferry on Green River, charging toll for conveying wagons across the river.[68]

Vasquez appears to have remained in business at Fort Bridger until 1855, when he sold the fort, or at least his interest in it, to the Mormons. The Mormon Church Historian's Office "Journal History" has this entry under date of October 18, 1858: "Louis Vasques of the firm of Bridger and Vasques, executed a bill of sale of Fort Bridger, and acknowledged receipt of $4,000 on Aug. 3, 1855, and $4,000 this day (Oct. 18, 1858).[69]

This was done at Salt Lake City, Vasquez probably having come out for the purpose of effecting a settlement. The "Mormon War" had been settled the previous summer and title to the Fort Bridger property was in controversy. While in the Mormon capital the old Mountain Man was interviewed by a Salt Lake correspondent of the *San Francisco Bulletin*. The resulting story, although garbled in chronol-

[66] Letter of Jim Baker: data given in a letter of J. C. Alter to me, November 29, 1932.

[67] *Millenial Star* (Liverpool, England), Nov. 21, 1849. "Louis Vasquez, associated with James Bridger at Fort Bridger, opened a branch store in Salt Lake City. He sold sugar at three pounds for $2." This note is from J. C. Alter. When Capt. Howard Stansbury visited Fort Bridger in August, 1849, Vasquez was in Salt Lake City. Stansbury, *Exploration and Survey of the Valley of the Great Salt Lake of Utah* (Washington, 1853), 76. On the homeward journey the next year the Captain met Vasquez and Bridger at their fort and received assistance from them; *ibid.*, 228.

[68] My interview in July, 1930, with Hiram Vasquez, stepson of Louis Vasquez; in *Colorado Magazine*, VIII (1931), 106-8.

[69] Also quoted in Alter, *James Bridger*, 257.

ogy and certain data, is an important item that deserves reproduction:

MAJOR VASQUEZ, THE DISCOVERER OF GREAT SALT LAKE. I have had the pleasure of meeting, during the past week, Major Vasquez, the oldest mountaineer in this country, and the discoverer of Great Salt Lake. He first entered this valley 36 years ago. In the fall of 1822, he, with a company of trappers, arrived in Cache Valley, where they determined to spend the winter, and trap in the numerous streams with which it abounds. The winter, however, became so severe – the snow falling to the depth of 8 feet – that they found it necessary to hunt out a better valley, in order to save their animals. Accordingly, Major Vasquez, with one or two of his party, started out, and crossing the divide, entered this valley, and discovered Great Salt Lake. This they at first took to be an arm of the Pacific Ocean. They found the valley free from snow, and well filled with herds of buffalo. Returning to their party, they guided them over into this valley, when they divided – one party, under Weber, wintering on the river which now bears his name; the other party wintering on Bear river, near its mouth. The following spring, Vasquez built a boat, and circumnavigated this sheet of brine, for the purpose of finding out definitely whether it was an arm of the sea or not, and thus discovered that it was in reality merely a large inland lake, without an outlet. Since that time, the lake has been gradually receding.[70]

Bill Hickman states: "The post was then [1857], and had been for two years owned by the [Mormon] church, and in possession of Mr. Robinson, who had had charge of the same from the time of its purchase, I having been one of the carriers of the heavy load of gold it took to purchase said place with the stock and goods thereon." [71]

Vasquez appears to have left the mountains in 1855, immediately after selling his interests at the fort. Hiram Vasquez states: "Mother had folks in Missouri and wanted

---

[70] *San Francisco Bulletin,* Oct. 29, 1858.

[71] *Brigham's Destroying Angel* (ed. by J. H. Beadle), 118. Hiram Vasquez says that one room or part of a room at Fort Bridger was the safe. He remembered seeing a pile of gold in it; interview had with Mr. Vasquez by me in July, 1930. The gold he saw could have been the purchase price of the fort.

to go back there. We returned to St. Louis when I was eleven or twelve. We went the Platte route. The buffalo were around us for fourteen days; there were millions of them. Father had a brick house in St. Louis, on Hickory Street." [72]

In 1859 "A. Pike Vasquez & Co." had a provision and grocery store in Denver. The business was owned in part by Louis Vasquez.[73] He no doubt financed his nephew in the project, and appears to have visited Denver to launch the business.[74] Louis Vasquez was living at Westport, Missouri, in September, 1859, where Jim Beckwourth visited him before coming to Denver to be employed at the Vasquez store.[75]

Hiram Vasquez says: "Father bought a brick house in Westport and we had a farm ten miles south of Kansas City and one mile east of the state line . . . Felix Bridger was about my age. We were raised together. He was a son of Jim Bridger by a Flathead squaw . . . In Missouri Bridgers lived within two miles of our place. From town out, there was William Bent's place, ours, and then Bridger's." [76]

When a road was being projected up Clear Creek (Vasquez Creek) in 1862 and it was decided that the pass over the continental divide should be called Vasquez Pass, the editor of the local newspaper wrote: "It is but simple justice that the name of old Louis Vasquez, the first white man who

---

[72] *Colorado Magazine,* VIII (1931), 107.

[73] W. N. Byers, "History of Colorado," in *Encyclopedia of Biography of Colorado,* 20. See also advertisements in the *Rocky Mountain News,* Dec. 1, 1859, and following dates.

[74] "Major Vasques arrived in town yesterday, having come in from his trading post in the mountains. He passed the vicinity of Cherry Creek and other mining localities"; Pease and Cole, *Guidebook for Pike's Peak,* quoting the *Kansas City Journal of Commerce.* See also the *Chicago Press-Tribune* of Jan. 13, 1859. He doubtless came to Denver enroute from Salt Lake City.

[75] *Rocky Mountain News,* Dec. 1, 1859.

[76] *Colorado Magazine,* VIII (1931), 107-8.

ever trod the plains, or climbed the mountains in this region, should be perpetuated." [77]

At his town house in Westport (now a suburb of Kansas City, Missouri) and on his farm nearby, Vasquez reared his family of seven children (born between 1847 and 1863) and two stepchildren.[78]

Louis Vasquez died in his Missouri home in September, 1868, and was buried in the old cemetery beside St. Mary's Church.[79] His widow spent her later years in Colorado with her sons Hiram and Louis and daughter Narcissa. She died in 1899 in Pueblo, Colorado, at the age of eighty, and is buried in the Masonic Cemetery in Walsenberg, Colorado.[80]

---

[77] *Rocky Mountain News,* Nov. 6, 1862.

[78] Bray's "Louis Vasquez," *op. cit.,* 10.

[79] The cemetery records give this: "On this 7th day of September A.D. 1868 was enterred Louis Vasquez aged about 72 years. – Bernard Donnelly." Rev. John J. Doyle, Secretary of Mt. St. Mary's Cemetery, 2305 Norton Avenue, Kansas City, Mo., wrote me on Dec. 22, 1932: "Since our present cemetery was not opened until January, 1877, Louis Vasquez was buried in the 'Old Cemetery' adjoining St. Mary's Church at 11th and Penn Sts. This 'Old Cemetery' was closed and all the bodies moved to the Mt. St. Mary's Cem. Most of them rest in unmarked graves in Section F."

[80] Bray's "Louis Vasquez," 17.

Walkara, Ute Chief

by GUSTIVE O. LARSON
Brigham Young University

The Ute war chief Walkara, anglicized into Walker, was first lifted into present day perspective in the summer, 1952, issue of *Western Humanities Review* in an article called "Walkara's Half Century." [1] The present writer introduced that article, which was based on original research, by saying:

> Walkara, Ute War Chief, deserves to be better known in American Indian Annals. He emerged from legendary origins to leave his mark on the history of the great Southwest during the second quarter of the nineteenth century. Boasting scars from battles with many tribes, he became a leading actor in the successive dramas of his country's exploration, conquest and settlement; he knew the mountain men in their heyday; conducted profitable trade with both Spanish and Oregon Trails; witnessed western reconnaissance and migration and influenced Mormon colonization. An opportunist in the changing pattern of the West, he was more notorious than great, more bandit than chief, feared from California to New Mexico. Yet the century since his burial with Ute honors has barely preserved his name even in the state called after his tribe.

Walkara's claim to a place among the Mountain Men rests not so much on direct contribution to fur gathering as on his association and trade with the trappers, traders and reconnaissance men. The fact that many trappers on the upper Snake and Green rivers in the 1830s and 1840s rode horses with Mexican and California brands was due in no small part to his well-organized raids into those localities. Trappers enjoyed Indian squaws through his hospitality and sought to imitate his successful trafficking in native slaves.

---

[1] Since then two books, based primarily on the same sources, have appeared about the chief: the first in 1954 by Paul Bailey, titled *Walkara, Hawk of the Mountains;* and the second in 1962 by Conway B. Sonne, titled *The World of Walkara.*

The chief's chameleon-like personality won varied descriptions from contemporaries. Most witnesses saw him as "a tall fine looking man," "a man of imposing appearance;" one characterized him as "the very beau ideal of nature's nobility," another described him as an "ugly looking speciman for an Indian Chief." It was generally agreed that he ruled through fear, but certainly his "wild cat fierceness" became "velvet-pawed" at will. He was well versed in several Indian dialects, spoke Spanish and made himself understood in English. When words failed him a highly developed art of pantomime came to his rescue. He was physically powerful and inured to hardship. His appetite for liquor was generally controlled when trading and when decisions required a clear head. He was subtile, vain, and cruel in the manner and custom of a Ute Indian.*

If the great mystery reserved some creature to become Walkara's "medicine" it must have been the horse, for his whole life was identified with it. The horse became the source of his wealth and power and the means of his ceaseless shuttling across the great Southwest. The horse's appearance among the Timpanogas roughly paralleled Walkara's. Father Escalante's horsemen visited the Timpanogos in the year 1776, and in 1805 the Spanish interpreter Mestas reported having traced stolen horses to their valley. Arze and Garces called on the Timpanogos in 1813, did some trading, and lost eight horses in a savage native attack.[2]

The Old Spanish Trail from Santa Fe into Ute country in the late eighteenth century gradually wormed its way over the Colorado River and the southern extremities of the

---

* See portrait sketch at page 19 of this volume.

[2] The above description is taken from the writer's earlier article on Walkara in *Western Humanities Review* (Summer, 1952), where the following appears in a footnote: "Walkara characterizations appear in S. N. Carvalho, *Travel and Adventure in the Far West* (New York, 1857), 188-94; William Lewis Manly, *Death Valley in '49* (Los Angeles, 1949), 87-96; Gwinn Harris Heap, *Central Route to the Pacific* (Philadelphia, 1854), 90-3; H. H. Bancroft, *History of Utah* (San Francisco, 1889), 473-4; and Thomas L. Kane, quoted in LDS Journal History (MS.), March 26, 1850." The work by Heap has since been reprinted (Glendale, Calif., 1957).

Great Basin into California. Horses and mules in uncertain numbers began to move eastward over the trail in the third decade of the nineteenth century. W. H. Ashley was able to purchase horses from the Utes at the Green River crossing in 1825. Jedediah Smith, after moving southward through Utah in 1827, followed the west end of the trail into California. William Wolfskill led a trading party from Santa Fe to Los Angeles in 1830 and en route traded horses to the Utes.

It is not known when Walkara began his raiding in Mexico and California. A letter from John Rowland to Emanuel Alvarez, dated Rancho de la Puente, Feb. 28, 1846, said, "It appears from Accounts that the Utes are very bad or have been so, but I hope by this time that the *Ventre Rouge* has chastized them enough, a party of Yutas from the Big Lake amounting to forty under the command of a chief named Walker paid a visit to this country some time ago, as soon as they could steal a few horses they put away to their own country, without any molestation from this people, because nobody followed them." [3] By 1840 residents of San Bernardino Valley, California, were already complaining that "the moon has come again and with it the dread 'Py-Utahs.'" [4] Father Juan Caballeria wrote, "The famous Ute Indian Chief Cuaka – best known as Walker – was very active about the time (1842-45) and his repeated depredations on the stock of the settlers was very annoying." [5] Cajon Pass served as a gateway in and out of the Mexican territory and most of the raids were conducted overnight. But when the stolen herds were large, with owners in hot pursuit, the Utes often divided their booty into several herds and lost

---

[3] Read Collection, Historical Society of New Mexico Papers, State Records Center and Archives, Santa Fe, Series I, no. 265, letter of Juan Roland [*sic*] to Emanuel Alvarez [Manuel Alvarez].

[4] W. D. Frazee, *History of San Bernardino County* (San Francisco, 1883).

[5] Father Juan Caballeria, *History of San Bernardino Valley* (San Bernardino, 1902), 103.

themselves in several canyons. Then in a day or two they would emerge on the desert side and reassemble on the Mojave River.

Sometimes the raids were strictly Ute affairs, sometimes in partnership with American trappers. Once, when operating alone with his band in Mexico, Walkara was pursued by armed Spaniards almost to the Colorado River. When the stolen horses refused to enter the cold water the chief separated several of them from the herd and, accompanied by a few warriors, drove them back to meet the Spaniards. Confident that he would not be recognized, he presented himself as having led a rebellion against Walkara and lost three men. He had managed to escape, he said, with part of the herd before the chief crossed the river. He felt that he was entitled to compensation for his losses in men and a reward for returning the animals to the Spaniards. The owners virtually bought back their own horses when they rewarded the chief and gave up the chase.[6]

There were dramatic moments in the early association of Walkara with Mountain Men like Jim Bridger and Peg-leg Smith. The three were about to cross the Green River to hunt buffalo when a band of Shoshones was discovered upstream. The chief insisted his friends first join him in driving out his traditional enemies. Peg-leg demurred on grounds of lacking a good horse. Walkara immediately volunteered one of his. In the attack the tough-bitted mount carried the trapper unwillingly into the very midst of battle. He wrested a war club from a Shoshone and fought with such ferocity that he became the hero of the day. Chief Walkara in great admiration for his bravery offered him any number of his squaws as reward. The trapper related that "being a very modest man I only took three." [7]

However, Walkara was not always so ready to give up his

---

[6] *Utah Historical Quarterly,* VI (October, 1933), 123.

[7] Philip A. Bailey, *Golden Mirages* (New York, 1948), 32.

squaws. "Dr. Lyman" came upon him in 1831 returning from an unsuccessful pursuit of one of his squaws who had fled across the San Juan River with her paramour. The chief was sad and kept muttering "Kah-che, Kai-yah, Mah-ru-ah," which Lyman later learned meant "very bad girl." The chief denied any intention of warring against his rival for he said he had "two other beauteous Helens who would console him for his loss." [8] Further, if we may believe his own accounts as related by Colonel Thomas L. Kane, "He has more than one black-eyed mistress there [Mexico] to whom he makes love in their own language." [9]

Walkara joined Peg-leg Smith and Jim Beckwourth in 1839-40 in what may have been the biggest raid of his career.[10] A half dozen white men and about 150 Indians were involved. Beckwourth preceded the others to spy out the land. He stopped at the Chino Ranch and familiarized himself with horse herds in the surrounding country. Then came Peg-leg and Walkara, and their followers, and every large ranch in southern California was visited overnight. About three thousand of the best horses and mules were driven away. The best yield came from San Luis Obispo, where the raiders got "1000 mares and the rest of the tame horses" amounting to a total of twelve hundred. Walkara and his men quietly cut an opening into the corral, tied up the guards and turned out the finest saddle horses. Trappings and saddles were also taken.

Knowing that they would be overtaken beyond Cajon Pass, Walkara sent the main party ahead with the horses. He hid himself with a few Utes in willows bordering a stream where he knew the Spaniards would stop to rest. Don

---

[8] Thomas J. Farnham, *Life, Adventures and Travels in California* (New York, 1840), quoted in J. Cecil Alter, *Utah, the Storied Domain*, I, pp. 35-6.

[9] "Journal History" (L.D.S. Church Historian's Office, Salt Lake City), Mar. 26, 1850.

[10] Eleanor F. Lawrence, "Old Spanish Trail," (MS., 1928, Bancroft Library, Univ. of Calif.), 138-40.

Palomares and his thirsty men dismounted, drank, and snatched an hour's sleep. The Utes crept in to take their horses and when safe from gunshot gave a great war whoop and rode off. The Spaniards were left to return on foot.

Santa Fe provided a lucrative market for Walkara's horses in his early career. It was also the source of equipment and adornment which transformed him from a buckskin-clad Ute to the grandiose chief described by Frémont and Thomas L. Kane. Frémont recorded on May 20, 1844:

> We met a band of Utah Indians, headed by a well-known chief who had obtained the American or English name of Walker by which he is quoted and well known. They were all mounted, armed with rifles and used their rifles well. The chief had a fusee which he carried slung, in addition to his rifle. They were journeying slowly toward the Spanish Trail to levy their usual tribute upon the great Californian caravans. They were robbers of a higher order than those of the desert. They conducted their depredations with form, and under the color of trade and toll for passing through their country. Instead of attacking and killing they affect to purchase – taking horses they like and giving something nominal in return. The chief was quite civil to me. He was personally acquainted with his namesake, our guide (Joseph Walker), who made my name known to him. He knew of the expedition of 1842, and as tokens of friendship and proof that we had met, proposed an interchange of presents. We had no great store to choose out of; so he gave me a Mexican blanket and I gave him a very fine one which I had obtained in Vancouver.[11]

Kane, in a lecture in 1850, described Walkara as he must have appeared only on occasion:

> His dress is a full suit of the richest broadcloth, generally brown and cut in European fashion, with a shining beaver hat and fine cambric shirt. To these he adds his own gaudy Indian trimmings, and in this way contrives, they say, to look superbly, when he rides at the head of his troop whose richly caparisoned horses, with their embroidered saddles and harness, shine and tinkle as they prance under their weight of gay metal ornaments.[12]

11 John Charles Fremont, *Memoirs of My Life* (Chicago and N.Y., 1887), 386.
12 Journal History, Mar. 26, 1850.

With the opening of the Oregon Trail in the 1830s and establishment of trading posts in the Wasatch and Uintah areas, Walkara's horse market shifted in that direction. He welcomed the change of scenery after kidnapping Spaniards for ransom became too risky.[13] With success in trade came expansion of business and in the 1840s, his lieutenants, principally his brothers, conducted raids independently but under his direction. Gwinn Harris Heap wrote of Walkara in 1853:

> Having an unlimited supply of fine horses, and being inured to every fatigue and privation he keeps the territories of New Mexico and Utah, the provinces of Chihuahua and Sonora and the southern portion of California in constant alarm. His movements are so rapid and his plans so skillfully and so secretly laid that he has never once failed in any enterprise, and he scarcely disappears from one district before he is heard of in another. He frequently divides his men into two or more bands which, making their appearance at different points at the same time, each headed, it is given out, by the dreaded Walkah in person, has given him with the ignorant Mexicans the attribute of ubiquity. The principal object of his forays is to drive off horses and cattle but more particularly the first; and among the Utahs we noticed horses with brands familiar to us in New Mexico and California.[14]

Chief Walkara also carried on a lucrative slave trade. Paiutes and Digger Indians readily sold their squaws and children in times of famine. Horse meat was preferable to eating their own flesh. But the chief did not depend on starvation for his slave traffic. He levied tribute on the weaker tribes and stole what he could not take otherwise. Daniel W. Jones wrote:

> . . . the people of New Mexico in 1851 were making annual trips commencing with a few goods, trading on their way with either Navajos or Utes for horses. . . These used-up horses were brought through and traded to the poorer Indians for children. . . This trading was continued into Lower California where the children bought on the down trip would be traded to the Mexican-Californians for

[13] Bancroft, *op. cit.*, 478.   [14] Heap, *op. cit.*, 92.

other horses, goods, or cash. . . All the children bought on the
return trip would be taken back to New Mexico and then sold, boys
fetching on an average $100, girls from $150 to $200. . . This
slave trade gave rise to cruel wars between native tribes from Salt
Lake down to the tribes of Southern Utah. Walker and his band raided
the weak tribes, taking their children prisoners and selling them to the
Mexicans. Many of the lower classes, inhabiting the southern deserts,
would sell their own children for a horse, and kill and eat the horse.[15]

American occupation of California in 1846-47 proved
disturbing to Walkara's economy. U.S. soldiers were stationed in Cajon Pass to block the main channel of raiding.
This increased the hazards of the chief's horse stealing and
made it necessary to bring smaller herds across the mountains by devious trails. The first guards stationed in the pass
were members of the Mormon Battalion under command of
Jefferson Hunt.

More disturbing was the appearance of these same Mormons on the Oregon Trail in the north. Several emigrant
parties had crossed the inhospitable salt desert in 1846
en route to California. But in 1847 the Mormons located in
the Salt Lake Valley itself. Jefferson Hunt hurried from
California to join his people in their new home. In June,
1848, others of the Battalion followed, bringing a wagon,
and gradually the route became the Mormon emigrant road
to California.

News of the Mormon invasion of Salt Lake Valley
reached Walkara in Spanish Fork Canyon where he was
camped with Chief Sowiette. Recalling the white man's
encroachment on other tribal lands, Walkara proposed driving them out before their settlement became a threat to Ute
hunting ground. When Sowiette opposed him the war chief
insinuated it was from fear.

"Dog, you call me a coward!" the peace-loving chief
growled. Before Walkara could reply Sowiette grabbed a

---

[15] Daniel W. Jones, *Forty Years among the Indians* (Salt Lake City, 1890), 49-50.

rawhide whip and lashed him across the shoulders. The young chief yielded before the prestige of his respected elder.[16]

It was fortunate for the Mormons that their first settlement was in the relatively unattractive "no man's land" between Utes and Shoshones; fortunate also that Chief Walkara was an opportunist. If he could not drive out the Mormons he would cultivate them and use them to his advantage as he had the Spaniards. He had long insisted that the outlying ranches in San Bernardino Valley were maintained for his special benefit.[17] Now trade had come to his own lands, and cattle and horses would multiply in the Wasatch. He promptly appeared in Salt Lake with several hundred horses for sale.[18]

Jim Bridger refused to let the Ute trade swing to the Mormons without a struggle. He wrote Brigham Young on April 14, 1849, informing him that Walkara was stirring up the Indians against the settlers.[19] At the same time he courted Walkara's friendship at his fort on the Oregon Trail. He warned the chief that the Mormons would gradually occupy the best Ute lands. When Walkara returned to Utah Valley he found Bridger's prediction coming true. The Mormons were building Fort Utah on a choice fishing stream of the Utes. The local Indians were beating war drums. A cannon boomed once in response. Brigham Young sent two rugged Mormons to talk peace with Walkara.[20] As Porter Rockwell and George Bean approached the Indian camp they heard the war chant and soon they caught glimpses of painted forms dancing wildly against a red fire. Bean was captured as he stood fascinated by the scene, but his fearlessness won Ute respect and soon he faced Chief Walkara with Brigham

[16] Orson F. Whitney, *History of Utah* (Salt Lake City, 1892), I, p. 398; *Tullidge's Quarterly Magazine,* III (July, 1884), 240-1.

[17] Caballeria, *op. cit.,* 103-4.   [18] Journal History, Sept. 5, 1848.

[19] *Ibid.,* April 17, 1849; Bancroft, *op. cit.,* 309.

[20] George W. Bean, *Autobiography* (Salt Lake City, 1945), 53-4.

Young's message. He insisted that the Mormons came only as friends and wanted to teach the Utes to plant and harvest. Rockwell came forward to corroborate Bean's message and Walkara was satisfied. He sent the following reply to Young: "The waters are mine. Mormons may use them. We want to trade. Brigham is our white father. Bridger wants to trade with us but we wait for you. You do not come so we come to you in Salt Lake." [21]

The chief called on Brigham Young two weeks later and on June 13 invited the Mormons to settle on his lands in San Pete and Little Salt Lake Valley. In August he piloted an exploring party into the former.[22]

Immediately following Walkara's invitation to the Mormons to occupy his lands the first waves of the "forty niners" swept across the Basin toward California. The late-comers, to whom the northern course was closed, backed and eddied around Fort Utah during the fall. Finally Jefferson Hunt relieved the situation in September by piloting them toward their destination over the southern or Mormon route to California. W. L. Manly became a part of that miscellaneous group as a result of Chief Walkara's timely assistance. Manly's party had come down the Green River by boat to the entrance of the Duchesne.

> They [some Utes] took us into their lodges and showed us blankets, knives, and guns and then with a suggestive motion said all was "Mormonee" by which we understood they had got them from the Mormons. An Indian in the back of the lodge looked very pleasant and his countenance showed a good deal of intelligence for a man of the mountains.[23]

---

[21] Journal History, June 2, 1849.

[22] Prior to leaving Salt Lake, Walkara attended Mormon 24th of July (Pioneer Day) festivities "with two hundred of his best dressed and mounted cavaliers, who stacked their guns and took up their places at the ceremonies and banquet with the quiet precision of soldiers marched to mass." Kane in Journal History, Mar. 26, 1850.

[23] Manly, *op. cit.*, 86-96.

The Manly party decided to pose as Mormons and:

> The fine looking Indian who sat as king in the lodge, now by motions and a word or two made himself known as Chief Walker. . . I asked him how many sleeps or days it was from there to Mormonee. In answer he put out his left hand and then put two fingers of his right hand astride of it, making both go up and down with the same motion of a man riding a horse. Then he shut his eyes and laid his head on his hand three times by which I understood that a man could ride to the Mormon settlement in three sleeps or four days.

The chief, upon learning the whites were bound for California, dramatically dissuaded them from continuing down the dangerous river and directed them overland to Utah Valley.

November 19, 1849, Bishop Isaac Morley led a Mormon colony into the San Pete Valley. A week later Parley P. Pratt, with a company of fifty horsemen, left Fort Utah to explore the land southward. Pratt found Walkara's band on the Sevier River in a sorry condition. Measles, the white man's gift to his people, was rampant and food was scarce. The man of a thousand horses was grateful for a sack of flour to be shared with his brother Arrapeen. A daughter of Arrapeen died of the fever and the Mormons watched the Utes kill a captive Paiute boy to share her grave. Not far up the river they came upon Walkara's aged mother dying alone according to custom.[24]

It was natural that the suffering Utes should migrate toward Morley's colony at Manti and become its ward during the severe winter. Walkara and Bishop Morley became fast friends and the chief was baptized a Mormon on March 13, 1850. The situation was fortunate for the colonists, for in their hospitable presence Walkara resisted pressure from two directions to turn their enemy. Some Mormons had killed a thieving Indian at Fort Utah and part of Walkara's tribe laid siege to the fort and called him a woman for not

[24] Journal History, Dec. 6-8, 1849.

joining an attack on it. He also confided to Bishop Morley that certain traders were trying to wean him away from the Mormons. Morley wrote Brigham Young at Walkara's request on April 21, 1950:

> Grant has written a letter to Vasquez and others to stir up the natives to go over into Uintah Valley. They say "We are your friends; we are rich, we will pay you for your land; the Mormons want to get it for nothing. We don't kill you for stealing from us or killing our cattle. The Mormons do what is wrong. We love you." Walker says, "It is not us they love, but our trade, the buck-skins." . . . The leaders wish to have the natives keep this consultation a secret but Walker says he will tell it as he wishes to be friends with all white people.[25]

The days of the Mountain Men were over. The trappers' rendezvous had given way to forts and trading posts in the 1840s. These in turn had dwindled to the few which now served the swelling flood of emigrants wheeling their way westward. Among these Walkara became increasingly involved with the Mormons, who were filling up the valleys of his homeland. An opportunist in every sense, he suppressed the urge towards expulsion and extended a hand of welcome. Early trading relations proved satisfactory, and he identified himself with the Mormons through membership in the church. But he was soon chafing under the limitations imposed by the white man's civilization. With American occupation of California in 1846, a barrier was raised against the source of his equestrian wealth and power. Five years later the interfering Mormons blocked his slave traffic with the Mexicans. The Walker War of 1853 represented a last futile effort to assert his native independence. But it came too late. Another year he moved among fort walls which shut him out and then passed away at Meadow, Utah, on January 25, 1855.

---

[25] *Ibid.*

William Wolfskill

by IRIS HIGBIE WILSON
Long Beach, California

Of that notable group of Mountain Men who afterwards became permanent and influential settlers in the Mexican province of California during the pre-gold rush era, William Wolfskill stands as an important member.[*] Born in Madison County, Kentucky, on March 20, 1798, of American parents descending from German and Irish ancestry, Wolfskill was a typical example of his generation's pioneer tradition.[1] In the fall of 1809, when Boonesborough, Kentucky, seemed to be overcrowded with newcomers, the Wolfskill family, numbering fourteen, set out for Missouri. With the encouragement of Daniel Boone, several Kentucky families cleared and fenced a small tract of land in Howard County, then beyond the fringe of any settled area. During the War of 1812, the Indians of the Missouri River region were particularly menacing and at the age of fourteen William Wolfskill could handle a Kentucky rifle with considerable skill.[2]

When the war ended in 1815, Wolfskill returned to Kentucky to attend school. Two years of "formal education" were adequate for the young frontiersman and he returned to the family homestead at Boone's Lick. In May of 1822, Wolfskill and several of his Howard County neighbors joined Captain William Becknell's second expedition to

---

[*] A full book-length biography of William Wolfskill, by the contributor of this sketch, is to be issued in 1965 by the publisher of the present series.

[1] James M. Guinn, *A History of California and an Extended History of Los Angeles and Environs* (Los Angeles, 1915), II, p. 24.

[2] *History of Howard and Cooper Counties, Missouri* (St. Louis, 1883), 92-6; Will C. Ferril, "Missouri Military in the War of 1812," *Missouri Historical Review,* IV (October, 1909), 38-41.

Santa Fe. When the party broke up in New Mexico, Wolfskill remained in the area and trapped beaver during the
summer and fall of 1822.[3]

In January of 1823, Wolfskill and a New Mexican with
whom he had trapped on the Pecos River the preceding
fall, set out on a trapping venture down the Rio Grande to
El Paso del Norte. During the course of the journey, the
two men found it necessary to build a small brush hut for
protection against the snow and bitter cold. A few nights
later, while sleeping in the hut, Wolfskill became the victim
of what he imagined was an Indian attack. He realized
that he had been shot in the chest with a rifle, but the force
of the ball had fortunately been slowed by passing through
a blanket and his right arm and left hand. Wolfskill left the
hut and made his way on foot to the nearest Mexican
settlement, Valverde, which lay at a distance of twenty-five
miles. Much to his amazement, his companion turned up a
few hours later with the story that he had been attacked by
Indians and his partner, Mr. Wolfskill, had been killed.
The New Mexican was arrested after the falsity of his
report was verified and Wolfskill, almost unable to believe
that a person would go to such trouble to steal a few beaver
traps and an old rifle, returned to Santa Fe as soon as his
strength permitted.[4]

By August of 1823, Wolfskill was back in the New Mexican capital. After some local trapping with a few trusted
companions, he journeyed to Taos, arriving in the valley at
Christmas time. During the month of February, 1824,
Wolfskill fitted out for a trapping expedition to the headwaters of the San Juan River and other tributaries of the
Colorado. The party was numerous at first, but as it con-

---

[3] Henry D. Barrows, "Story of an Old Pioneer [William Wolfskill]," Los Angeles
World, Sept. 24, 1887.

[4] Henry D. Barrows, "William Wolfskill, the Pioneer," Annual Publications of
the Historical Society of Southern California, v (1902), 290.

tinued around the west side of the Sierra Madre, various members worked down different streams until Wolfskill remained with just two companions, Isaac Slover and Ewing Young. They remained out until beaver season was over and returned to Taos in June with furs worth almost ten thousand dollars.[5]

In November of 1824, Wolfskill left Taos to go south with a party led by a Captain Owens for the purpose of buying horses and mules to take to Louisiana. They bought the animals in the northwestern part of Chihuahua and drove them as far as the Presidio del Norte. Near this point the party was attacked by Indians and several of the men, including Captain Owens, were killed. Several of the animals which had not been captured by the Indians were recovered by Wolfskill and another member of the party. With money left by Captain Owens, Wolfskill purchased some additional mules and the two men started home to Missouri.[6]

Because of the danger of Indian attacks, Wolfskill and his companion thought it best to return home by way of the Mexican settlements along the Gulf. They started down by way of the Rio Grande and hoped to eventually gain passage on a schooner bound for New Orleans. Failing to make connections, Wolfskill continued on alone by land to Natchitoches, Louisiana, and then caught a steamer which took him to St. Louis. Weary from his long journey and in poor health because of his chest wound, the young adventurer arrived at his father's home in Boone's Lick in June of 1825. Several months later, Wolfskill traveled to San Felipe de Austin to rejoin his companion who was waiting with the mules. They drove the Mexican animals, which later became known as "Missouri Mules," across Louisiana and

---

[5] Joseph J. Hill, "Ewing Young in the Fur Trade of the Far Southwest, 1822-1824," *Oregon Historical Quarterly,* xxiv (March, 1923), 7.

[6] Barrows, Los Angeles *World,* Oct. 1, 1887.

Mississippi to Greenborough, Alabama, where they sold them at a good profit. Wolfskill remained in Alabama for the winter, but in March of 1826 returned to Missouri by way of Mobile and New Orleans. Once again in Boone's Lick, Wolfskill gave the proceeds of the sale to Captain Owens' family.[7]

After remaining in the Missouri area until the summer of 1826, Wolfskill joined Ewing Young on another venture to New Mexico for the purpose of trapping the Rio Gila. Upon their arrival in Santa Fe, Young took sick and the leadership of the expedition fell to Wolfskill. Among the original eleven members of the party were Milton Sublette and George Yount, both of whom had arrived with the Santa Fe caravan of that summer. The group was later joined by five trappers led by Thomas L. "Peg-Leg" Smith and Maurice Le Duc.[8] After two or three weeks on the Gila River, the expedition ran into difficulty with Indians and was unfortunately forced to return to Santa Fe empty-handed. Wolfskill then drove a band of horses from Sonora, Mexico, to Independence, Missouri, and spent the next year in the United States.

In 1828 Wolfskill left Missouri for the last time, making his third trip westward over the Santa Fe trail. Once in New Mexico he sold the majority of his trade goods to Ewing Young, and these two men entered into a partnership with Solomon Houck for the purpose of fitting out a party to trap the waters of "the California valley."[9] Young, however, made another trip to the Rio Gila while Wolfskill went to El Paso in the spring of 1829 to purchase a supply

---

[7] Ibid.

[8] Joseph J. Hill, "New Light on Pattie and the Southwestern Fur Trade," Southwestern Historical Quarterly, XXVI (April, 1923), 253; "The Story of an Old Trapper. Life and Adventures of the Late Peg-Leg Smith," San Frarncisco Daily Evening Bulletin, Oct. 26, 1866.

[9] J. J. Warner, "Reminiscences of Early California from 1831 to 1846," Annual Publications of the Historical Society of Southern California, VII (1907-08), 190.

of wines, brandy and other goods which could be sold in Taos. Wolfskill remained in Taos the balance of the year awaiting the return of Young, who with eighteen men including Kit Carson, had continued on to California.[10]

In March of 1830, Wolfskill made legal application for Mexican citizenship [11] and in July of that year prepared for an expedition to California to hunt beaver. He also expected to find Young somewhere on the Pacific Coast. Wolfskill's party consisted of about twenty men whose names can be found in the ledger of financial transactions which were made during the trip.[12] Among those who definitely accompanied Wolfskill to California were John Lewis, Zachariah Ham, Ziba Branch, Alexander Branch, Francisco Le Fourri, Baptiste St. Germain, Samuel Shields, José Archuleta, George Yount, Love Hardesty, Martin Cooper and Lewis Burton. Eleven members of the company were employees of Wolfskill and the others were free trappers under the leadership of Yount.

The route which Wolfskill's party followed after its departure from Taos was not recorded at the time, but it can be generally traced through descriptions made in later accounts by several of the participants. Wolfskill's own statement, which his son-in-law Henry Barrows faithfully recorded, is the most succinct, although it may have been edited by Mr. Barrows:

> Last of Sept., 1830, the party, with Mr. Wolfskill at its head, left Taos for this then far off Territory of California. They came by a route farther north than that usually adopted by the Spaniards in

10 Edwin L. Sabin, *Kit Carson Days, 1809-1868* (New York, 1935), 39ff; Christopher Carson, "Kit Carson's Story as Told by Himself," MS., n.d., Bancroft Library.

11 José Guillermo Wolfskill to the Governor of New Mexico, Petition for Citizenship, San Gerónimo de Taos, March 25, 1830; Mexican Archives of New Mexico, no. 2496b; Recommendation for Approval of Citizenship, March 25, 1830, Mexican Archives of New Mexico, no. 2497; Santa Fe, New Mexico.

12 William Wolfskill, "Ledger of Accounts, 1830-1832," MS., photostat, Huntington Library, San Marino, Calif. For a complete discussion of this expedition see LeRoy R. and Ann W. Hafen, *The Old Spanish Trail* (Glendale, Calif., 1954).

traveling between California and New Mexico – their object being to find beaver. They struck the Colorado just below the mouth of the Dolores, at the head of the "Great Cañon," where they crossed; entering the Great American Basin, striking the Sevier; thence southward to the Rio Virgin, which they followed down to the Colorado; thence descending the Colorado to the Mojave; where they hoped to obtain some provisions of which they were in want, and also to find beaver. From there they took across to the sink of the Mojave River, through the Cajon Pass to San Bernardino, and finally to Los Angeles, where they arrived in February, 1831.[13]

In contrast to the somewhat vague and circuitous routes of previous expeditions, Wolfskill's group charted a track which traversed the entire distance across the Great Basin and led directly into southern California. Explorers and fur traders such as Father Garcés and Fathers Domínguez and Escalante in 1776, Jedediah Smith in 1826-27, Ewing Young in 1829, and Antonio Armíjo in 1829-30 had followed parts of the same trail, but to Wolfskill belonged the honor of having marked the first route feasible for pack trains which covered the entire distance from Taos to the Pacific.[14] Wolfskill's path was called the "Old Spanish Trail" because it was considered to be a continuation of a trail used by the Spaniards since 1765, but in reality it was a new route discovered during the Mexican period.

Several of the members of Wolfskill's party, after reaching California, advantageously disposed of their woolen blankets, called *serapes* or *fresadas,* to the rancheros in exchange for mules. These blankets were typical of the region of New Mexico and frequently used by trappers and other travelers out of Santa Fe. They were very thick, almost impervious to water, and their high quality impressed the Californians. At the same time, the mules of California were much larger and of finer form than those used in the Mis-

---

13 Wilmington *Journal,* Oct. 20, 1866. See also Charles L. Camp (ed.), "The Chronicles of George C. Yount," *California Historical Society Quarterly,* II (April, 1923), 38ff.

14 Gloria Griffen Cline, *Exploring the Great Basin* (Norman, 1963), 165.

souri and Santa Fe trade. Their appearance in New Mexico caused quite a sensation, especially when it was learned that they had been received in trade for blankets. Juan José Warner later wrote that out of the bargain made by Wolfskill's men "there sprang up a trade, carried on by means of caravans or pack animals between the two sections of the same country, which flourished for some ten or twelve years." [15] On the other hand, a more recent source states that these trappers should not be thought of as having begun the caravan trade over the Old Spanish Trail because two months after Wolfskill's arrival in California "30 men from New Mexico, merchants in wool, bringing passports" appeared in Los Angeles. Since these businessmen apparently had no other purpose in going to California except to trade merchandise for mules, their transactions were those which actually began the new commerce. [16]

The Wolfskill party reached the ranch of Don Antonio María Lugo on the outskirts of Los Angeles on February 5, 1831. Here the accounts of the various trappers were settled. Financially, the expedition was not successful as a trapping venture, and Wolfskill was left in debt. Rather than continue hunting the elusive beaver, he and George Yount associated themselves with Samuel Prentice, Nathaniel M. Pryor and Richard Laughlin to build a vessel in which to hunt sea otter. This enterprise was made possible through a confusion of Spanish terms. Wolfskill had been granted a license to hunt *nutria* by the Governor of New Mexico. *Nutria* in California correctly meant "otter," whereas it was a provincialism of New Mexico to use the same word to mean "beaver." [17]

[15] J. J. Warner, *An Historical Sketch of Los Angeles County* (Los Angeles, 1876), 33.

[16] Eleanor F. Lawrence, "Mexican Trade between Santa Fe and Los Angeles, 1830-1848," *California Historical Society Quarterly*, x (March, 1931), 27-9.

[17] Warner, "Reminiscences of Early California," 192; George W. Beattie and Helen P. Beattie, *Heritage of the Valley* (Pasadena, Calif., 1939), 27.

With the aid of Father José Sánchez of Mission San Gabriel, who supplied both material and Indian laborers, Wolfskill and his associates built a schooner under the direction of Joseph Chapman, an apprenticed ship-builder originally from Boston, with timber cut and hauled from the San Bernardino Mountains. The schooner, perhaps the first built in California, sailed from San Pedro harbor in January of 1832.[18] Wolfskill and his partners worked the vessel from as far south as Cedros Island to north of Point Conception, but the former Mountain Men failed as sea otter hunters. They sold the schooner to Captain William S. Hinckley, who sailed her to the Hawaiian Islands.

William Wolfskill decided at this time to settle down in the pueblo of Los Angeles and direct his energies toward the cultivation of the soil. After successfully petitioning for a tract of land, Wolfskill worked part-time as a carpenter while his newly planted crops took root. Within a few years, he became one of the leading vineyardists of the country, having affirmed his belief that a vine, "if well cared for, would flourish one hundred years."[19] William and his brother John, who had reached Los Angeles from Santa Fe in 1838, acquired a vineyard in March of that year which contained four thousand vines and the two planted thirty-two thousand additional vines during the next few years. Through the acquisition of adjacent lands, William – called "Don Guillermo" by his Hispanic neighbors – increased his holdings to 145 acres in the central part of Los Angeles and eventually planted eighty-five thousand vines.[20]

In the year 1841 Wolfskill planted a two-acre orange orchard, the first commercial enterprise of that kind in Cal-

---

[18] Barrows, "William Wolfskill" (1902), 293, says the vessel was named *Refugio,* but Alfred Robinson, *Life in California* (San Francisco, 1891), 132, gives the name as *Guadalupe.* Bancroft in his Marine List (*History of California,* III, p. 382) cites the *Guadalupe* as weighing 60 tons, built by Joseph Chapman and launched at San Pedro in 1831. The schooner probably had two names.

[19] Harris Newmark, *Sixty Years in Southern California* (New York, 1930), 199.

[20] John H. Hittell, *The Resources of California* (San Francisco, 1863), 200.

ifornia, on land which was later occupied by a passenger depot of the Southern Pacific Railroad. Obtaining the young trees from the Mission San Gabriel, Wolfskill experimented in the cultivation of lemons, limes and other citrus fruits in addition to some deciduous varieties. During the early 1850s he acquired a tract of land along the San Gabriel River and by 1857, when there were not more than one hundred orange trees bearing fruit in the whole county, Wolfskill planted several thousand and thus established the largest orange orchard in the United States. Many of the seeds for these trees came from the Hawaiian Islands.[21]

Also in 1841 William Wolfskill journeyed to northern California to look for a ranch on the then-vacant public domain. At the suggestion of his friend Juan José Warner, Wolfskill selected lands lying on both sides of Putah Creek, the course of which ran along the western border of the Sacramento Valley in present-day Yolo and Solano Counties. In 1842 he petitioned Governor Juan Bautista Alvarado for a grant of land containing four square leagues, or about eighteen thousand acres.[22] His brother John drove a herd of livestock northward to put on the ranch and when the grant was finally confirmed, John purchased one-half of the land. During the gold rush, John Wolfskill made large profits in the cattle business and at one time sold one thousand head of cattle for $40,000 cash. In 1856 William Wolfskill sold his half of the ranch to his brother Mathus and two other purchasers for $71,000.[23]

[21] J. Albert Wilson, *History of Los Angeles County* (Oakland, Calif., 1880), 183; John L. Von Blon, "Here Oranges like Ruddy Lanterns Shine," *Touring Topics,* xxv (November, 1933), 13.

[22] *The United States vs. William Wolfskill,* Case no. 232, U.S. District Court Records, Northern District of California, San Francisco.

[23] A sketch of the active part taken in the historical development of California by John R. Wolfskill, Sarchel Wolfskill and William Wolfskill, typescript with notes in the handwriting of David R. Sessions (Bancroft Library, Univ. of Calif.), Deed of Wm. Wolfskill to A. and G. B. Stevenson, Mathus Wolfskill and Edward McGary, July 5, 1856.

By the early 1840s Wolfskill had constructed a large rambling adobe ranch house on his Los Angeles property and was active in the local affairs of the pueblo. In January of 1841 the ex-trapper married Doña Magdalena Lugo, daughter of Don José Ignacio Lugo and Doña Rafaela Romero de Lugo of Santa Barbara, and the couple became the parents of six children. Two of Wolfskill's sons, Joseph and Luis, were especially interested in agriculture, and the boys assisted in the cultivation of such new plants as the eucalyptus tree from Australia, the soft-shelled almond, the chestnut and the persimmon tree, all of which were unknown in California.[24] In addition, Wolfskill was successfully engaged in the wine-making industry, which had proven to be a profitable venture. In 1859 when the total vintage for California was reported to be 340,000 gallons of wine, William Wolfskill produced 50,000 gallons, or a little over fifteen percent of the total.[25] The value of Wolfskill's vineyards and orchards was placed at $80,000 by the Los Angeles County Assesor's office in 1858.[26]

Wolfskill always maintained a firm interest in education and established a private school in his home during the 1850s for members of his family and the children of his neighbors. The curriculum of the school included a thorough course in English and Spanish as well as basic mathematics and a study of music. Among the students in his school were the sons of other former Mountain Men such as John Rowland and Lemuel Carpenter, who had settled on nearby ranches. Wolfskill also subsidized the first public school in Los Angeles which threatened to close after the completion of its first term in 1854.[27]

---

24 Newmark, *op. cit.*, 125, 562.

25 Henry D. Barrows, "Letter from Los Angeles," San Francisco *Daily Evening Bulletin*, Oct. 24, 1859.

26 *The Southern Vineyard*, Sept. 18, 1858. Property was assessed then as now at a figure much lower than its actual value.

In 1860 Wolfskill bought Rancho Lomas de Santiago, eleven square leagues of pasture land in present-day Orange County, for $7,000. He maintained the rancho to graze his large herd of cattle and horses. When the drought of 1863-64 hit the majority of southern California livestock, Wolfskill drove his herds through Cajon Pass to grassy Mojave River bottom lands and managed to save all but about twenty-five percent of his animals. In spite of this successful move, Wolfskill sold the rancho, plus an interest which he held in the neighboring Rancho Santiago de Santa Ana, to Flint, Bixby, and Company and James Irvine in 1866. He received the same price for the property that he had paid six years before.[28]

Wolfskill also bought Rancho Santa Anita, which consisted of between nine and ten thousand acres in Los Angeles County, for $20,000 in 1865. Wolfskill used the land for agricultural purposes and eventually left it to his son Luis, who sold it for $85,000 in 1872. Another piece of property which came into the hands of William Wolfskill was Rancho San Francisco, the site of present-day Newhall, which was sold to the Philadelphia Oil Company during the first California oil boom for seventy-five cents an acre.[29]

On October 3, 1866, William Wolfskill died at his Los Angeles residence. His sixty-eight years had spanned not only the important epoch of the far western fur trade, but had witnessed the founding of an Anglo-Californian society. The former Mountain Man contributed his share to the economic and cultural development of the Far West. Perhaps as the result of his many activities, Wolfskill spent little time writing. All that exist today from his own hand

[27] Roy M. Cloud, *Education in California* (Stanford, Calif., 1952), 32; Joseph E. Pleasants, "Los Angeles in 1856," *Touring Topics,* XXII (January, 1930), 37.

[28] Robert Glass Cleland, *The Irvine Ranch of Orange County* (San Marino, Calif., 1962), 53.

[29] Ruth Waldo Newhall, *The Newhall Ranch* (San Marino, Calif., 1958), 44-7.

are a few business letters and his account books. If he kept a diary, it has not been discovered, and he passed away before Hubert Howe Bancroft began compiling information for his "Pioneer Register and Index." It has been possible, however, to gain an insight into the character of William Wolfskill through the writings of his contemporaries, who agreed without exception that he was a man of intelligence, sincerity and resourcefulness. Major Horace Bell, one of the early California rangers, summed up the prevailing opinions when he commented that "Mr. Wolfskill was a very remarkable man; in fact, he was a hero – not the kind of a hero poets like to sing about, but still a hero. A man of indomnitable will, industry and self-denial; an American pioneer hero; one who succeeds in all he undertakes, and is always to be trusted, of the kind of men who enrich the country in which they live." [30]

[30] Major Horace Bell, *Reminiscences of a Ranger* (Santa Barbara, Calif., 1927), 58. A portrait of Wolfskill appears at page 20 of the present volume.

John Work

by RAY M. REEDER
Provo, Utah

The maps of the Far West reflect the lives and travels of the early fur traders and explorers. In the Southwest one is aware of the Spanish influence and in the Northwest there are numerous Scotch, English, French, as well as American names which accurately indicate the nationalities of the earliest white travelers in the area. Irishmen are often associated with big city life of the East, but few of them seem to have been fur traders. John Work was an exception.

Work was an employee of the Hudson's Bay Company who came into the Oregon country in 1823 and lived in the area for the rest of his life. His career spanned the pioneer and settlement era of the Northwest. He is not well known as a Mountain Man and is pretty well forgotten, especially in the United States. One reason for this perhaps is because the greater part of his activities were on the Canadian side of the border. Nevertheless he was an important man in the Hudson's Bay Company and became intimately acquainted with the Oregon territory and northern California. He ought to be recognized as an explorer, trader, journalist, brigade leader, factor, miner, farmer, and largest landholder on Vancouver Island.

The name of Work is an Anglicized version of the Irish name of Wark. John Work and brother, Joseph, changed their surname but the rest of the family retained the original spelling. John was born about 1792 in County Donegal, the son of Henry Wark. He was the eldest of six children. Another brother, David, became prominent in New Brunswick and served in the Canadian Senate.

John Work's contract with the Hudson's Bay Company is

dated at Stromness, June 15, 1814.[1] His first assignment was to the Hudson's Bay area, where he worked as a steward at York Factory and Severn House. He seems to have been highly regarded by his employers, as he survived the reorganization of the company when it merged with the North West Company in 1821. Many of the younger men were not retained. Prior to 1823 Work was a clerk, but in that year he was sent to the Columbia District where he spent the rest of his life, always in the employ of the company. His assignments changed greatly in the new activity.

Work was an excellent journalist, not solely for his own interest and satisfaction, but also because the company instructed their men to keep records in order that they would be useful to others who followed their trails.[2] His "Journals" were written carefully and contain many interesting observations of the practices of the fur traders, Indian culture, and natural resources of the areas through which he traveled. The available "Journals," fifteen in number, cover the years 1823 to 1835. There are some gaps in this period, but when they occur Work's activities can be determined in part by the records of the posts where he served, as well as by the accounts and letters of his contemporaries. He kept journals before 1823, but they seem to be unavailable.[3] Record keeping in the field was difficult. The entries were probably made at night when fatigue, cold, campfire smoke, or mosquitoes, etc., made comfort an unknown feature of brigade life. The picturesque and obscure vocabulary of the traders produces problems of meaning and intent but adds to the interest of the accounts. Work's "Journals" are typical of these observations. A characteristic of the writing

---

[1] Henry Drummond Dee, "An Irishman in the Fur Trade: The Life and Journals of John Work," in *British Columbia Historical Quarterly*, VII (Oct., 1943), 229.

[2] *Ibid.*, 231.

[3] "The journals which Work kept during this period are in existence, in the Hudson's Bay Company Archives in London, but are as yet inaccessible." *Ibid.*, 230. (Written in 1943).

of John Work is that he always recorded the weather conditions as the first notation of each day's entry. This practice was faithfully followed in all of the "Journals" that are presently available.

Peter Skene Ogden was in charge of the group that left York Factory, July 18, 1823, of which Work was a member. There were eight men in the party that traveled by canoe.[4] Their route was the familiar one of the Hudson's Bay men: Lake Winnepeg, the Saskatchewan, Athabaskan, and Columbia rivers to Spokane House. They had problems of delays, food shortages, and the like which were common to travel in primitive areas. Work was once sent ahead to Edmonton to obtain food for the men. This was no small assignment for one who was completely unacquainted with the area. It may be noted that he lost his way; the company reached the post almost before he did.

John Work was among the early traders that Hudson's Bay sent to Oregon after the merger with the North West Company. The area had not been previously exploited by the great English concern and the trading activities were organized in the familiar pattern that had been used elsewhere. Dr. John McLoughlin was appointed chief factor and he made Fort Vancouver his headquarters. From this point he dispatched fur brigades into the interior and from their successful ventures he was able to send great quantities of furs to Europe. The brigades were colorful institutions of the Oregon country before the settlers developed an agricultural empire out of the primitive valleys. A description of the trading company is most interesting:

At the head of the brigade rode the leader, a chief trader of the Hudson's Bay Company, astride a strong limbed Nez Perce horse and armed to the teeth with the best weapons of the day. Directly behind him rode his Indian wife gaily attired in the finest London broadcloth, with a wide brimmed, feather trimmed hat atop her wealth of long,

[4] Dee states the party consisted of two canoes, four men to each. See *ibid.*, 233.

shining, black hair. The bells of her leather leggings made a musical note as her pony jogged lazily along. At her saddle bow, in a basket of native weave, hung her youngest offspring. Other children on spotted cayuses rode at her side or close behind. Proud was the Indian girl chosen to be the consort of a "gentleman of the company." Security and honor were hers.

The French Canadian trappers wore bright red, knitted toques, but here and there among them might be seen the coonskin cap of an American free trapper who was welcome to the party because of his yankee ingenuity and his prowess with the long rifle. All the men were clad in deerskin and were well equiped with the weapons then in vogue. At his side along with his bright-beaded tobacco pouch, each man carried the long knife of the trapper and hunter.

. . . The leader of the fur brigade had to be a man of parts. Not only was he a dictator, the sole law and authority, but he was a military commander in case of attack by hostile Indians. He was physician in case of illness, linguist with a knowledge of many native tongues, and diplomat to negotiate with the Spaniards, Russians, and Americans, his rivals for the harvest of furs. Above all he must be a highly competent trapper and trader, in order that he might return to headquarters with a highly satisfactory yield of beaver and otter skins for shipment to the London market of his employers.[5]

At Spokane House on Spokane River, John Work spent the winter of 1823-24. In the spring he was made a member of the brigade that traveled to Fort George.[6] Supplies were low at the fort because the supply ship for the season had not yet arrived. Work was assigned to lead part of the men to the Indian tribes who lived upstream on the Columbia in order that they might trade with the natives for provisions. This was his first experience as a brigade leader. Food was not the only item that Indians could offer the men. Work recorded the following: "As usual, some women arrived in the evening for the purpose of hiring themselves to the people for the night."[7] Tobacco and buttons were

[5] Herbert E. Bolton in *Fur Brigade to Bonaventura, 1832-33,* ed. by Alice Bay Maloney (San Francisco, 1945), pp. iv-v.

[6] Fort Astoria was re-named Fort George and was still used as headquarters for the Company prior to the move to Vancouver.

[7] Dee, *op. cit.,* 237-8.

items of exchange and before long it was estimated that there were only two dozen buttons left among the traders.

The brigades usually started near the end of the summer and before the men were sent off they were given a chance to enjoy a last drinking party. They were sent off by themselves where there would be little chance for them to get into trouble. Work's "Journals" make several references to the practice of drinking the regale, as they were called, and sometimes the scheduled departure was delayed until all of the men had recovered.

In the early fall of 1824 Work led a party of thirteen men into the Flathead country to trade with the Indians, and upon his return to Fort George he was sent on an exploring expedition to the Fraser River. The purpose was to discover the mouth of that stream and to determine if the river was navigable. Work was with a group that discovered the Cowlitz Portage, and the route between the Columbia and Fort Nisqually was thus laid out. Some of the notations Work made in his "Journals" on Indian life are very enlightening. His description of native homes is detailed:

> The people's houses are constructed of planks set on end neatly fastened at the top, those in the ends lengthening toward the middle to form the proper pitch, the roofs are cased in with planks, the seams between are filled with moss, a space is left open all the way along the ridge which answers the double purpose of letting out smoke and admitting the light. About their habitations there is a complete bank of filth and nastiness. At this wet season it is complete mess mixed with offal of fish and dirt of every kind renders it surprising that human beings can reside among it.[8]

The following day he again commented upon the repugnant life of the Indians:

> The filth about these houses exceeded that we saw yesterday. About and even in the houses were literally alive with maggots which had generated in the off all [sic] of fish and the stench was most offensive.

---

[8] T. C. Elliott, "Journal of John Work, November and December, 1824," in *Washington Historical Quarterly*, III (July, 1912), 206 (notation for Nov. 26, 1824).

Canoes of these people accompanied us from one village to another, many of them were quite naked regardless of the rain. . .[9]

When Dr. McLoughlin moved Hudson's Bay headquarters from Fort George to Fort Vancouver, Work was one of those who helped transfer the goods and supplies to the new site on the north side of the Columbia River.

In June, 1825, Work was assigned to an interior brigade and later was given temporary charge of the Spokane House. Governor Simpson wanted him to have more experience before he was made responsible for the great brigades. Hudson's Bay was now encouraging the development of agriculture near the various posts in order to make them more self-sustaining. Work was an early leader in the development of farming [10] and on July 21, 1825, at Spokane House he records: "The garden looks remarkably well, the potatoes are bigger than eggs." [11] A year later, August 5, 1826, he speaks of potatoes, barley, wheat, Indian corn, green peas, turnips, cabbages, horses, cattle, and pigs as being part of the farming enterprise at Kettle Falls.[12]

One of the first assignments Work received at Spokane House was to abandon the post and transfer it to a new location at Kettle Falls on the Columbia, which was to be called Fort Colvile.[13] Governor Simpson ordered the move as this seemed to be a more favorable location for the regional fur post. It would then be possible to avoid the sixty-mile pack-horse trip from the Columbia to Spokane House.[14] Work placed one of the subordinates in charge of

---

[9] *Ibid.,* 207.

[10] Several references speak of Work as being the first to farm in the Oregon area. See Elliott, *ibid.,* 27, also Maloney, *op. cit.,* p. xvi.

[11] Elliott, *WHQ,* v (April, 1914), 97.

[12] *Ibid.,* vi (January, 1915), 27.

[13] William Stanley Lewis and Paul Chrisler Phillips (eds.), *The Journals of John Work, A Chief Trader of the Hudson's Bay Company* (Cleveland, 1923), 75.

[14] Spokane House was located at the junction of Little Spokane River and the main river, nine miles northwest of present day Spokane. See Elliott, *op. cit.,* v (April, 1914), 97.

the construction at Fort Colvile while he was employed in other activities. The work on the new post was slow and the foreman in charge did not accomplish much while Work was absent. During the winter of 1825-26 Work spent time between Spokane House and Flat Head House in western Montana. During this time his account first mentions his wife Josette Legace, a Spokane woman.[15] In April, 1826, Work closed Spokane House and activities ceased there.

From 1826 to 1830 Work's assignments were centered at Fort Colvile. He was sent on many short expeditions to nearby localities for a number of different errands. Several times he journeyed to the Snake River to obtain horses from the Indians and these would be used in the brigades. In 1830 he drove fifty head of horses to Fort Vancouver and forced them to swim the Columbia River; only two head were lost on the entire trip. On another occasion he rushed three boat loads of merchandise to the Flathead Indians when he heard that Americans were in the area. H.B.C. was determined to keep the Americans out of the Oregon country and it was the policy of the company to create a fur desert to discourage the Yankee traders from penetrating into what the British regarded as their exclusive domain. Peter Skene Ogden had been in charge of the Snake River brigades and his men had trapped the area thoroughly. By the late 1820s the best fur harvests had been taken. In 1830 John Work replaced Ogden as head of the Snake River brigade. It is evident from his "Journals" that he felt a frustration for not being able to garner a greater harvest of furs with his brigade. But in spite of the handicaps his expeditions were profitable and the company regarded him highly.

Work led three major brigades in the years between 1830 and 1833. These were in the Snake River area, along the Clark's Fork and the headwaters of the Missouri and

---

[15] Dee, *op. cit.*, 244.

Salmon River, and the last one on the Sacramento River in California. His "Journals" record the details of each of these trips. It was on these expeditions that Work truly became a "Mountain Man." After the year 1834 his activities were confined to the coastal trade and to the company's interests in British Columbia.

Work's Snake River expedition, which began in the fall of 1830, consisted of 41 men, 74 women and children, and 242 horses.[16] His records tell the routine of the brigade and give interesting detail on its operations. The brigade traveled ten to twenty miles daily in a predetermined direction and smaller parties fanned out from the main camp to trap on the various streams. Sometimes these parties would be gone for several days at a time. Travel was adjusted to the requirements of camp life. When delays came for sickness or other causes, Work readily made concessions for the convenience of his people. Two days were allowed for the women in labor before the brigade moved on.[17] Danger and risk were always present and Work describes this peril:

> Thus are people wandering through this country in quest of beaver continually in danger of falling into the hands of these ruthless savages and certain of losing their lives in the most barbarous manner, independent of the privations and hardships of every other kind they subject themselves to.[18]

Several men lost their lives on this expedition.

The route of this brigade was from Walla Walla to the Boise River, and in November the expedition was on the Salmon River. An American party had been following them but the Hudson's Bay men lost the competitors. Winter cold induced the group to turn from the Salmon to the Snake River waters, and the more severe months were passed in the area of the Blackfoot Hills.[19] Work had expected to take six or seven hundred beaver in the area but he was

---

[16] *Ibid.*, 247.   [17] *Ibid.*, 248.   [18] *Ibid.*, 248.   [19] *Ibid.*, 249.

disappointed because of the deep snow which prevented free movement. However, on one small stream near the American Falls the trappers took fifty beaver in spite of the fact that Americans had trapped the area the previous fall.

After a severe winter the snow lay upon the land and spring was late in coming. On May 4, 1831, the brigade moved to the Raft River which enters the Snake from the south, a few miles west of American Falls. Work's "Journal" describes this stream in its flood stage and tells of beaver and buffalo in the area. At the present time the stream is practically non-existent in its lower course because of its utilization in irrigation. The men were urged to procure a stock of buffalo meat as "we have a long way to march through a country nearly destitute of animals of any kind and this is the last place where we are likely to find any buffalo." [20] Bison along the Raft and Snake rivers were in adequate numbers to supply the brigade with meat but there were some in the party who were indifferent to future needs.

> Some of them want no provisions themselves and are indifferent whether others have it in their power to get any or not. By missing the opportunity of collecting a little provisions now the people would be obliged to eat several of their horses before reaching the Fort [Ft. Nez Perce] as animals of any kind are uncertain.[21]

On May 14, Work recorded, "[We] encamped on a small river on Mr. Ogden's usual road to Ogden's [present Humboldt] river." [22] From these quotations it is evident that the brigade had Ogden's records or at least were supplied with definite information on the nature of the area they planned to traverse.

On May 13 the expedition left the headwaters of Raft River and crossed the mountain to Dove Creek, which is a

---

[20] "Journal of John Work's Snake Country Expedition of 1830-31, Second Half" (ed. notes by T. C. Elliott), *Oregon Historical Quarterly,* XIV, p. 287.

[21] *Ibid.,* 288.   [22] *Ibid.,* 291.

few miles west of Park Valley, Utah. He was now in the Great Basin.[23] On May 16 Work described the area:

> On reaching the plain it appears to be eastward like an immense lake with black, rocky hills, here and there like islands large tracts of the plain appear perfectly white and destitute of any kind of vegetation it is said to be composed of white clay. A small lake appears in it at some distance. To the South E. is the Utah Lake and river, to the Southward (? ? ?) is said to be destitute of water for a long way, yet snow capped mountains appear in that direction.[24]

From this point the route led through a desolate area with little water until they reached the Humboldt, or Ogden's River.[25] This area is extremely arid and Work's impression of it was not favorable. The Indians are described as "naked and wretched." [26] Few animals of any kind were found and improvident hunters were soon obliged to kill horses for food. Work mentions the paucity of animal life, including beaver, even after they reached the Humboldt. "This is miserable poor country, not even an antelope to be seen." [27] With little trapping to be done the company moved on to the John Day River and by July 20 the expedition was over. Work summarized the trip as covering more than 2000 miles, with a loss of 82 horses and as having produced a poor harvest of furs because of previous exploitation of the country. Awaiting him at headquarters was his commission as chief trader; it was dated at London, November 3, 1830.[28]

---

23 Work is often given credit for entering the Salt Lake Valley. The use of this term is misleading in present-day nomenclature. The Salt Lake Valley is now regarded as the area where Salt Lake City is located. Work had entered the northern edge of the Salt Lake desert.

Elliott (*op. cit.,* 291) states that Work entered the Great Basin near Kelton, Utah. This would have taken him over the pass at Strevell, Idaho. However in David E. Miller, "Peter Skene Ogden's Trek into Utah, 1828-29," *Pacific Northwest Quarterly,* vol. 51 (January, 1860), 18, Work's route is traced to an area miles to the west. Miller's suggestion seems more plausible.

24 "Journal of John Work's Snake Country . . ." etc. *op. cit.,* 292.

25 See Miller, *op. cit.,* 20, for a map of Work's route.

26 "Journal of John Work's Snake Country . . ." etc. *op. cit.,* 293-4.

27 *Ibid.,* 305.   28 Dee, *op. cit.,* 250.

Company officials now decided to give the Snake River area a rest and Work asked if he might lead a brigade to the Arrow Stone, or Clark's Fork River.[29] The request was granted rather reluctantly because this area had also been heavily trapped. Malaria had broken out on the lower Columbia and many of the men were ill, but Work proceeded with his plans. The season was growing late and because of this the departure could not be delayed. The first leg of the trip was by boat and "every boat was like a hospital." [30] But conditions improved with cool weather.

The route was along the Lolo Trail to the Bitterroot River and from here to Hellgate Canyon near present Missoula, Montana. Work had planned to trap in American territory on the upper waters of the Missouri, even though it was against company policy, but he was deterred by the reports of a large party of Americans in the area. This was the land of the treacherous Blackfeet Indians. The brigade was not immune to their attacks and on October 31 a small party was ambushed and two men were killed. This event turned the group toward the Big Hole and Beaverhead rivers. This was still Blackfoot country, but the company needed to hunt buffalo, which abounded in this vicinity. On November 21, Work noted, "There is little necessity for our hurrying on as the danger from the Blackfeet is the same wherever we can go." [31]

Americans were also in the area and the brigade moved away from them. Between the Indians and the Yankees the trapping results were disappointing. The Indians attacked several times and on one of these raids, November 24, one of the men was shot through the breast. He was carefully nursed and when the expedition moved on, a litter was made and the injured man was carried on the shoulders of his companions. On December 8 Work wrote:

[29] *Ibid.*   [30] Quoted in *ibid.,* 250.
[31] Lewis and Phillips, *Journal of John Work, op. cit.,* 106.

J. Desland, the wounded man, insisted on going on horseback alone, it is to be feared it will injure him. He is recovering very slowly, and is becoming so peevish tempered that the people who attend him can scarcely bear him.[32]

On January 30, 1832, a party of three hundred Blackfeet Indians attacked the brigade. Work details the event:

At break of day this morning we were attacked by a party of at least three hundred Blackfeet, they continued the battle to noon when they retired, and were pursued by a party of our people but were too numerous to be attacked successfully, and after some sharp firing were allowed to retire (we retired). They commenced the attack this morning by a war yell and discharge of guns, and were promptly met by part of our people and the Indians who returned the fire with effect which made them retire a little, and take positions in the woods and on the hills overlooking the camp. Some of them were wounded and several killed at the offset. Two of our men, W. Raymond and Bt. Gadipre were wounded, one of our Indians was killed and two wounded. A brisk fire was kept up on both sides to noon, at one time they had surrounded our camp, but kept at a considerable distance. Our cannon burst the third discharge, one of the killed was scalped by our people, he is supposed to be a chief from the efforts they made to recover his body, four or five others were killed, and several wounded, but they succeeded in carrying them off. Our loss is a F(lat)head killed and three wounded, two whites, W. Raymond wounded dangerously, and my little W(alla) W(alla) I(ndian) house-keeper dangerously wounded, S. Kanato slightly wounded in the foot, and myself slightly in the arm. The F(lat)heads have six and us five horses killed and several wounded. Nearly the whole of them were armed with guns, and well supplied with ammunition, as they were enabled to keep up a brisk and continued fire upon us for upwards of five hours. The old chief (La Bunte) had two horses killed under him. They were repulsed.[33]

On February 1 this note was made by Work which describes the Indian use of dogs: "These two days some of the B(lack)feet's dogs have been taken with bundles of shoes, and other articles tied upon them, there was some ammunition also." [34] On March 14 he tells of the death of

---

[32] *Ibid.*, 111.   [33] *Ibid.*, 127-8.   [34] *Ibid.*, 128.

one of the wounded men.[35] A week later a young man ate
hemlock root and died a short time afterwards. In view of
these incidents it is apparent that Work's comment on the
dangerous life of the trapper was very appropriate.

The hostility of the Blackfeet turned the brigade away
from the Missouri waters and the company retreated to the
headwaters of the Salmon River for the remainder of the
season. Here relations with the Snake Indians were better:

> Monday (May) 21 The two Snakes who were brought to the camp
> yesterday were kindly treated, and received little presents, with which
> they were much pleased. They returned today accompanied by two
> more men and three women. They also received little presents.[36]

As the trappers returned to Walla Walla that summer
they attempted to augment the meager stock of furs they had
taken by having a part of the group work the Burnt River.
But misfortune dogged the men and one of them was killed
by the Indians. Two others drowned in the Salmon River
as a party of four attempted to descend this river in boats.
Work was greatly disappointed in the season's catch, but
McLoughlin expressed confidence in him in his report to
the company.[37]

The next assignment given to Work was to lead an expedition toward the Spanish settlements to the south. He was not
happy with the prospects of the trip, as seen by this comment in a letter:

> I am going to start with my ragamuffin freemen to the southward
> towards the Spanish settlements but with what success I cannot say.
> I am tired of this cursed country, Ned, and becoming more disatisfied
> every day with the measures in it; things don't go fair, I don't think I
> shall remain long, my plan is to hide myself in some out of the way
> corner, and drag out the remainder of my days as quietly as possible.
> Susette (Josette) is well, we have now got three little girls, they
> accompanied me these last two years, but I leave them behind this one,

---

[35] *Ibid.,* 137.

[36] *Ibid.,* 156.   [37] Dee, *op. cit.,* 252-3.

the misery is too great, I shall be very lonely without them but the cursed trip exposes them to too much hardship.[38]

The route of this brigade was from Walla Walla across the Blue Mountains, along the John Day River to the Silvas, and then to the Sacramento River. The men were plagued with sickness as they had been the year before and Work had to exercise severe discipline at times to keep the camp moving. On September 10 he recorded, "One of the men Rocquebin refused to go and seek after the stray horses tho three of them were his own. I was obliged to knock him down and give him a beating." [39] Several days later one of the trappers was ambushed by Indians and killed, yet Work recorded the following on October 14:

> I had given orders to the people that should they fall in with any of the natives to use them kindly and endeavor to bring them to camp so that we might get information from them.[40]

On the Sacramento River the trappers were prevented from making large catches because of high water and the fact that Americans had worked the area ahead of them. To add to the chagrin of the brigade it was soon discovered that another expedition under Lafromboise had disregarded orders to hunt the coast and had already worked on the inland river. Eventually the two parties merged, with Work acknowledged as leader. Sometime later Work divided the group and his contingent went to the shores of San Francisco Bay to explore the area. He spent Easter with the Spanish padres but he was not favorably impressed with them.

From the Bay he turned northward up the coast and continued his almost fruitless efforts at trapping. At Fort Ross he dined with the Russians and they told him of the uselessness of continuing along the coast. Against their council he stayed with his original plans until the rugged coast terrain

---

[38] Maloney, *Fur Brigade to the Bonventura*, p. xvii. In spite of Work's resolutions his wife and family did accompany him on the trip.

[39] *Ibid.*, 4.   [40] *Ibid.*, 11.

and absence of large rivers forced him inland to the Sacramento River. His fortunes did not improve here and before
long half or more of the brigade was ill with fever. Indians
continued to harrass the company and the sickness was such
that it was October before they reached Fort Vancouver. In
spite of the poor results of trapping, the brigade still showed
a small profit. Work describes the prospects of the Sacramento Valley as "the country is now so exhausted that little
can be done in it." [41]

Work was among those that were ill with fever and he
suffered the effects of it for the rest of his life. He states:

> I was reduced to a perfect skeleton and so much exhausted and
> debilitated that I could scarcely walk, being thus overtaken by sickness
> far out of the reach of any Establishment or the means of procuring aid
> in a wild country, . . . great numbers of the natives were swept
> off by this scourge.[42]

During most of the winter of 1833-34 Work remained at
Fort Vancouver in order to recover from this illness. After
he had recovered he made a short trip up the Umpqua
River. This was the last of his brigade assignments, as he
now succeeded Ogden in having charge of the coastal trade.
Headquarters for this enterprise was at Fort Simpson on
McLoughlin Bay and most of the trading was done on the
British Columbia coast. This assignment directed Work's
activities away from what was to be inland America and his
subsequent career was thus centered in Canada. In 1839,
however, he helped survey property for the Puget Sound
Agricultural Company, which was a Hudson's Bay affiliate
for fostering farming activities.

Work remained at Fort Simpson until 1845 and during
most of this time he seemed to have been forgotten by Hudson's Bay. He did not get along well with McLoughlin over
the use of the ship *Beaver,* which was the company boat for
the coastal trade. But Work was not entirely overlooked

---

[41] *Ibid.,* 107.   [42] *Ibid.,* 107.

and in 1846 he replaced John McLoughlin as chief factor. In 1849 he became a member of the Board of Management for the Columbia District.

Work's interest now led him to develop coal mining and in 1850 it centered on gold. In some of these investigations around Queen Charlotte's Island he discovered that this body of land was really two islands. The discovery of gold caused a small rush in Queen Charlotte but the results were disappointing and the excitement was soon over.

In 1853 Work made his home at Victoria. His health was not good and years of rugged living had their effect upon him. From this time on he devoted his energies to farming, being chief factor of the company, and to public service. He soon became the largest landholder on Vancouver Island and because of these activities he was appointed to the Legislative Council in 1853. He remained a member until his death. He held other responsible positions also.

In 1856, he and James Douglas organized the Fur Trade Branch of Hudson's Bay Company in order to obtain land and sell it in small allotments to settlers. In this way they were able to attract settlers that did not want to purchase larger acreages which the law required. Work's own holdings of over a thousand acres were farmed or used to good purposes. His home became noted for its hospitality and his family and friends made it a mecca.

In 1849, Work had his marriage solemnized by the Church of England. He and Josette were the parents of eleven known children.

Work's health declined because of a number of weaknesses, and death came to him in December, 1861. His wife survived until 1896. The memory of Work is largely forgotten today; he seems overshadowed by others of the fur traders, yet his work ranks him among the great pioneers.[43]

---

[43] A portrait of John Work appears at page 20 of this volume.

Ewing Young

by HARVEY L. CARTER
Colorado College, Colorado Springs

Ewing Young, one of the most considerable figures of the fur trade of the Far West, was born near Jonesboro, Washington County, in eastern Tennessee, at least as early as 1794 and, more probably, as early as 1792.[1] He was the son of Charles and Mary Rebecca (Wilkins) Young, who had taken up land there in 1790. His grandfather, Robert Young, was an early Watauga Valley settler and a veteran of the battle of King's Mountain.[2] Although his father died in 1796, it is evident that his son, Ewing, received some education and it is also known that he was apprenticed to learn the carpenter's trade.

When and under what circumstances Young left his native state are unknown but, on January 18, 1822, he bought a farm, in partnership with Thomas P. Gage, at Charitan, Missouri, on the north bank of the Missouri River. On May 24, 1822, they sold the farm and, on the next day, Ewing Young joined William Becknell, who was about to set out on his second trip to Santa Fe.[3] Becknell had twenty-one

---

[1] Kenneth L. Holmes, "Ewing Young, Enterprising Trapper" (Unpublished doctoral dissertation, University of Oregon, 1963), 4-5. The researches of Dr. Holmes turned up a will of Charles Young dated May 28, 1794 (Will Book no. 1, Washington County, Tennessee, p. 176) in which mention is made of his "sons Wilken and Ewen and dater Giny." Thus, Ewing Young's birth was prior to May 28, 1794 and, if an inference may be drawn from the order of the mention of the children, Ewing was probably born during the year 1792. Prior to the investigations of Dr. Holmes, the date 1796 had been accepted for Young's birth because of his baptismal record in Taos in 1831, which gave his age as 35 years at that time.

[2] Samuel C. Williams, *Tennessee during the Revolutionary War* (Nashville, 1944), 157, reports the legend that Robert Young shot Major Ferguson at the battle of King's Mountain, with his rifle, "Sweet Lips."

[3] Holmes, *op. cit.*, 16-22. Here again Dr. Holmes has discovered material enabling a correction to be made. Young could not have been with the first Becknell expedi-

men and three wagons for this trip. This was undoubtedly the first use of wagons on the Santa Fe trail. Young had invested whatever he had from the sale of his farm in trade goods and thus made the journey as a partner in the venture. The only other members known are William Wolfskill and John Ferrell. The latter had been in the gunpowder-making business at Boone's Lick with John Day and Benjamin Cooper, and he and Young proposed to engage in this business in New Mexico.[4] The route they followed left the Missouri at present Kansas City and struck the Arkansas at the Great Bend. Joined by a party under John Heath, they continued on the Cimarron route and arrived at San Miguel twenty-two days after leaving the Arkansas.[5] The gunpowder scheme with Ferrell failed to materialize for lack of an adequate supply of nitre. Young turned instead to beaver trapping, inviting Wolfskill to join him. They trapped the Pecos River in the fall of 1822 and thus was begun his notable career as a trapper and trader.[6]

There is no record of Young's movements in the year 1823 but it is likely that he trapped on some of the more frequented streams of New Mexico and matured his plans for going farther afield, for he told Wolfskill that he wanted "to get outside of where trappers had ever been." [7] In pursuance of this aim, he organized and led a party westward to the San Juan River in February, 1824. The party was loosely organized and gradually broke up, but Young, Wolfskill, and Isaac Slover stuck together until June, 1824, when they returned to Santa Fe with over ten thousand dollars worth of furs.[8]

tion in 1821, as had previously been believed, because his involvement with land transactions precludes such a possibility.

[4] *Ibid.*, 24-5.

[5] William Becknell, "Journal of Two Expeditions from Boone's Lick to Santa Fe," in *Missouri Historical Review* (January, 1940), IV, pp. 79-80.

[6] Holmes, 42.   [7] *Ibid.*, 44.

[8] Joseph J. Hill, "Ewing Young in the Fur Trade of the Far Southwest, 1822-1834," in *Oregon Historical Society Quarterly* (March, 1923), XXIV, p. 7.

Ewing Young now had some capital with which to operate and he returned to St. Louis in the fall of 1824, possibly with Augustus Storrs, although this is conjectural. Here he purchased a supply of trade goods worth $1,206.40 in Mexican dollars. He made the return trip to Santa Fe very early in the spring of 1825 and paid $301.50 customs duty on the goods, which were itemized and valued by the Mexican authorities on April 11, 1825. The goods consisted chiefly of cotton and silk cloth, handkerchiefs, ladies' slippers, metal buttons and combs, but also included knives and hoes.[9] Young returned to Missouri with M. M. Marmaduke, leaving Santa Fe May 31, 1825, which may indicate that his goods found a ready market and that his stock needed replenishing. This time he took a number of mules, some of which were stolen by the Osage Indians. He received $216, the amount he requested, from the federal government as indemnification. The Marmaduke party arrived in Franklin, Missouri, on August 5, 1825.[10] Young must have returned to New Mexico after a very short stay in Missouri, for Major Sibley recorded in his *Journal* that he permitted one of his men, Benjamin Robinson, to go trapping with "Mr. E. Young" on November 27, 1825. Robinson died before they had gone far, and Young himself returned to Taos in ill health by January 22, 1826.[11]

While recovering his health, Young again teamed up with his old partner, William Wolfskill, who set out to trap the western rivers while Young returned once more to Missouri, this time with Major Sibley. They set out on February 26, 1826, and reached Missouri early in April. Young started back with more goods from Fayette, Missouri, on May 20,

[9] Young's list of trade goods is in the Ritch Collection of the Henry E. Huntington Library, doc. no. R181. See Holmes, 47-8.

[10] M. M. Marmaduke, "Journal," in *Missouri Historical Review* (October, 1911), VI, pp. 1-10.

[11] A. B. Hulbert, *Southwest on the Turquoise Trail, Overland to the Pacific Series,* II, pp. 147, 153.

1826.[12] Arriving in Taos in the late summer he found that
Wolfskill's trapping venture had been unsuccessful because
of trouble with hostile Indians.[13]

Young now decided to organize a trapping party strong
enough to defend itself against the Indians and to recover
the losses suffered at their hands. However, he was by no
means the only leader of a fur brigade headed for the tributary streams of the Colorado River in the year 1826.
Governor Narbona had issued licenses by August 31 of that
year to Isaac Williams, Ceran St. Vrain, Michael Robidoux,
and John Rowland as well as to "Joaquin Joon," as Young
is styled in the Mexican documents. These separate parties
amounted to over a hundred men, and probably more went
than were actually licensed to go.[14]

Young originally led a party of eighteen licensed trappers
in 1826, including Milton Sublette and Thomas L. (later
"Peg-Leg") Smith. But he had consolidated with a group of
sixteen men, of whom George Yount was one, who accepted
his leadership. This large party was in the neighborhood of
the junction of the Salt and Gila rivers when it encountered
three survivors of a group of thirty French-American trappers, the rest of whom had been set upon and killed by
Papago Indians. These three, Michael Robidoux, the leader,
young James Ohio Pattie, and one other were glad to join
Young's band.[15]

Stirred by the news of the massacre of the Robidoux
party, Young set a successful ambush for the Papagos and

[12] Holmes, 53-4.   [13] Ibid., 55.

[14] See Thomas Maitland Marshall, "St. Vrain's Expedition to the Gila" in Southwestern Historical Quarterly (January, 1916), XIX, pp. 251-60. Marshall over-
estimates the role of St. Vrain. The New Mexico records usually refer to Young as
Joaquin Joon, Jon, or Jong; the California records used also the designation of
Joaquin or Joachim Joven.

[15] Joseph J. Hill, op. cit., 9-15. This reconstruction of events, first made by Mr.
Hill, has been accepted universally by historians. There seems to be no doubt that
Young was the "genuine American leader" referred to by Pattie. See also Robert
G. Cleland, This Reckless Breed of Men (New York, 1952), 179-81.

exacted a heavy toll of lives for those of the dead trappers, whose mutilated bodies they gathered and buried. Having done this, Young divided his band into two equal groups to trap the Salt and Gila rivers to their headwaters. Both groups then returned to the junction of these rivers and were reunited. They then trapped down the Gila to its junction with the Colorado, which brought them among the Yuma Indians, with whom they had no trouble. As they moved up the Colorado River they enjoyed good beaver trapping. However, when they came among the Mojave Indians, Young was aware at once that they were menacingly hostile, and he built a stockade in anticipation of trouble. When a chief shot an arrow into a tree, Young put a bullet into the arrow with his rifle. The Indians, unimpressed by this display of marksmanship, attacked the trappers at daybreak but were repelled with a loss of sixteen. Young continued up river for four days, keeping men posted at night. Then, thinking the Indians had given up the chase, he relaxed his guard. Immediately the Mojaves attacked, killing two and wounding two before they were driven off. Eighteen of the trappers pursued them on horseback and killed a number, whom they hanged from trees to discourage the others. At the confluence of the Bill Williams Fork with the Colorado, Young lost three more men, who were scouting for beaver sign. The Indians were found roasting and eating their victims but managed to get away.[16]

Young now led his men along the south rim of the Grand Canyon until they reached the Navajo country south of the San Juan River. Here, for reasons not very clear, it was decided to continue northward and trap the Grand River (now the Colorado). Pattie's narrative becomes extremely vague and untrustworthy from this point. It is certain they could not have been on the Yellowstone and on Clark's Fork

[16] *The Personal Narrative of James Ohio Pattie,* ed. by Milo M. Quaife (Chicago, 1930), 136-50.

of the Columbia as he declares. The most probable reconstruction is that they crossed the continental divide from the
headwaters of the Grand (Colorado) in the vicinity of
Long's Peak and got upon the South Platte. Then they may
have swung in a big circle, going to the Laramie, the North
Platte, the Sweetwater, the Little Snake, the Yampa, and
finally, up the Eagle to the headwaters of the Arkansas in
the central Colorado Rockies.[17] In the process, four more
men were lost to Indians, but the remainder of the party
crossed from the Arkansas to the Rio Grande and so, back
into New Mexico, heavily laden with furs worth perhaps
$20,000.

Young must have learned that Narbona was no longer
governor and that the new governor, Armijo, was hostile to
American trappers, for he left twenty-nine packs of beaver
in the village of Peñablanca, in the care of a Mexican named
Cabeza de Baca, before proceeding to Santa Fe.[18] Governor
Armijo learned where the furs were and, in June, 1827, sent
men to confiscate them. They did so, killing Cabeza de
Baca in the process. At Santa Fe, Milton Sublette managed
to seize the two bales of beaver belonging to him and to get
away with them. Young was thereupon thrown in jail for a
time. When questioned he gave no information that would
aid in apprehending Sublette and was soon discharged.
Meanwhile, the beaver pelts had received poor care and
were sold at a low rate, but it is not thought that Young and
his men ever recovered anything despite the fact that they
had been duly licensed to trap.[19] In order to protect himself
better in the future, Young procured a passport from the
American State Department signed by Henry Clay, then
Secretary of State. He also applied for Mexican citizen-

---

[17] *Ibid.,* 150-9. Pattie's dates are unreliable as well as his geography. See also
Hill, *op. cit.,* 17-18.

[18] Cleland, *op. cit.,* 218-19.

[19] *Ibid.,* 219-24.

ship, in company with four other Americans, on April 26, 1828.[20]

Meanwhile, he opened a store in Taos in partnership with Wolfskill, who had just brought in a fresh lot of goods from St. Louis, and outfitted a trapping party which he sent to the Gila River. This party, not having Young's redoubtable leadership, soon returned because of trouble with the Apaches.[21] He now began to make plans for an extensive trapping expedition, which he would lead in person, all the way to California. Doubtless the recent return of his good friend Richard Campbell from California had made him acquainted with the opportunities that lay in this direction. But before he set out he was to perform a signal service for other traders. The regular Santa Fe caravan had been escorted to the border by Major Bennett Riley and there turned over to the protection of Mexican troops. Although the Mexican guard was 120-strong and the traders themselves numbered sixty, word came in to Taos that the caravan was beleagured by a much larger force of Indians. Young set out, with forty men, to the rescue, but on receiving fresh news, returned and augmented his force to ninety-five men. The Indians rode off when Young and his hunters appeared; the wagon train was saved and decided to go to Taos instead of Santa Fe.[22]

In August, 1829, Young led forty trappers north from Taos into the San Luis Valley. This was to give the impression that they planned to trap in the central Rocky Mountains on American soil. Actually they never got out of Mexican territory but doubled back across western New Mexico to the Zuni pueblo. From here they went to the

---

[20] Ritch Collection, Henry E. Huntington Library, doc. R199. Young's passport was dated March 20, 1828. He applied for Mexican citizenship in order to get a Mexican provincial passport as well.

[21] Holmes, 85.

[22] William Waldo, "Recollections of a Septuagenarian" in *Missouri Historical Society Quarterly* (April, June, 1938), v, pp. 64, 77, 78.

familiar trapping waters of the Salt River. They trapped
down that stream and up the Verde River with considerable success, driving off and killing some interfering
Apaches along the way. Now Young divided his party and
sent half of the men back to New Mexico with the furs,
while he himself led the other half to California. Among
the latter was young Kit Carson, who had worked as a cook
for Young in Taos and who was now out on his first real
trapping expedition.[23]

Leaving the headwaters of the Verde (San Francisco)
River, they struck out for the Colorado just below the Grand
Canyon, camping at a place long after known as Young
Spring, near present Truxton, Arizona. After crossing the
Colorado, finding themselves short of food, they bought
from the Mojaves a mare about to foal and ate both the mare
and the foal. Their route lay up the dry course of the Mojave
River for several days, then down through Cajon Pass to
the mission at San Gabriel, California. Here they stayed
only for one night, so eager were they to get upon the beaver
streams of California.[24]

They passed on to the San Fernando Valley and over the
Tehachapi range to the San Joaquin River. This was the
beaver paradise for which they had been heading, but as
they worked down the stream they became aware that it had
been trapped by another party. This turned out to be Peter
Skene Ogden and his Hudson's Bay Company brigade,
whom they overtook after a while. They trapped the Sacramento, as far as what is now Redding, together with Ogden's
group without any argument developing. Here they parted
and Young returned downstream with his party, augmented
by a man who had left British employment to join him.[25]

It was now July of 1830. Young aided the San José mis-

---

23 Kit Carson, *Autobiography*, ed. by Milo M. Quaife (Chicago, 1935), 9.

24 *Ibid.*, 10-14. Young was the fourth American to lead an overland party to
California. He was preceded by Jedediah Smith in 1826, the Patties in 1827, and
by Richard Campbell in 1827.

25 Hill, *op. cit.*, 25.

sion to recover runaway Indians, who had run off into the
Sierra Nevada Mountains, sending Carson with ten men to
accomplish this service for the mission. He also sold his furs
to a ship captain, Don José Asero, and purchased more
horses and mules. Soon after this, Indians stole sixty horses
but, by swift pursuit, all but five were recovered. At this
time also, three of Young's men went to Monterey to secure
passports to return to Taos, but they were forced by the
others to rejoin the party.[26]

In September, 1830, they started back to New Mexico,
but went by way of Los Angeles where most of the men got
drunk. In the course of this spree, James Higgins shot and
killed James Lawrence. Young, who was not drunk, sensed
bad trouble with the authorities and got the men to ride out
of Los Angeles in a hurry. They went down the Colorado
River to the Gulf of California, then up the river to the
Gila and up that river to its source, trapping with considerable success as they went. Young now employed a stratagem
by going to the Santa Rita copper mines and leaving the
furs with Robert McKnight, who was working the mines.
He then proceeded to Santa Fe, where he procured a license
to trade with the Indians at Santa Rita. He then sent back
for the furs. There was over a ton of beaver skins, and he
was taking no chances of losing this catch by confiscation.[27]

It was April, 1831, when Young paid off his men in Taos.
During the twenty months that had elapsed since he had set
out for California, three other expeditions had made their
separate ways there – those of Antonio Armijo, William
Wolfskill, and Peg-Leg Smith. Young's first California expedition, besides being profitable, must be credited with the
effective opening of trade with California. It is also notable
that Kit Carson served his apprenticeship as a Mountain
Man under so experienced a leader as Ewing Young and

---

[26] *Ibid.*, 23. The three would-be deserters were Francois Turcote, Jean Vaillant,
and Anastase Carier.

[27] *Ibid.*, 27.

that Young was quick to recognize both the ability and the reliability of the younger man.

On May 11, 1831, Young was baptized by Father Martinez at Taos, but he did not apply for naturalization. He lived with Maria Josepha Tayfoya, but did not contract a legal marriage with her. Young was planning to go to California a second time and considering whether he wanted to settle there. While at San José on his first trip, he had become acquainted with John R. Cooper, with whom he had since had some correspondence in which was discussed both the possibility of developing the mule trade between California and New Mexico and the possibility of Young's settling in California.[28]

On July 4, 1831, the wagons of Smith, Jackson, and Sublette reached Santa Fe. Jedediah Smith had been killed by Indians on the Cimarron, but the other two partners brought in the goods. On July 31, 1831, William Sublette paid Ewing Young $2,484.82 owed to him by William H. Ashley. About the same time, Young formed a partnership with Dr. David Waldo and David Jackson for the purpose of beginning the mule trade Young had in mind and continuing the trade in beaver pelts.[29]

David Jackson went ahead with a letter from Young to John R. Cooper which was to facilitate his buying of mules. He set out on August 25, 1831, and arrived in San Diego early in November of that year with eleven men. Meanwhile, Young had received a passport on August 21 to travel to Chihuahua, but instead of using it he organized a party of thirty-six trappers and set out for California in October, 1831. Among them was Job F. Dye, to whom we are indebted for the following list of men who were in the party: Sidney Cooper, Moses Carson, Benjamin Day, Isaac Sparks, Joseph Gale, Joseph Dofit, John Higans, Isaac Williams,

28 Holmes, 126-7.
29 Sublette Papers, Missouri Historical Society, St. Louis, Missouri.

James Green, Cambridge Green, James Anderson, Thomas Low, Julian Bargas, José Teforia, and John Price. They stopped at the Zuni pueblo for supplies and then trapped down the Salt River, catching beaver in large numbers. There were other adventures as well. Young and Dye had a scrape with a grizzly bear. They fought Apaches and Young himself killed their chief. Then Cambridge Green, usually called Turkey – a small man, but mean – killed big Jim Anderson, who bullied him once too often. By January 1, 1832, they had moved down the Gila and were camped on the Colorado River.[30]

Young took ten men and went to Los Angeles, arriving February 10, 1832. He turned Green in to the authorities for homicide. The rest of the men did not come in until March 14, 1832. Where they spent the intervening time is not known. Early in April, Jackson came in from the north with six hundred mules and one hundred horses. This was only about a fourth of what they had hoped to buy. So instead of all driving them to New Orleans, as had been planned originally, Jackson drove them to Santa Fe and Young remained in California to hunt sea otter.[31] Father Sanchez at the San Gabriel Mission had a vessel built for this purpose which was transported now by ox-cart to San Pedro harbor and assembled there. Young and Jonathan Warner and several others, including two Kanakas, engaged in the otter hunt; but Young did not like being dumped in the surf and, after being spilled several times, left the hunt and went to Monterey.

This was in early July and, by early October, Young had organized fourteen men to trap the San Joaquin. There is no record of Young's movements during this three-month period. It has been supposed that he stayed in California.

---

[30] Job F. Dye, *Recollections of a Pioneer, 1830-1852* (Los Angeles, 1951), 18-29.

[31] Holmes, 142-52. Professor Holmes points out that Alfred Robinson, *Life in California* (New York, 1846), 140-41, almost certainly describes Young's landlubber experiences while hunting sea otter, although Young is not identified by name.

However, Maria Josepha Tafoya, back in Taos, on April 8, 1833, gave birth to a son whose paternity was attributed to Young and never denied by him. It would have been possible for Young to have returned to Taos during the summer of 1832, and if he was the true father of Joaquin Young, who later inherited his property, it is essential to assume that he did so.[32]

Regardless of Young's whereabouts during the summer it is clear that in early October, 1832, he led fourteen trappers out from Los Angeles into the San Joaquin Valley. When they reached the Fresno River they saw signs indicating that a large band of trappers had been there very recently. So they hastened on to the Sacramento, where they found a Hudson's Bay Company brigade under Michael La Framboise, who was soon joined there by another band under John Work. The combined Hudson's Bay Company party amounted to 163 persons, although only forty were trappers, the rest being women and children and Indians.[33] John Turner, one of the survivors of the massacre of Jedediah Smith's men on the Umpqua in 1827, was working for La Framboise but, after talking with Young, he openly transferred to him. Turner interested Young in going farther north than he had intended. In March, 1833, they went to the Pacific coast, about seventy-five miles above Ft. Ross, and continued north as far as the Umpqua River. Ascending

---

[32] The alternatives to the conclusion that Young revisited Taos in the summer of 1832 are: (a) Father Martinez, Maria Tafoya, Kit Carson, Richard Campbell, and Manuel Lefevre were all mistaken in certifying Young's paternity; or (b) Maria Tafoya experienced a pregnancy of eighteen months. The baptismal record is dated April 12, 1833, and states that the infant was four days old at that time. It is in the Chancery office, State Records Center, Santa Fe, New Mexico. However, the entry does not appear in the normal consecutive order for that date but is written on an insert, stuck in at the bottom of the page. This irregularity may provide still a third alternative, namely, that this insert was made some years later 'than the normal entries and that it may not be accurate as to the date of birth and baptism of Joaquin Young.

[33] Alice Bay Maloney, *Fur Brigade to the Bonaventura* (San Francisco, 1945), 22 ff.

this to its source, they crossed to the northwest shore of Klamath Lake and thence to the Klamath and the Pitt rivers, past Mt. Shasta and back to the upper waters of the Sacramento, thus completing a big circle through most difficult country. By November 13, 1833, the night of the great meteoric shower, they were camped on the shores of Tulare Lake, whence they returned to Los Angeles.[34] Young had some conversation at San Pedro with Abel Stearns about starting a sawmill, but soon they went on to trap once more on the Gila, in the winter of 1833 and 1834.[35]

When he returned to San Diego and Los Angeles, Young was discouraged by the poor results of his last trapping expedition and by his inability to get either men or tools to engage in lumbering. It was at this time, near San Diego, that he met the eccentric Oregon enthusiast, Hall J. Kelley of Massachusetts, who was temporarily stranded on his way to "the promised land." Nevertheless, after listening to Kelley expound the wonderful future of Oregon, Young declined to accompany him thither. Kelley went on to Monterey and was surprised to have Young, with seven men, turn up there during the last of June, 1834, with the declaration that he was ready to go and settle in Oregon and that, if Kelley had deceived him, "woe be unto him." [36]

They started their northward journey with over forty horses and mules belonging to Young. At San José, they stopped for five days to secure provisions, and Young went to San Francisco to get more horses, which he had contracted for before leaving Monterey. When they left San

---

[34] Holmes, 161-7. Both in the Sacramento and San Joaquin valleys, where Indian population had been plentiful, they now found many dead of a great pestilence which had ravaged those regions during their absence in Oregon.

[35] Abel Stearns Papers, Henry E. Huntington Library. A letter of Young's to Stearns dated March 14, 1834, indicates that Young had not yet given up the project for a sawmill at that time.

[36] Fred Wilbur Powell, *Hall J. Kelley on Oregon* (Princeton, 1932), 100. Kelley wrote that they first met "in Pueblo, near the port of St. Diego." This may refer to Los Angeles.

José, Young had seventy-seven horses and mules, and Kelley and the other men with Young had twenty-one, all of which Young swore were fairly bought. However, either at San José or just north of it, they were joined by nine men with fifty-six horses, of which Young said he did not know whether they were bought or stolen.[37]

This accession to the party was to be the cause of much trouble for both Kelley and Young upon their arrival in Oregon. Governor José Figueroa wrote on September 9, 1834, from Santa Clara Mission to Dr. John McLoughlin at Fort Vancouver, charging Young and the members of his party with having driven two hundred stolen horses out of California and asking McLoughlin's aid in recovering them.[38] There is no proof that Young acquired any of his stock dishonestly. On the contrary, he had always shown a disposition to cultivate good relations with the authorities in California, had helped the missions to recover stock and Indians, had given up a number of horses in his possession in 1833 upon identification of brands, and had refused to give up others.[39] This would seem to be adequate refutation of the charge that Young was a horse thief. His mistake lay in allowing the marauders to join up with him.

Young's party was overtaken in the Umpqua valley by La Framboise and his returning Hudson's Bay Company brigade. At this time, Kelley was extremely ill and Young was glad to allow him to travel with the Hudson's Bay Company captain, who was better equipped to give him medicinal care. Kelley thus arrived at Fort Vancouver a little before Young did, late in October, 1834.[40]

---

[37] *Ibid.,* 300, 351. These are the men whom Kelley called "marauders." There is not much doubt that their animals were stolen. Two of them were deserters from Joseph R. Walker's famous expedition to California in 1833. Kelley says further that these marauders tried to kill him but were prevented by Young. Their number is variously given as five, seven, and nine.

[38] A copy of this letter is in the Archives of the Hudson's Bay Company in London. The transcript of it was furnished to me by Professor Kenneth L. Holmes.

[39] Hubert Howe Bancroft, *History of California,* III, pp. 394, 410.

We do not know precisely what occurred between Ewing Young and Dr. John McLoughlin, but we know that McLoughlin had circulated Figueroa's charge of thievery against Young and that he refused to have any business dealings with him. Young felt a keen resentment over this treatment. He denied the charge and eventually received a retraction of it. But meanwhile, he had to shift for himself. It is no small tribute to his character and ability that he was able to survive in spite of the tremendous power and influence of the Hudson's Bay Company. Looking about for a likely place to settle, he pre-empted fifty square miles of land in the Chehalem valley and built a hillside cabin overlooking his domain. Here for the next two years he managed to exist, entirely independent of the hostile fur company, which refused all his overtures to trade, though willing, on occasion, to offer charity, which Young was too proud to accept. He told Lt. Slacum, in 1836, that "a cloud hung over him so long, through Dr. McLoughlin's influence, that he was almost maddened by the harsh treatment of that gentleman." [41]

But doubtless he was able to trade furs for supplies from American ships that came up the Columbia from time to time and, in 1836, he began the erection of a sawmill with Sol Smith, who had come to Oregon with Nathaniel Wyeth in the same year that Young had arrived. Also, in 1836, he announced his plans to start a whiskey distillery, with Lawrence Carmichael as partner, and bought from Wyeth's trading post, after Wyeth's departure, a large cauldron or

[40] Powell, 262-4. Kelley remained in Oregon until March, 1835, when he took ship for the Hawaiian Islands. He was given adequate care by Dr. McLoughlin but was segregated and not admitted to table at the fort. His account of this period is found in Powell, 181-9. It should be said that McLoughlin's treatment of Young and Kelley was an exception to his usual policy of open handed hospitality. Young's spread was located southwest of modern Portland and about twenty miles almost directly west of Oregon City.

[41] "Slacum's Report on Oregon, 1836-1837" in *Oregon Historical Society Quarterly* (June, 1912), XIII, p. 196.

copper kettle for this purpose. A temperance society was already in existence among the American settlers, having been organized February 11, 1836. Jason Lee and other missionaries asked him to abandon his plans to operate a distillery. The Hudson's Bay Company had a strict monopoly of liquor, as well as nearly everything else, up to this time. Young may have seriously intended to break into this monopoly. Or he may have foreseen the objection of the American temperance people and acted as he did for the purpose of winning their good opinion and so lessening the power of the company. At any rate, he consented to their request and stopped the erection of the distillery. He refused to take $51 which the temperance society had raised to compensate him, but later he sold the kettle to them for $50, which was a high price. It is not certain that Lt. William A. Slacum had arrived before this matter was settled, but if so he may have influenced Young's decision not to persist against the wishes of the community.[42]

Slacum, a naval lieutenant, had been ordered by President Jackson to look into affairs in Oregon. He noted the dependence of American settlers on the British company, especially in the matter of cattle. The company would lend a cow to a settler but refused to allow any to pass into private hands. In discussing the situation with Ewing Young, Slacum learned that there were many cattle in California and that some might be brought to Oregon from there. Thus was organized the Willamette Cattle Company. Young agreed to take ten men and go to California, purchase cattle, and drive them to Oregon. Slacum would transport the men to California. Settlers subscribed money for the purchase, and even Dr. McLoughlin was drawn into the scheme by the able lieutenant.[43] The *Loriot*, Slacum's brig, reached the

---

[42] Miss A. J. White, *Ten Years in Oregon* (Ithaca, 1848), 78-9. See also Courtney Walker, "Sketch of Ewing Young," in *Transactions of the Oregon Pioneer Association, 1880*, 56-7.

Russian Post, Fort Ross, February 20, 1837, and a week later sailed into San Francisco Bay, carrying Young and the cattle company treasurer, Philip Leget Edwards, and their men.[44]

In the course of his negotiations with California officials regarding the cattle deal, Young found it necessary to continue to Monterey, where he landed March 2, 1837. To secure final permission, he had to go overland to Santa Barbara. The officials wanted their palms greased and apparently Young applied the unguent by purchasing more cattle than he actually took out of California. At all events, he returned to Monterey, where he met Edwards on May 10, 1837, and took time out to visit his old friend and employee, Job F. Dye, at his still house near Monterey.[45] Then, having been authorized by General Vallejo to purchase one thousand head of cattle, he seems to have bought seven hundred at three dollars per head at San Solano and five hundred more at San José, both purchases being negotiated through the government. However, after they started north on July 27, 1837, Edwards estimated, on August 14, that they were driving 729 head. On September 9, near Mt. Shasta, they still had about 680 head. The cattle were mostly heifers and Young refused to allow any to be killed for food until August 27. They followed the Hudson's Bay Company fur brigade's old trail over the Siskiyous and reached the Rogue River, where they encountered some Indian trouble.[46] Here Edwards ceased keeping his diary but we know they reached the settlements on the Willamette early in October

[43] "Memorial of William A. Slacum" in *Senate Document no. 24,* 25 Cong., 2 sess., pp. 12-13.

[44] Philip Leget Edwards, *California in 1837* (Sacramento, 1890), 7.

[45] *Ibid.,* 20. See also Doyce B. Nunis, editor, *The Diary of Faxon Dean Atherton* (1964), 55-6.

[46] *Ibid.,* 20-47. The route lay over rough country where, as Edwards wrote, the mountains "appear every day to grow more difficult. Hills peep over hills, and Alp on Alp."

with about 630 head. The total cost amounted to about $8.50 per head.[47]

Of the cattle he brought through, 135 head belonged to Young himself, making him the most considerable owner of livestock in the Oregon settlements. He was now able to expand his lumbering operations on Chehalem Creek, where he cut planks from Douglas fir and oak. He built himself a larger cabin. He constructed a grist mill, too, since he farmed more than 150 acres of wheat himself and since other settlers had need of one. Of course, he continued his fur trade on a small scale. The business records that he kept were very complete and they indicate that he acted in the capacity of banker for many of the settlers.[48] There was every indication that he was the leading citizen among the American settlers and that his old troubles with the Hudson's Bay Company were over.

In 1838 he was visited by John Augustus Sutter, who was soon to settle in California on a more princely domain than Young had carved out for himself in Oregon. Father Blanchet arrived in that year and borrowed money from Young. Thomas Jefferson Farnham came overland to Oregon in 1839 and visited Young on November 12 of that year.[49] One of Farnham's men, Sidney Smith, went to work for Young and lived with him. Through the Hudson's Bay Company, Young made arrangements to import some Kanakas from Hawaii, in 1839, to augment his labor force. In 1840, he found some gigantic bones of prehistoric animals and arranged to send them by ship to Boston, where they could and did receive study from those versed in such matters.[50]

---

[47] Hubert Howe Bancroft, *History of Oregon*, I, pp. 139-150.

[48] F. T. Young, "Ewing Young and his Estate" in *Oregon Historical Society Quarterly* (September, 1920), XXI, pp. 197-315. Young's "Day Book" and his "Register" are given here.

[49] Thomas Jefferson Farnham, *Travels in the Great Western Prairies, the Anahuac and Rocky Mountains, and in the Oregon Territory* (New York, 1843), 95.

[50] Holmes, 249-60.

However, Young had for several years been troubled with what was called dyspepsia. The ailment seems to have persisted from the time of his first arrival in Oregon. His records show that he received medicine for it from several doctors. Early in February, 1841, he had a particularly bad attack. He lingered a short while in delirium before he died. A post mortem examination was made and it was reported "that a sack of water had formed on his brain" and "that his stomach was destroyed by acid he was accustomed to take for his indigestion." [51] It is difficult to avoid the conclusion that he had suffered for years from an ulcer of the stomach, which probably also caused his death.

Ewing Young was at least forty-seven but probably not more than forty-nine years of age when he died. His death raised a problem in the American settlement in Oregon. There was no governmental authority to take charge of the disposition of his property. His death caused the first steps toward a provisional government to be taken. His property was disposed of at public auction, with Joe Meek acting as auctioneer. Sidney Smith bought up his land claim and much of his livestock. Old Mountain Men like Doc Newell, Joe Gale, and John Turner bought tools and livestock. George Gay bought seven books for a dollar and Courtney Walker paid $3.50 for a two-volume set of Shakespeare.[52] Some have supposed that Young carried this set with him in all his wanderings, but the price indicates it was in good condition and it seems more likely that he had bought it off some New England ship during his Oregon years. His estate was probably worth a good bit more than it actually sold for.

The government used some of the money to build a jail, as it was allowed to use it until final disposition could be made. Finally, in 1854, a young man arrived in Oregon

---

[51] *Ibid.*, 266.
[52] F. T. Young, *op. cit.*, 171-97.

bearing the name Joaquin Young and armed with creden-
tials from Taos setting forth that he was the son of Ewing
Young and Maria Josepha Tafoya. In addition to these
documents, sworn to by Charles Beaubien, Christopher
Carson, and Manual Lefevre, of Taos, testimony was heard
in Oregon. Joseph Gale certified that he knew of Young's
connection with Maria Tafoya and that the young man
resembled Young very much. Robert (Doc) Newell testified
that Young had told him he had a son in New Mexico. So
Joaquin Young was awarded and paid $4,994.64 by the
Territory of Oregon.[53] Joaquin Young left Oregon for
California, where his inheritance was soon dissipated.

The only physical description that has been recorded of
Ewing Young is that of the Oregon missionary, Elijah
White, who said he was "a large finely built man six feet
and perhaps two inches in height." [54] Farnham referred to
him as "the excellent old Captain" and evidently enjoyed his
company, but told nothing of his appearance. Hall Kelley
refers to him as "bold and enterprising" and speaks of having listened to the thrilling events of his eventful life but
unfortunately he did not set down any of these events in his
writings. Kelley considered that Young had lost some of the
refinements of civilization and more than once indicates that
he stood in some fear of him. At the same time, he admired
the way Young stood up to McLoughlin and he characterized him as of undoubted patriotism.[55] In this connection,
it is to be remembered that, although Young applied for

[53] *Ibid.*, 199-202. During the summer of 1954, while teaching a course in Western
History at Western State College, Gunnison, Colorado, the writer had in his class
two women named Romero, the wives of a grandson and a great-grandson of
Joaquin Young. They knew of his Oregon inheritance and said that he lost most of
it in gambling. They did not know of Ewing Young except through learning of him
in my course.

[54] White was interviewed by Frances Fuller Victor in San Francisco, February
18 and 21, 1879. W. H. Gray referred to Young as "a stirring ambitious man" and
Courtney Walker characterized him as "a candid and scrupulously honest man
. . . thorough going, brave and daring."

[55] Powell, 183-4.

Mexican citizenship for business reasons, he did not complete the process.

Young's attitude towards Indians was condemned by Hall Kelley, who gave instances of the death of Indians he believed to be innocent, at the hands of men traveling with Young. Two things need to be said regarding Kelley's charges. First, Kelley, who believed the Indians innocent, was afraid to speak up in their behalf. Secondly, Young merely permitted the action of others and did not initiate it himself.[56] Young's attitude with regard to Indians was much the same as that of other Mountain Men. He did not trust them because his experience told him this was a mistake. He also believed, and acted upon his belief, that Indians should never be allowed to have the upper hand and that retaliatory action should be swift and sure. Young was not, by choice, an Indian fighter or an adventurer. He was a business man. He took only so much action in the discipline of Indians, or for that matter, the discipline of his own men, as would enable him to continue with his business in an unhampered manner.

As a business man, Young was successful in a modest way from beginning to end. Had he lived longer he might have been successful in a much bigger way. He started with very little capital and succeeded in spite of some hard financial reverses. He was extremely independent and had the habit of command. It is notable that he was the leader of every expedition that he accompanied after his arrival in New Mexico. Sometimes he sent out men whom he did not accompany but, when he was along, he was in charge. When he acted in partnership with others, he seems to have been always at least an equal partner and more often a dominating one, after his first expedition with Becknell, where he was a minor partner.

---

[56] Powell, 351-3.

Young had a good eye for business opportunity. He sensed the necessity of exploiting new and untrapped areas for the fur trade. His mule venture, though not highly successful, was soundly based. He was the pioneer Oregon cattleman, wheat man, and lumber man.[57] These were the three products for which the Pacific Northwest became most famous, and that one man should have been responsible for the beginning of all three is an indication of a high degree of business acumen on the part of that man. Young's most outstanding traits were his unerring business judgment, his marked organizational ability, and his unyielding determination in the face of adversity. For this last quality, a rare one among men, he is much to be admired.

Except for a few letters, preserved by those to whom he wrote, Ewing Young left no records to aid the historian, beyond his expense accounts in Oregon. Had he left a journal of events on even one of his many trapping expeditions, he would loom much larger in the fur trade than he does. He operated in Mexico where such records might be a liability in relations with the government and, being his own boss, he did not need to render a report to anyone.[58] But the fact that we know as much as we do about his career, and that our knowledge comes almost entirely from those who crossed or joined his path in one way or another, are indication of the magnitude of his importance in the history of the American frontier. It is also significant that what was recorded about him by others was never what he said, but what he did.

Only Jedediah Smith and Peter Skene Ogden can be said to have surpassed Ewing Young in terms of penetration of wide areas of the Far West and sheer distance covered. They

[57] F. T. Young, *op. cit.*, 171 ff. Small amounts of wheat had been grown by French-Canadians prior to Young's acreage. He was the first American to grow wheat in Oregon.

[58] Cleland, *op. cit.*, 215-16.

surpassed him in terms of priority in time, but Young surpassed them in terms of independent individual enterprise as opposed to company enterprise. Even in chronological sequence, Young was right on their heels and probably more effective in opening routes to be followed by others.[59] In the southwest, he was already experienced before such eminent characters as St. Vrain and Carson had got started. He cannot be said to have furnished so dramatic a leadership as many of the principal characters of the fur trade were able to give. Nor can it be said that he was the hero of celebrated individual exploits to the extent that even minor characters were at certain stages of their careers. But it is doubtful if anyone connected with the fur trade touched the historical development of the American Far West at more frequent or more vital points than Ewing Young.

When we think of this grandson of a pioneer on the Watauga in eastern Tennessee coming to the end of his career in the Chehalem valley of far-off Oregon, before that land had become part of the United States, and when we consider that he came to that extreme westerly spot by strenuous marches through the borderlands of what was then northern Mexico, we must realize not only the enormous geographical distance traversed but also the tremendous span of American history encompassed in the career of Ewing Young.[60]

---

[59] Holmes, 3.

[60] Archer Butler Hulbert, *Frontiers; The Genius of American Nationality.* (Boston, 1929), 56.

*The final volume of the series will provide
an index-directory to the biographies
and introductory materials in
all volumes of the work.*

The Series—

THE MOUNTAIN MEN AND THE FUR TRADE OF
THE FAR WEST is a project estimated to run to six or more
volumes of 375 to 400 pages each. The publication will contain carefully prepared biographies of some four hundred Mountain Men.

More than fifty scholars will cooperate in the project through their
signed contributions of biographical sketches of participants in the fur
trade drama. The biographies will run from one to twenty-five pages
each, depending on the importance of the subject and the available
source materials. Each sketch will give not only the subject's experience as a fur man, but a brief account of his full life span, to the
extent that dependable information can be found.

The areas of exploration and activity will include the present states
of California, Oregon, Washington, Idaho, Montana, Wyoming,
Nevada, Utah, Colorado, Arizona, New Mexico, the Dakotas,
Kansas, Nebraska, Missouri, Oklahoma, and Iowa, as well as the
Provinces of southwest Canada.

The volumes will be issued at intervals of approximately six
months, the first volume appearing in early 1965. Subscription orders
for the entire series may be placed, or individual volumes may be
ordered as each is published. The publisher will furnish descriptive
material or other detailed information on request.